THE SYSTEMATIC DESIGN OF INSTRUCTION

THIRD EDITION

Walter Dick

FLORIDA STATE UNIVERSITY

Lou Carey

UNIVERSITY OF SOUTH FLORIDA

 HarperCollins*Publishers*

Library of Congress Cataloging in Publication Data

Dick, Walter,
    The systematic design of instruction / Walter Dick, Lou Carey. — 3rd ed.
      p.   cm.
    Includes bibliographical references.
    ISBN 0-673-38772-0
    1. Instructional systems—Design.   I. Carey, Lou.   II. Title.
  LB1028.35.D53   1990
  371.3'94—dc20   89-28474
                                                      CIP

7 8 9 10 11   97 96 95 94

ISBN 0-673-38772-0

PREFACE

During the thirteen years since the original publication of *The Systematic Design of Instruction*, the field of instructional design has continued to grow, both as an area of study and as a profession. More and more colleges and universities are offering courses in instructional design and more industries are adding instructional designers to their staffs.

The amount of change that has occurred with regard to the process of instructional design became more apparent as the authors launched into this revision of the text. There have been no major changes in the components of the systematic design process in recent years, but rather an expansion of our knowledge about each particular step in the systems approach model. Those familiar with the second edition will find that this third edition has expanded the treatment of nearly every topic, especially goal analysis, instructional analysis, media selection, instructional strategies, and formative evaluation.

An additional change in the past decade has been the emergence of the microcomputer as an instructional tool and of the video disc as a device that has intrigued instructional designers. It is our belief that the use of these tools will only be as good as the instructional design planning that precedes their implementation. The use of the systematic design process is every bit as critical with these delivery systems as it has been with other media.

The systems approach model used in this book was first taught in a course at Florida State University in 1968. Since that time hundreds of students have taken the course and have developed instructional materials that have had demonstrated effectiveness with learners. The systems approach model is not a simplistic model, nor is it so highly complex that instructors could not use it in their work. The model has been most heavily influenced by the work of Robert Gagné, Leslie Briggs, Robert Mager, Robert Glaser, and Lee Cronbach. It is a behaviorally oriented model stressing the identification of skills students need to learn, and the collection of data from students to revise instruction.

During the more than twenty years we have taught the instructional design course, we have had the valuable opportunity to observe our students' work and thus to refine our presentation of the concepts and procedures associated with each step in the model. This book is the culmination of a carefully conceived instructional strategy and of the many years of practical experience in implementing it. From the publication of the first edition in 1978, we have been able to obtain valuable feedback from instructors and students who have used the book, and we are most grateful for their helpful comments.

In this third edition we retain the features that seem most important to readers of the previous editions. For example, perhaps the most important feature of this book is the regular linking of the theoretical descriptions of the concepts with numerous illustrations of their application. The examples have been carefully selected to represent a wide range of important skills. The examples and practice exercises have been designed to lead the reader from an initial understanding of concepts to their practical application, resulting eventually in his or her own instructional design project.

The reader will find that each of the chapters, after the introduction, is structured in a similar manner. We hope this structure will facilitate the learning of the concepts and procedures associated with the instructional design model. The description of the model's components in each of the chapters includes the following sections:

OBJECTIVES: The major objectives are listed for each chapter. They describe what the reader should be able to do after completing the chapter. They are stated in relatively general terms.

BACKGROUND: This portion of each chapter provides the reader with a brief statement of the background, research and development, and/or problems that led to the development of the procedures associated with each particular component of the model.

CONCEPTS AND PROCEDURES: This section includes both definitions of critical concepts associated with the components as well as a description of "how to do it." It indicates how to carry out the procedures associated with each particular component.

EXAMPLES: In each chapter we provide examples of ways the processes described for each component can be applied. We use a variety of examples in the hope that the reader will be able to apply each procedure to the content area in which he or she is interested.

SUMMARY: This section is specifically provided for those readers who will be developing instructional materials as they study these chapters. It summarizes the concepts and procedures discussed in each chapter. By presenting the material in this manner, we hope to illustrate the interrelatedness of the various components of the model.

PRACTICE AND FEEDBACK: We also provide a series of practice activities in which the reader is required to apply the process to a variety of examples. Readers will receive feedback to their responses to indicate if they understand the principles described in the chapter and to correct any difficulties they may be having. The examples used to illustrate procedures in the book have been purposefully kept simple. The reader should not have to learn the content related to an example to understand the procedure, which is the main focus.

REFERENCES: A brief listing of the most relevant references appears at the end of each chapter. These are annotated to direct the reader to those resources that may help to amplify points made in the chapter.

The authors wish to extend their appreciation to Dennis C. Myers of the University of Toledo for his assistance with various aspects of the third edition of this book, and to James Russell, Donald Stepich, and their students at Purdue University for developing the first draft of the glossary, which precedes the appendix.

In the spirit of constructive feedback, always an important component of the systematic design process, the authors welcome reactions from readers about ways in which the text may be strengthened to better meet their needs.

Walter Dick
Tallahassee, Florida

Lou Carey
Tampa, Florida

TO THE INSTRUCTOR FROM THE AUTHORS

Based on our experience teaching instructional design, we have developed a number of methods and materials we believe you will find useful as you determine your approach to using this book in your course. We hope these teaching suggestions and procedures will help you to effectively use *The Systematic Design of Instruction*, Third Edition.

There are two general ways in which a course in instructional design may be taught: a "knowledge" approach or a "product" approach. The most basic decision that you, the instructor, must make is which to use.

In the knowledge approach, students are expected to be able to state the principles of instructional design. In the product approach, students are expected to apply these principles to design instructional materials. The text readily lends itself to both approaches.

When knowledge is the course goal, the text serves as a source of information. The role of the instructor is to amplify the principles presented in the materials, to provide examples, and to evaluate students acquisiton of the knowledge. *The Systematic Design of Instruction* is well suited to this type of instruction. It provides students with an instructional design model they can use to understand a variety of concepts in the field of education. Such ideas as "performance objectives" and "formative evaluation" can be presented and understood in terms of the overall design, delivery, and evaluation of instruction.

The product approach to teaching instructional design requires that students not only know about designing instruction but, in addition, develop instructional materials. It is this approach that we personally have found to be most successful in teaching instructional design. From our experience, students learn more through actually developing instruction. Concepts that appear to be academic in the text become very real to students as they grapple with such decisions as how many test items they need or how many practice exercises to use. The personal motivation and involvement of students also tends to increase with each succeeding assignment as they begin to produce instruction in their own content area. By the time students reach the stage of one-to-one formative evaluation of their materials, they usually become increasingly enthusiastic because, as a result of the analysis and revision of their materials and procedures, they are able to strengthen their instruction and improve their students' learning. If at all possible then, we recommend that students be encouraged to develop their own instructional materials according to the model presented in the text.

Sequence of Model Components

The second major decision you, the instructor, need to make in teaching instructional design is the sequence in which the model components are presented. The text presents the model components in the sequence typically followed when designing instruction. If the knowledge approach to the course is used, it is likely that the components in the model will be presented as they appear in the text. However, if the product approach is used, the component sequence might be changed.

The first sequence we used was to have students learn about a component in the model and then complete the developmental assignment related to that component. For example, after students read the chapter on instructional goals, they selected their own instructional goal. Then, after reading about instructional analysis procedures, they would do an instructional analysis for their selected goal. This read-develop, read-develop process continued until they completed the model. Even though this approach seems quite rational, students often commented that they would have done things very differently in the beginning of the development of their instructional materials if they had been knowledgeable about the components at the end of the model. Many students also indicated that they needed more knowledge about the design process before making a significant commitment to developing instruction for a particular topic.

An alternative sequence, and one we now prefer, is to have students study the entire model first and then develop an instructional product after they know about the developmental process they are expected to undertake. We have used this sequence a number of times, and it seems very acceptable to students. Students basically read and then are tested on the entire text on a knowledge level. They read the text, study the examples, and complete the practice and feedback sections for the entire instructional design process in a relatively short period of time. After they complete the text and pass a knowledge examination, they select their own instructional goal and proceed through the model again, this time developing each component of their instruction as they move ahead. The advantage of this approach is that students are fully aware of all the steps in the model. With this knowledge, they can make appropriate adjustments in their instructional goal and related design tasks.

The selection of the knowledge or product approach to instruction has significant implications for course management strategies and, particularly, for the use of class time. If the knowledge approach is chosen, the course will focus primarily on the knowledge objectives that are stated at the beginning of each chapter in the text. The pace of classroom activities can be slow enough to allow for discussion time and the opportunity to talk about various examples and practice and feedback exercises. Students may learn the concepts best if they are required to provide their own examples.

If the product approach is used, a great deal of time will be required for students to design, develop, and evaluate their instruction. Students who have used the product approach indicate that they spend approximately one hundred hours out of class from the beginning to the end of the course.

Evaluation of Student Products

The students' design for their instruction can be evaluated in several ways. Each design can be reviewed to determine whether there is consistency among the various components in the design including the instructional goal, terminal and subordinate objectives, and test items. After reviewing the students' designs, you may wish to meet individually with students who appear to be having problems with the design process.

We also have found that many students benefit from reviews of their design by a small group of peers. Students, in turn, should describe their instructional goal and their design for it. The other students can critique the goal and design and make suggestions as to how the components can be improved.

As a further step in formatively evaluating the design, students can construct pretests using items from the Design Evaluation Chart to be administered to target pupils to validate the instructional analyses and validate the knowledge of their target population. Students may discover at this point, before instructional development, that members of the target group already have all the identified subskills or have mastered patterns of subskills from the analysis. In cases such as this, students should either change target groups or adjust the subskills they plan to teach and identify those actually needed by the target group. The testing of selected members from the target group should not be undertaken until after the design has been reviewed by content experts, the instructor, and/or peers. See Table 1 for a list of suggested criteria.

One of the most important aspects of the systematic design of instruction is the documentation of the process that is used to design, develop, and evaluate the instruction. Table 2 contains a Checklist students may use to guide their documentation activities. The Checklist also can serve as a useful outline for students in preparing the documentation report of their activities.

For the instructor, the Checklist provides a convenient outline of the content that should be included in the documentation report and the relative weighting of sections of the report for evaluation purposes. If a component of a student's report fully meets a stated criterion, then the total points for the component should be assigned to the student. If some of the criteria are not met, then points should be deducted from the component accordingly. If the component is not included in the student's report, then no points should be given for it.

TABLE 1

CRITERIA FOR EVALUATING INSTRUCTIONAL DESIGNS

1. Is the instructional goal clearly stated; does it include a behavioral verb?
2. Are the subskills parallel to those in the Design Evaluation Diagram?
3. Is the behavior required clearly stated in each subskill?
4. Does the behavioral objective directly parallel the behavior indicated in the matching subskill?
5. Does the behavioral objective contain the conditions of performance (given what), the performance (do what), and the criteria for judging mastery (how well)?
6. Does the test item(s) enable the student to perform the behavior specified, under the conditions specified, to meet the criteria specified?
7. Are there enough test items for the pretest, embedded tests, and the posttest?
8. Are test items for the same objective parallel?
9. Is the sequence assigned for subskills in the Design Evaluation Diagram appropriate?
10. Is the Design Evaluation Diagram accurate in illustrating the relationship among subskills identified in the Design Evaluation Chart?

TABLE 2

PRODUCT EVALUATION CHECKLIST

Course Objectives	Points	Your Points
I. Instructional Goal		
A. rationale for topic (criteria used for selecting instructional goal)	2	
B. statement of instructional goal	1	
II. Instructional Analysis		
A. rationale for methodology selected	1	
B. completeness of diagram of subskills	3	
C. clarification between subskills included as entry behaviors and those included as skills to be learned through materials	2	
III. Description of Target Population		
A. description of general characteristics of target population and implications these have for instructional materials	2	
IV. Performance Objectives		
A. derivation from instructional analysis	2	
B. statement of the objectives	3	
V. Criterion-Referenced Tests		
A. relationship of items to performance objectives	2	
B. appropriate tests based upon materials and target population (pretest, posttest, embedded test)	3	
VI. Instructional Strategy		
A. preinstructional activities	1	
B. information presentation	2	
C. student participation activities	2	
D. testing (covered in No. V)		
E. follow-through activities	1	
F. materials congruent with strategy	3	
VII. Formative Evaluation		
A. description of one-to-one data collection procedures	2	
B. results and revisions based upon one-to-one testing	3	
C. description of small-group evaluation procedures		
1. sample group characteristics	1	
2. design of formative evaluation study	2	
3. instruments and procedures used for data collection	2	
4. data summary and display	4	
VIII. Suggested Revisions		
A. materials	2	
B. tests	2	
C. procedures	1	
TOTAL 49 Points		

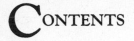ONTENTS

CHAPTER **6**

CHAPTER **7**

CHAPTER 11

REVISING INSTRUCTIONAL MATERIALS   260

CHAPTER 12

SUMMATIVE EVALUATION   288

THE
SYSTEMATIC
DESIGN
OF
INSTRUCTION
THIRD EDITION

INTRODUCTION TO INSTRUCTIONAL DESIGN

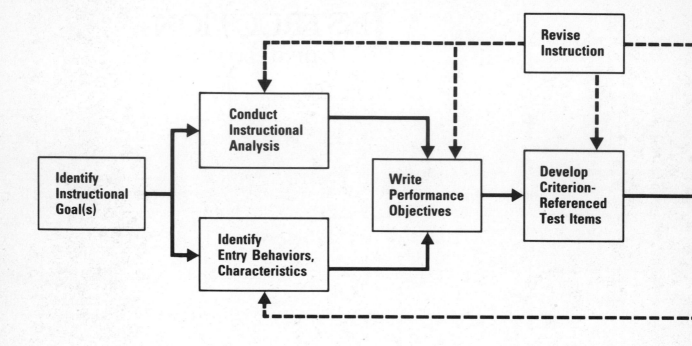

THE DICK AND CAREY SYSTEMS APPROACH MODEL FOR DESIGNING INSTRUCTION

The instructional process has traditionally involved instructor, learners, and textbooks. The content to be learned was contained in the text, and it was the instructor's responsibility to "teach" that content to the learners. Teaching could be interpreted as getting content from the text into the heads of learners in such a way that they could retrieve the information for a test. With this model, the way to improve instruction is to improve the instructor (i.e., to require the instructor to acquire more knowledge and to learn more methods for conveying it to learners).

A more contemporary view of instruction is that it is a systematic process in which every component (i.e., teacher, students, materials, and learning environment) is crucial to successful learning. This perspective is usually referred to as the systems point of view, and advocates of this position typically use the systems approach to design instruction.

Let's consider what is meant by a system, then consider the systems approach. The term *system* has become very popular as more and more of what we do is interrelated with what other people do. A system is technically a set of interrelated parts, all of which work together toward a defined goal.

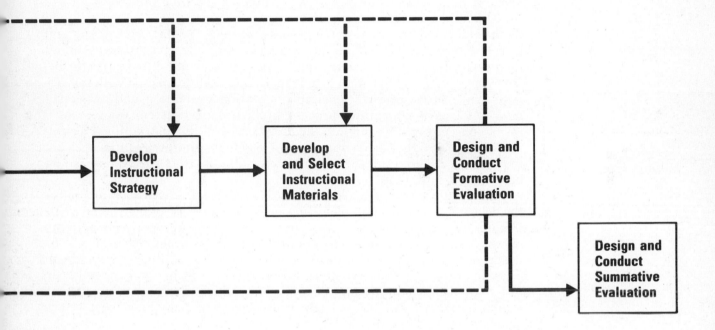

The parts of the system depend on each other for input and output, and the entire system uses feedback to determine if its desired goal has been reached. If it has not, then the system is modified until it does reach the goal. The most easily understood systems are those we create rather than those that occur naturally. For example, you probably have a heating or cooling system in your home that consists of various components that work together to produce warmth or coolness. The thermostat is the feedback mechanism through which the thermometer constantly checks the temperature and signals the system when more heat or cold is needed. When the desired temperature is reached, the system shuts itself off.

How is this related to instruction? First, the instructional process itself can be viewed as a system. The purpose of the system is to bring about learning. The components of the system are the learners, the instructor, the instructional materials, and the learning environment. These components interact in order to achieve the goal. For example, the instructor reviews sample problems in the textbook or manual with the learners in a quiet classroom. To determine whether learning is taking place, a test is administered.

This is the instructional system thermostat. If learner performance is not satisfactory, then there must be changes enacted in the system to make it more effective, and to bring about the desired learning outcomes.

The result of using the systems view of instruction is to see the important role of all the components in the process. They must all interact effectively, just as the parts in a heating or cooling system must interact effectively in order to bring about the desired outcomes. There is not an overemphasis of any one component in the system, but a determination of the exact contribution of each one to the desired outcome. And it is clear that there must be both an assessment of the effectiveness of the system in bringing about learning, and a mechanism to make changes if learning fails to occur.

Thus far, our discussion of the instructional process has focused upon the interactive component of the process, namely, the time instructors and learners come together with the hope that learning will occur. But what about the preparation for the instructional process? How does the instructor decide what to do, and when? It is not surprising that the person with the systems view sees the preparation, implementation, evaluation, and revision of instruction as one integrated process. In the broadest systems sense, a variety of sources provides input to the preparation of the instruction. The output is some product or combination of products and procedures that are implemented. The results are used to determine whether the system should be changed, and, if so, how.

The purpose of this book is to describe a systems approach model for the design, development, implementation, and evaluation of instruction. This is not a physical system such as a furnace or air conditioner or heat pump (which will do both), but a procedural system. A series of steps will be described, all of which will receive input from the preceding steps and will provide output for the next steps. All of the components work together in order for the user to produce effective instruction. The model includes an evaluation component that will help determine what, if anything, went wrong, and how it can be improved.

While our model will be referred to as a systems approach model, we must emphasize that there is no single systems approach model for designing instruction. There are a number of models that bear the label "systems approach," and all of them share most of the same basic components. The systems approach model presented in this book is less complex than some, but includes the major components included in other models.

The systems approach models are an outgrowth of more than twenty-five years of research into the learning process. Each component of the model is based upon theory and in most instances research that demonstrates the effectiveness of that component. The model brings together in one coherent whole many of the concepts that you may have already encountered in a variety of educational situations. For example, you undoubtedly have heard of behavioral objectives and may have already developed some yourself. Such terms as criterion-referenced testing and formative evaluation may also be familiar. The model will show how these terms, and the processes associated with them, are interrelated and how these procedures can be used to produce effective instructional materials.

The model, as it is presented here, is based not only upon theory and research, but also a considerable amount of practical experience in its application. We suggest that the novice instructional designer use the model principally in the sequence and manner presented in this chapter because students who have done so have produced effective instructional materials.

On the other hand, we acknowledge that in particular circumstances and with increased design experience, you may be required to change the model. Also, we expect that more research and experience will help amplify the procedures associated with each component of the model.

In the section that follows, we will present the general systems approach model in much the same way as a cookbook recipe—you do this and then you do that. When you begin to use a recipe in your own kitchen, however, it takes on greater meaning, just as the model will when you begin to develop your own instruction: you select a topic for which instruction is needed, you develop your own instructional resources, you select your own set of learners, and so on. Your perspective on the model will probably change greatly. In essence, your use of your own kitchen, your own ingredients, and your own personal touch will result in a unique product.

The model that will be described in detail in succeeding chapters is presented on pages 2 and 3. The model includes nine interconnected boxes and a major line that shows feedback from the last box to the earlier boxes. The boxes refer to sets of procedures and techniques employed by the instructional designer to design, produce, evaluate, and revise instruction. The steps will be briefly described in sequence below and in much greater detail in subsequent chapters.

COMPONENTS OF THE SYSTEMS APPROACH MODEL

IDENTIFY AN INSTRUCTIONAL GOAL The first step in the model is to determine what it is that you want students to be able to do when they have completed your instruction. The definition of the instructional goal may be derived from a list of goals, from a needs assessment with regard to a particular curriculum, from practical experience with learning difficulties of students in the classroom, from the analysis of someone who is already doing a job, or from some other requirement for new instruction.

CONDUCT AN INSTRUCTIONAL ANALYSIS After you identify the instructional goal, you will determine what type of learning is required of the student. The goal will be analyzed to identify the subordinate skills that must be learned and any subordinate procedural steps that must be followed to learn a particular process. This analysis will result in a chart or diagram that depicts these skills and shows the relationship among them.

IDENTIFY ENTRY BEHAVIORS AND CHARACTERISTICS In addition to identifying the subordinate skills and procedural steps that must be included in the instruction, it will be necessary to identify the specific skills that students must have prior to beginning instruction. This is not a listing of all the things learners *can* do, but the identification of the specific skills they *must be able to do* in order to begin. It is also important to identify any specific characteristics of the learners that may be important to consider in the design of the instructional activities.

WRITE PERFORMANCE OBJECTIVES Based on the instructional analysis and the statement of entry behaviors, you will write specific statements of what it is the learners will be able to do when they complete your instruction. These statements, which are derived from the skills identified in the instructional analysis, will identify the skills to be learned, the conditions under which the skills must be performed, and the criteria for successful performance.

DEVELOP CRITERION-REFERENCED TEST ITEMS Based on the objectives you have written, you develop assessment items that are parallel to and measure the learner's ability to achieve what you described in the objectives. Major emphasis is placed on relating the kind of behavior described in the objectives to what the items require.

DEVELOP AN INSTRUCTIONAL STRATEGY Given information from the five preceding steps, you will identify the strategy that you will use in your instruction to achieve the terminal objective. The strategy will include sections on preinstructional activities, presentation of information, practice and feedback, testing, and follow-through activities. The strategy will be based upon current outcomes of learning research, current knowledge of the learning process, content to be taught, and the characteristics of the learners who will receive the instruction. These features are used to develop or select materials, or to develop a strategy for interactive classroom instruction.

DEVELOP AND/OR SELECT INSTRUCTION In this step you will use your instructional strategy to produce the instruction. This typically includes a learner's manual, instructional materials, tests, and an instructor's guide. The decision to develop original materials will depend upon the type of learning to be taught, the availability of existing relevant materials, and developmental resources available to you. Criteria for selecting from among existing materials are provided.

DESIGN AND CONDUCT THE FORMATIVE EVALUATION Following the completion of a draft of the instruction, a series of evaluations is conducted to collect data that are used to identify how to improve it. The three types of formative evaluation are referred to as one-to-one evaluation, small-group evaluation, and field evaluation. Each type of evaluation provides the designer with a different type of information that can be used to improve the instruction. Similar techniques can be applied to the formative evaluation of materials or classroom instruction.

REVISE INSTRUCTION The final step (and the first step in a repeat cycle) is revising the instruction. Data from the formative evaluation are summarized and interpreted to attempt to identify difficulties experienced by learners in achieving the objectives, and to relate these difficulties to specific deficiencies in the instruction. The line in the figure on p. 2 and 3 labeled "Revise Instruction" indicates that the data from a formative evaluation are not simply used to revise the instruction itself, but are used to reexamine the validity of the instructional analysis and the assumptions about the entry behaviors and characteristics of learners. It is necessary to reexamine statements of performance objectives and test items in light of collected data. The instructional strategy is reviewed and finally all this is incorporated into revisions of the instruction to make it a more effective instructional tool.

CONDUCT SUMMATIVE EVALUATION Although summative evaluation is the culminating evaluation of the effectiveness of instruction, it generally is not a part of the design process. It is an evaluation of the absolute and/or relative value or worth of the instruction, and occurs only after the instruction has been formatively evaluated and sufficiently revised to meet the standards of the designer. Since the summative evaluation usually does not involve the designer of the instruction, but instead involves an independent evaluator, this component is not considered an integral part of the instructional design process, per se.

The nine basic steps represent the procedures that one employs when the systems approach is used to design instruction. This set of procedures is referred to as a systems approach because it is made up of interacting components, each having its own input and output, which together produce predetermined products. A system also collects information about its effectiveness so that the final product can be modified until it reaches the desired quality level. When instructional materials are being developed, data are collected and the materials are revised in light of these data to make them as effective and efficient as possible.

Before concluding our discussion of the systems approach model, it should be made clear that, as it stands, this is not a curriculum design model. In order to design a curriculum many more steps would be required before identifying the instructional goals. Some of these techniques are known as needs assessment and job analysis. The model described here is intended to be used at that point when the instructor is able to identify a specific instructional goal. The model is used in curriculum development projects after the instructional goals have been derived.

USING THE SYSTEMS APPROACH MODEL

Now that you have read about this model, you should consider several very important questions about its use. These are discussed in the sections that follow.

WHY USE THE SYSTEMS APPROACH? Few of the formal research studies that appear in the literature address the question of the effectiveness of the systems approach. While much research has been done on component parts of the model, it is extremely difficult to do rigorous studies that involve the total model. The few studies that have been published tend to provide strong support for the approach. The primary support comes from designers who have used the process and have documented their success with learners.

It appears that there are a number of reasons that systematic approaches to instructional design are effective. The first is the focus, at the outset, on what the learner is to know or be able to do when the instruction is concluded. Without this precise statement, subsequent planning and implementation steps can become unclear and ineffective.

A second reason for the success of the systems approach is the careful linkage between each component, especially the relationship between the instructional strategy and the desired learning outcomes. Instruction is specifically targeted on the skills and knowledge to be taught and supplies the appropriate conditions for the learning of these outcomes. Stated in another way, instruction does not consist of a range of activities only some of which may be related to what is to be learned.

The third and perhaps most important reason for the success of the systems approach is that it is an empirical and replicable process. Instruction is designed not to be delivered once, but for use on as many occasions as possible with as many learners as possible. Because it is "reusable," it is worth the time and effort to evaluate and revise it. In the process of systematically designing instruction, data are collected to determine what part of the instruction is not working, and it is revised until it does work.

Because of these characteristics, the systems approach is valuable to instructors who are interested in successfully teaching basic and higher level competencies to learners. The competency based approach has been a very natural and widely adopted approach among vocational educators. Similarly, perhaps the most numerous applications of the systems approach may be found in industry and the military services. In these environments there is a premium on both efficiency of instruction and quality of student performance. The payoffs in both situations are quite obvious.

WHAT IS THE BASIC FORMAT OF SYSTEMATICALLY DESIGNED INSTRUCTION? When the systems approach is used, there is almost always the creation of some form of instructional materials. These materials were initially referred to as programmed instruction. As the format changed, they became learning activity packages (LAPs) and modules. We will tend to use the latter term, or simply refer to *instruction*. A module is usually a self-instructional printed unit of instruction that has an integrated theme, provides students with information needed to acquire and assess specified knowledge and skills, and serves as one component of a total curriculum. While printed modules are still quite popular as a format for instruction, more and more designers are choosing to use computers as the mechanism for delivering at least part of their instruction.

Most designers would agree with the definition of a module given above. However, they would differ on a number of specific characteristics. For example, the length of time required for learners to study a module may vary from one to fifteen hours. Even less time may be required for very young children. Some designers will insist that a module of instruction should include at least two alternative conceptual presentations of the instructional materials and preferably two or more modes of presentation to accommodate individual differences. Other designers would not agree that all these alternatives are necessary.

In addition, some instructors would argue that a module should be strictly self-contained. That is, a learner should be able to achieve all the objectives stated in the module without interacting with the instructor or other individuals. Other instructors will specifically include in the design of the module the participation of peers, instructors, and outsiders in order to involve the learner in a variety of interactive activities.

Many instructors even differ on whether learners should be informed of the major objectives for a module. Some insist that learners should receive precise statements of the objectives while others argue that objectives should be reworded at a level more appropriate for the individual, or that objectives may be omitted altogether.

Regardless of the issues listed above, most modules require the learners to interact actively with the instructional materials rather than simply allowing them to read the materials passively. The learners are asked to perform various types of learning tasks and receive feedback on that performance. There is some type of testing strategy that tells the learners if they achieved mastery of the content and what they should do if they did not.

Based upon the description of prior paragraphs, how would you recognize a module if you saw one? In its most simple form, a module might be a typewritten statement to students that says what it is they are about to learn and how they will be tested. It would provide printed or typed instructional materials as well as some practice exercises. A self-test that might be used prior to taking a terminal test could also be included.

The most complex module might contain all of the items listed above, but might also incorporate a number of alternative sets of materials from which the learner could choose the one most appropriate. Alternative media forms such as audiotapes or filmstrips could also be included. In addition, the learner might go to a laboratory to conduct an experiment or go outside the learning environment to gather information.

FOR WHICH MEDIA IS THE SYSTEMS APPROACH APPROPRIATE?

The systems approach to the design of instruction includes the planning, development, implementation, and evaluation of instruction. As a part of this process, the method of delivery of this instruction must be chosen. In some instances, it is most appropriate to have the instructor deliver the instruction, while in other situations, a variety of media may be employed. Most recently it seems that every new instructional effort tends to include a computer. In every instance, the systems approach is an invaluable tool for identifying what is to be taught, determining how it will be taught, and evaluating the instruction to find out whether it is effective.

The procedure that will be described for developing an instructional strategy is a generic one. It is most directly applicable to the development of print instruction. However, the procedure can be easily modified to fit the conditions of the selected medium of instruction, such as television or computers. Media specialists in these areas, for example, could use the instructional strategy statements to create story boards or screen displays. The use of the systems approach prevents the designer from trying to create instruction for a medium prior to a complete analysis of what is to be taught and how. Most research suggests that it is the analysis process, and not the delivery mode, that determines the success of the instruction.

DOES THE USE OF THE SYSTEMS APPROACH IMPLY THAT ALL INSTRUCTION WILL BE INDIVIDUALIZED? From our discussion of

the development of printed modules and computer-based instruction, the reader might assume that systematically designed instruction is the same as individualized instruction: it is not. Let's assume, for the sake of discussion, that individualized instruction permits each learner to progress at his or her own rate. (This is considered the minimal definition of individualized instruction!) A well-designed print module or computer-based lesson could certainly be used in this manner. So the systems approach can be used to design individualized instruction. However, it can also be used to design group-based instruction—if we may use this term in contrast with individualized instruction. The systems approach can be used to incorporate all types of instructor-led and interactive group activities. In fact, it is often the case that these are precisely the conditions that are most effective and efficient for bringing about the desired learning outcomes.

The reader should be careful to distinguish between the process of designing instruction and the delivery of that instruction. The systems approach is basically a design process while instructors, modules, computers, and television are delivery mechanisms. These delivery mechanisms can be used with one or many learners at the same time. A major part of the design process is to determine how the instruction can be delivered most effectively.

The beneficiary of the application of the systems approach to the design of instruction is the individual learner. Careful attention is paid to what it is that must be learned and what must already be known in order to begin the instruction. The instruction is focused on the skills to be learned and is presented under the best conditions for learning. The learner is evaluated fairly with instruments that measure the behaviors described in the objectives, and the data are used to revise the instruction so that it will be even more effective with succeeding learners. Following the process causes the designer to focus on the needs and abilities of the individual learner and results in the creation of the best possible instruction.

WHO SHOULD USE THE SYSTEMS APPROACH? As you study the model and, hopefully, use it to design some instruction, you will find that it takes both time and effort. You will probably find yourself saying "I could never use this process to prepare all the instruction I need to use," and you would probably be correct. The individual instructor who has day-to-day instructional responsibilities can use the process to develop only small amounts of written instruction at any given time. However, the process can also be used effectively and efficiently to select from among existing materials, and for designing nonmaterials based instruction.

In addition, the authors have found that almost every instructor who has studied the process has come away with two reactions. The first is that they will certainly begin immediately to use some of the components in the model, if not all of them. The second reaction is that their approach to instruction will never be the same after the insights which they have gained from using the process. (The reader may be somewhat skeptical at this point; be sure to consider your own reactions after *you* have used this approach.)

There is a second group of users of the systems approach, which is growing quite rapidly. They are typically referred to as instructional designers since they are trained to use a systematic approach to designing new instructional systems or improving already existing systems. Their full-time job is to create replicable instructional programs that are effective with a particular learner population.

In contrast to the instructor who may be working alone, the instructional designer often works with a team of specialists to develop the instruction. The team would typically include a content specialist, a media specialist, an evaluation specialist, and a manager. (When the instructor works alone, he or she usually must fill all of these roles.) The team approach draws on the expertise of specialists to produce a product that none could produce alone. In these settings there is a high premium on interpersonal skills because seemingly everyone has ideas on how best to do what needs to be done.

This book has been written for both the instructor who would like to know more about the systems approach to instruction and the beginning instructional designer who may pursue a career in this field. The book is also intended for the public school teacher, the university professor, the industrial trainer, and the military instructor. We are convinced that the model and procedures are equally applicable in both school and nonschool settings.

Therefore, in our examples of various aspects of the application of the systematic design process, we have included instruction that is intended for all age groups, from young children to mature adults. In addition, we will use the terms *teacher, instructor,* and *designer* interchangeably throughout the book because we truly believe they are.

References and Recommended Readings

At the end of each chapter in this book, several carefully selected references are listed. The books and articles supplement the description in the chapter, or focus in more detail on an important concept that has been presented.

The references listed for this first chapter are somewhat different. These are books in the field of instructional design or ones that have direct implications for the practice of instructional design. Many of the topics in this book also appear in these references. The books vary in depth and breadth of coverage of topics, but they should all help to expand your knowledge and understanding of the instructional design field.

AECT Task Force on Definitions and Terminology (1979). *Educational technology: A glossary of terms.* Washington, DC: Association for Educational Communications and Technology.

Banathy, Bela H. (1968). *Instructional systems.* Palo Alto, CA: Fearon Publishers.

Banathy, Bela H. (1973). *Developing a systems view of education.* Seaside, CA: Intersystems.

Bass, Ronald K., & Dills, Charles R. (Eds.) (1984). *Instructional development: The state of the art, II.* Dubuque, Iowa: Kendall/Hunt Publishing Co.

Briggs, Leslie J. (Ed.) (1977). *Instructional design: Principles and applications.* Englewood Cliffs, NJ: Educational Technology Publications.

Briggs, Leslie J., & Wager, Walter W. (1977). *Handbook of procedures for the design of instruction* (2nd ed.). Englewood Cliffs, NJ: Educational Technology Publications.

Davis, Robert H., Alexander, Lawrence T., & Yelon, Stephen L. (1974). *Learning system design: An approach to the improvement of instruction.* New York: McGraw-Hill.

Dick, Walter, & Reiser, Robert A. (1989). *Planning effective instruction.* Englewood Cliffs, NJ: Prentice-Hall.

Fleming, Malcolm L., & Levie, W. Howard (1978). *Instructional message design.* Englewood Cliffs, NJ: Educational Technology Publications.

Gagné, Robert M. (1985). *The conditions of learning* (4th ed.). New York: Holt, Rinehart and Winston.

Gagné, Robert M. (Ed.) (1987). *Instructional technology: Foundations.* Hillsdale, NJ: Lawrence Erlbaum Associates.

Gagné, Robert M., Briggs, Leslie J., & Wager, Walter W. (1988). *Principles of instructional design* (3rd ed.). New York: Holt, Rinehart and Winston.

Gagné, Robert M., & Driscoll, Marcy P. (1988). *Essentials of learning for instruction* (2nd ed.). Englewood Cliffs, NJ: Prentice-Hall.

Kemp, Jerrold E. (1977). *Instructional Design: A plan for unit and course development* (2nd ed.). Belmont, CA: Fearon Publishers.

Knirk, Frederick G., & Gustafson, Kent L. (1986). *Instructional technology: A systematic approach to education.* New York: Holt, Rinehart and Winston.

Mager, Robert F. (1984). *Preparing instructional objectives* (2nd ed.). Belmont, CA: Pitman Learning, Inc.

Mager, Robert F. (1988). *Making instruction work.* Belmont, CA: David S. Lake Publishers.

Markle, Susan (1978). *Designs for instructional designers.* Champaign, IL: Stripes.

Romiszowski, A. J. (1981). *Designing instructional systems.* London: Kogan Page.

Romiszowski, A. J. (1984). *Producing instructional systems.* London: Kogan Page.

2

IDENTIFYING
AN INSTRUCTIONAL GOAL

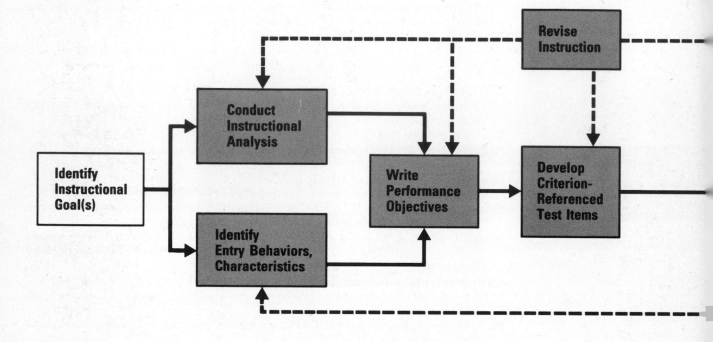

OBJECTIVES

- Identify an instructional goal that meets the criteria for initiating the design of effective instruction.
- Write an instructional goal that meets the criteria for initiating the development of instructional materials.

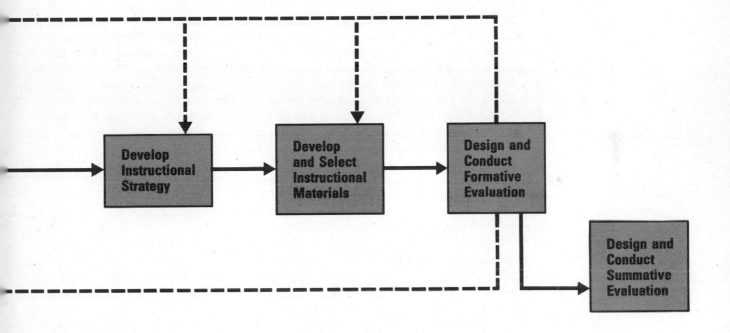

BACKGROUND

Instruction is the solution to a problem. The instructional design process begins with the identification of one or more problems. The problem identification process is typically referred to as needs assessment. Kaufman and English (1979) describe a very complete process for incorporating the viewpoints of students, parents, and community members as well as educators in the identification of problems that should be resolved.

This technique focuses on the "what is" and "what should be" in a particular situation. In other words, a need is expressed as the gap between the way we would like things to be and the way they presently are. For example, the application of the needs assessment process within a large corporation might indicate a requirement to service various microcomputers. A quick check indicates that at present there are no persons in the company with these skills. Therefore, a goal might be to obtain the services of the required number of microcomputer technicians. The technicians would meet the need by filling the gap between what is and what should be and thus solve the problem of servicing the computers. What remains to be decided is whether the company should train these personnel or obtain their services elsewhere.

As another example, we might want 95 percent of the students in our school district to pass the functional literacy examination. However, our records indicate that only 81 percent are passing the test. There is a gap of 14 percent between what is and what should be. Therefore, a goal might be to increase the percentage of students passing the functional literacy examination by 14 percent, to a level of 95 percent passing.

It should be noted that these goals focus on what learners will be able to do. While it may not be clear exactly what the skills are that make a person "functionally literate" or a "microcomputer technician," at least we would have some idea of how we would proceed to derive more specific skills that would, *in toto*, represent these goals. Notice also that the goals describe the outcomes of instruction and not the process of instruction. A need statement should not refer to "a need to use computers in our instruction," or "a need for more third grade teachers." These are part of the process of achieving some goal, but do not represent good instructional design goal statements. The use of computers in a business and more teachers in a school is a means to an end and should not become ends in and of themselves.

Typically, the goals used by an instructional designer have been derived from some type of needs assessment, either formal or informal, and have been further refined by either a job or curriculum analysis. Consider the goal of obtaining the services of 25 microcomputer technicians. The question you should immediately ask is, "Must we train these people from among our present staff, hire new people who will be trained, or would it be less expensive to hire people who are already trained?" In other words, the designer should always try to determine if there is a *noninstructional* solution to the problem that might be less costly and equally effective. Not all problems are solved with instruction!

If it were determined that the training of the technicians is to take place in-house, then a curriculum for that training would be developed. The most likely way to identify the skills that should be taught would be to undertake a job analysis. Elaborate techniques have been developed for identifying what skills job incumbents use and how frequently they use them. Based on the data from a large number of people who are performing the job, it is possible to identify the skills that seem to be the critical ones for inclusion in the curriculum. The general goal would be represented by many skills, which become subgoals, such as to be able to maintain a computer keyboard. This seems like a much more manageable instructional task than simply training a microcomputer technician.

Now consider the goal of raising the functional literacy scores. One set of information that should be obtained is the description of skills that are tested. With this list it is possible to determine where each skill is presently taught in the curriculum. Some skills may not be taught at all. Others may only be taught at the elementary level, and probably have been forgotten. It could be decided that in order to get 14 percent more of the students to pass the examination, a new course must be established to serve the needs of potentially low performing students.

The goals for the new course would probably be in the areas of mathematics and language. These will be further broken down into topic areas, units, and ultimately into lessons. The process of identifying the topics to be included often seems to involve making sure that as much content as possible is covered, rather than determining exactly what it is that learners need to know. These can be two somewhat different things. In our example, the existence of the functional literacy examination helps define the topic areas to be covered in the course. However, a copy of such an examination is often not present and, therefore, other means must be used for establishing what is to be included in the course. Experience has shown that it is almost inevitable that an attempt is made to cover the most content in the shortest period of time. The end result is a set of goals that the designer will use as the starting point for the design process.

In summary, instructional goals are ideally derived through a process of needs assessment that establishes rather broad indications of the problem that must be solved. Then an analysis of that goal is undertaken, either in the context of a curriculum proposal or a job analysis. As a result, more refined specific statements emerge and focus on what learners will be able to do when they complete their instruction.

CONCEPTS

Needs Assessment Strategies

It is generally accepted that the instructional design process begins with the identification of a need—a gap between what is and what should be. Who should be involved in identifying that gap? In our previous examples of the functional literacy examination and the maintenance of computers, it was the unstated assumption that "someone" in the system identified the need. Kaufman and English have indicated that educators, parents, and community members should participate along with the learners who are representative of those who will be directly affected by instruction.

The focus throughout the instructional design process is on the learner, and researchers like Rossett (1987) stress the importance of collecting needs assessment information directly from the learners for whom the instruction would be intended. This emphasis applies to both adult and public school learners.

When a needs assessment is conducted, instruments must be developed to collect data from the learners. It is important to know exactly what can be discovered from the questions asked. Rossett has identified five different types of questions that can be asked of learners in order to identify the specific needs for which your instruction may be a potential solution. The broadest type of question is used to identify problems that people who are being assessed may be experiencing. These items place few restrictions on the respondents: "What problems have you recently had on the job?"

If you ask a question like "What problems have you experienced on the job recently?" you will undoubtedly receive a wide range of answers, not all of which will have implications for training. The answers can be categorized into those that deal with: interpersonal skills, equipment failures, or lack of information. Given these categories it might be important to repair certain key equipment and publish a weekly information sheet for employees. It may be found that only the interpersonal skills problems require training. Instructional designers must always be sensitive to the criticism that they want to solve all problems with some type of training. The designer should look for less costly and potentially more effective solutions to problems before initiating an instructional program.

The second type of item asks learners to express priorities among possible topics or skills that might be included in a course: "Rate each of the following skills in terms of your need for them to improve your effectiveness in the office."

The third approach to data collection is to ask learners to demonstrate particular skills. This amounts to giving the learners a pretest for a possible course: "Write the following sentence in shorthand." Many other skills could also be tested in a similar manner.

Rossett's fourth type of item is one that tries to uncover the feelings that learners have about a particular course or skill. For example, learners might be asked, "How interested would you be in a workshop on telephone etiquette?" or "Would you like to participate in a management seminar with your supervisor?"

The last type of item which might be used in a needs assessment study is one that lets the learners identify what they think are the best solutions to a problem. Consider this type of item: "It has been found that many people are not receiving their office messages or understanding the ones they do receive. Which of the following would improve our communication?" A list of alternative strategies would include training in receiving and communicating messages. As with any problem situation, this last type of item allows the learner to identify noninstructional solutions that may be much more cost-effective than instruction.

Needs assessment is becoming an increasingly important component of the total design process. Trainers and educators are aware of the tremendous cost of creating instruction for which there is no need; therefore, more emphasis is being placed on "front-end" analysis and other approaches for identifying needs more accurately. In the past it was common for survey instruments to be the major means of identifying and documenting training needs. Today surveys are being supplemented or surplanted with more insightful interviews and direct observations of performers. The "performers" may be either the audience with the potential problem or experts who demonstrate how a particular task is to be performed on new equipment.

It is not our purpose in this book to explain or demonstrate how to conduct a complete needs assessment, because the books by Rossett (1987) and Kaufman (1988) provide the conceptual background and procedural details for performing this assessment. Therefore, we begin the instructional design process at the point following goal identification. We are in no way minimizing the importance of the process used to identify appropriate goals. Regardless of the procedure that is used to generate a goal, it is almost always necessary for the designer to clarify and sometimes amplify the goal in order for it to serve as a firm starting point for the instructional design process. Many goals are really fuzzy, and designers must learn how to cope effectively with a "fuzzy."

Clarifying Instructional Goals

Mager (1972) has described a procedure that the designer can use when a fuzzy is encountered. A fuzzy is generally some abstract statement about an internal state of the learner like "appreciating," "having an awareness of," "sensing," etc. These kinds of terms often appear in goals, but the designer doesn't know what they mean because there is no indication of what learners would be doing if they achieved this goal. Designers assume that at the successful completion of their instruction, students should be able to demonstrate that they have achieved the goal. But if the goal is so fuzzy that it is not apparent what performance would represent successful achievement, then further analysis must be undertaken.

To analyze a fuzzy goal, first write down the goal. Then write down the things a person would do to demonstrate that he or she had achieved that goal. Don't be too critical at first; just write everything down that occurs to you. Next, sort through the statements for those which best represent what is meant by your fuzzy goal. These should be indications of what learners would be doing when they achieved your goal. Now incorporate each of these indicators (there may be one or quite a few) into a statement that tells what the learner will do. As a last step, examine the goal statements and ask yourself if learners achieved or demonstrated each of the performances, would you agree that they had achieved your goal? If the answer is yes, then you have de-fuzzied the goal; you have developed one or more goal statements that collectively represent the achievement of an important, yet fuzzy, goal.

The designer should be aware of this type of goal analysis procedure because many critical educational and training goals are not initially stated as clear, concise descriptions of performances of learners. They often are stated in terms that are quite meaningful (in general) to the originator, but have no specifics that the designer can use for developing instruction. Such goals should not be discarded as being useless. An analysis should be undertaken to identify specific performance outcomes that are implied by the goal. Often it will be helpful to engage a group in the process so that you see the range of ideas that can emerge from a fuzzy goal and the need for a consensus on specific behaviors if truly successful instruction is to be developed.

Criteria for Establishing Instructional Goals

Sometimes the goal-setting process is not totally rational; that is, it does not follow a systematic needs assessment process. The instructional designer must be aware that all instructional design takes place in a specific context. That context includes a number of political and economic considerations, as well as technical or academic ones. Stated in another way, powerful people often determine priorities, and finances almost always determine the limitations of what can be done on an instructional design project. Any selection of instructional goals must be done in terms of the following concerns: (1) Are there sufficient people and time to complete the development of instruction for this goal? (2) Are these goals acceptable to those who must approve this instructional development effort? And, most important, (3) Will the development of this instruction solve the problem that led to the need for it? These questions are of great importance to the institution or organization that will undertake the development.

There are additional questions that the designer should examine when contemplating an individual project. Assuming that a need has been established and that time and resources are available, then the designer should determine if the content is stable enough to warrant the cost of developing it. If it will be out of date in six months, then extensive instructional development is probably not warranted.

Another concern is the availability of learners. The instructional design process involves the use of these individuals to try out the instruction. If the designer cannot get access to appropriate learners, it will be impossible to implement the total design process. A small number of learners should be available to receive the instruction. If they are not, then one should reconsider the validity of the need.

The final concern is the designer's own expertise in the area in which the instruction will be developed. Certainly experienced designers often work on teams in which, at least initially, the content area is totally foreign to them. A great deal of content learning must take place before the designer can work effectively. For novice designers, it is preferable to begin by working in a content area in which they already have subject matter expertise. It is a lot easier to learn one new set of skills, namely, instructional design skills, than it is to learn two new sets of skills—both content and process—at the same time.

If you have chosen (or are required) to design an instructional package as you work through the chapters in this book, you will undertake a process that will consume many hours of your time. Therefore, before you select or identify an instructional goal, review the criteria listed in this chapter. It is particularly important (1) that you have the expertise to deal with the subject matter, (2) that learners are available to you to help evaluate and revise the instructional materials, and (3) that you have selected a goal that can be taught in a reasonable amount of time. With regard to the third condition, if you are designing instruction for young children in preschool, kindergarten, or first grade, you may wish to design activities that require no more than twenty to thirty minutes of the children's time because of their limited attention span. On the other hand, adults are often motivated to study for two hours or longer without taking a break.

EXAMPLES

Two examples of the procedures used to develop instructional goals may help you formulate or evaluate your own goals. Both examples are based upon an identified problem, needs assessment activities, and a prescribed solution to a problem. Each example has its own scenario to help clarify the context of the problem and the process used to identify the goals.

The first example is based upon a common problem identified by classroom teachers in elementary, middle, and high school. Parents complain to teachers and administrators that their children are unable to write clearly. Teachers recognize that although their students can communicate orally and can perform reasonably well on grammar tests, their students cannot write effective compositions, either long or short. Administrators complain that graduates of the district do not score well on composition tests often required to enter college.

During a middle school faculty meeting called to discuss the composition problem, teachers decided to conduct a needs assessment study. Each teacher assigned a short essay for his or her students, to be written on a common topic. A newly formed evaluation team of teachers reviewed the themes to identify possible common problems. They reported that, generally, students use one type of sentence—namely, declarative, simple sentences to communicate their thoughts rather than varying their sentence structure by purpose or complexity. Additionally, punctuation other than periods and commas was absent from the students' work, and commas were rare.

The evaluation team reported their findings to the faculty. To solve the problem, a new, semester-long, written composition class was planned.

The instructional goal for the new class was stated by the evaluation team:

To offer a new course in written composition in which no less than one theme each week is assigned, written, graded, and returned to students for refinement.

A new task force of teachers was selected to develop the course based upon the stated instructional goal and a one semester time-frame.

The task force team began by analyzing the stated instructional goal. What problems do you believe they encountered with it? Remember that the list of criteria for a good instructional goal includes the following:

- That it contains a clear, general statement of learner outcomes
- That it is related to an identified problem and needs assessment
- That it can be achieved through instruction rather than some more efficient means such as enhancing motivation of employees

The first problem they encountered was that the goal mostly described what the administration and teachers rather than the learners would accomplish. The administrators would create a special new course in written composition, and the teachers would assign, grade, and return one theme each week. Students were required to write and refine one composition weekly. However, the goal did not focus on what learners were expected to achieve through their writing efforts. They were simply to write and refine. Although the goal was based upon a real problem and a needs assessment that provided necessary information to help the task force refine the instructional goal, they decided to reserve judgment on whether the goal could be achieved through instruction until they had revised and clarified it.

After reviewing the needs assessment report of the evaluation team, the task force identified several intentions of the language arts faculty, which they believed could be useful in refining the goal. First, they wanted students to practice written composition by writing and revising one theme weekly. Second, they wanted students to learn to use a variety of sentence types that they could classify by purpose. Third, they wanted students to vary their sentences by complexity. And fourth, they wanted students to use a variety of punctuation that was appropriate for the sentence purpose and complexity.

Using these intentions gleaned from the evaluation team report, can you write an instructional goal for the new course? Write one on a scratch sheet of paper and compare it with the following example. Your goal may not be stated exactly like ours, but you can judge whether the intentions are the same.

Students will write one short composition each week and focus their writing skills on the following: (1) a variety of sentence types based upon sentence purpose, (2) a variety of sentence structures that varies in complexity, and (3) a variety of punctuation matching sentence type and complexity.

The task force returned their revised instructional goal to the faculty to determine whether their revisions in the statement more clearly reflected the intentions for the course related to the expected learner outcomes. The faculty approved the revisions as they were written and agreed that the refined goal reflected the following:

- A clear, general statement of learner outcomes
- A logical agreement between the identified problem of weak written composition and particular shortcomings identified through the needs assessment process
- A problem that could best be addressed through instruction rather than otherwise

At this point, the instructional goal is clear enough to provide guidance for the task force charged with developing the new course. Other criteria the teachers should consider before progressing are the following:

1. The expertise of those charged with developing the course
2. The stability of the content over a period of time
3. The time required to develop the instruction and teach the skills
4. Whether the goal describes two or more related or separate kinds of behavior
5. The availability of students to test the instruction

The first criterion was met because the teachers on the special task force were all language arts specialists. The second criterion was also met since criteria for well-written compositions were not expected to change during the foreseeable future. The third criterion, time required to develop instruction and teach the skills, posed a problem. It was a sizable instructional goal covering a course rather than a smaller unit of instruction. The goal as stated would require many hours of instruction during a semester of study. The course goal would have to be broken down into modules or units of a manageable size in order to accomplish the task. This discovery was related to the fourth criterion, a complex goal that described two or more kinds of behavior. The fifth criterion was met since there were many students available in the school who could be used to test the instructional materials.

The single criterion that posed a problem was the size of the instructional goal. The task force decided to perform further analysis to identify the required learner behaviors for smaller units of instruction. They would then write each as an instructional goal for a unit and determine the best order for sequencing them.

Suppose you were a member of the task force and were asked to brainstorm with the group to identify categories of learner behaviors implied by the instructional goal. You would begin by reviewing the instructional goal to identify clusters of behaviors that could be combined into manageable unit goals.

There appear to be four natural breaks in the implied skills. So you could write each as a separate instructional goal.

1. In written composition, students will use a variety of sentence types based upon the purpose for the sentence.
2. In written composition, students will vary the complexity of sentence structure.

3. In written composition, students will use a variety of punctuation marks to match the purpose and mood of the sentence.
4. In written composition, students will use a variety of punctuation marks to combine simple sentences, clauses, and phrases into compound, complex, and compound-complex sentences.

After reviewing the four unit-level instructional goals, the teachers decided to sequence them relative to which should be taught first, second, and so forth. Which order do you believe would be best, and why? Perhaps instructional goal one should be first, three should be second, two should be third, and four should be fourth. This order is suggested because goals one and three are closely related; it would be hard to teach sentence type without the accompanying punctuation. Likewise, goals two and four are natural companions since teaching students to combine sentences without the appropriate punctuation would also be impossible.

Based on this logic, the task force decided to combine goals one and three and goals two and four into two goals. They are the following:

1. In written composition, students will use a variety of sentence types and accompanying punctuation based upon the purpose and mood of the sentence.
2. In written composition, students will use a variety of sentence types and accompanying punctuation based upon the complexity or structure of the sentence.

The task force then considered sequence. Should they write instruction for goal one or goal two first? They decided to select goal one first because it appeared to thgem to be less complex in content and skills than goal two and because students did not need to master the skills in goal two before they could learn the skills implied in goal one. Therefore, the committee would begin their instructional project with the first instructional goal.

This scenario has demonstrated that selecting an instructional goal for a unit of instruction includes a series of decisions and refinements. It cannot be stressed too much that careful planning and analysis at the instructional goal stage of development may save hours of work later.

A second example of how to "defuzzy" an instructional goal will be helpful. Remember, simply because a goal is fuzzy does not mean it is not worthwhile. Just the opposite—it may be very worthwhile. For this example we have selected a goal common to many banks:

Personnel will know the value of courteous, friendly service.

Although we can all agree that the intentions of this goal are sound, it can be classified as fuzzy and should be clarified.

First, the phrases "will know the value of" can be changed to "will demonstrate" in order to communicate better what is expected of personnel. Second, we must determine exactly what personnel are expected to demonstrate. We can begin this task by dividing the comprehensive term *service* into more interpretable main parts. We chose to define service as: (1) a greeting to the customer, (2) a business transaction, and (3) a conclusion. Even with these two relatively minor changes, the goal is much more clear.

Original Goal	*Restated Goal*
Personnel will know the value of courteous, friendly service.	Personnel will demonstrate courteous, friendly behavior while greeting customers, transacting business, and concluding transactions.

Although the goal is much better in the new form, there are still two terms, *courteous* and *friendly*, that remain to be defuzzied. By relating two concepts to each of the three stages of service that have been identified, we can further defuzzy the goal.

Before we continue, remember the six steps included in making a fuzzy goal more clear are the following:

1. Write the goal on paper.
2. Brainstorm to identify the behaviors learners would demonstrate to reflect their achievement of the goal.
3. Sort through the stated behaviors and select those that best represent the goal.
4. Select indicators of the behaviors.
5. Incorporate each indicator into a statement that describes what the learner will do.
6. Evaluate the resulting statement for its clarity and relationship to the original fuzzy notion.

To help with the brainstorming process to identify behaviors implied by *courteous* and *friendly*, we identified the behaviors specific to each of the three stages of service. We also decided to consider behaviors that could be classified as discourteous and unfriendly in a bank setting. The lists of behaviors bank personnel *could* demonstrate and *should not* demonstrate to be considered courteous and friendly are the following:

GREETING THE CUSTOMER

Do	*Don't*
1. Initiate greeting to customer, e.g., "Hello" or "Good morning."	1. Wait for customer to speak first.
2. Say something to customer to make service appear personal: (a) use customer's name whenever possible, (b) say, "It's good to see you again" or "We haven't seen you for a while."	2. Treat customer like a stranger or someone you have never seen before.
3. If you must complete a prior transaction before beginning work, smile, verbally excuse yourself, and say you will only need a moment to finish your current task.	3. Simply continue working on a task and fail to look up or acknowledge a customer until you are ready.
4. Inquire, "How may I help you today?"	4. Wait for customer to initiate conversation about service needed.

TRANSACTING BUSINESS

Do	*Don't*
1. Attend to the customers currently waiting in your line. If you must leave your station, simply inform *newly arriving* customers that your line is closing and invite them to *begin* waiting in an alternate line.	1. Shuffle customers to another line after they have waited in yours for a while.
2. Listen attentively to customer as he or she explains problem or service desired.	2. Interrupt customers even though you believe you know what they are going to say and can see by the paperwork the type of transaction they wish.
3. Keep customer's business as the primary focus of attention during transaction.	3. Chat with employees or other customers thereby delaying current customer.
4. Complete any missing information on the form yourself explaining to the customer what you have added and why.	4. Simply inform customers they have incorrectly or incompletely filled out form thereby making it their problem.
5. Give complete, clear instructions for additional forms that the customer should complete.	5. Simply say, "Complete these other forms and then come back."

CONCLUDING TRANSACTION

Do	*Don't*
1. Inquire whether there are any additional services they need today.	1. Dismiss a customer by focusing your eyes on the next customer in line.
2. Thank the customer for his or her business.	2. Act like you have done him or her a favor by completing the transaction.
3. Verbally respond to any comments that the customer may have initiated, e.g., the weather, a holiday or upcoming vacation, your outfit or haircut, new decorations, etc.	3. Let customer-initiated comments drop as though unnoticed.
4. Conclude with a wish for their well-being, e.g., "Take care," "Have a nice trip," "Have a nice day," or "Hurry back."	4. Allow customers to walk away without a final comment or wish for their well-being.

The lists of courteous and discourteous behaviors can be given to bank administrators for additions, deletions, and further clarification.

After the list of representative behaviors is as complete as you can make it, review the list at each stage of service to identify key behaviors that best represent the instructional goal. Based upon the sample list, we would restate the instructional goal as follows. All three forms of the goal are included to enable you to compare them for completeness and clarity.

Original goal
Personnel will know the value of courteous, friendly service

Revised version
Personnel will demonstrate courteous, friendly behavior while greeting customers, transacting business, and concluding transactions

Final goal
Personnel will demonstrate courteous, friendly behavior while greeting customers, transacting business, and concluding transactions by initiating conversation, personalizing comments, focusing attention, assisting with forms, and concluding with a "thanks" and a wish for the customer's well-being.

Although the final goal reflects only a subset of the behaviors generated during the brainstorming process, those selected convey the basic intention of the instructional goal. The complete list of courteous and discourteous behaviors that was generated should be saved as input for subsequent instructional analysis activities.

These two examples demonstrate that instructional goal definition and refinement can be a lengthy, complex process which incorporates many people in the identification of problems, needs assessment, solutions, and statements of clear instructional goals. However, if instruction is to address real problems that a school or organization is facing and reflect actual goals, then this process is necessary. The second example related to clarifying a "fuzzy" goal demonstrates that while a goal clarification process can result in a clearer instructional goal, it can still remain open to interpretation by instructional designers or instructors. It must be further clarified by defining the actual behaviors to be demonstrated within each of the general categories included in the instructional goal.

A final concern when identifying instructional goals is the context in which the behavior will be performed. In our one example, the written composition goal would be achieved in a classroom with the hope that the behavior will transfer to other writing situations. The instructional goal for sales personnel implies that the ultimate performance will be with customers in a salesroom. The context of the performance of the goal will have important implications for the instructional strategy.

SUMMARY

Instructional goals are clear statements of behaviors that learners are to demonstrate as a result of instruction. They are typically derived through a needs assessment process and are intended to address problems that can be resolved most efficiently through instruction. They provide the foundation for all subsequent instructional design activities.

Instructional goals are selected and refined through a rational process that requires answering questions about a particular problem and need, about the clarity of the goal statement, and about the availability of resources to design and develop the instruction.

Questions you should answer about the problem and need include whether:

1. The need is clearly described and verified.
2. The need is foreseeable in the future as well as presently.
3. The most effective solution to the problem is instruction.
4. There is logical agreement between the solution to the problem and the proposed instructional goals.
5. The instructional goals are acceptable to administrators and managers.

Questions you should answer related to the clarity of the instructional goal include whether:

1. The behaviors reflect clearly demonstrable, measurable behaviors.
2. The topic area is clearly delineated.
3. The content is relatively stable over time.

Questions to be answered related to resources include whether:

1. You have the expertise in the instructional goal area.
2. The time and resources required to complete the project are available to you.
3. A group of learners is available during the development process in order for you to evaluate and refine your instruction.

Frequently the instructional goal will be a very general statement of behaviors and content that must be clarified before some of the preceding questions can be answered. The procedure recommended for clarifying instructional goals includes:

1. Write down the instructional goal.
2. Generate a list of all the behaviors the learners should perform to demonstrate that they have achieved the goal.
3. Analyze the expanded list of behaviors and select those that best reflect achievement of the goal.
4. Incorporate the selected behaviors into a statement or statements that describe what the learners will demonstrate.
5. Examine the revised goal statement and judge whether learners who demonstrate the behaviors would be considered to have accomplished the initial broad goal.

An appropriate, feasible, and clearly stated instructional goal should be the product of these activities. Using this clarified statement of learner outcomes, you are ready to conduct a goal analysis, which is described in chapter 3.

PRACTICE

1. The following list contains several instructional goals that may or may not be appropriate based upon the criteria for writing acceptable instructional goals stated in this chapter. Read each goal and determine whether it is all right as written or should be revised. If you believe it can be revised given the information available, revise it and compare your work with the revisions provided in the Feedback section that follows.
    a. The district will provide in-service training for teachers prior to the administration and interpretation of standardized tests.
    b. Students will understand how to punctuate a variety of simple sentences.
    c. Salespersons will learn to use time management forms.
    d. Teachers will assign one theme each week.
    e. Students will understand how to balance a checkbook.

2. The first step in developing a unit of instruction is to state the instructional goal. Several criteria can be used to help you select a suitable topic. From the following list of possible considerations for selection of an instructional goal, identify those that are relevant to a designer's selection of an instructional goal.
    _____ 1. Personal knowledge and skills in content area
    _____ 2. Stable content area
    _____ 3. Time required for writing instruction versus the importance of students possessing that knowledge or skill
    _____ 4. Students available to try out materials for clarity and revision purposes
    _____ 5. Areas in which students have difficulty learning
    _____ 6. Few materials available on the topic though instruction is considered important
    _____ 7. Content area is fairly logical
    _____ 8. Topic can be organized to fit the time available for both writing the instruction and for students using it

3. An instructional goal must be stated as clearly as possible. Below is a list of considerations for writing instructional goals. Select those within each section that are important for writing instructional goals.
    a. Behavioral Versus Nonbehavioral
        _____ 1. Behavior required of the student is obvious in the goal
        _____ 2. Behavior in the goal can be observed
        _____ 3. Behavior in the goal can be measured to determine whether students have reached the goal
    b. Clear Versus Fuzzy Goals
        _____ 1. Instructional goal with a topic and intended behavior is stated clearly
        _____ 2. Any limitations which will be imposed on the behavior or the topic is stated clearly
    c. Time
        _____ 1. Approximate instructional time required for students to reach goal
        _____ 2. Approximate writing time you can devote to writing and revising instruction

4. Write an instructional goal for which you would like to develop a unit of instruction.

═ FEEDBACK ═

1. Following are suggestions for revising the instructional goals presented in the practice exercises:
   a. Instructional goal a. should be revised because it describes what the district is expected to accomplish rather than the teachers. The goal could be rewritten in the following way to reflect two units of instruction commonly provided by school districts. Notice the behavior to be exhibited by teachers has been clarified.
      - Teachers will administer selected standardized tests according to the procedures described in the test manual.
      - Teachers will interpret student performance on both individual and class profile sheets that are provided by the test maker.
   b. Goal b. should be revised since the words "will understand" are too general. The goal could be rewritten to clarify exactly the behavior students will use to demonstrate that they understand how to punctuate sentences. Additionally, the specific punctuation marks to be included in the lesson and used by students are included in the goal.
      - Students will punctuate a variety of simple sentences using periods, question marks, and exclamation points.
   c. In goal c., "learn to use" states the intended outcome of instruction, but behavior used to describe what sales personnel will actually do might be clarified as follows:
      - Sales personnel will complete time management forms using a daily, weekly, and monthly schedule.
   d. Goal d. is not an instructional goal, but a description of the process teachers will use to enable students to practice composition skills; it totally ignores the nature of the skills students are expected to acquire during practice. Not enough information is included in the statement to enable the instructional goal to be rewritten.
   e. The term "will understand" in goal e. is imprecise. The instructional goal could be clarified as follows:
      - Given cancelled checks, a check register, and a monthly bank statement, students will balance a checkbook.

2. If you answered yes to all of the criteria listed, you are correct. Each of these criteria is an important consideration in developing an instructional goal.

3. All of the considerations listed in question 3 are important.

4. Refer back to the criteria listed in the answer to question 2. Evaluate your topic using each criterion statement.
   - Does your goal meet each criterion?
   - If it does not meet a particular criterion, can it be revised to do so?
   - If it does not meet a particular criterion and cannot be revised to do so, you may want to write another instructional goal and try again.

You may need help in determining whether your goal meets some of the criteria for topic selection such as need or interest. You might discuss these issues relative to your goal with colleagues and students. Libraries are another good source for determining whether materials on your topic are available and the nature of the available materials. Revise and rewrite your instructional goal as needed to meet the above criteria.

You may check the clarity of your goal by asking colleagues and intended learners to interpret verbally the instructional goal you have written. Do they interpret the goal and the required behavior exactly as you intended? You may need to revise.

If your goal is too big for the instructional time available (thirty minutes, one hour, two hours, etc.), you may want to divide the goal into its logical major parts, reword each part as an instructional goal, and then select the part most suited to your needs and time constraints.

If your goal is too small for the amount of time you desire, consider the skills the student will need to enter your instruction and the skills the student will be ready to learn as a result of completing it. By considering skills related to your goal in this fashion, you can identify the appropriate instruction to include for a specific period of time. Of course you will want to revise your instructional goal to include more skills or information as required.

Rewrite your instructional goal if necessary, and begin chapter 3 after you have developed a clear, behaviorally stated instructional goal that you estimate will require the desired amount of instructional time.

References and Recommended Readings

Dick, W., & Carey, L. M. (1977). Needs assessment and instructional design. *Educational Technology,* 17 (11), 53–59. This article describes procedures for using the output of a needs assessment to begin the instructional design process.

Gagné, R. M., Wager, W. W., & Briggs, L. J. (1988). *Principles of instructional design* (3rd ed.). New York: Holt, Rinehart and Winston, 1988, 39–52. Educational goals are related to instructional outcomes, especially as they relate to different categories of learning.

Kaufman, R. (Ed.) (1977). Special issue: Needs assessment. *Educational Technology,* 17 (11). An entire issue of this journal is devoted to a wide range of applications of needs assessment.

Kaufman, R. (1988). *Planning educational systems.* Lancaster, PA: Technornic Publishing Company. This book describes a total educational planning process, which includes a detailed assessment of educational needs.

Kaufman, R., & English, F. W. (1979). *Needs assessment: Concept and application.* Englewood Cliffs, NJ: Educational Technology Publications. One of the most complete and consistent descriptions of needs assessment concerns and procedures.

Mager, R. F. (1972). *Goal analysis.* Belmont, CA: Fearon Publishers. This brief book describes a process used by the author to help groups clearly identify goals for their instruction.

Miller, R. B. (1962). Task description and analysis, in R. M. Gagné (Ed.), *Psychological principles in system development.* New York: Holt, Rinehart and Winston, 187–230. This chapter is an early effort in relating job-analysis techniques to the development of training systems.

Rossett, A. (1982). A typology for generating needs assessments. *Journal of Instructional Development,* 6 (1), 28–33. Rossett relates the various purposes of a needs assessment to the types of instruments that can be used, and provides several items that might be used in needs assessment instruments.

Rossett, A. (1987). *Training needs assessment.* Englewood Cliffs, NJ: Educational Technology Publications. An excellent description of various needs assessment techniques and supporting tools.

C 3

ONDUCTING
A GOAL ANALYSIS

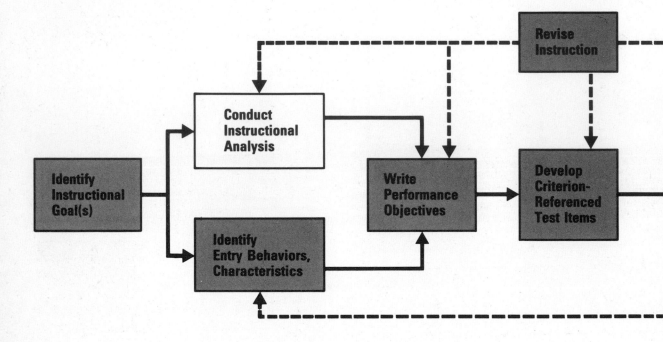

OBJECTIVES

- Classify instructional goals in the following domains: intellectual skill, verbal information, psychomotor skill, and attitude.
- Analyze an instructional goal in order to identify the major steps required to accomplish it.

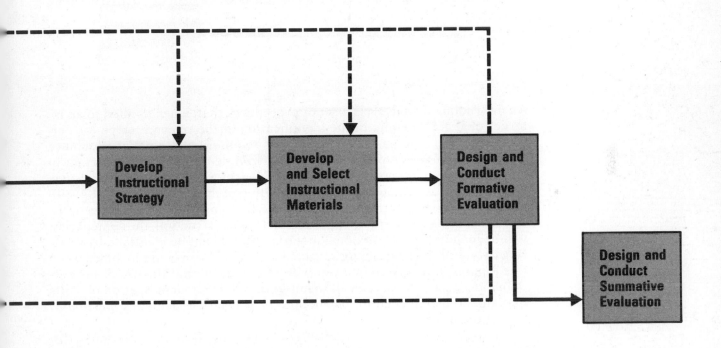

BACKGROUND

It has been customary for the content of textbooks and manuals to be determined by experts who have developed a structure for knowledge that makes up a particular discipline. Experienced instructors, using these textbooks, often have varied the instructional approach, sequence, or content as they proceeded to teach learners on a trial-and-error basis.

In recent years, researchers have tried to develop more effective procedures for identifying the appropriate skills and knowledge that should be included in instructional materials for students to efficiently and effectively achieve an instructional goal. For example, can you imagine the frustrations of a group of employees at a two-week training session on how to use a computer, who spend the first week studying the history and theory of computers? Not until the second week do they get to sit at a terminal and begin to experience the excitement of doing their own programming. This is an example of not only destroying learners' motivation, but also of not having a procedure for identifying the skills that are *really* required to achieve the instructional goal.

Likewise, rather than describing the content of a course on Shakespeare in terms of ten plays that a student might read, there has been an effort by instructional designers, through the use of goal analysis, to identify precisely what it is that students will be able to do (not what they will have read) when they complete their course on Shakespeare. This chapter will focus on these procedures.

It should be stressed that while it is not claimed that the goal analysis approach is the only way to identify content that should be included in a set of instructional materials, the use of this approach does result in the identification of skills that effectively leads to the achievement of an instructional goal.

CONCEPTS

An instructional analysis is a set of procedures that, when applied to an instructional goal, results in the identification of the relevant steps for performing a goal and the subordinate skills required for a student to achieve the goal. A subordinate skill is a skill that, while perhaps not important in and of itself as a learning outcome, must be achieved in order to learn some higher or superordinate skill. The acquisition of the subordinate skill facilitates or provides positive transfer for the learning of superordinate skills.

When using the systems approach to design instruction, the content that will be included in instructional materials should not be identified by referring to typical reference materials that indicate what is always included when this topic is taught. We hope you will be convinced that the use of instructional analysis procedures will result in the effective identification of skills that should be included in instruction for learners to achieve a particular instructional goal.

In the presentation in this chapter and chapter 4, we have chosen to discuss first the analysis of the *goal statement* per se, that is, how we determine exactly what it is that the learner will be able to do; then we discuss the instructional analysis process that is applied to identify the *subordinate (or prerequisite) skills* that must be learned in order to reach the goal. The overall process will be referred to as instructional analysis; it includes both a goal analysis and a subordinate skills analysis.

Goal analysis includes two fundamental steps. The first is to classify the goal statement according to the kind of learning that will occur. (The different categories of learning are referred to as *domains of learning*.) The second step is to describe exactly what a student will be doing when he or she is performing the goal.

Examine the following list of abbreviated goal statements:

1. The learner will be able to set up and operate a video camera.
2. Given a bank statement and a checkbook, the learner will be able to balance the checkbook.
3. Given a list of cities, the learner will be able to identify the state of which each is the capital.
4. The learner will choose to make decisions about his or her life-style that reflect positive lifelong health concerns.

Each of these goals might serve as the starting point for an instructional program. The question is: How do we determine what skills must be learned in order to achieve these goals? The first step is to categorize the goal into one of Gagné's (1985) domains of learning. The goal should be classified into one of the domains in order to identify the appropriate subordinate skills analysis techniques discussed in chapter 4. Therefore, we will consider each of the four goals in turn and classify the goal under consideration.

Psychomotor Skills

The first goal we listed involved the setting up and operation of a video camera. This would be classified as a psychomotor goal because it involves mental and physical activity. In this case there is equipment that must be manipulated in a very specific way to successfully produce a video image.

The characteristics of a psychomotor skill are that the learner must execute muscular actions, with or without equipment, to achieve specified results. In certain situations there may be a lot of "psycho" in the psychomotor goal. That is, there may be a great deal of mental or cognitive activity that must accompany the motor activity. However, for purposes of instructional analysis, if the learner must learn to execute new, nontrivial, motor skills, or performance is dependent on the skillful execution of a physical skill, we will refer to it as a psychomotor goal.

Intellectual Skills

Now let's consider the goal which deals with balancing a checkbook. By nearly anyone's definition, this is a problem-solving task and therefore is classified as an intellectual skill. Intellectual skills are those that require the learner to do some unique cognitive activity—unique in the sense that the learner must be able to solve a problem or perform an activity with previously unencountered information or examples. There are four types of intellectual skills: discriminations, concepts, rules, and problem solving.

With these skills the learner can determine whether two things are alike or different, can classify things according to labels and characteristics, can apply a rule, and can select and apply a variety of rules in order to solve problems. Therefore, any goal that requires a learner to manipulate symbolic information in some way will be an intellectual skill. So, in addition to our problem-solving goal, the following would also be classified as intellectual skills: being able to apply the rule for computing sales tax, being able to classify a variety of creatures as either animals or fish, and being able to determine if two musical tones are similar or different. Carefully note the difference between intellectual skills and the domain of verbal information described in the next section.

Verbal Information

One of our sample goals required the learner to list the state for which each of the cities is the capital. The task for the learner is to list the state that corresponds with each capital city. There are many ways to teach such a skill and several ways the learner might try to learn it. But basically there is only one answer for each question and only one basic way to ask each question.

There is no symbolic manipulation—no problem solving or rule applying. In essence, verbal information goals require the learners to provide specific responses to relatively specific stimuli.

You can usually spot a verbal information goal by the verb that is used. Often the learner must state, list, or describe something. It is assumed that the "something" that is to be stated or listed will be taught in the instruction. Therefore, the learner is storing the information during the instruction and retrieving it for the test.

Attitudes

If we express a goal statement in terms of having learners choose to do something, then that goal should be classified as an attitudinal goal. Attitudes are usually described as the tendency to make particular choices or decisions to act under particular circumstances. For example, we would like individuals to choose to be good employees, choose to protect the environment, choose to eat nourishing food, etc. The goal we stated at the beginning of the chapter was that learners would choose to make life-style decisions that reflect a positive concern for their health. To identify an attitudinal goal, determine whether the learners will have a choice to make, and if the goal indicates the direction in which the decision is to be influenced.

Another characteristic of attitudinal goals is that they probably will not be achieved at the end of the instruction. They are quite often long-term goals that are extremely important, but very difficult to evaluate in the short term.

As you examine an attitudinal goal, you will find that the learner expresses an attitude by doing or expressing something. That "something" will be a psychomotor skill, intellectual skill, or verbal information. Therefore, instructional goals that focus on attitudes can be viewed as: influencing the learner to choose, under certain circumstances, to perform an intellectual skill, psychomotor skill, or stating certain verbal information.

Goal Analysis

It is important to recognize that the amount of instruction required to teach an instructional goal will vary tremendously from one goal to another. Some goals will represent skills that can be taught in less than an hour while others will take many hours to achieve. The smaller the goal, the easier it is to do a precise analysis of what is to be learned. After we identify the domain of the goal, it is necessary to be more specific in indicating what the learner will be doing when performing the goal.

The best technique for the designer to use in analyzing a goal is to describe, in step-by-step fashion, exactly what a person would be doing when performing the goal. This is not as easy as it at first sounds since the things that the person does can be either physical activities, as in a psychomotor skill, which are easy to observe, or they can be "mental steps," which must be executed before there is any overt behavior, as in an intellectual skill. For example, it would be quite easy to observe the steps used to clean a paintbrush and spray equipment, but almost impossible to observe all the steps that a person might follow to determine how much paint would be required to cover a building.

As you go through the process of describing the exact steps that a person would take in performing your goal, you may find that one of the steps requires a decision followed by several alternate paths that can be pursued (and, therefore, must be learned). For example, with the cleaning of a paint-brush, you might find at one point in the cleaning process that the paint will not come out, so an alternative technique must be applied. Similarly, in attempting to solve the mathematics problems related to area and required paint, it may be necessary to first classify the problems as "type A" or "type B." Based on that outcome, one of two very different techniques might be used to solve the problem. The point is that the learner has to be taught both how to make the decision and how to perform all of the alternative steps required to reach the goal.

Therefore, goal analysis is the visual display of the specific steps the learner would do when performing the instructional goal. You might simply list the steps: 1, 2, 3, etc. It is even better to represent each step in a box in a flow diagram:

If reaching the goal includes decision making, the decision point step can be shown in a diamond with the alternate paths shown leading from the diamond.

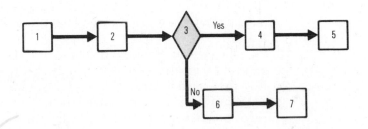

Notice that the numbers do not necessarily indicate the sequence in which all of the steps will be performed because, as in the example diagramed above, if a person does steps 4 and 5 as a result of the decision made at 3, then the person would not do steps 6 and 7. The opposite would also be true. Also note that step 3, because it is in a diamond, *must* be a question, the answer to which leads one to *different* steps or skills. The answers to the questions are written on the pathway to the next steps. If a decision is made but, regardless of the decision, the next step is always the same, then a diamond is not used, just a box.

As you analyze your goal, you may find that you have difficulty knowing exactly how much should be included in each step. As a general rule, at this stage, you would typically have at least three to five steps, but not more than fifteen. If you have fewer than three to five, perhaps you have not been specific enough in describing the steps. If you have more than fifteen steps, then you have either taken too large a "chunk" to be analyzed, or you have listed the steps in too much detail. The recommendation is to review and revise the steps until you have between five and fifteen.

One special note should be made about the goal analysis of a verbal information goal. If you begin the process by thinking, "Now let's see, what will the student be doing? I guess I will ask them to list the major bones in the body, to describe the major causes of bone injuries, etc. I'll just ask them on a test to do this, and they'll write down their answers." In a sense, there is no intellectual or psychomotor procedure other than the presentation of a test question and the retrieval of the answer. There is no problem solving with the information nor any decision making required of the learner. Therefore, the goal analysis indicates only the specific cues the learner might use to retrieve the desired information, but there is no sequence of steps, per se.

In the section that follows, you will see how goals can be described in a sequential, step-by-step fashion. This procedure provides both a clear statement of what the learner will be able to do, and helps the designer with the next step in the process, namely, identifying the subordinate skills necessary for reaching the goal.

The goal analysis is an extremely important step in the instructional design process, because all subsequent design activities depend on the skills that are identified. If it is difficult to think of your goal in terms of sequential steps, perhaps it has not been clearly stated in terms of the outcome behavior required. If it has, and you still have difficulty, there are several procedures you can use to help identify the steps. The first suggestion is to describe for yourself the kind of test item or assessment you would use to determine whether the learners could perform your goal. Now, think about the steps the learner would have to go through to respond to your assessment or test. Another suggestion is to "test" yourself; that is, observe yourself, both in the physical and mental sense, performing the goal. Note each of the steps you go through and the decisions you have to make. Although these procedures may seem very simple to you, remember that you are the subject-matter expert; they will not be so simple or obvious to the uninformed learner.

One precaution must be noted. It has been our experience with goal analysis that the person doing the analysis often falls into the trap of saying, "Well, first they need to know this, and then this, and then this . . ." This is definitely not what is desired, because focusing on what learners need to know often leads to a list of concepts, not behavioral steps the learner must do. The trick is to concentrate on the steps in *performing* the goal rather than on what you think learners need to know—that will come later.

EXAMPLES

The first phase of performing an instructional analysis involves two major steps: (1) classifying the goal into a domain of learning, and (2) identifying and sequencing the major steps required to perform the goal. Table 3.1 includes five sample instructional goals and a list of the four learning domains previously described. First, we will classify each goal into one of the domains and then identify and sequence the major steps required to perform the goal. The letter of the corresponding learning domain is written in the space provided to the left of each goal statement.

The first instructional goal presented in the table, putting a golf ball, should be classified as a psychomotor skill since both mental planning and physical execution of the plan are required to putt the ball into the cup. Neither banging the ball around the green nor simply "willing" the ball into the cup will accomplish the task. Rather, mental planning and calculating com-

TABLE 3.1

SAMPLE INSTRUCTIONAL GOALS AND LEARNING DOMAINS

Domain Letter	Sample Goals	Learning Domain
C	1. Putting a golf ball.	A. Verbal information—stating facts, providing specific information, e.g., naming objects.
B	2. Determining the distance between two specified places on a state map.	
D	3. Choosing to maximize personal safety while staying in a hotel.	B. Intellectual skills—making discriminations, learning concepts, using rules, and solving problems.
A	4. Naming the command keys used to move the cursor around the screen in a specified direction and speed (word processing).	C. Psychomotor skills—physical activity which usually includes mental activity as well.
B	5. Writing a theme that includes a variety of sentence types based upon the purpose of the sentence and the idea being communicated.	D. Attitudes—making particular choices or behaving in a manner that implies an underlying belief or preference.

bined with accurately executing the stroke based upon mental calculations are required.

Now that we have the putting goal classified by domain, we should proceed to identify and sequence the major steps learners would take to execute the goal. Figure 3.1 contains the major steps, in sequence, required to accomplish the goal. As we watch a golfer preparing to putt the ball, we notice some mental planning activities appear to occur. The steps identified that follow planning simply provide a broad overview of the complete task from beginning to end. The sequence we have at this point provides us with the framework we will need to identify the subordinate skills required to perform each of the steps already identified.

Return to the second goal listed in Table 3.1, determining distances between specified places on a state map. This goal is classified as an intellectual skill because learners will be required to learn concepts, follow rules,

FIGURE 3.1

GOAL ANALYSIS FOR A PSYCHOMOTOR SKILL

GOAL:
Putting a golf ball

TYPE OF LEARNING:
Psychomotor

GOAL ANALYSIS:

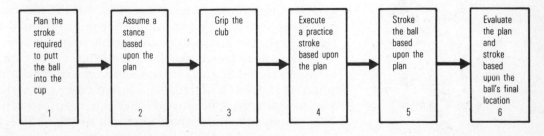

Plan the stroke required to putt the ball into the cup	Assume a stance based upon the plan	Grip the club	Execute a practice stroke based upon the plan	Stroke the ball based upon the plan	Evaluate the plan and stroke based upon the ball's final location
1	2	3	4	5	6

and solve problems in performing the goal. With the goal classified, we should identify major steps required to perform the goal and the best sequence for the steps. A good way for the designer to proceed is to identify the type of test item that would be used to determine if a student could perform this skill. You could obtain a copy of a state map and review how this task can be accomplished using the map as a reference. Checking the map, one sees that there are obviously three separate and distinct ways to determine distance between specified places. One is to use a mileage table, another is to use a mileage scale, and yet another is to add miles printed along highways between the cities. Therefore, if the student is to be able to use all three methods, there will be three main methods included in the goal analysis.

Another task would be to decide which of the three identified methods is most appropriate to use in a particular situation. This task implies that there is a decision to be made; therefore, the criteria necessary to make the decision must be learned. Figure 3.2 contains the major steps required to perform the goal. If learners need to determine the distance between major cities within a state, they will perform tasks 1, 2, 3, and 4. If they need to determine the distance between distant towns or a city and a town, they will use tasks 1, 2, 3, 5, and 6. Similarly, if they need to determine the distance between relatively close cities and towns, which would be the situation if the answer to the first two questions were "no," they will use steps 1, 2, 3, 5, and 7. When a choice or decision must be made in order to perform a goal, then when and how to make the decision must be learned together with the other steps. Simply teaching learners to use each of the three procedures would not be adequate. At this point we have the instructional goal analyzed to provide a framework that will enable us to identify the subordinate skills required to accomplish each major task.

The third goal listed in Table 3.1, choosing to maximize personal safety while staying in a hotel, is classified as an attitudinal goal since it implies behavior based upon an underlying attitude or belief. What would learners be doing if they were exhibiting behavior that showed they were safety conscious while staying in a hotel? The first step to building a framework for this goal would be to visit several hotels and inquire about safety features provided by them. This activity would probably result in identifying the three main areas of concern.

1. Follows safety precautions for hotel fires.
2. Follows safety precautions for personal safety while in room.
3. Follows safety precautions for securing valuable possessions.

Figure 3.3 shows the major steps for the first goal related to hotel fires. This series of steps reflects the actual behaviors that a person would perform if they *choose* to follow safety precautions for hotel fires. Each of these major steps could be broken down further, but, for now, they indicate what a person would be doing if he or she performs the first part of this goal. A similar analysis would be done for the second and third components of the goal related to personal safety and protecting valuable possessions.

The fourth instructional goal in Table 3.1, naming the command keys used to move the cursor around the screen of a microcomputer in a specified direction and speed (which is related to word processing), is classified as a verbal information goal, because learners are required to name a specific command key required to move the cursor in a specified direction. The cursor is a line or dash of light that indicates where on the screen the next character can

FIGURE 3.2

GOAL ANALYSIS FOR AN INTELLECTUAL SKILL

GOAL:
Determine distance between specified cities and towns on a state map

TYPE OF LEARNING:
Intellectual skill

GOAL ANALYSIS:

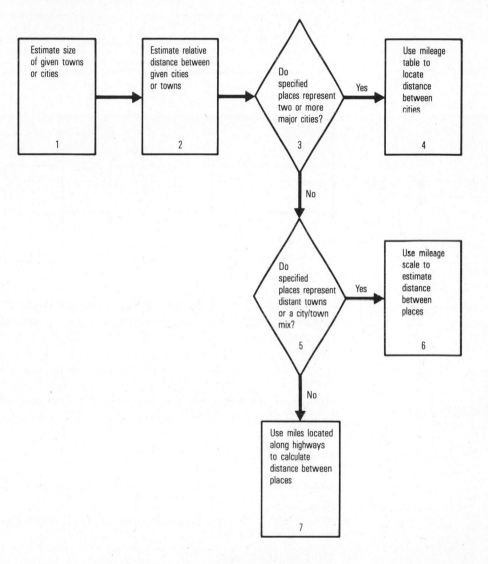

be typed. Knowledge of four topics is required to perform this goal; they are illustrated in Figure 3.4. There is no mandated order inherent in the information. Note that for a verbal information goal these are not "steps" in the sense that one goes from one activity to the next. Thus, the goal analysis simply indicates the major topics of information that must be covered in the instruction.

Now turn your attention to the fifth instructional goal in Table 3.1, writing a story that includes a variety of sentence types based upon the purpose

FIGURE 3.3

GOAL ANALYSIS FOR AN ATTITUDINAL GOAL

GOAL:
Chooses to maximize personal safety while staying in a hotel

TYPE OF LEARNING:
Attitude

GOAL ANALYSIS:

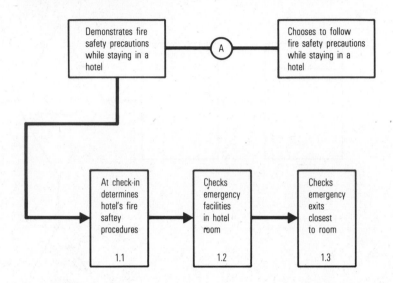

of the sentence and the idea being communicated. This goal is classified as an intellectual skill since it requires learning concepts and rules as well as solving problems. The nine steps identified to perform this goal and the planned sequence are included in Figure 3.5. There is a natural flow of tasks from left to right since the product developed at each step becomes input for the subsequent one. Notice also that a feedback loop for continued revision has been included. This step-by-step explanation of the general instructional goal will make subsequent instructional analysis activities much easier.

FIGURE 3.4

GOAL ANALYSIS FOR A VERBAL INFORMATION GOAL

GOAL:
Able to name the command keys used to move a cursor in a specified direction and speed around a screen

TYPE OF LEARNING:
Verbal information

GOAL ANALYSIS:

Describe the cursor and its movement around the screen	Describe the control key and its relationship to cursor	Name the command keys used to control cursor direction	Name the command keys used to control cursor speed
1	2	3	4

FIGURE 3.5

GOAL ANALYSIS OF INSTRUCTIONAL GOAL ON STORY WRITING

GOAL:
In writing short stories, use a variety of sentence types and punctuation based upon sentence purpose and the idea or mood being communicated

TYPE OF LEARNING:
Intellectual skill

GOAL ANALYSIS:

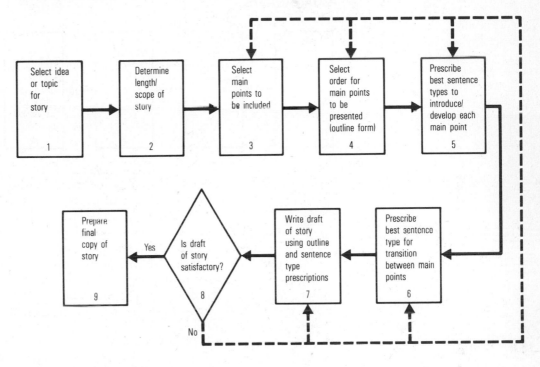

Typical First Approach to Goal Analysis

When writing a text like this, the instructional goal diagrams illustrated appear in the text as though they simply flowed from the pens (or word processors) of the authors. When the reader initially applies the process, however, it doesn't always seem to work well. Therefore, it might be useful to show a typical "first pass" at goal analysis and to point out some of the problems that can be avoided.

Examine Figure 3.6, which shows the analysis of a wordy goal, related to the initial use of a word processor. It appears that the analyst did not say, "How would I perform this goal?" but seemed to ask: "How would I teach this goal?" We might want to explain a few concepts before we get started, which may be appropriate as part of the instructional strategy. At this point, however, we only want to list the steps in actually performing the goal. So, if the designer were performing the goal in Figure 3.6, he or she would not start with an explanation of DOS; thus, step 1 should be eliminated.

Step 2 appears to be a general step related to getting the system up and running. It should be revised to express what the learner would be doing, namely, insert disk and turn on power. Step 3 indicates some of the DOS

FIGURE 3.6

**FAULTY GOAL ANALYSIS OF AN INTELLECTUAL SKILL
RELATED TO WORD PROCESSING**

GOAL:
Students will be able to boot up the PCs with DOS, execute some systems commands, and create, edit, and print a document using a word processing system

TYPE OF LEARNING:
Intellectual skill

GOAL ANALYSIS:

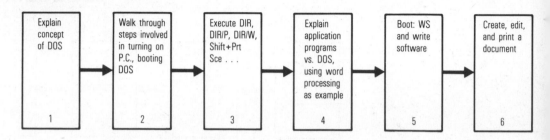

system start-up commands and probably should be stated that way. Those familiar with word processing will note that there are actually *two* goals here—one related to DOS commands and one related to the use of word processing. Therefore, we recommend dropping step 3 (as shown in Figure 3.6) completely and moving to the next step.

In step 4, the expert who was performing the goal would never stop to explain what an application program is. This may be a subordinate skill somewhere in the instruction, but it doesn't belong here; thus, it too should be eliminated. All we want to do is note the steps in getting the word processing application working.

Now on to step 5: Boot WS and write software. Now we are back on track of using the word processing system, since "boot WS" will bring the word processing system up on the screen. However, what is meant by "write software"? It should be dropped because the substance of the goal is included in step 6.

The final step, step 6, includes writing, editing, and printing a document. This is much too large a step for a goal analysis. It should be broken down into the following separate steps: create a file, enter a paragraph of prose, edit a paragraph, and print a paragraph.

Given this analysis, we would rewrite the goal as follows: Students will be able to operate a word processing system by entering, editing, and printing a brief document. The revised steps are shown in Figure 3.7. It looks considerably different from the initial one in Figure 3.6. Also note as you review the steps necessary to carry out the goal, that no one step is equivalent to performing the goal; *all* the steps must be performed in sequence in order to demonstrate the ability to perform the goal.

SUMMARY

The goal analysis process is begun only after you have a clear statement of the instructional goal. The first step in the goal analysis process is to classify the goal into one of the four domains of learning. It will be either an

FIGURE 3.7

REVISED GOAL ANALYSIS FOR A WORD PROCESSING GOAL

GOAL:
Students will be able to operate a word processing system by entering, editing, and printing a brief document

TYPE OF LEARNING:
Intellectual skill

GOAL ANALYSIS:

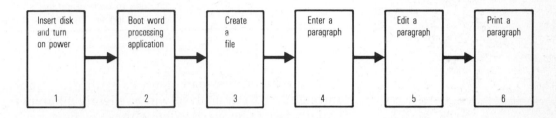

attitude, an intellectual skill, verbal information, or a psychomotor skill. This classification step is necessary because each type of goal requires a different goal analysis technique.

The second step in goal analysis is to identify the major steps learners must perform to demonstrate they have achieved the goal. These major steps should include both the behavior and relevant content, and they should be sequenced in the most efficient order. For intellectual skill and psychomotor goals, a chronological list of the steps to be taken is best. The best sequence for the behaviors within attitude and verbal information goals is also chronological when a natural chronology can be identified. When there is no natural chronology among the steps, however, they should be sequenced based on the inherent relationships among them, e.g., spatial, easy-to-complex, familiar-to-unfamiliar, common content areas, etc.

It is important to remember that perfect frameworks of skills required for a goal are rarely created following the first attempt. Your initial product should be viewed as a draft and should be subjected to evaluation and refinement. Specific problems to look for during the evaluation include steps that are unnatural in the process, that are too small or too large, and that are misplaced in the sequence.

The final product of your goal analysis should be a framework of skills that provides an overview of what learners will be doing when they perform the instructional goal. This framework is the foundation for the subordinate skills analysis described in chapter 4.

PRACTICE

1. Table 3.2 contains a list of learning domains and sample instructional goals. Read each goal in column two, and classify it using the learning domains listed in column one. Space is provided in column three for you to write the rationale you need to classify each goal. Check your work with the examples provided in Table 3.3 in the Feedback section.

2. On separate sheets of paper, identify and sequence the major areas of activity implied by each of the instructional goals shown in the first prac-

TABLE 3.2

Learning Domain	Sample Instructional Goal	Rationale
A. Psychomotor Skill B. Intellectual Skill C. Verbal Information D. Attitude	_____ 1. Open and maintain a checking account _____ 2. Label parts of the human body using common terminology _____ 3. Separate an egg yolk from the egg white, using the shell as a tool _____ 4. Choose to behave safely while flying on airplanes	

tice activity. Check your analysis with those provided in Figures 3.8 through 3.11. Your analysis will be slightly different from ours since there usually is no one way to define these goals.

FEEDBACK

Compare your responses to Table 3.2 and your decisions about what constitutes the major steps and sequences for each of the four instructional goals listed in the table with Table 3.3 and Figures 3.8 through 3.11.

In deciding the major steps and sequence for the tasks related to opening and maintaining a checking account, a simple chronological order for main events was used. You cannot deposit money into an account that has not been opened, you cannot keep a register of activities if none has occurred, and you cannot withdraw money from an account if none has been deposited. These major steps and the order identified using the instructional goal will provide the framework necessary for you to identify subordinate skills required to accomplish each step.

The second goal, locating and labeling parts of the human body, did not have a chronology of events that could be used to develop a logical framework. Therefore, an organizing method needed to be identified that would

FIGURE 3.8

GOAL ANALYSIS FOR AN INTELLECTUAL SKILL

GOAL:
Open and maintain a checking account

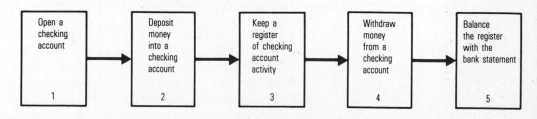

FIGURE 3.9

GOAL ANALYSIS FOR A VERBAL INFORMATION GOAL

GOAL:
Locate and label various parts of the human body

LOCATE AND LABEL:

1. Head	2. Arm	3. Hand	4. Trunk	5. Leg	6. Foot
1.1 Ear	2.1 Upper arm	3.1 Back	4.1 Spine	5.1 Thigh	6.1 Heel
1.2 Eye	2.2 Elbow	3.2 Palm	4.2 Shoulder blade	5.2 Knee	6.2 Sole
1.3 Nose	2.3 Forearm	3.3 Thumb	4.3 Buttocks	5.3 Calf	6.3 Arch
1.4 Mouth	2.4 Wrist	3.4 Finger	4.4 Collarbone	5.4 Shin	6.4 Big toe
1.5 Forehead		3.5 Knuckle	4.5 Shoulder	5.5 Ankle	6.5 Toes
1.6 Eyebrow		3.6 Fingernail	4.6 Chest		
1.7 Cheek			4.7 Waist		
1.8 Chin			4.8 Stomach		
			4.9 Pelvic bone		

enable us to cluster or group tasks in a logical manner. We chose to organize the content using main areas of the body. We then selected a sequence for the areas by moving from the top to the bottom—for example, head, arms, trunk, legs, and feet. Note that the boxes are not connected because these are not sequential steps that must be performed.

The psychomotor skill required to crack an egg and separate the yolk from the white also had a natural chronology of events. The shell could not be pulled apart until it was broken, and the egg white could not be separated until the shell was pulled apart. Like most psychomotor tasks, this one requires practice. The only way your mind can tell your hands how hard to

FIGURE 3.10

GOAL ANALYSIS FOR A PSYCHOMOTOR SKILL GOAL

GOAL:
Using the shell as a tool, separate an egg yolk from the egg white

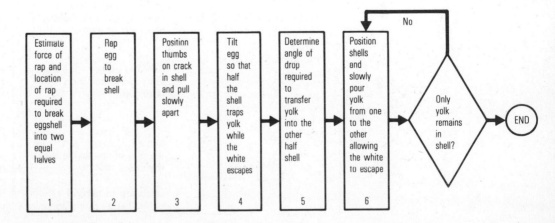

FIGURE 3.11

GOAL ANALYSIS FOR AN ATTITUDINAL GOAL

GOAL:
Choose to follow safety precautions while traveling on airplanes

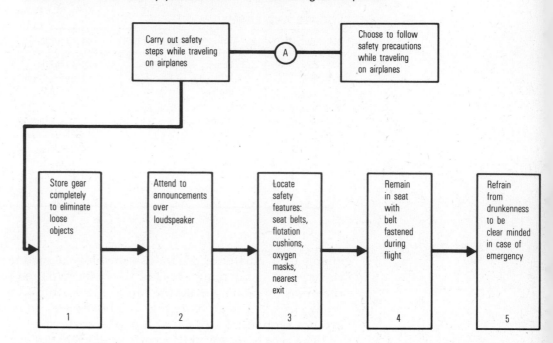

tap the shell or how fast to pour the yolk is to practice the skill. Incorrect estimations and translations result in squashed shells and broken yolks.

The instructional goal on airplane safety has a sequence of sorts that does help with this goal. Carry-on items are stored and then attention is given to safety announcements. They will help in locating safety features on the plane. Then it is necessary to keep the seat belt on and to limit one's alcoholic intake.

TABLE 3.3

Learning Domain	Sample Instructional Goal	Rationale
A. Psychomotor Skill B. Intellectual Skill C. Verbal Information D. Attitude	_B_ 1. Opening and maintaining a checking account	Requires a complex set of discriminations, concepts, and rules to make decisions and solve problems.
	_C_ 2. Labeling parts of the human body using common terminology	Requires associating a name with a part of the body. Each part of the body has one name. It does not require anything but recalling labels or names.
	_A_ 3. Separate an egg yolk from the egg white, using the shell as a tool	Requires mental planning and accurate translation of mental plans into physical actions.
	_D_ 4. Choosing to behave safely while flying on airplanes	Behavior implies an underlying attitude about safety.

References and Recommended Readings

Briggs, L. J., & Wager, W. (1981). *Handbook of procedures for the design of instruction* (2nd ed.). Englewood Cliffs, NJ: Educational Technology Publications, 85–100. Excellent resource for developing information maps that include two or more types of goals.

Davis, R. H., Alexander, L. T., & Yelon, S. L. (1974). *Learning system design*. New York: McGraw-Hill, 129–158. The coverage of instructional analysis emphasizes techniques for examining procedural, sequential types of learning tasks.

Gagné, R. M. (1985). *Conditions of learning* (4th ed.). New York: Holt, Rinehart and Winston. This book is a classic in regard to many aspects of instructional design, including the domains of learning and hierarchical analysis.

Gagné, R. M., Briggs, L. J., & Wager, W. W. (1988). *Principles of instructional design* (3rd ed.). New York: Holt, Rinehart and Winston. Provides a number of examples of the application of hierarchical analysis to intellectual skills.

Hannum, W. H. (1980). Task analysis procedures. *NSPI Journal*, 19 (3), 16–17. A comparison of several procedures for identifying subordinate skills.

Journal of Instructional Development (1983). Vol. 6, no. 4. This is a special theme issue on instructional analysis, which includes discussions of current trends and alternative methods of task and instructional analysis.

Levine, E. R. (1983). *Everything you always wanted to know about job analysis*. Tampa, FL: Mariner Publishing Co. This is a paperback introductory text on job analysis.

Magee, R. F. (1988). *Making instruction work*. Belmont, CA: David S. Lake Publishers. Discusses goal analysis and shows the use of a flow diagram to clarify a goal.

Merrill, P. F. (1978). Hierarchical and information processing tasks analysis: A comparison. *Journal of Instructional Development*, 1, 35–40. Merrill explains the information processing approach to analyzing a task in terms of the sequence of mental steps required of the person performing the task.

Merrill, P. F. (1980). Analysis of a procedural task. *NSPI Journal*, 19 (2), 11–15. Merrill uses flow-charting methods to identify the subordinate skills of a complex intellectual skill.

4
CONDUCTING
A SUBORDINATE SKILLS ANALYSIS

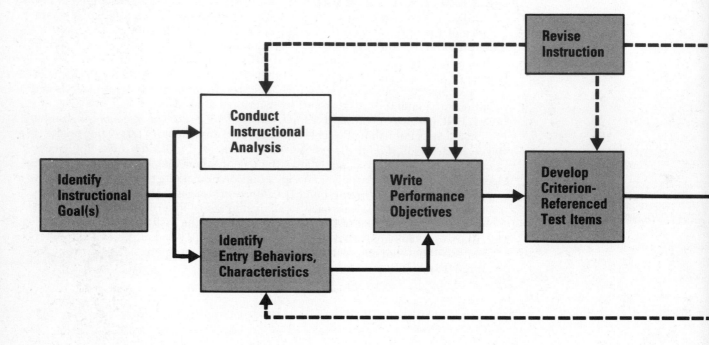

OBJECTIVES

- Identify and describe hierarchical, procedural, cluster, and combination approaches to subordinate skills analysis.
- Describe the relationship among the subskills identified through an analysis.
- Apply subordinate skills analysis techniques to identify subskills required to reach an instructional goal.

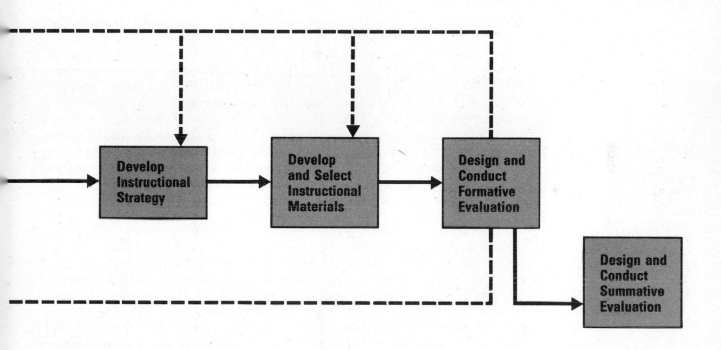

BACKGROUND

A goal analysis indicates the steps and decisions learners would carry out if they were performing the goal. In the most basic instructional situation, we could instruct the learner how to do step 1, then step 2, etc. However, this is usually not feasible for two reasons: either the step is too large to be taught as stated and must be broken down into smaller steps. or the learner must acquire some preliminary information prior to learning a particular step in the instructional goal. The skills that must be mastered prior to learning how to perform the steps in the goal are referred to as subordinate skills.

The major problem is the identification of the appropriate set of subordinate skills. If required skills are omitted from the instruction, then many students will not have the background required to achieve the goal, and thus the instruction will be ineffective. On the other hand, if superfluous skills are included, the instruction will take more time than should be required, and the unnecessary skills may actually interfere with learning the required skills. The identification of both too many or too few skills can be a problem.

The processes used to identify subordinate skills are directly related to the various domains of the goals. We will describe each of the techniques and indicate how they can be applied to various types of goals. We will begin with "pure" goals, that is, goals in which the steps are only intellectual skills or only psychomotor skills. Complex goals, however, often involve several domains. A combination approach that can be used with complex goals will also be described.

CONCEPTS

Hierarchical Approach

The hierarchical approach is used to analyze goals that are classified as intellectual skills. To understand the hierarchical approach, consider an instructional goal that requires the student to justify the recommendation that a particular piece of real estate should be purchased at a particular time. This is an intellectual skill goal, and it requires students to learn a number of rules and concepts related to the assessment of property values, the effect of inflation on property values, the financial status of the buyer, and the buyer's short- and long-term investment goals. The skills in each of these areas would depend upon an understanding of the basic concepts used in the financial and real estate fields. In this example, it would be extremely important to identify and teach each of the critical rules and concepts prior to teaching the steps for analyzing a particular situation and making a recommendation.

How does the designer go about identifying the subordinate skills a student must learn in order to achieve a higher level intellectual skill? The hierarchical analysis technique suggested by Gagné consists of asking the question, "What must the student already know so that, with a minimal amount of instruction, this task can be learned?" By asking this question, the designer can identify one or more critical subordinate skills that will be required of the learner prior to attempting instruction on the final task. After these subordinate skills have been identified, the designer then asks the same question with regard to each of them, namely, "What is it that the student must already know how to do, the absence of which would make it impossible to learn this subordinate skill?" This will result in the identification of one or more additional subordinate skills. If this process is continued with lower and lower level subordinate skills, one quickly reaches a very basic level of performance such as being able to recognize whole numbers or being able to recognize letters.

To get a visual understanding of how the designer "builds" the hierarchical analysis, consider the generic hierarchy shown in Figure 4.1. Here two "rules" serve as the immediate subordinate skills required to learn a particular problem-solving skill. It is important to understand that box 7 represents all the steps in performing the goal. This technique can also be applied to only *one* step in the goal, if that step is an intellectual skill. After the two rules have been identified (boxes 4 and 6), the designer then asks, "What must the student know how to do in order to learn the first rule?" The answer is that the student must learn two "concepts," which are represented in boxes 3 and 2. The same question for rule two results in the identification of one concept, which is shown in box 5. When asked, "What must the student know how to do to learn the concept in box 3?" the answer is "nothing," so no additional skills are listed. The same is true for box 5. For box 2, the question results in the identification of a relevant discrimination. Figure 4.1 represents how the analysis would appear when laid out in a diagram.

Figure 4.1 is consistent with Gagné's hierarchy of intellectual skills. Gagné has noted that in order to learn how to perform problem-solving skills, the learner must first know how to apply the rules that are required to solve the problem. Thus, the immediate subskills to the instructional goal are the rules that must be applied in the problem situation.

Further, Gagné has noted that rules are based upon recognizing the components or concepts that are combined in the rules. In other words, in order to learn the relationship among "things," you must be able to classify them. Therefore, the subordinate skills required for any given rule are typically classifying the concepts that are used in the rules. Finally, the learner must be able to discriminate whether a particular example is relevant to the concept.

This hierarchy of skills is helpful to the designer because it can be used to suggest the type of specific subordinate skills that will be required to support any particular instructional goal or step in the goal. If the goal is a problem-solving skill (or selecting and using a number of rules), then the subskills should include the relevant rules, concepts, and discriminations. If, however, the application of a single rule is being taught, then only the subordinate concepts and discriminations would be taught.

FIGURE 4.1

HYPOTHETICAL HIERARCHICAL ANALYSIS OF A PROBLEM-SOLVING GOAL

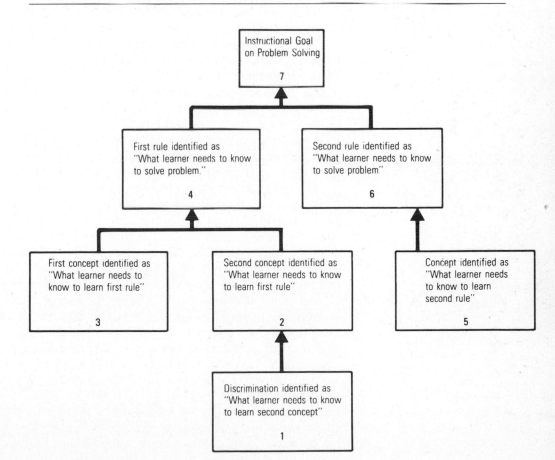

In Gagné's work with hierarchical analysis, he began the analysis with the instructional goal described in a single box at the top of a page. As the analysis procedure is carried out, the subordinate skills are then listed in appropriately connected boxes beneath the instructional goal. You may choose to use this technique, or a modified approach which is based on your goal analysis.

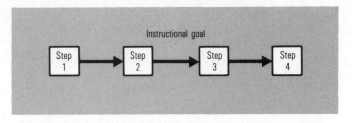

In order to relate the hierarchical analysis technique to the goal analysis in chapter 3, assume that the various steps in the goal are shown in boxes, and then a large box is drawn around all of them:

The execution of all the steps represents the goal, as does the larger box. It helps, in doing the hierarchical analysis, to have the individual steps shown in the box so that the designer can be certain to identify all of the skills that must be learned before instruction can begin for the instructional goal. Note that in many examples in this book of hierarchical analysis, the top box representing the instructional goal will, as Gagné has done, include only a statement of the goal and not all the component steps. This is a shorthand method used for space purposes. It is assumed that all of these "boxes" include all the component steps in the goal statement.

To apply the hierarchical approach to the steps in the goal analysis, the designer uses exactly the same approach as with the intact goal statement, but now applies it to *each step* in the execution of the goal. The question is asked, "What would the student have to know in order to learn to do the *first step* in performing the goal?" The question is repeated for each of the subskills for the first step, and then for each of the remaining steps in the information-processing representation of the goal. If this approach were used with the hypothetical problem-solving goal which was shown in Figure 4.1, the result might resemble that shown in Figure 4.2.

Observe that in Figure 4.2 the same subskills have been identified as in the original methodology suggested by Gagné: The fact that there are no subskills listed for steps 1, 3, and 4 indicates that the designer has determined that there are no relevant skills that the learner must master before being taught these steps. Often this may be a perfectly reasonable assumption. However, when the steps in the goal analysis are used, it may be found that there are more subskills than those identified through the original approach.

An example of the result of using the hierarchical instructional analysis technique appears in Figure 4.3. In the diagram it can be seen that the instructional goal requires the student to estimate to the nearest one-hundredth of a unit (plus or minus one one-hundredth) a designated point on a linear scale marked only in tenths. Given this goal, three subordinate skills have been identified. These are related to estimating a point to the nearest hundredth on a scale marked only in tenths units, dividing that scale into subunits, and identifying a designated point on a particular scale. Each of these skills has subordinate skills which are identified.

The use of the goal analysis approach to hierarchical analysis is illustrated in Figure 4.4. Notice that the cognitive task performed by the learner

FIGURE 4.2

HYPOTHETICAL HIERARCHICAL ANALYSIS OF STEPS IN A PROBLEM-SOLVING GOAL

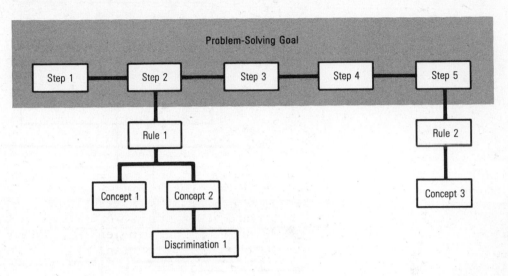

is stated somewhat differently in the four successive steps labeled 1, 2, 3, and 4. In this particular example, the subordinate skills are the same as those identified for the same skill in Figure 4.3; however, it should be noted that they are organized somewhat differently.

These particular analyses were not devised on the basis of one attempt at the process, or even two or three. It takes a number of attempts at identifying the vertical subordinate skills and their interrelationships before you can be satisfied that you have identified all the relevant skills and have stated them appropriately—and it is almost impossible to know when an appropriate and valid hierarchical analysis of an instructional goal has been achieved.

After you are satisfied that you have identified all the subskills required for students to master your instructional goal, you will want to diagram your analysis. The following conventions are used when diagramming a hierarchical analysis:

1. The instructional goal and/or steps in the goal appear in a box at the top of the hierarchy.
2. All subordinate intellectual skills appear in boxes that are attached via lines coming from the tops and bottoms of boxes.
3. Verbal information and attitudinal skills are attached to intellectual and motor skills via horizontal lines, as will be shown in subsequent sections.
4. Arrows should indicate that the flow of skills is upward toward the goal.
5. If two lines should not intersect, then use an arch as shown for the line between box 2 and box 7 in Figure 4.3. The interpretation is that the skill in step 2 is required for steps 5 and 7, but not step 6.
6. Statements of all subordinate skills should include verbs that indicate what the student must be able to do. Avoid boxes that include only nouns.
7. Hierarchies, in the real world, are not necessarily symmetrical, and they can take on all kinds of shapes. There is no "one" correct appearance for a hierarchy.

FIGURE 4.3

SUBORDINATE SKILLS ANALYSIS FOR SCALE-READING EXAMPLE

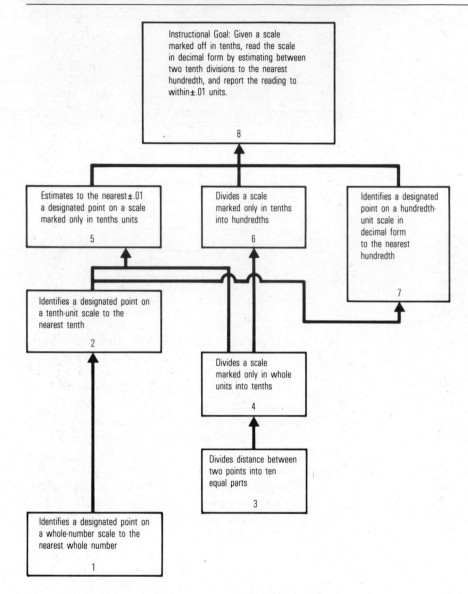

8. If one of the steps in the goal analysis is a question and is represented by a decision diamond, it is necessary to determine if there are subordinate skills required to make that decision.

Developing a hierarchy is not an easy task. We are not accustomed to thinking about the content of instruction from this point of view. One way to proceed is to ask, "What mistake might students make if they were learning this particular subordinate skill?" Often the answer to this question is the key to identifying the appropriate subordinate skills for the one in question. The kinds of "misunderstandings" that students might have will indicate the "understandings," also known as skills, which they must have. For example, if students might do an improper analysis because they become

FIGURE 4.4

HIERARCHICAL ANALYSIS OF AN INFORMATION-PROCESSING REPRESENTATION OF AN INSTRUCTIONAL GOAL

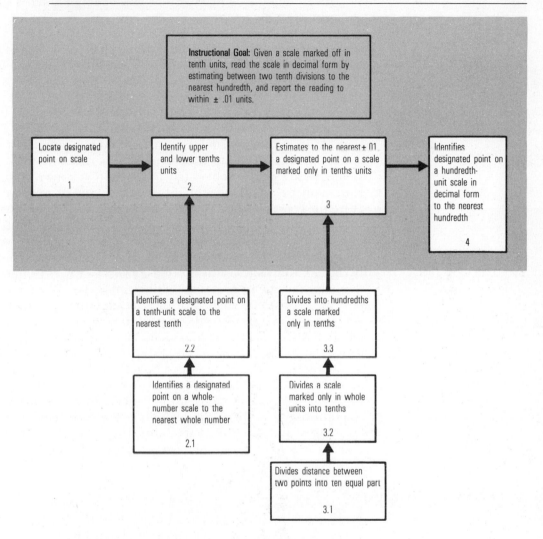

confused between stalactites and stalagmites, then an important subordinate skill would be the ability to classify examples of these two entities.

It is important to review your analysis several times, making sure that you have identified all the subskills required for students to master the instructional goal. At this point you should again use the backward-stepping procedure, from the highest, most complex skill in your hierarchy to the lowest, simplest skills required by your learners. This will allow you to determine whether you have included all the necessary subskills. It may be possible to check the adequacy of your back-stepping analysis by starting with the simplest skills in your hierarchy, and working upward through the subskills to the most complex skills. You should also ask the following questions:

1. Have I included subskills that relate to the identification of basic concepts, such as objects or object qualities? (Example: Can a tetrahedron be identified?)

2. Have I included subskills that enable students to identify abstractions by means of a definition? (Example: Can the student explain what a city is, or show what an emulsion is?)
3. Have I included subskills that will enable students to apply rules? (Example: Making sentence verbs agree with subjects, simplifying mixed fractions.)
4. Have I included subskills in the analysis that will enable students to learn how to solve problems required to demonstrate mastery of the instructional goal?

You may be able to identify subskills you have omitted by using these questions to evaluate your instructional analysis. You may also make another type of interesting discovery, namely, that your instructional goal is limited to having students learn how to make discriminations or identify concepts. While these skills are obviously important, you may want to modify the goal statement by requiring students to use a rule or to solve problems that require the concepts and discriminations that you originally stated in your goal.

You may also find that you have included skills that are "nice to know" but are not *really* required in order to achieve your goal. Many designers begin with the attitude that these skills are important and should be included. In the end, superfluous tasks often confuse learners or unnecessarily increase the length of the instruction, which can cause the instruction for more important tasks to be rushed or omitted due to time constraints. Don't think you should include everything you know about a topic in a hierarchy. The whole point of using the hierarchical approach is to identify just what the learner must know to be successful—nothing more and nothing less. Although it is sometimes tempting not to do so, our best advice is to let the analysis identify the skills for you. It is absolutely the best starting point.

As a final step, we suggest that you explain your hierarchy to a colleague to point out how subordinate skills are interrelated and how they support learning of the superordinate skills. If the explanation does not sound convincing to you or your colleague, more work needs to be done.

Procedural Analysis

Procedural analysis is the technique used to identify the subordinate skills in a psychomotor goal. It is a method employed to expand the description of each component in the psychomotor goal by asking, "What would the learners be doing when they do this step?" The answer to this question may be, for example, a four-step procedure. This would be shown in the instructional analysis as follows:

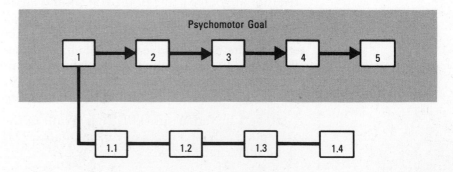

In other words, the procedural analysis of step one indicates that the learner must actually do four activities that, taken together, represent doing component 1 of the sequential analysis. As an example, step one may have been "set up TV camera," while the four procedural steps might involve securing the camera, locating the power source, removing the camera parts from the case, and assembling the camera. This procedural analysis would continue for each step in the original sequential analysis. Note that the activities that are being identified in this manner are not really *subordinate* skills, but are more detailed statements of the skills described in the goal.

Therefore, in order to complete the analysis of the psychomotor skill, it is necessary to ask, with regard to each step in the analysis, "What does the student need to know or be able to do in order to efficiently perform this step?" The answer to this question could be a single psychomotor skill or an intellectual skill required to carry out the psychomotor skill. Therefore, the complete analysis of a psychomotor skill might look like this:

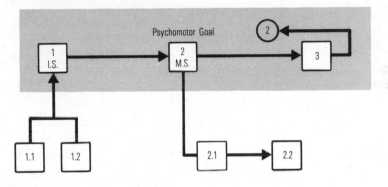

This diagram indicates that the psychomotor goal has three main steps. When the procedural analysis was applied to each of the steps, it was found that step two could best be expressed as two activities that are connected horizontally. Neither skill 2.1 nor 2.2 is skill 2; rather, by doing 2.1 then 2.2, skill 2 has been performed. When the designer asked what the learner needed to know to learn step one, it was found that it has two subordinate intellectual skills, and that the third skill could be taught without knowledge of additional subordinate skills.

Note the following conventions, when you are diagramming a procedural analysis:

1. Each step or separate act is represented by a separate box.
2. Each box has a separate identifying number.
3. The instructional goal statement and steps appear in a box above the analysis.
4. All connecting lines with arrows between main steps in the procedural analysis flow from the vertical side of each box.
5. At certain points in the goal, several activities may follow a given decision. Each separated activity should be described in the analysis.
6. Occasionally, the result of a step will be the decision to go back and repeat one or more steps in the activity. This can be done by using a line that points backward from the box, with a number which indicates the "return" box. See box 3 in the preceding diagram.

Cluster Analysis

We demonstrated previously that it makes little sense to try to do a goal analysis of a verbal information goal since no logical procedure is inherent in the goal. Instead, you move directly to the identification of information needed to achieve the goal.

How do you identify the subordinate skills that should be taught? The answer is almost always apparent from the statement of the goal itself. If the student must be able to identify the states associated with each capital city, then there are fifty subskills, one associated with each state and its capital. It would be useless to write those out as part of the analysis. They could easily be reproduced from a text. However, sometimes the subskills are not as apparent, as in the goal, "List five major causes of inflation." The answer may be dependent on a particular economic theory. In this case, it might be worth listing the five major reasons as part of what we will refer to as a cluster analysis.

The most meaningful analysis that the designer might do of a verbal information goal is to identify the major categories of information that are implied by the goal. Are there ways that the information can be clustered best? The state capitals might be clustered according to geographic regions; the bones of the body might be clustered by major parts of the body such as head, arms, legs, and trunk. If the goal were to be able to list all the major league baseball cities, they might be clustered by American and National Leagues and then by divisions.

How do you diagrammatically represent a cluster analysis? One way is to use the hierarchical technique with the goal at the top and each major cluster as a subskill. If this is done, it should be clearly labeled as a verbal information cluster analysis, and not a hierarchy. It would be just as easy to use an outline format and simply list each of the clusters.

It is sometimes embarrassing for teacher-designers to find that when instructional analysis techniques are used, an instructional goal that they have often taught in the past and for which they would like to develop systematically designed instruction is, in fact, simply verbal information. They feel guilty that they are not teaching rules and problem solving. Sometimes this guilt is misplaced.

There are times when the acquisition of verbal information is critically important. For example, learning vocabulary in a foreign language is verbal information that is the foundation of learning a very complex set of communication skills. The verbal information we must learn as children or as adults is the vehicle we use to develop much more complex concepts and rules. Therefore, verbal information goals should not be automatically discarded upon discovery, but considered for their relevance to other important educational goals. Verbal information is the knowledge base called upon when we execute our how-to intellectual skills.

Instructional Analysis Techniques for Attitude Goals

In order to determine the subordinate skills for an attitudinal goal, the designer should ask, "What must the learner do when exhibiting this attitude?" and, "Why should they exhibit this attitude?" The answer to the first question is almost always a psychomotor skill or an intellectual skill. The purpose of the goal is to get the learner to choose to do either a psychomotor or an intellectual skill. Therefore, the first half of the analysis for an attitudinal goal is to use either the procedural or hierarchical analysis to identify the subskills that will be required *if* the learner chooses to do them. If the learner is to choose to jog, then it is necessary to teach the learner to jog. If the learner is to choose to appreciate a certain body of literature, then the student must learn to comprehend and analyze it.

The second part of the analysis is, "Why should the learner make a particular choice?" The answer to this question is usually verbal information. The verbal information may either by analyzed using a separate cluster analysis, or it may be integrated, as verbal information, into the basic procedural or hierarchical analyses that were done for the first half of the analysis. The verbal information constitutes the persuasive part of attitude shaping, along with modeling and reinforcement, and it should be included as an integral part of the instructional analysis.

In order to represent an attitude on an instructional analysis chart, simply write the attitude goal in a box *beside* the procedural or intellectual skill goal that will be analyzed. Connect the two main boxes with a line like this:

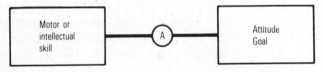

This connecting line shows that the motor or intellectual skill is supporting the attitudinal goal. The verbal information required to support the attitude can be attached to the procedural or hierarchical analyses at the appropriate point, via a line connecting the boxes like this:

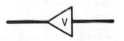

At this point it is obvious that we are beginning to combine the various analysis techniques. These combinations, which have been developed by Briggs and Wager (1981) and called information maps, are described in the following section.

Combining Instructional Analysis Techniques

We have just described how an attitudinal goal can be analyzed by the use of a procedural or hierarchical analysis, and that a psychomotor skill can have intellectual skills as subordinate skills. It is quite common to find that the instructional analysis process results in identifying a combination of subordinate skills from several domains for a goal that was classified as belonging to only one domain.

Consider, for example, the combination of intellectual skills and verbal information. It is not unusual when doing a hierarchical analysis to identify knowledge that the learner should "know." Just "knowing something" is not an intellectual skill as we have defined it here and therefore would not, by the rules, appear on an intellectual skills hierarchy. But often it is important that this knowledge, which is verbal information, appear as a part of the analysis of what must be learned to achieve the instructional goal. Therefore, Briggs and Wager (1981) suggest that the verbal information be shown in a box with a connecting line like this:

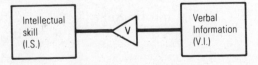

This indicates that the verbal information in the right-hand box is used in support of the intellectual skill in the left-hand box. In a hierarchy, it might look like this:

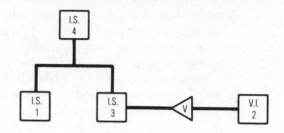

Boxes 1, 3, and 4 represent intellectual skills, while box 2 includes verbal information.

What happens if you put all the diagramming techniques together? It might be conceivable that a psychomotor skill with an attitude component might require subordinate intellectual skills and verbal information! It would look something like this:

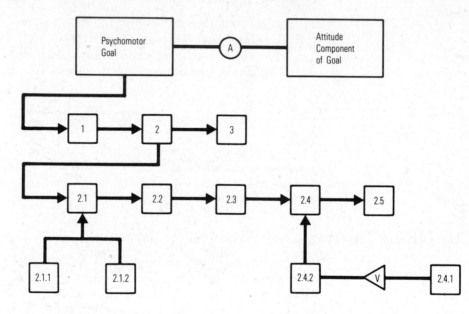

Instructional Analysis Diagrams

At this point we will review the diagramming procedures for doing an instructional analysis. The first step, of course, is to classify your instructional goal and perform a goal analysis. Then select the appropriate technique(s) for identifying the subordinate skills.

Type of Goal or Step	*Type of Analysis*
Intellectual skill	Hierarchical
Psychomotor skill	Procedural
Verbal information	Cluster
Attitude	Procedural, hierarchical, and/or cluster

As the designer proceeds with the analysis, the subordinate skills are visually displayed in diagrams. The basic appearance of the procedural and hierarchical analysis are shown below. When diagrammed, any particular set of subskills required to reach a terminal objective can have a variety of structural appearances. Traditionally, procedural tasks are placed in a straight line to indicate that none is dependent upon or subordinate to another. The following diagram is generally used to represent a procedural analysis. There are no subordinate learning-dependent subskills, so all the skills are diagrammed in one continuous line.

It is also traditional to place learning-dependent subskills above the skills upon which they are dependent. In this way, the reader will automatically recognize the implied learning relationship of the subskills. This is illustrated in the following diagram. Notice that subskills 1.1, 1.2, and 1.3 are not dependent upon each other, but that learning objective 4 requires the previous learning of 1.1, 1.2, and 1.3. Objectives 2, 3, and 4 are not interdependent; 4.1 and 4.2 must be learned prior to 4.

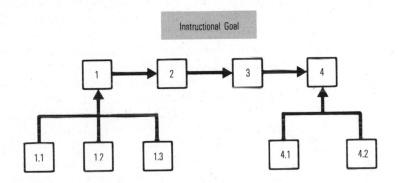

The following diagram illustrates the dependence of subsequent skills upon those preceding them.

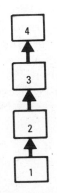

The student must learn subskill 1 before being able to learn to perform subskill 2. Likewise, before subskill 4 can be learned, subskills 1, 2, and 3 must be mastered. Thus, these skills form a hierarchy.

In addition, we noted that attitudinal goals can be indicated by the following:

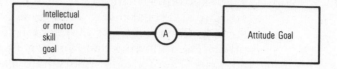

Verbal information can be indicated as follows with the verbal information appearing in the right-hand box:

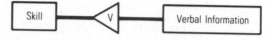

An understanding of these diagramming conventions should help you grasp the implied relationship of subskills in an instructional analysis diagram. The order for learning each skill is also implied through the sequencing of skills.

Note should be taken of the numbers that have appeared in the various diagrams of subordinate skills. Do not interpret them to mean more than they do. At this point in the instructional design process, the numbers in the boxes are used simply as a shorthand for referring to the box. Using these numbers, we can discuss the relationship between box 7 and box 5 without describing the skills that are involved. The numbers, at this point, do *not* represent the sequence in which the skills will be taught. We should not be thinking about how we will teach these skills, but rather, ensuring that we have the correct skills included in our analysis. At a later point in the design process, it will be necessary to decide on the instructional sequence for the skills. At that time you may wish to number the skills in that sequence. Until that time, however, the numbers are simply identifiers.

Why is the instructional analysis process so critical to the design of instruction? It is a process the instructional designer can use to identify those skills really needed by the student to achieve the terminal objective, and to help exclude unnecessary skills. This may not appear to be a terribly strong argument when considered in light of a particular instructional goal which you might select. You might feel that you are so thoroughly familiar with the content and skills required of the student that this type of analysis is superfluous. You may be assured, however, that as you become involved in a variety of instructional design projects you cannot be a subject-matter expert in all areas. It will be necessary to engage in analytic processes of this type with a variety of subject matter personnel to identify the critical skills that will result in efficient and effective instruction.

EXAMPLES

Hierarchical Instructional Analysis of an Intellectual Skill

Topic

Simple sentence structure and punctuation based upon function or purpose of the sentence in short stories.

Instructional Goal

In writing short stories, use a variety of sentence types and accompanying punctuation based upon the purpose of the sentence and the idea being communicated.

In chapter 3, this instructional goal was classified as an intellectual skill, and initial analysis of the goal (Figure 3.5) resulted in nine sequential steps to be accomplished in performing the goal. To continue the instructional analysis, each of these steps must be broken down into its subordinate skills. Since a complete hierarchical analysis of this complex goal would require an elaborate substructure for *each* of the steps, we selected only one of them to illustrate: step 5, prescribing the best sentence types for introducing main ideas.

The hierarchical approach was selected to continue the analysis of this step since students cannot prescribe the best types of sentences to use without first being able to select the best sentence type to convey a specified mood or emphasis. Likewise, they cannot select sentences without learning the purpose for each type and how to write it using the correct punctuation. At this point we should specify exactly the types of sentences students will be using. There are four different kinds of sentences involved: declarative, interrogative, imperative, and exclamatory. We took liberty with the order in which each type of sentence would be encountered by students since it appears to be *possible* to learn to write an exclamatory sentence prior to learning to write a declarative one. However, we chose a logical order based upon frequency of use to present each of the four sentence types. The four types of sentences were placed horizontally in the diagram to illustrate that the relationship among them is not hierarchical. However, writing each of these four types of sentences should be accomplished prior to encountering instruction on the superordinate skill of selecting the best sentence type to convey a specified mood or emphasis. This section of the analysis would be illustrated in the following manner:

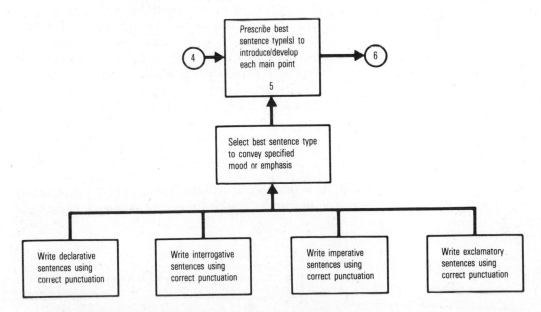

At this point, we can continue the hierarchical analysis by backing down again from the current level of skills to identify those considered subordinate to each of the four sentence writing tasks. For this we should focus on one of the sentence types at a time, so we will begin with writing declarative sentences using correct punctuation. What would students have to be able to do before they can write a declarative sentence using correct punctuation? They would need to *recognize* a declarative sentence with correct punctuation when they saw it. They could not possibly construct one without knowing what it looks like. Therefore our next subordinate skill is to recognize a declarative sentence with correct punctuation.

Analysis of this skill enables us to identify two obvious subcomponents included within it: recognizing a declarative sentence and recognizing the correct punctuation for a declarative sentence. In our step-down process, should one of these tasks come before the other, or should they be placed side by side indicating independence? It would be difficult for students to punctuate a declarative sentence if they were unsure about whether the sentence was declarative. Using this logic, we will place punctuation superordinate to recognizing a declarative sentence. So far our hierarchy looks like this:

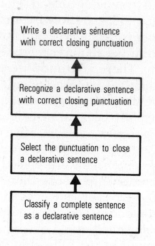

Let us now concentrate on the third subtask down the list. What would a student need to know before being able to select the correct punctuation for a declarative sentence? The student would need to know the rule: Declarative sentences are closed using a period. This could be learned as a fact or statement so it could be learned as verbal information. The rule for including verbal information in the skills hierarchy is to place the information in a box beside the skill it supports and connect the two boxes using this symbol:

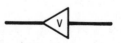

So the task and the accompanying verbal information would be illustrated in the hierarchy in the following manner:

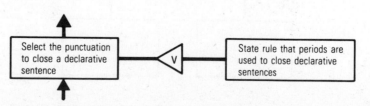

Not let's turn our attention to the next task on the list: Classify a complete sentence as a declarative one. To demonstrate this skill, a student would need to know the purpose or function of a declarative sentence. Stating the purpose of a declarative sentence could be learned as verbal information. The student would need to know that the purpose of a declarative sentence was to convey information to the reader. This would need to be stated in the hierarchy in a manner that indicates what the learners will do to demonstrate that they know the purpose. This skill and the supporting information could be diagrammed as follows:

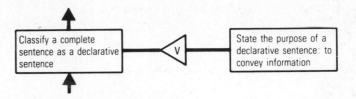

Besides the definition required to identify the purpose of a declarative sentence, are there other subskills implied in the task statement? Yes. Students would need to be able to recognize a complete sentence. How would they do it? They would need to have the definition of a complete sentence. The skill to recognize a complete sentence and the supporting definition could be diagrammed in the following manner:

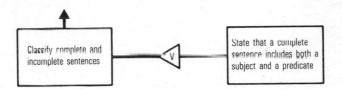

Next, we should identify the skills required to learn our latest task of classifying sentences as either complete or incomplete. Analyzing this task should lead you to the conclusion that in order to accomplish it, students would have to be able to recognize subjects and predicates when they see them. Therefore, the next task down on the list should read: Recognize subjects and predicates in sentences. Now, what would a student need to know to be able to accomplish this task? They would need to know definitions for subjects and predicates before they could recognize them in a sentence. The definitions for these terms could be taught as verbal information, and the relationship among these tasks could be diagrammed as follows:

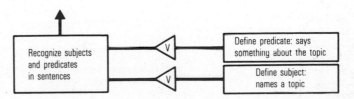

A completed draft of the analysis thus far is included in Figure 4.5 to demonstrate the previously described relationship among subtasks in the hierarchy. First, notice that the original nine steps that provide an overview and step-by-step sequence for the instructional goal have been enclosed in a large box at the top of the diagram. Second, notice the hierarchical substructure beneath step five. This substructure identifies the subordinate skills in the hierarchy for only this step. Third, notice that the four sentence types

FIGURE 4.5

HIEARCHICAL ANALYSIS OF DECLARATIVE SENTENCE PORTION OF STORY-WRITING INSTRUCTIONAL GOAL

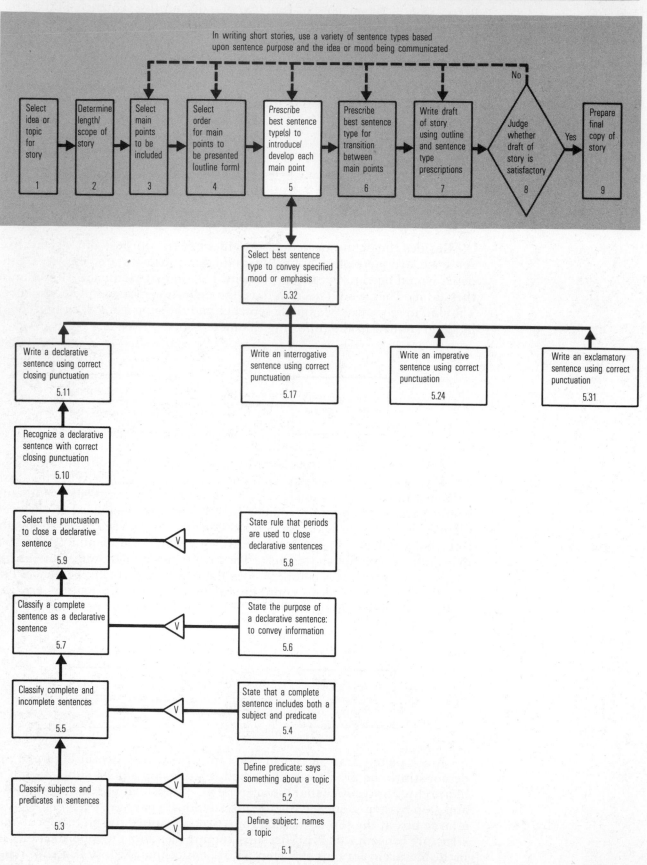

specified have been arranged horizontally (subordinate skills 5.11, 5.17, 5.24, and 5.31), which implies that they are not hierarchically related. Fourth, notice that the subordinate skills for *only* the declarative sentences are illustrated (skills 5.1 through 5.10). To complete the analysis of step five, you would simply identify the subordinate skills for each of the remaining three sentence types. Likewise, to complete the entire analysis for the instructional goal, you would identify the subordinate skills for each major step named in the instructional goal. As you can see from this example, a thorough analysis of an intellectual skill can become quite elaborate.

Analysis of a Psychomotor Skill

Topic
Golf

Instructional Goal
Putt a golf ball into the cup.

Psychomotor skills usually require a combination of intellectual and motor skills, and the intellectual skills often require supporting verbal information. The chronological procedure to follow in putting a golf ball was illustrated in Figure 3.1. At this point we need to continue the instructional analysis to identify the subordinate skills and information required to perform each step previously identified in the procedure. As an illustration, we will first analyze the subordinate skills required to perform step one: Plan the stroke required to putt the ball into the cup. The analysis appears in Figure 4.6.

Note in the diagram that the subordinate skills required to plan the stroke are all intellectual skills, or the "psycho" component of the psychomotor skill. The "motor" component occurs when the golfer translates the plan into action. As an observer of someone putting, the designer can readily see the motor part of the skill, whereas the mental part remains hidden. However, all of the mental activity required to plan the stroke should be completed prior to moving to step two: Assume a stance based upon the plan.

The first step in this psychomotor skill is an intellectual skill, so we apply the hierarchical analysis procedure (even though the overall goal is a motor skill). In response to the question, "What would the student need to be able to do in order to plan the stroke?", it is determined that the plan consists of predictions on the direction the ball should be hit and the force with which it should be hit. In turn, direction of the putt depends on knowledge of the required trajectory of the ball, which in turn depends on knowledge of the "lay of the land." A similar analysis has been used to identify the subordinate skills associated with determining how hard to hit the ball.

Two items are of importance in this example. The first is that the first step in the goal, namely, making a plan about how to hit the ball, is a step that must be taught. However, it cannot be taught until students have learned about direction and force and their accompanying subordinate skills. Then, these skills can be combined into the step of making a plan. Also of note, again, is that although this is a motor skill, the first subordinate skill analysis was hierarchical because the step is an intellectual skill. Contrast this with the analysis of step 4 in the next paragraph.

Step 4 is the psychomotor skill of taking a practice swing. This large step is broken down into: position the club face, mentally trace the trajectory the

FIGURE 4.6

INTELLECTUAL SKILLS SUBORDINATE TO FIRST STEP IN PSYCHOMOTOR SKILL OF PUTTING A GOLF BALL

GOAL:
Putting a golf ball

TYPE OF LEARNING:
Psychomotor

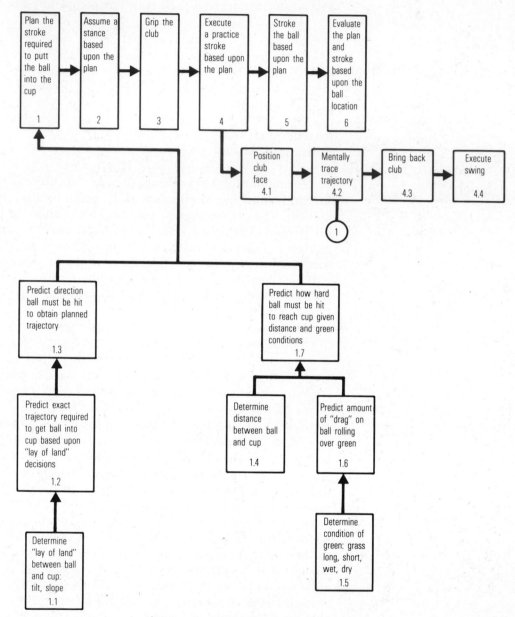

ball is to follow, bring the club back, execute the swing. These four steps appear under step 4 in Figure 4.6. Note the difference between the way in which these boxes are arranged compared with the boxes beneath step 1. The boxes beneath step 4 are horizontal and are connected from the side. This indicates that these four substeps, when executed in sequence, are equivalent to doing step 4. This was not the case with the subordinate intellectual skills for step 1, which had to be learned *prior* to learning step 1.

Now examine the four subskills beneath step 4. You should again go through the process of determining if each is an intellectual skill, and, if so, whether further hierarchical analysis is required. If it is a motor skill, further procedural analysis may be required. Steps 4.1, 4.3, and 4.4 are motor skills that should require no further analysis. However, step 4.2 is an intellectual skill that requires the use of the plan, and all the accompanying subordinate skills, listed for step 1. It is not necessary to repeat all these skills in the chart. This dependency can be noted by simply putting 1 in a circle under step 4.2 to indicate that all of step 1 must be learned *before* this step.

Each of the other steps in the putting procedure would need to be analyzed to identify the subordinate skills required to perform it. Skill is acquired through both accurate mental predictions and practice at translating the prescriptions into physical actions. Much practice is required for accurate translations.

Subordinate Skills Analysis of a Goal that Requires Both Intellectual Skills and Verbal Information

Topic
Banking

Instructional Goal
Open and maintain a checking account.

The major steps identified for opening and maintaining a checking account were illustrated previously in Figure 3.8. Step 2, deposit money into a checking account, was selected to demonstrate the analysis required to identify subskills for this task. They are included in Figure 4.7. Note in the figure that another goal analysis has been carried out because the step is so large. Steps 2.1 through 2.12 are the steps to perform if one were performing the goal of depositing money in a checking account.

The tasks were identified and sequenced using a chronological approach. After obtaining a sample deposit slip for reference, we identified what should be done first, second, and so forth to complete the form. Steps 2.1 through 2.12 illustrate the process of depositing money into a checking account. Step 2.3 shows that a decision must be made based upon the type of transaction that is desired. An individual may wish to deposit: (a) cash only, (b) checks only, (c) cash and checks, or (d) checks only, and have a portion of the total returned as cash during the transaction. The exact steps to take will be determined by the nature of the money to be deposited.

Why do we have the steps arranged horizontally rather than vertically as we did in the theme writing and the putting examples? Because it is possible to learn how to complete a deposit slip without first learning how to obtain a deposit slip. We could simply give learners a deposit slip and provide instruction on how to complete it. This is not the case in the theme writing unit. Students could not learn to write complete declarative sentences without first learning all the subordinate skills. Likewise, a golfer cannot predict a path for a putt without first knowing the influence the lay of the land will have on the ball's direction. This basic difference, whether the learner must have subordinate skills prior to achieving the current task, helps us determine whether tasks should be arranged sequentially or hierarchically.

FIGURE 4.7

SUBORDINATE SKILLS ANALYSIS FOR CHECKING ACCOUNT GOAL

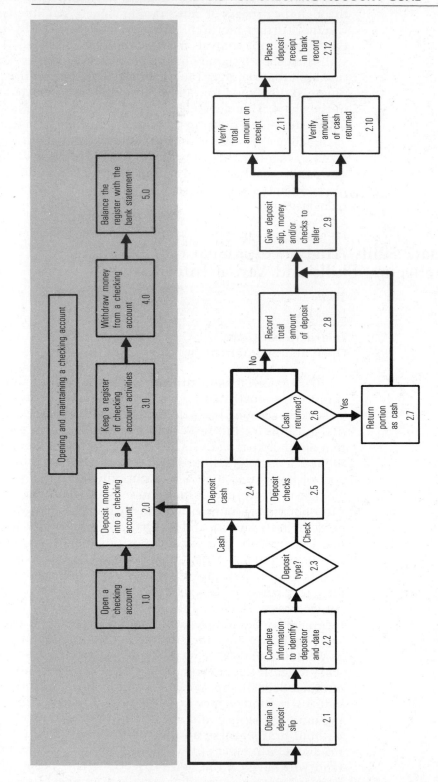

Next, we further analyzed the steps a student would have to take to deposit cash (2.4), checks (2.5), and checks with money returned (2.7). This analysis appears in Figure 4.8. Notice in these procedures that a combination of procedural and hierarchical tasks appears. For example, a student cannot possibly total the amount of cash to be deposited without learning the subordinate skill of addition. Similarly, the learner cannot determine the total amount of the deposit after subtracting the amount of cash to be returned without first learning to subtract. However, students can learn where to enter checks on a deposit slip without first learning that they should sign each check and record their account number on it. The learning relationship between any two tasks in the analysis is the determining factor related to whether they are hierarchical or procedural.

Cluster Analysis for Verbal Information Goal

Topic
Word processing command keys used to move the cursor around the screen

Instructional Goal
You will be able to name the command keys used to move the cursor in a specified direction and speed on the screen

Many businesses and schools have purchased computers with word processing programs to facilitate the work of secretaries, teachers, and other employees who need word processing support. One of the first lessons usually taught to employees who are learning to use the program are the commands required to move the cursor on the screen. In this example we will analyze and cluster the background verbal information necessary to learn to actually move the cursor. The first step in the analysis would be to break the instructional goal into logical segments or clusters of information, and second, to sequence the clusters using some type of rationale.

Our preliminary analysis of the "clusters" of information implied by the goal, and their sequence, was described in Figure 3.4. We will continue the instructional analysis by further identifying and sequencing the commands required to control the direction of the cursor, which was box 3 in Figure 3.4. In Figure 4.9 we have identified the major directions as right, left, down, and up.

Begin by identifying all the different ways the cursor can be moved to the right on one line. It can be moved across the whole line at once, it can be moved right to the next word, and it can be moved right to the next character. A sequence for learners to encounter this information should be determined. How would you sequence it and why? We selected commonality of use as our rationale and decided to make character first, word second, and line third. This order also represents a natural progression based upon the size of the movement from smallest to largest. We followed the same logic to identify and sequence the commands required to move the cursor to the left on one line. These two clusters of information are illustrated in Figure 4.9. The same procedure would be followed to identify information required for clusters three and four in Figure 4.9.

As noted in the Concept section, verbal information instructional goals usually support more complex tasks. The purpose of this verbal information lesson is to provide learners with the information they will need to actually move the cursor in a word processing program.

FIGURE 4.8

DETAILED INSTRUCTIONAL ANALYSIS OF STEPS 2.3, 2.4, AND 2.5 FROM
DEPOSITING MONEY GOAL

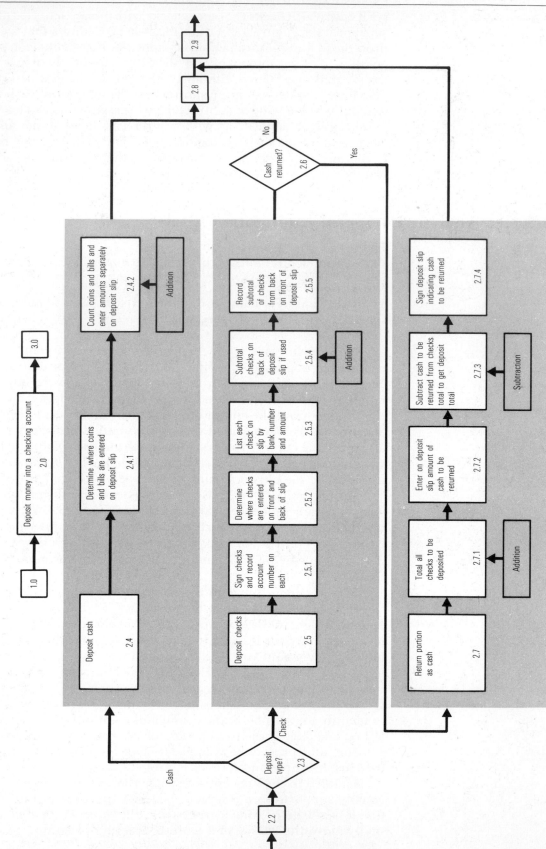

FIGURE 4.9

CLUSTERS OF INFORMATION IDENTIFIED FOR THE WORD PROCESSING GOAL ON COMMANDS FOR MOVING THE CURSOR

GOAL:
Name the command keys used to control cursor direction

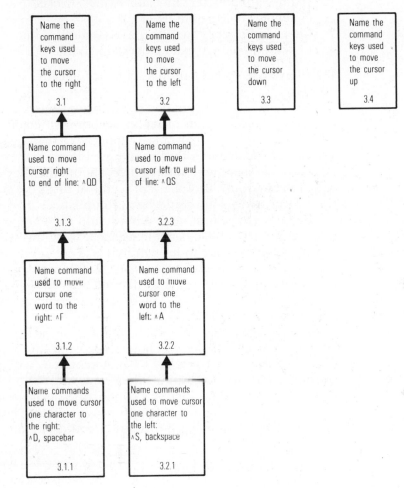

Attitudinal Subordinate Skills Analysis

The attitudinal goal analysis example that follows will illustrate one technique you could use to develop an instructional analysis for such a goal. Starting with the goal statement, the necessary procedures and information are identified in a step-by-step sequence.

Topic
Personal safety while staying in a hotel.

Instructional Goal
The learner will choose to maximize personal safety while staying in a hotel.

The choice to follow safety precautions while registered in a hotel requires that learners know about potential dangers to themselves, know the procedures to follow, and then *actually* follow the procedures. The attitudinal instructional goal was introduced in chapter 3 and preliminary analysis and sequence decisions were illustrated in Figure 3.3.

To continue the analysis, we focus only on fire hazards. What procedures should a hotel occupant follow to minimize the risk of being harmed during a hotel fire? We identified a procedure which contains three basic steps:

1. Inquire about hotel's fire safety rules, procedures, and precautions when checking into the hotel.
2. Check emergency facilities in assigned room.
3. Check emergency exits closest to room.

They have been placed in this sequence because it fits the natural order of events.

The next step is to analyze the information, procedures, or skills the individual would need in order to accomplish each step in the procedure. Remember that one important component of shaping an attitude, and thereby increasing the chances that people will demonstrate the desired behavior, is to provide them with information about why they should act in a certain way. In your analysis of these procedural tasks, be sure to include information about why each should be accomplished.

Begin with the first task. Why should someone request fire safety information? Information to help them choose to do this would include facts about death and injury due to fires in hotels. Facts about the frequency of hotel fires, additional hazards in high-rise hotels, or perhaps the number of persons killed or injured annually in hotel fires could be included. The purpose of this information is to get their attention and help them realize that they too are at risk while registered in hotels.

They would require other information for the first task as well. They must be able to judge whether the hotel's reported safety precautions and procedures are adequate. To make this judgment, they will need information about routine fire safety precautions they can expect to find in hotels. So, the first task in our procedure includes supporting information about why patrons should do it and what they should expect to find. The first step in the procedure and the supporting information could be diagrammed as follows:

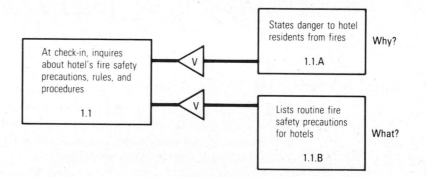

If we were to observe hotel patrons inquiring about fire safety procedures while checking into the hotel, we could correctly infer that they were choosing to maximize their personal safety while staying in the hotel (our original attitudinal goal).

From here, move to the second step in the desired procedure: check emergency facilities in assigned room. Again, they will need to know why they should do this and what they could expect to find. This information is diagrammed in the following manner:

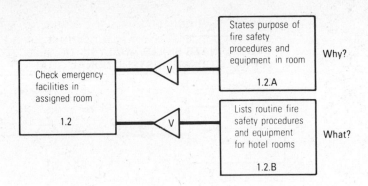

The last step in the procedure remains. Why should hotel guests check emergency exits close to their assigned rooms, and what should they expect to see? This information appears in the next illustration.

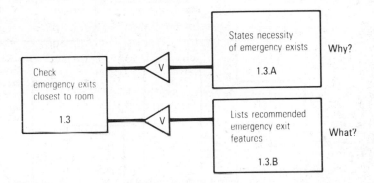

A completed analysis for the fire precaution component appears in Figure 4.10. Notice in the diagram that the main steps in each of the three procedures are placed horizontally on a line and that they are connected by arrows that indicate the desired progression. Blocks of information required to perform each step in the procedure are connected to the appropriate box using this symbol:

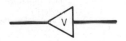

The placement of the sets of procedures on the page and the numbering system suggest that the fire safety procedures could be taught first, room security second, and valuables security last.

After completing steps two and three, it would be wise to check each procedure and the steps within each to determine whether they are related to the original attitudinal goal. If patrons were performing the tasks as specified, could we infer that they were demonstrating an attitude toward maximizing their personal safety while staying in a hotel? If the answer is yes, then we have not strayed from our original goal.

SUMMARY

In order to begin a subordinate skills analysis, it is necessary to have a clear description of the main tasks learners need to perform in order to accomplish the instructional goal. The derivation of these major steps was described

FIGURE 4.10

SUBORDINATE SKILLS ANALYSIS OF SELECTED COMPONENT OF AN ATTITUDINAL INSTRUCTIONAL GOAL

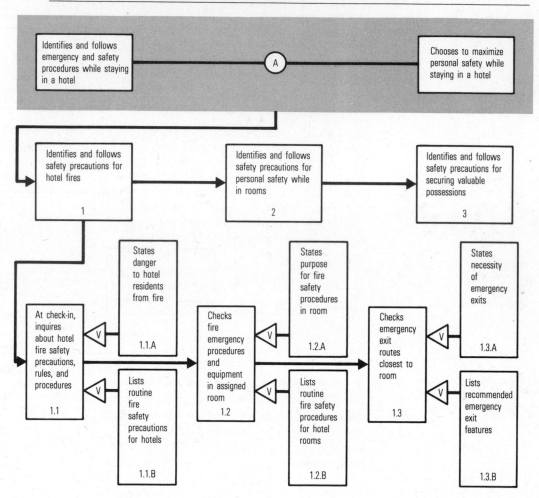

in chapter 3. To conduct a subordinate skills analysis, you must analyze each of these major steps.

The first judgment to be made about each task is whether it represents verbal information, an intellectual skill, or a psychomotor skill. Each type of skill requires a different analysis procedure to identify its subordinate skills.

Once steps are classified, you are ready to identify the subordinate skills. If the step is a verbal information task, a cluster analysis would work best to identify and cluster bodies of information that must be learned to perform the step. Intellectual skill steps should be analyzed to identify the hierarchy of rules, concepts, and discriminations required to accomplish the task. Psychomotor skills are best analyzed by identifying the intellectual and physical procedures learners would follow to accomplish each main step in the goal.

Recall that the goal analysis procedure for an attitude resulted in identifying the behaviors learners would exhibit if they held the attitude. During the subordinate skills analysis phase, each of these behaviors would need to be classified as either psychomotor or intellectual skills, and then either a procedural or hierarchical analysis would be applied respectively. Verbal information required to perform either the intellectual or psychomotor skill would be placed within the framework to support the related steps in the hierarchy or procedure. This information might include what to expect and why a particular action should be performed.

For each of the skills identified during this subordinate skill analysis, the process is repeated. That is, each of the identified subordinate skills is classified by domain and then analyzed using the recommended procedure to identify its respective skills. This step-down process is used until you believe that no further subordinate skills remain to be identified.

The final product of the subordinate skills analysis is a framework of the subordinate skills required to perform each main step of the instructional goal. The total instructional analysis includes the instructional goal, the main steps required to accomplish the goal, and the subordinate skills required to accomplish each main step. This framework of skills is the foundation for all subsequent instructional design activities.

It is important to evaluate the analysis of learning tasks before proceeding to the next phase of design activities, because many hours of work remain to be completed. The quality of the analysis will directly affect the ease with which succeeding design activities can be performed and the quality of the eventual instruction. Specific criteria to use in evaluating the analysis includes whether all relevant tasks are identified, superfluous tasks are eliminated, and the relationships among the tasks are clearly designated through the configuration of tasks on the chart and the placement of lines used to connect the tasks. Producing an accurate, clear analysis of tasks typically requires several iterations and refinements.

PRACTICE

In the exercises that follow, you will be asked to complete a subordinate skills analysis for psychomotor, intellectual, and verbal information goals. The topics and goals used in the examples are purposely different from those used in previous examples. Working with new goals at this point will provide you with a broader base of experience that should be beneficial when you select a topic and goal of your own.

Work through each example, and then compare your analysis with the sample one in the Feedback section. If your analysis is different, locate the differences and determine whether you would like to make any revisions in yours. You may like your analysis better than the sample provided, but you should be able to explain and justify the differences.

I. Procedural Analysis for a Psychomotor Skill

Topic
Changing a tire.

Instructional Goal
Change a tire on an automobile.

The psychomotor skill selected for a procedural analysis can be accomplished by first identifying the *major* steps in the process. Once you identify the major steps, select the step of jacking up the car to continue the analysis at a more detailed level for that task. To complete the procedure required for jacking up the car, you may need to analyze one or two of the other tasks that occur *during* the jacking process.

Complete your analysis on paper, check to make sure your steps are in the order you desire, and then compare your analysis with the example in Figure 4.11.

II. Hierarchical Analysis for an Intellectual Skill

Demonstrate your ability to do a hierarchical analysis by identifying the subordinate skills required to perform each of the four main steps for the following instructional goal on map reading.

GOAL:
Use a map of (your town) to locate specific places and determine the distance between them

TYPE OF LEARNING:
Intellectual skill

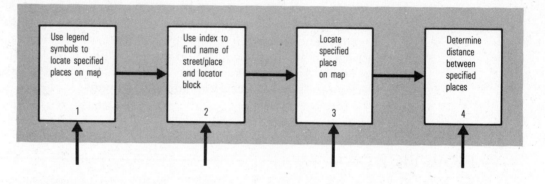

To aid your analysis, you may want to obtain a copy of a local city map and use it to perform each of these main steps. As you work, note what tasks you must perform and what information and skills you need to perform each one.

When you complete your hierarchical analysis, compare your hierarchy with the one in Figure 4.12. Analyze and try to explain any differences.

III. Cluster Analysis for Verbal Information

Topic
Parts of the body.

Instructional Goal
Label the parts of the body using common terminology.

One strategy for this analysis might be to proceed from the top to the bottom, or head to feet. Another format consideration might be to use a combination task box and outline format to avoid repeating the word label many times. Compare your cluster analysis with the one in Figure 4.13.

FIGURE 4.11

PROCEDURAL ANALYSIS FOR CHANGING AN AUTOMOBILE TIRE

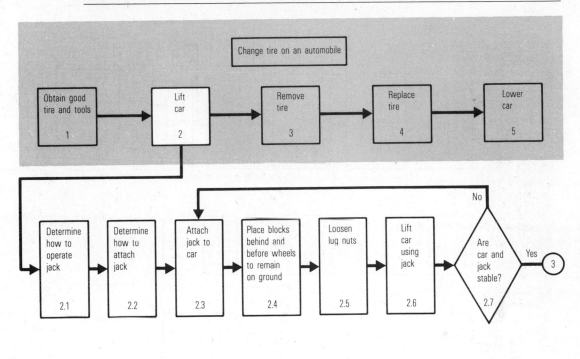

FEEDBACK

Compare your procedural analysis, hierarchical analysis, and cluster analysis with Figures 4.11, 4.12, and 4.13 at the end of this chapter if you have not already done so.

References and Recommended Readings

Briggs, L. J., & Wager, W. (1981). *Handbook of procedures for the design of instruction.* (2nd ed.) Englewood Cliffs, NJ: Educational Technology Publications, 85–100. Excellent resource for developing information maps which include two or more types of goals.

Davis, R. H., Alexander, L. T., & Yelon, S. L. (1974). *Learning system design.* New York: McGraw-Hill, 129–158. The authors' coverage of instructional analysis emphasizes techniques for examining procedural, sequential types of learning tasks.

Gagné, R. M. (1985). *Conditions of Learning.* (4th ed.) New York: Holt, Rinehart and Winston. This book is a classic in regard to many aspects of instructional design, including the domains of learning and hierarchical analysis.

Gagné, R. M., Briggs, L. J., & Wager, W. W. (1988). *Principles of instructional design.* (3rd ed.) New York: Holt, Rinehart and Winston. A number of examples of the application of hierarchical analysis to intellectual skills are provided.

Hannum, W. H. (1980). Task analysis procedures. *NSPI Journal,* 19 (3), 16–17. A comparison of several procedures for identifying subordinate skills.

Journal of Instructional Development. (1983). vol. 6, no. 4. This is a special theme issue on instructional analysis, which includes discussions of current trends and alternative methods of task and instructional analysis.

FIGURE 4.12

INSTRUCTIONAL ANALYSIS FOR MAP READING GOAL

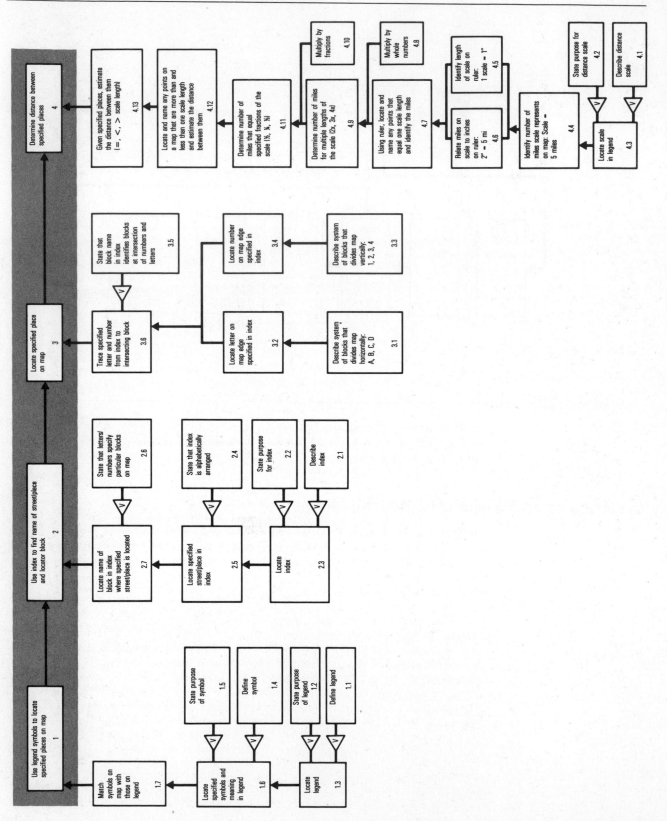

FIGURE 4.13

CLUSTER ANALYSIS OF A VERBAL INFORMATION TASK

GOAL:
Locate and label various parts of the human body

TYPE OF LEARNING:
Verbal information

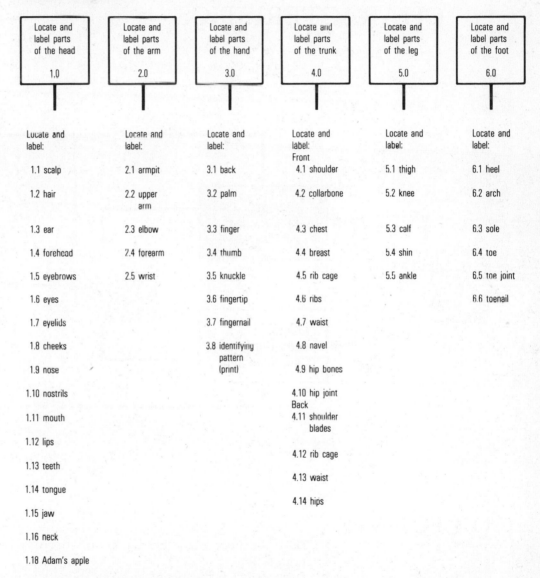

Locate and label parts of the head 1.0	Locate and label parts of the arm 2.0	Locate and label parts of the hand 3.0	Locate and label parts of the trunk 4.0	Locate and label parts of the leg 5.0	Locate and label parts of the foot 6.0
Locate and label:	Locate and label:	Locate and label:	Locate and label: Front	Locate and label:	Locate and label:
1.1 scalp	2.1 armpit	3.1 back	4.1 shoulder	5.1 thigh	6.1 heel
1.2 hair	2.2 upper arm	3.2 palm	4.2 collarbone	5.2 knee	6.2 arch
1.3 ear	2.3 elbow	3.3 finger	4.3 chest	5.3 calf	6.3 sole
1.4 forehead	2.4 forearm	3.4 thumb	4.4 breast	5.4 shin	6.4 toe
1.5 eyebrows	2.5 wrist	3.5 knuckle	4.5 rib cage	5.5 ankle	6.5 toe joint
1.6 eyes		3.6 fingertip	4.6 ribs		6.6 toenail
1.7 eyelids		3.7 fingernail	4.7 waist		
1.8 cheeks		3.8 identifying pattern (print)	4.8 navel		
1.9 nose			4.9 hip bones		
1.10 nostrils			4.10 hip joint Back		
1.11 mouth			4.11 shoulder blades		
1.12 lips			4.12 rib cage		
1.13 teeth			4.13 waist		
1.14 tongue			4.14 hips		
1.15 jaw					
1.16 neck					
1.18 Adam's apple					

Levine, E. R. (1983). *Everything you always wanted to know about job analysis.* Tampa, FL: Mariner Publishing Co. This is a paperback introductory text on job analysis.

Merrill, P. F. (1978). Hierarchical and information processing tasks analysis: A comparison. *Journal of Instructional Development,* 1, 35–40. Merrill explains the information processing approach to analyzing a task in terms of the sequence of mental tasks required of the person performing the task.

Merrill, P. F. (1980). Analysis of a procedural task. *NSPI Journal,* 19 (2), 11–15. Merrill uses flow-charting methods to identify the subordinate skills of a complex intellectual skill, which he refers to as a *procedure.*

5
IDENTIFYING ENTRY BEHAVIORS AND CHARACTERISTICS

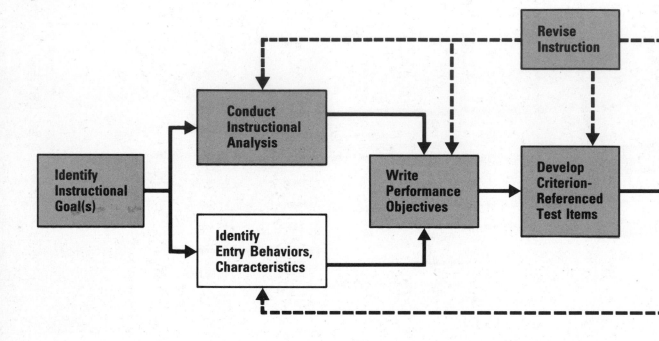

OBJECTIVES

- Describe how entry behaviors are derived for students in a target population.
- Derive entry behaviors when given an instructional analysis and a specific target population.
- Describe the general characteristics of a target population which would be important to consider when developing instruction.

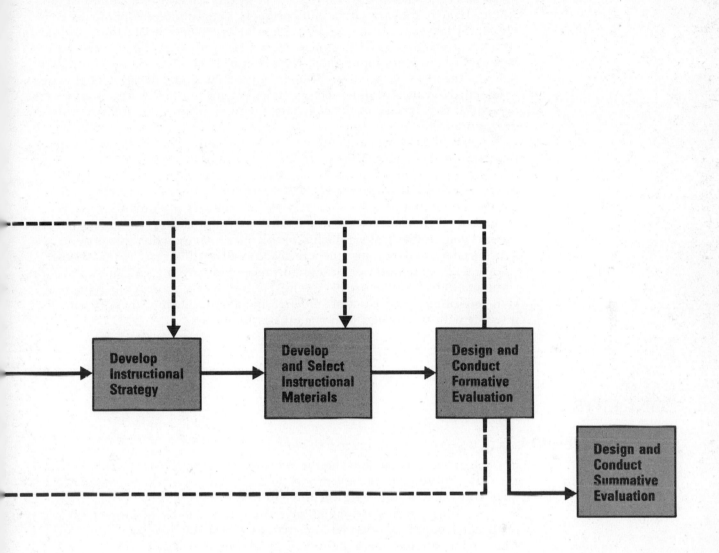

BACKGROUND

Have you ever picked up a textbook that you were highly motivated to read, but found you could not get past the first few pages? Or have you ever enrolled in a course and found that you already knew much of the information that was being taught? These are typical examples of mismatches between instruction and the abilities of students. In the chapters on instructional analysis we were concerned with identifying the skills that must be learned in order to achieve an instructional goal. In this chapter, we will begin looking at the other side of that coin—the skills students must have learned before they begin instruction. In order to have effective instructional materials or, for that matter, any type of successful instructional experience, there must be a match between students and instruction.

Perhaps one of the most costly mismatches between students and materials occurred in the late 1950s and in the 1960s in the United States when a large number of curriculum projects were funded to update the content of the textbooks being used in high schools. The textbooks that resulted from those projects were extremely effective for only the top high school students. Most students found them too difficult. It is interesting to note that many of the ideas we are presenting in our instructional design model were researched during that time, and that at least some of the new processes were developed in response to the criticisms of curriculum development efforts during that era.

The problem of overestimating or underestimating the ability of learners is still of great concern. Most instructional designers are far removed either by age, expertise, or socioeconomic status from the learners whom they hope to serve through their materials. Therefore, to design effective instruction, the designer must identify the entry skills required of students as well as their general characteristics, which may have implications for the design of the instruction. Several significant problems can arise when this is done inappropriately, and the consequences of each will be illustrated in this chapter.

We will highlight the critical importance of identifying specific skills that a student must have before beginning a unit of instruction, identifying relevant general characteristics of students, and identifying how these two might interact with the format of instructional materials.

CONCEPTS

Target Population

Let's begin by considering who the learners are for any given set of instruction. We will refer to these learners as the *target population*—they are the ones you want to "hit" with the appropriate instruction.

Sometimes the target population is also referred to as the target audience or target group. It is referred to using descriptors such as age, grade level, topic being studied, job experience, or job position. For example, a set of materials might be intended for kindergarten children, fifth-grade reading classes, junior high school football classes, or principals. These examples are typical of the descriptions usually available for instructional materials. But the instructional designer must go beyond these general descriptions and be much more specific about the skills required of the learners for whom the materials are intended.

It is important to make a distinction between the target population and what we will refer to as *try-out learners*. The target population is an abstract representation of the widest possible range of users, such as college students, fifth graders, or adults. Try-out learners, on the other hand, are those learners who are available to the designer while the instruction is being developed. It is assumed that these try-out learners are members of the target population, that is, they are college students, fifth graders, and principals, respectively. But the try-out learners are *specific* college students, fifth graders, or principals. While the designer is preparing the instruction for the target population, the try-out learners will serve as representatives of that group in order to plan the instruction and to determine how well the instruction works after it is developed.

Entry Behaviors

The task of the instructional designer at this point in the design process is to identify the entry behaviors or skills that must be mastered by learners from the target population before beginning instruction. Entry behaviors are not simply a list of things that these students know or can do, but only those skills necessary to begin your instruction.

The procedure used to identify entry behaviors is directly related to the subordinate skills analysis process. You will recall that with the hierarchical analysis you ask, "What does the learner need to know in order to learn this skill?" The answer to this question is one or more subordinate skills. If you continue this process with each successive set of subordinate skills, the bottom of the hierarchy will contain very basic skills.

Assume you have such a highly developed hierarchy. It represents the array of skills required to take a learner from the most basic level of understanding up to your instructional goal. It is likely, however, that your target population already has some of these skills, and therefore it will not be necessary to teach all the skills in the extended hierarchy. In order to identify the entry behaviors for your instruction, examine the hierarchy, or the results of other forms of instructional analysis (e.g., procedural or cluster analysis), and identify those skills that a majority of the population will have already mastered before beginning your instruction. Draw a dotted line above these skills in the analysis chart. The skills that appear above the dotted line will be those you must teach in your instruction. Those that fall below the line are called entry behaviors.

Why are entry behaviors so important? They are defined as the skills that fall directly below the skills you plan to teach. Therefore, they are the initial building blocks for your instruction. Given these skills, learners can begin to acquire the skills presented in your instruction. Without these skills, a learner will have a very difficult time trying to learn from your instruction. Entry behaviors are a key component in the design process.

An example of how entry behaviors can be identified through the use of a hierarchy appears in Figure 5.1. This is basically the same hierarchy that appeared in the preceding chapter as Figure 4.3, but we have added some skills.

Notice in Figure 5.1 that three more skills have been added to the analysis chart, and a dotted line has been drawn across the page. The dotted line indicates that all skills above the line will be taught in the instructional materials. All the skills listed below the line will be assumed to be skills already attained by students before beginning the instruction.

Each skill below the line was derived directly from a superordinate skill that already appeared on the instructional analysis chart. Each was derived by asking the question, "What does the learner have to be able to do in order to learn this skill?" Note that even the entry behaviors identified in Figure 5.1 have a hierarchical relationship to each other. The skills that have been derived include the ability to interpret whole and decimal numbers. These are skills that *must* be mastered in order to learn skills 1 and 7, and they will not be taught in this instruction. Therefore, students will have to have mastered these skills *before* they begin the instruction on reading a scale.

FIGURE 5.1

INSTRUCTIONAL ANALYSIS FOR SCALE READING EXAMPLE

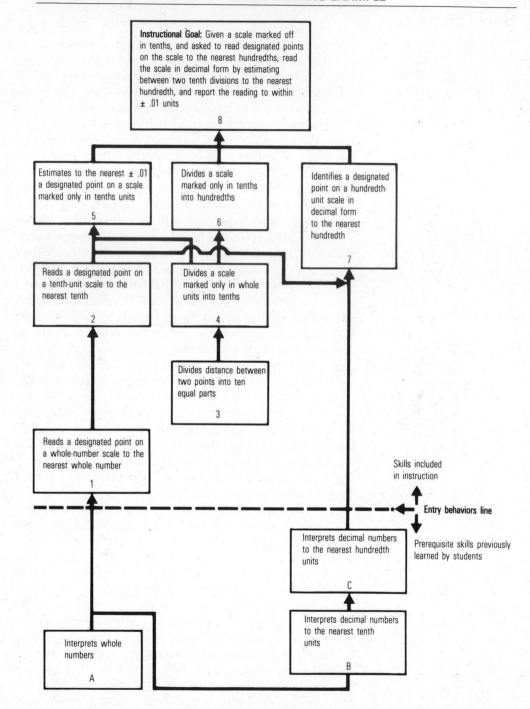

Instructional designers should identify expected entry behaviors of learners by continuing the instructional analysis to the point that skills identified become basic for their target population. The designer must assume that most, if not all, of the learners in the target population will have these skills. It is then a matter of simply drawing a dotted line through the instructional analysis chart to separate those skills to be included in the instruction from those skills that learners in the target population are assumed to have already mastered.

The description thus far has related entry behaviors to a hierarchical instructional analysis. This same approach can be taken with the procedural, cluster, and combination analyses. If a procedural analysis has a sequence of previously attained skills that must be linked together, the assumption is made explicitly that learners already have the individual skills, and the designer's task is simply to show how to link the skills together. The skills would be included in the statement of entry behaviors as well as in the task itself. If a cluster or combination approach is used in which subordinate skills and knowledge are identified, then the identification process can be continued until basic skills are identified, and so indicated by the dotted line.

You should be aware that the examples we have used have been rather clear-cut in that they describe specific skills related to specific instructional goals. There are some descriptors of learners that may be considered as either entry skills for a particular instructional unit or as descriptive of the general target population. Consider the question of students' reading levels.

It is apparent that instructional materials typically depend heavily upon the reading ability of students; students must have some minimum level of reading ability to become involved with the materials. Is the specification of reading level a description of a general characteristic of the target population or is it a specific entry behavior that students must possess before beginning instruction? Clear arguments could be made on either side of this issue. You may be able to identify other skills that would produce similar problems.

A technique you might employ to identify the appropriate category for such an ability is to determine whether you think it would be worthwhile or feasible for an instructor to test a learner for that particular skill prior to permitting the learner to begin the instruction. If the answer to that question is "yes, it would be worth the time to test the learner," then you have probably defined a specific entry behavior. If, on the other hand, it would seem to be inappropirate to test the skill of the learner (such as giving a reading test) before instruction, then the factor you have identified is probably better classified as a characteristic of the target population for which the unit is intended.

How you go about identifying the specific entry behaviors for your materials will depend upon where you stopped when you conducted your instructional analysis. If you identified only those tasks and skills that you plan to include in the instructional materials, then you will need to take each of the lowest skills in the hierarchy and determine the subordinate skills associated with it. These would be listed on your instructional analysis chart beneath a line that clearly differentiates them from subordinate skills that will be included in the instructional materials.

If your subordinate skills analysis were carried out to the point of identifying basic, low-level skills, then it should be possible for you simply to draw a line through the chart above those skills that you assume most learners in the target population have already acquired.

Also note that when developing instructional materials about topics of general interest that emphasize information objectives, there sometimes are apparently no required entry skills other than the ability to read the materials and to use appropriate reasoning skills to reach the instructional goal. If you find that you have identified such an area, then it is perfectly legitimate to indicate that, while the materials are intended for a certain target population, there are no specific entry behaviors required to begin the instruction.

The Tentativeness of Entry Behaviors

As one of our colleagues has indicated to us, the identification of entry behaviors is one of the real danger spots in the instructional design process. His point is that the designer is making assumptions about both what the learners must know and should already know. Obviously, the designer can err in one of two directions, and each has its consequences. The first problem was alluded to earlier when we said that some curriculum materials were designed for only the brightest students in the target population. This situation would be reflected in a subordinate skills analysis in which the dotted line separating skills to be taught from skills assumed to be known is placed relatively high on the chart, which suggests that target population learners already have most skills described on the chart. When the assumed entry behaviors are not already mastered by the majority of the target population, the instructional materials lose their effectiveness with a large number of learners. Without adequate preparation in the entry skills, learners' efforts are inefficient and the materials are ineffective.

The second error occurs when the dotted line is drawn too low on the instructional analysis. In this situation it is presumed that learners have few or none of the skills required to achieve the instructional goal. An error of this type is costly both in terms of developing instructional materials that are not really needed by learners, and in terms of the time required for learners to study objectives they have already mastered.

It should be noted that the designer is making a set of assumptions at this point about the target population. If time is available, try-out group members should be tested and interviewed to determine if most of them have the entry behaviors derived from the subskills analysis. Procedures for doing this will be discussed in later chapters. If time does not permit this, then the assumptions will have to be tested at a later time in the development process. Delaying this verification of the entry behaviors can lead to a situation in which a lot of development has taken place improperly with a mismatch between the target population and the instruction.

A fundamental question must be answered at this point. Is specific content being taught or is the target population being taught? If it is the former, then little or no change is required in entry behaviors. One simply keeps looking until a group of learners with the right entry behaviors is found. Your instruction is for them! However, if your purpose is to teach a specific target population, then the instruction must be modified, by the addition or subtraction of instruction, to match the entry behaviors that do exist within the group. There is no one correct answer to this dilemma. Each situation must be considered in light of the needs assessment that resulted in the creation of the instructional goal.

In the same manner, it is often found that only a portion of the target population has the entry behaviors. What accommodation can be made for this situation? It may be possible to have several "starting points" within the instruction. Learners' scores on entry behavior tests can be used to place learners at the appropriate starting point. Or the solution may again be that the instruction was designed for learners with certain entry behaviors. Those who do not have these skills must master them somewhere else before beginning the instruction. There are usually no easy answers to this all-too-common situation.

General Characteristics of Learners

General characteristics of the target population are much more inclusive than entry behaviors and are not derived from the subordinate skills analysis. For example, mathematics materials are often described as being appropriate for first-grade students or fourth-grade students, and a home economics text might be for seventh graders. This is a general description of a target population for whom instructional materials should (or might) be appropriate. We use the word *might*, because it is possible that a number of students who would be included in the target population lack the specific entry behaviors required for beginning an instructional unit. If a mathematics textbook is intended for use in fourth grade, but a majority of a particular fourth-grade class has not yet learned to add two-digit numbers, it is clear that, while the students are technically in the fourth grade, they would probably not have the critical entry behaviors to begin using the textbook. Grade level is not the prerequisite of importance.

It is important to identify the major characteristics of the target population so that potential users of instructional materials will have such a description. At this stage it is even more important to identify these characteristics because of their implications for the instructional development process. It is imperative that instructors consider the characteristics of the target population for whom instruction is being planned.

Too often designers make references about the characteristics of the learners without actually verifying them. Based upon stereotypes of the learners it might be assumed that fourth-grade boys would be interested in baseball and adults would be interested in the stock market. Quite often these assumptions reflect the interests of the designer or those of his or her children and are not at all reflective of the target population. Therefore, it is important to observe and interview members of the target population to determine not only their status vis-à-vis the entry behaviors, but their general ability level, previous experiences, and expectations about instruction.

Similar types of information about the physical and emotional characteristics of the target population can be used to draw implications about possible interests and skills. This information should be taken into consideration during the instructional development process, and such information is even more critical when the designer is planning for a special subgroup of learners such as the handicapped or the intellectually gifted. Their special characteristics must be considered when formulating any instructional strategy.

Learner characteristics is a very broad area, which can include everything from home environment to attitudes toward school to cognitive styles. All of these topics have been investigated, in terms of their relationship to student learning. Some studies examine individual differences among learners on these variables and their relationship to performance in learning situations.

We are all aware of our own characteristics, such as our preference for written instruction over lectures, and we intuitively believe that individual differences among learners are important. Our problem as designers is that the majority of the instruction we create is *not* created for individual learners, but for groups of learners. Given that fact, we must design instruction for the typical student in our target population.

While motivating learners and using presentation formats that they enjoy are important, the factor that research has indicated is most predictive of success in an instructional situation is a learner's prior knowledge of the content area that is going to be taught. Psychologists often encourage designers to determine the extent and the context of the knowledge that students already possess about a particular topic. This information can then be used to determine how to "bridge" the new knowledge to be learned with that which already exists. This approach is consistent with the concern for knowledge of entry behaviors and knowledge of the skills that are to be taught. If the student has no previously established schema upon which to associate the new information, the designer will have to identify more remote concepts that can be used to help the student acquire and retain it.

EXAMPLES

Identifying entry behaviors and learner characteristics is a very important early step in designing instruction for a specified target population. In this section we will consider entry behaviors first and then focus on learner characteristics.

Let's review the subordinate skills analyses developed in the Examples section of chapter 4 and identify entry behaviors for each analysis for specific target populations. Remember, identifying the exact entry point for a target group requires speculation on the designer's part.

Entry Behaviors

First, consider the procedural instructional analysis on banking skills included in Figures 4.7 and 4.8. Suppose you were asked to identify the entry points for the following target groups: (a) eighth-grade students, (b) college-bound seniors, and (c) the general population who uses banking services. Which of the tasks in the procedures do you believe should be entry behaviors for eighth-grade students? Go back and review each of the steps in the procedure. We would include all steps in the procedure in our instruction and label the addition and subtraction skills in Figure 4.8 as entry behaviors. Now consider the second target population, college-bound seniors. Which tasks would you cite as entry behaviors and which would you include in the instruction? We would keep the same pattern: all steps in the procedure would be included in instruction, and the arithmetic intellectual skills would be considered entry behaviors. We would maintain the same strategy for the population at large. It would be impossible to teach an individual to open and accurately maintain a checking account before he or she had mastered addition and subtraction of decimal numbers in multiple columns. This is an example of the type of skill described earlier in which the students, regardless of age, location, or motivation, all need the same entry skills prior to learning the banking procedure. Figure 5.2 repeats the subordinate skills analysis from Figure 4.8. Notice in the new diagram that broken lines have been added to indicate that addition and subtraction are considered entry behaviors and, as such, they will not be taught during instruction.

FIGURE 5.2

ENTRY BEHAVIOR LINES ADDED TO INSTRUCTIONAL ANALYSIS ON DEPOSITING MONEY INTO A CHECKING ACCOUNT

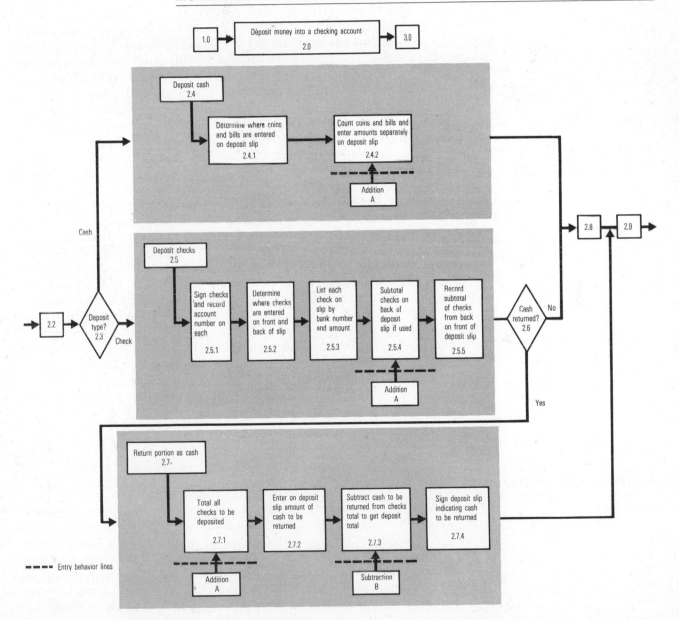

Next consider the hierarchical instructional analysis on writing declarative sentences in Figure 4.5. Estimate those tasks that should be labeled as entry behaviors for (1) fifth-grade students, (2) tenth-grade students, and (3) adult basic education students. For fifth-grade students you might want to draw the broken line under "classifying a complete statement as a declarative sentence" (5.7) and assume that tasks 5.1 through 5.5 are basic or common knowledge for fifth-grade students.

Where would you draw the entry behavior line for tenth-grade students? Did you draw the line between 5.9 and 5.10? We did, and assumed that all skills below 5.10 were common knowledge for tenth-grade students. This assumption could easily be tested using a short constructed response test for skills 5.6 through 5.9. If students could perform all the tasks through 5.9, then the instruction would start with 5.10. You may want to include subskills through 5.11 on the entry behaviors test to ensure that students need instruction on 5.10 and 5.11.

Where would you place the entry behaviors line for adult basic education students? Because of the wide variety of backgrounds and skills found in adult basic education classes we could draw the entry behaviors line below task 5.1 and include all tasks in instruction. Students would need to be tested individually to locate the entry point of each in the instruction.

Figure 5.3 contains the task analysis from Figure 4.5 with the entry behavior lines for each of the three hypothetical target groups included. The subordinate skills analysis of required skills remains the same while the entry behaviors line simply shifts location on the analysis to indicate the most appropriate entry point for the majority of students in each target group.

Third, turn your attention to the verbal information instructional analysis on commands to move a cursor in a word processing program in Figure 4.9. Where would you draw the entry behavior line on this analysis? We would place it below the bottom boxes for each cluster since only basic information is included in the analysis. Perhaps it would be wise to add: (1) describe the cursor and its movement around the screen, and (2) describe the control key and its relationship to cursor movement. These entry behaviors would be placed best before the 1.0 cluster. The diagram from 4.9 is repeated in Figure 5.4. The entry behaviors line and the newly identified entry behaviors have been added.

Now, review the attitude instructional analysis on personal safety in a hotel that is included in Figure 4.10. Where would you place the entry behaviors line? We would assume that all steps in the procedures and the information required for each step were all needed. Therefore, no entry behaviors line needs to be included in the diagram.

Learner Characteristics

In addition to specific entry behaviors that can be identified for a particular target group, information about the group's general characteristics can be very helpful in planning instruction tailored to the group's needs. These characteristics are not found on the instructional analysis chart, but they must be inferred from what the designer or others familiar with the group actually know about it. Caution must be taken to ensure that characteristics descriptive of a particular target population are indeed those of the group instead of stereotypical misconceptions of a group's characteristics.

FIGURE 5.3

ENTRY BEHAVIOR LINES ADDED TO INSTRUCTIONAL ANALYSIS FOR STORY WRITING GOAL

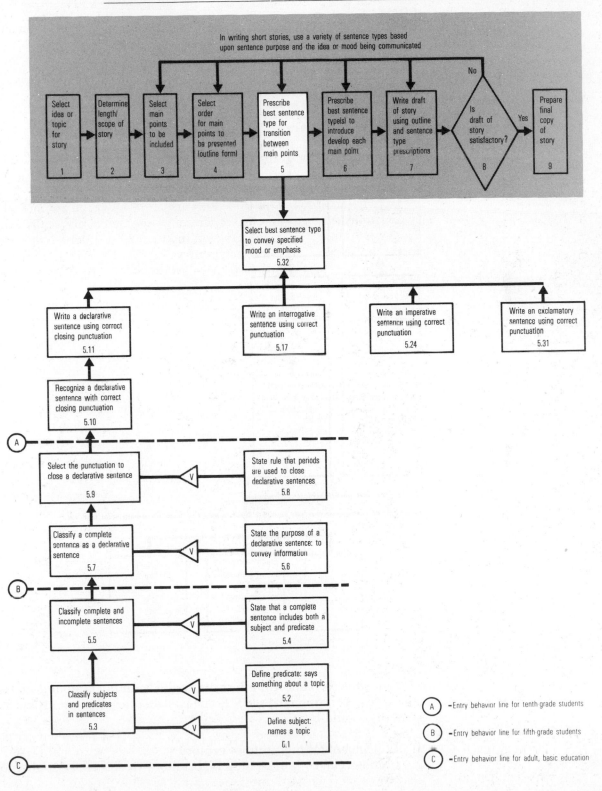

FIGURE 5.4

ENTRY BEHAVIORS FOR VERBAL INFORMATION INSTRUCTIONAL ANALYSIS ON WORD PROCESSING

GOAL:
Name the command keys used to move the cursor in a specified direction and speed around the screen

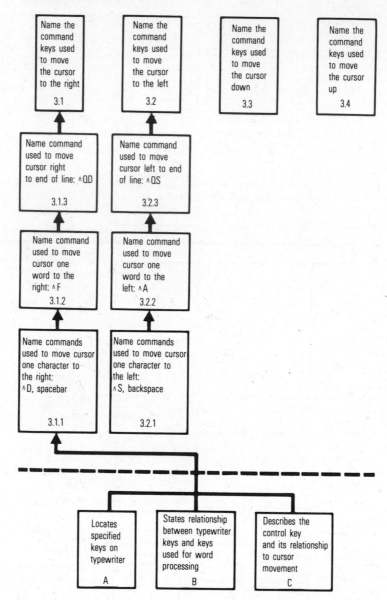

Consider the subordinate skills analysis on opening and maintaining a checking account in chapter 3. Some possible target populations for that instruction could be:

1. College-bound high school seniors
2. Commercial or work-study high school freshmen or sophomores

3. Any person inquiring about opening an account, either personal or commercial, from a bank
4. Sixth-grade students using a simulation of the exercise as a realistic practice in mathematics class

The designer would proceed differently through the instruction for these different groups. There would be differences among the groups in purposes, entry skills, motivation, and attention span. The designers would need to provide a more detailed description of the target population before beginning. Target population 3 above, any person, would result in the most general type of instruction, while instruction directed to either college students or work-study groups would differ in vocabulary, problems, practical examples, practice, and amount of feedback.

General characteristics of target populations can be described using general group descriptors such as age, grade, interests, professions, health, motivation, achievement level, abilities, socioeconomic status, or foreign-language status.

Target population 1 above, college-bound high school seniors, might be further described as having a high reading level, as not requiring math review, as good problem solvers, and as interested in the subject due to its relevance to their new money-management responsibilities.

Target population 2, commercial or work-study students, might be further described as having a limited vocabulary and reading skills, limited math skills, moderate problem-solving skills, and a general disinterest in school related activities.

Target audience 4, sixth-grade students, might further be described as having a limited vocabulary, limited math skills, limited understanding of banking, good to poor problem-solving techniques, a limited attention span, and little if any experience with banking or other types of forms.

By carefully defining the general characteristics of the target populations, using general predictors of ability and interests, it will be easier to determine whether you have indeed selected the correct population and to determine what type of approach or vocabulary you will need to use in tests and in instruction.

Broad general descriptions of target populations such as the example in 3, any person seeking to open a checking account, will make the resulting instruction more general and therefore more applicable to a wider audience, but it might lose its relevance for particular groups. Decisions must be made about whether the effort to design relevant material and the resultant learning are worth the additional effort and cost of designing very specific materials for a limited audience.

SUMMARY

To begin this stage of instructional design, you should have completed the goal analysis and the subordinate skills analysis. You should also have general ideas about the target population for which instruction will be developed. These ideas usually include general descriptions such as kindergarten children, seventh graders, college freshmen, ambulance drivers, or automobile operators convicted of reckless driving following a serious accident.

During this phase of the design process, your first task is to identify the entry behaviors required to begin your instruction. Entry behaviors are specific skills selected from the subordinate skills included in the overall analysis of tasks. Subordinate skills that you judge all or most members of the target population already possess should be classified as entry behaviors. The dividing line above entry behaviors indicates where instruction will begin. Thus, errors in judgment about learners' current knowledge and skill levels will result in inefficient instruction. It is a good idea to verify the accuracy of these judgments by testing representative members of the target population for these entry behaviors.

The second task is to identify the general characteristics that members of the target population bring to the instruction. These characteristics include descriptions such as reading levels, attention span, previous experience, motivation levels, attitudes toward school or work, and performance levels in previous instructional situations. Another important characteristic is the extent and context of related knowledge and skills that members of the target population already possess.

One outcome from these target group analysis activities is a description of the entry behavior learners must have to enter the instruction. Another outcome is information about the students' characteristics that will facilitate later design considerations such as appropriate contexts, motivational information and activities, materials formatting, and the amount of material to be presented at one time.

With the learning tasks divided into entry behaviors and subordinate skills to be taught, and the groups' characteristics described, you are ready to begin the next design phase: writing performance objectives for the specified target population. This phase is described in chapter 6.

══ PRACTICE ══

1. Review the procedural analysis on changing a tire in Figure 4.11. Assume that your target population is high school juniors with a temporary driver's license. Identify any steps in the procedure for the entry behaviors that you believe are relevant for this analysis. Modify the procedural analysis in the diagram to reflect your work. Check your diagram with Figure 5.5 in the Feedback section.

2. Review the hierarchical analysis on reading a map located in Figure 4.12. Assume that your target population is sixth-grade students who are below average, average, and above average in reading and arithmetic skills. Which tasks in the analysis would you predict are entry behaviors and which do you believe should be included in instruction for the sixth-grade group? Modify the diagram in Figure 4.12 to reflect your work, and compare your work with the analysis in Figure 5.6 in the Feedback section.

3. Consider the verbal information on locating and labeling parts of the human body in Figure 4.13. Assume that your target population is third-grade students. Which tasks do you believe should be considered entry

behaviors? Remember that the task requires students not only to locate, but also to label parts, which requires spelling. Modify Figure 4.13 to show your work, and compare your work with the analysis in Figure 5.7 in the Feedback section.

4. From the statements below, select those that might refer to general characteristics of the target population (GC) and those that might refer to descriptions of specific entry behaviors (EB).

    _____ 1.   To identify examples of fur-bearing animals
    _____ 2.   To define performance objectives
    _____ 3.   Highly motivated beginning swimmers
    _____ 4.   Frightened nonswimmers
    _____ 5.   To float facedown for thirty seconds
    _____ 6.   Twelfth-grade chemistry students
    _____ 7.   Beginning typing
    _____ 8.   To type at least thirty words per minute
    _____ 9.   Undergraduate business majors
    _____ 10.   High-school sophomores
    _____ 11.   To park a car between markers within ten inches of the curb
    _____ 12.   To write terminal objectives for instruction

You may check your responses with those in the Feedback section.

FEEDBACK

For questions 1, 2, and 3, see Figures 5.5, 5.6, and 5.7 that follow.

4. 1. EB; 2. EB; 3. GC; 4. GC; 5. EB; 6. GC; 7. GC; 8. EB; 9. GC; 10. GC; 11. EB; 12. EB.

FIGURE 5.5

PROCEDURAL ANALYSIS FOR CHANGING AN AUTOMOBILE TIRE

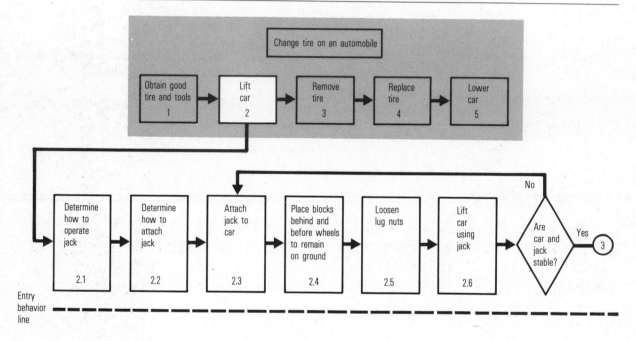

Given the target population, there are no particular entry behaviors for these skills.

FIGURE 5.6

INSTRUCTIONAL ANALYSIS FOR MAP READING WITH ENTRY BEHAVIOR LINE ADDED

GOAL:
Use a map of (your town) to locate specified places and determine the distance between them

TYPE OF LEARNING:
Intellectual skill

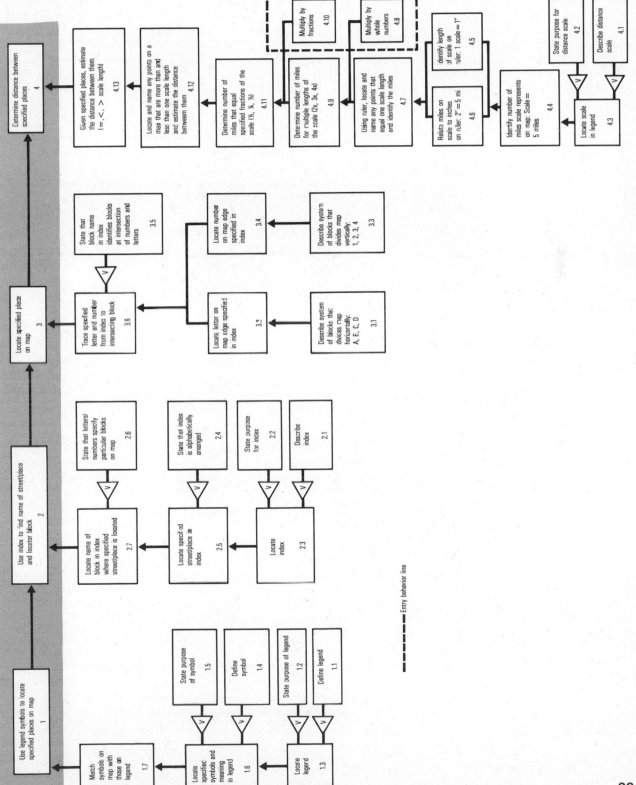

FIGURE 5.7

CLUSTER ANALYSIS OF A VERBAL INFORMATION TASK WITH ENTRY KNOWLEDGE ADDED

GOAL:
Locate and label various parts of the human body

TYPE OF LEARNING:
Verbal information

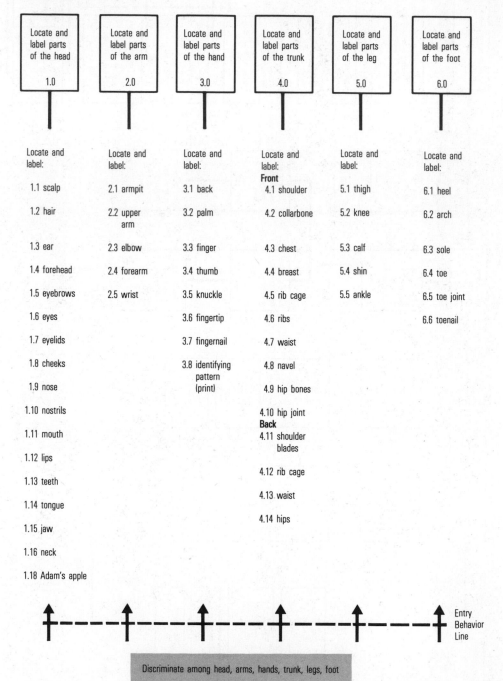

Locate and label parts of the head 1.0	Locate and label parts of the arm 2.0	Locate and label parts of the hand 3.0	Locate and label parts of the trunk 4.0	Locate and label parts of the leg 5.0	Locate and label parts of the foot 6.0

Locate and label:	Locate and label:	Locate and label:	Locate and label: **Front**	Locate and label:	Locate and label:
1.1 scalp	2.1 armpit	3.1 back	4.1 shoulder	5.1 thigh	6.1 heel
1.2 hair	2.2 upper arm	3.2 palm	4.2 collarbone	5.2 knee	6.2 arch
1.3 ear	2.3 elbow	3.3 finger	4.3 chest	5.3 calf	6.3 sole
1.4 forehead	2.4 forearm	3.4 thumb	4.4 breast	5.4 shin	6.4 toe
1.5 eyebrows	2.5 wrist	3.5 knuckle	4.5 rib cage	5.5 ankle	6.5 toe joint
1.6 eyes		3.6 fingertip	4.6 ribs		6.6 toenail
1.7 eyelids		3.7 fingernail	4.7 waist		
1.8 cheeks		3.8 identifying pattern (print)	4.8 navel		
1.9 nose			4.9 hip bones		
1.10 nostrils			4.10 hip joint **Back**		
1.11 mouth			4.11 shoulder blades		
1.12 lips			4.12 rib cage		
1.13 teeth			4.13 waist		
1.14 tongue			4.14 hips		
1.15 jaw					
1.16 neck					
1.18 Adam's apple					

Entry Behavior Line

Discriminate among head, arms, hands, trunk, legs, foot

References and Recommended Readings

Bloom, B. S. (1976). *Human characteristics and school learning.* New York: McGraw-Hill, 30–72. Bloom has conducted and summarized extensive research on the importance of cognitive and other entry skills for successful learning performance.

Davis, R. H., Alexander, L. T., & Yelon, S. L. (1975). *Learning system design.* New York: McGraw-Hill, 93–98; 1984–1991. The authors describe entry behaviors and characteristics of students and relate them to the task-analysis process.

DeCecco, J. P. (1968). *The psychology of learning and instruction: Educational psychology.* Englewood Cliffs, NJ: Prentice-Hall, 54–82. This is perhaps the most complete description available of the concepts of entry behaviors and student characteristics and how they are related to the design of instruction.

Gagné, Robert M., & Driscoll, Marcy P. (1988). *Essentials of learning for instruction* (2nd ed.). Englewood Cliffs, NJ: Prentice-Hall. This book discusses the cognitive psychology approach to understanding the learner.

McCombs, B. L. (1982). Transitioning learning strategies research and practice: Focus on the student in technical training. *Journal of Instructional Development, 5* (2), 10–17. This research stresses the importance of considering the entry knowledge and learning skills that learners bring to the instructional setting.

6

WRITING PERFORMANCE OBJECTIVES

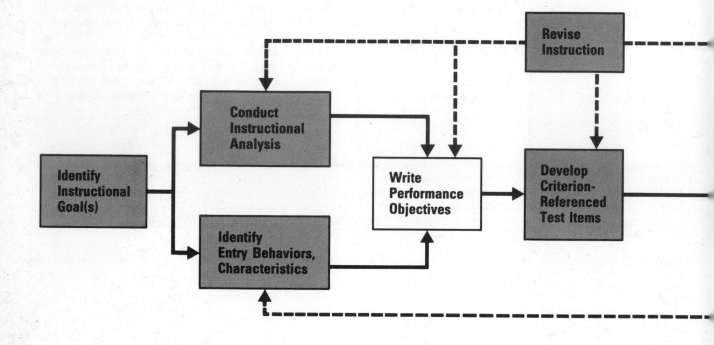

OBJECTIVES

- Identify and describe the components of a properly written performance objective.
- Write performance objectives for skills that have been identified in an instructional analysis. These objectives should include the conditions under which the skill will be performed, the skill to be performed, and the criteria for assessing the performance.

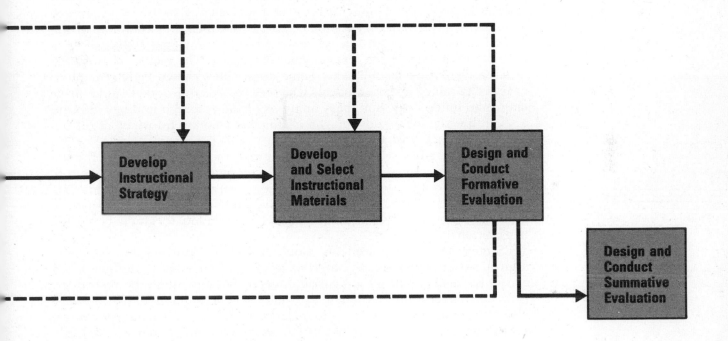

| Develop Instructional Strategy | Develop and Select Instructional Materials | Design and Conduct Formative Evaluation |

Design and Conduct Summative Evaluation

BACKGROUND

Perhaps the best-known component of the instructional design model is the writing of performance objectives, or, as they are more commonly called, behavioral objectives. Since publication of his book on objectives in 1962, Robert Mager has influenced the total educational community through his emphasis on the need for clear, precise statements of what students should be able to do when they complete their instruction. The term *behavioral objective* became familiar to many educators in the 1960s.

During that time, workshops were set up for public school teachers throughout the country. Thousands of teachers were trained to write behavioral objectives in order to become accountable for their instruction. However, two major difficulties emerged with this approach to instruction. These difficulties arose when the process of defining objectives was not included as an integral component of a total instructional design model.

Without such a model it was difficult for instructors to determine how to derive objectives. Therefore, although instructors could master the mechanics of writing an objective, there was no indication as to what was to serve as the stimulus for writing the objective. As a result, many teachers reverted to the tables of content of textbooks to identify topics for which they would write behavioral objectives.

The second and perhaps more critical concern was what to do with the objectives after they were written. Most instructors were simply told that objectives should be incorporated into their instruction, and that they would be better teachers because they now had them for their instruction. In reality, thousands and thousands of objectives were written and then placed in desk drawers, never to have an impact on the instructional process.

A number of researchers have asked whether it makes any difference if objectives are used. In almost all the research studies, this question has been asked in the context of an operational instructional setting. In a typical experiment, one group of students receives a sequence of instruction preceded by statements of what they should be able to do when they complete the instruction. A control group receives the same instructional materials, but without the statements of the instructional objectives. The results of this type of research have been ambiguous. Some studies have shown significant differences in learning for those students who receive objectives; other studies have shown no differences. Summary analyses of the research findings indicate a slight but significant advantage for students who are informed of the objectives for their instruction.

While these investigations are of interest, they do not address the importance of objectives in the design and development of instruction. The objectives guide the designer in selecting content and developing the instructional strategy. Therefore, objectives are critical to the design of instruction, regardless of whether they are presented to students during instruction.

Statements of what students should be able to do when they complete a given set of instructional materials are useful not only to designers but also to students, instructors, curriculum supervisors, and administrators. If objectives for a unit or course are made available to students, they have clear-cut guidelines for what is to be learned and tested during the course. Few students are likely to be lost for long periods of time, and more are likely to master the instruction when they know what they are supposed to be learning.

Objections to the use of behavioral objectives have been raised. For example, instructors can point to seemingly trivial objectives that appear in some instructional materials. Often, however, these objectives are not based on a carefully conducted instructional analysis illustrating the relationship of each new behavior to ones previously acquired. Similarly, many educators acknowledge that writing objectives in some areas, such as humanities, is more difficult than in others. Instructors in these areas, however, do evaluate student performance. The use of objectives requires instructors in these disciplines to perform the following tasks: (1) specify the behaviors they will teach, (2) determine the strategy for instruction, and (3) establish criteria for evaluating student performance when instruction ends.

While some instructors may see objectives as detrimental to free-flowing classroom discussion, they actually serve as a check on the relevance of discussion. Objectives also can increase the accuracy of communication among instructors who must coordinate their instruction. Statements describing what students should be able to do when they complete their instruction provide a clear description of what students will be "covering," thus helping prevent instructional gaps or duplication. Objectives can also indicate to parents and administrators what students are being taught. General course goals, which are often used for this purpose, may sound interesting and challenging, but seldom indicate what it is that students will know or be able to do when a course is completed.

CONCEPTS

Performance Objective

The most important concept associated with this chapter is that of a performance objective. A performance objective is a detailed description of what students will be able to do when they complete a unit of instruction. First, it should be pointed out that there are three terms often used synonymously when describing student performance. Mager first used the term *behavioral objective* to emphasize that it is a statement that describes what the student will be able to do. Some educators have strongly objected to this orientation. Other, perhaps more acceptable, terms have been substituted for *behavioral*. You will therefore see in the literature the terms *performance objective* and *instructional objective*. When you see these you can assume that they are synonymous with behavioral objectives. You should not be misled to think that an instructional objective describes what an instructor will be doing. It describes the kind of behavior that the instructor will be attempting to produce in learners.

We have said previously that the instructional goal describes what learners will be able to do when they complete a set of instructional materials. Similarly, the skills derived through an analysis of the instructional goal are called *subordinate skills*. The objectives that pave the way to the achievement of the terminal objective are referred to as *subordinate objectives*. When you convert the instructional goal to a behavioral objective, it is referred to as the *terminal objective*. The terminal objective describes exactly what the student will be able to do when he or she completes a unit of instruction. Though this paragraph may seem to be filled with jargon, these terms will become meaningful as you use the instructional design model.

Performance objectives are derived from the skills in the instructional analysis. At least one or more objectives can be written for each of the skills identified in the instructional analysis. This includes the writing of objectives for the skills identified as entry behaviors.

Why should objectives be written for entry behaviors if they are not included in instruction? The most important reason for having objectives for entry behaviors is that the objective is the basis for developing test items. It will be necessary to have test items to determine if, in fact, students do have the entry behaviors you assumed they would have. Therefore, items should be written to assess the skills stated in the performance objectives for your entry behaviors. In addition, it will be useful for the designer to have these objectives should it be determined that learners in the target population do not have the entry behaviors, and it becomes necessary to develop instruction for these behaviors.

COMPONENTS OF AN OBJECTIVE Given that there will be objectives for the goal statement, subordinate skills, and entry behaviors, how are they written? The work of Mager has been the continuing standard for the development of objectives. His model for an objective is a statement that includes three major components. The first component describes the skill or behavior identified in the instructional analysis. The objective must describe what it is the learner will be able to do.

The second component of an objective describes the conditions that will prevail while a learner carries out the task. Will the learners be allowed to use a dictionary? Will they be given a paragraph to analyze? These are questions about the conditions under which the learner will perform the desired behavior.

The third component of the objective describes the criteria that will be used to evaluate learner performance on the objective. The criterion is often stated in terms of the limits, or range, of answers or responses that will be acceptable. The criterion answers the question, "Does an answer have to be exactly correct?" The criterion indicates the tolerance limits for the response. The criterion may also be expressed in terms of a qualitative judgment such as the inclusion of certain facts in a definition or a physical performance judged to be acceptable by an expert.

The following statement contains all three components of an objective: "Given two points on a line, the learner will divide the distance into ten equal parts by drawing nine equidistant lines between the two points. This will be done with an error of less than 10 percent." In other words, the behavior to be exhibited is "divide the distance into ten equal parts by drawing nine equidistant lines between the two points." The conditions are "given two points on a line." The criterion is explicit: "draw equidistant lines that are within a tolerance of 10 percent."

One problem that sometimes occurs is that although an objective may not convey any real information, it may meet the criteria for being an objective. For example, consider the following objective: "Given a multiple-choice test, complete the test and achieve a score of at least nine out of ten correct." While this may be a slightly exaggerated example, it can be referred to as a universal objective in the sense that it appears to meet all the criteria for being an objective and is applicable to almost any cognitive learning situation. It says nothing, however, in terms of the actual conditions or the behavior that is to be learned and evaluated. You should always make sure that your objectives are not universal objectives.

Derivation of Behaviors

It has been stated that objectives are derived directly from the instructional analysis. Thus they must express precisely the type of behavior already identified in the analysis. If the subskill in the instructional analysis includes, as it should, a clearly identifiable behavior, then the task of writing an objective becomes simply the adding of criteria for behavioral assessment and describing the conditions under which the behavior must be performed. For example, if the subskill is "divides a scale into tenths," then a suitable objective might be stated thus: "Given a scale divided into whole units, divide one unit into tenths. The number of subunits must be ten, and the size of all units must be approximately the same."

Sometimes, however, the designer may find that subskill statements are too vague to write a matching objective. Therefore, the designer should carefully consider the verbs that may be used to describe behavior. Most intellectual skills can be described by such verbs as discriminate, identify, classify, demonstrate, or generate. These verbs, as described by Gagné, Briggs, and

Wager (1988), refer to such specific activities as grouping similar objectives, distinguishing one thing from another, or solving problems. Note that the list does not include such verbs as *know* or *understand.*

The instructor must review each objective and ask, "Could I observe a learner doing this?" It is impossible to observe a learner "knowing" or "understanding." Often these verbs are associated with information that the instructor wants the students to learn. To make it clear to students that they are supposed to learn certain skills, it is preferable to state in the objective exactly how students are to demonstrate that they have learned the skills. For example, the learner might be required to state that New York and California are approximately three thousand miles apart. If students are able to state (or write) this fact, it may be inferred that they know it.

Gagné, Briggs, and Wager (1989) have suggested that intellectual skill and verbal information objectives should describe not only the actual behavior to be observed, but the intent of the behavior, a distinction also made by Mager (1975). For example, students might demonstrate their ability to identify Latin words by circling such words in a mixed list of English and Latin words. This statement of an objective not only describes what the students will be doing, namely, "circling a response," but it also describes the capability that will be demonstrated, namely, "identifying." In other words, the intent of the objective is not to have the students demonstrate their ability to draw circles, but to demonstrate their ability to identify examples of Latin words.

Objectives that relate to psychomotor skills usually are easily expressed in terms of a behavior (e.g., running, jumping, or driving). When objectives involve attitudes, the learner is usually expected to choose a particular alternative or sets of alternatives or to complete an attitude questionnaire. Or, it may involve the learner making a choice from among a variety of activities.

Derivation of Conditions

With the behavioral component of the objective clearly identified, you are ready to specify the conditions part of the objective. In selecting appropriate conditions you need to consider both the behavior to be demonstrated and the characteristics of the target population. You should also distinguish among the functions that the conditions component serve. These functions include specifying: (1) the cue or stimulus that learners will use to search the information stored in memory, (2) the characteristics of any resource material required to perform the task, and (3) the scope and complexity of the task.

Consider first the cue or stimulus provided for learners. This is an especially important consideration for testing verbal information tasks. Suppose you wanted to ensure that learners could associate a particular concept with its definition, or vice versa. It is common to find the conditions for this type of task simply written as, "From memory, define . . . ," or as "Given a paper and pencil test, define . . ." Neither of these examples identifies the cue or stimulus the learners will use to search their memory or schema for the related information.

There are several conditions that could be used to describe the stimuli learners will be given to aid their recall of verbal information. Consider the following list of stimuli (conditions) and behaviors, each of which could enable learners to demonstrate that they know or can associate the concept with the definition.

Condition	*Behavior*
Given the term, ⟶	write the definition.
Given the definition, ⟶	name the term.
Given the term and a set of alternative definitions, ⟶	select the most precise definition.
Given an illustration of the concept, ⟶	name and define the object illustrated.
Given the term, ⟶	list its unique physical characteristics.
Given the term, ⟶	list its functions or roles.

While each of these conditions is "from memory," it more clearly specifies the nature of the stimulus material or information learners will be given in order to search their memory for the desired response. Each condition also implies a paper and pencil test, but merely specifying a paper and pencil test as the condition leaves the issue of an appropriate stimulus undefined.

The second function of the conditions component of an objective is to specify any resource materials that are needed to perform a given task. Such resource materials might include: (1) illustrations such as tables, charts, or graphs; (2) written materials such as reports, stories, or newspaper articles; (3) physical objects such as rocks, leaves, slides, machines, or tools; and (4) reference materials such as dictionaries, manuals, or textbooks. Besides naming the resources required, the conditions should specify any unique characteristics the resources should possess.

The third function of the conditions component is to control the complexity of a task in order to tailor it to the abilities and experiences of the target population. Consider how the following conditions control the complexity of a map reading objective.

1. Given a neighborhood map containing no more than six designated places, . . .
2. Given a neighborhood map containing no more than 12 designated places that are spaced one inch apart, a locator grid and index, and a scale with one inch equal to one mile, . . .
3. Given a commercial map of a city, . . .

Such conditions limit the complexity of the same task to make it appropriate for a given target group.

In deciding the conditions that should be specified, the primary considerations should be the nature of the stimulus material and the characteristics of the target population. Special resources required and limitations on task complexity are both conditions that are directly related to the nature of appropriate stimuli and the capabilities of the group.

While the preceding examples have focused on intellectual skills and verbal information, conditions appropriate for demonstrating psychomotor skills and attitudinal choices should also be considered carefully. Related to psychomotor tasks, you will need to consider the nature of the context in which the skill will be performed and the availability of any required equipment for performing the task. For example, if learners are to demonstrate that they can drive an automobile, you need to consider whether automatic or standard transmissions should be required. You also need to consider whether the driving demonstration will involve inner-city freeways, interstate highways, downtown streets, two-lane country roads, or all of these. Such decisions will influence the equipment required, the nature of instruction, the time required for practicing the skills, and the nature of the driving test.

Specifying the conditions under which learners will demonstrate that they possess a certain attitude also requires careful consideration. Three important issues are the context in which the choice will be made, the nature of the alternatives from which the learner will choose, and the maturity of the target population. These considerations are important because choices may be situation specific. For example, choosing to demonstrate good sportsmanship during a tennis match may depend upon the importance of the match in terms of the consequences for winning or losing. It may also depend on the player's sense of freedom to "act out" feelings of frustration and anger without negative repercussions. It will also depend on the age and corresponding emotional control of the players. Demonstrating the true acquisition of a sportsmanlike attitude would require a competitive match free from fear of reprisal. Simply stating the appropriate behavior on a pencil and paper test or demonstrating it under the watchful eye of the coach will not suffice.

Specifying conditions for both psychomotor skills and attitudinal choices can be tricky. An appropriate set of conditions may be difficult to implement in the instructional and testing setting. For this reason, compromises and simulations are sometimes required. When they are, the designer must remember that the actual demonstration of the attitude has been compromised.

Derivation of Criteria

The final part of the objective is the criteria for judging acceptable performance of the skill. In specifying logical criteria, you must consider the nature of the task to be performed. Many intellectual skill and verbal information tasks have only one response that would be considered correct. Examples include adding or subtracting whole numbers, matching the tense or number of subjects and verbs, and naming state capitals. In such instances, the criteria are that learners can produce the precise response sought. Some designers add the criterion "correctly" to this type of objective, whereas others state no criterion and assume that it is implicit in the conditions and behavior. However you choose to treat such objectives, you should keep in mind that specifying the number of times that learners are to perform the task (e.g., two out of three times or correctly 80 percent of the time) does not indicate the objective criterion. The question of "how many times" or "how many items correct" and similar statements are questions of mastery. The designer must determine how many times a behavior must be demonstrated in order to be sure that learners have mastered it. This decision is usually made when test items are developed. The important point is that the criterion in the objective describes what behavior will be acceptable or the limits within which a behavior must fall.

Many intellectual skills and verbal information tasks do not result in a single answer, and learners' responses can be expected to vary. Examples include dividing a line into equal parts and estimating distance using a scale. In these types of instances the criteria should specify the tolerance allowed for an acceptable response. Other tasks that result in a variety of responses include defining terms, writing paragraphs, answering essay questions on any topic, or producing a research report. The criteria for such objectives should specify any information or features that must be present in a response for it to be considered accurate enough. For complex responses, a checklist of response features may be necessary to indicate the criteria for judging the acceptability of a response.

The criteria for judging the acceptability of a psychomotor skill performance may also need to be specified using a checklist to indicate the expected behaviors. Frequency counts or time limits might also be necessary. A description of the body's appearance as the skill is performed may need to be included (e.g., the position of the hands on a piano keyboard).

Specifying criteria for attitudinal goals can also be complex. Appropriate criteria will depend on such factors as the nature of the behavior observed, the context within which it is observed, and the age of members of the target population. It might include a tally of the number of times a desirable behavior is observed in a given situation. It could also include the number of times an undesirable behavior is observed in the situation. You may find that a checklist of anticipated behaviors is the most efficient way to specify criteria for judging the acquisition of an attitude. A frequent problem with criteria for attitude measurement is the evaluator's ability to observe the response within a given time period and circumstance; thus, compromise may be necessary.

One problem that can arise in certain instructional settings is to state that expert judgment or instructor judgment is the criterion for judging student performance. It is wise to begin with a determination to avoid listing this as the criterion for an objective. It is not helpful to you or to the learners. It only says that someone else will judge their performance. In situations in which a judge must be used, try to consider what types of things you would look for if you were the expert who was judging the performance. Develop a checklist of the types of behaviors and include these in the statement of the objective to ensure a clear understanding of the criteria.

Evaluation of Objectives

A good way to evaluate the clarity and feasibility of an objective you have written is to construct a test item that will be used to measure the learners' accomplishment of the task. If you cannot produce a logical item yourself, then the objective should be reconsidered. Another way to evaluate the clarity of an objective is to ask a colleague to construct a test item that is congruent with the behavior and conditions specified. If the item produced does not closely resemble the one you have in mind, then the objective is not clear enough to communicate your intentions.

You should also evaluate the criteria you have specified in the objective. This may be done by using the criteria to evaluate existing samples of the desired performance or response. These may be samples produced by yourself, by colleagues, or by anyone who has performed the task. You should specifically attend to whether each criterion named is observable within the specified conditions and time frame. Determining the observability of criteria usually is easier for verbal information and intellectual skill tasks than it is for psychomotor skill and attitudinal objectives, as you might suspect.

While writing objectives, the designer must be aware that these statements will be used to develop tests for the instruction. Therefore, the designer might again check objectives by asking, "Could I design an item that indicates whether a learner can successfully do what has been described in the objective?" If it is difficult to imagine how this could be done in the existing facilities and environment, then the objective should be reconsidered.

Objectives should be written for each of the skills identified in the instructional analysis, including the instructional goal and all entry behaviors. The relationship between the skill and the objective should be obvious. You may find that sometimes it will require two or three objectives to describe adequately the types of behavior represented by a skill in the instructional analysis. The need for four or more objectives suggests that the task itself is too large and should be reanalyzed into subordinate skills in order to provide a more fine-grained analysis of what it is that you are attempting to teach.

Another suggestion that may be helpful is that you should not be reluctant to use two or even three sentences to adequately describe your objective. There is no requirement to limit objectives to one sentence. Also you should avoid using the phrase "after completing this instruction" as part of the conditions under which a student will perform a skill as described in an objective. It is assumed that the student will study the materials prior to performing the skill. Objectives do not specify *how* a behavior will be learned.

One final word: Do not allow yourself to become deeply involved in the semantics of objective writing. Many debates have been held over the exact word that must be used in order to make an objective "correct." The point is that objectives have been found to be useful as statements of instructional intent. They should convey to the designer or subject matter specialist in the field what it is that the student will be able to do. However, objectives have no meaning in and of themselves. They are only one component in the total instructional design process and only as they contribute to that process do they take on meaning. Therefore, the best advice at this point is to write them in a meaningful way and then move on to the next step in the instructional design process.

The Function of Objectives

It is worth noting that objectives serve a variety of functions, not just as statements from which test items are derived. Objectives have quite different functions for designers, instructors, and learners, and it is important to keep these distinctions in mind. For the designer, objectives are an integral part of the design process. They are the means by which the skills in the instructional analysis are translated into complete descriptions of what students will be able to do after completing instruction. Objectives serve as the input documentation for the designer or test construction specialist as they prepare the test for the instruction and the instructional strategy. It is important that designers have as much detail as possible for these activities.

After the instruction has been prepared for general use, the objectives are used to communicate to both the instructor and students what it is that may be learned from the materials. To accomplish this, it is sometimes desirable to either shorten or reword the objectives so that they express ideas that can be understood by the students based upon their knowledge at that point in the instruction. Therefore, designers should be aware of this shift in the use of objectives, and reflect this distinction in the materials they create.

Consider how a comprehensive list of objectives created during the design process is modified for inclusion in instructional materials. How do these embedded objectives differ from those used by designers? First, few of the objectives that were used during the development of materials typically appear in them. Generally only the major objectives are included in the publication. Second, the wording of those objectives appearing in the materials is modified. The conditions and criteria from the objectives are often omitted in order to focus learners' attention on the specific behaviors to be learned, resulting in better communication of this information. Finally, students are more likely to attend to three to five major objectives than to a lengthy list of 30 or more subordinate objectives.

EXAMPLES

This section contains examples of performance objectives for verbal information, intellectual skills, psychomotor skills, and attitudes. To aid your analysis of each example, the conditions are highlighted using the letters (CN), the behaviors are identified with a (B), and the criteria are indicated using the letters (CR). You would not include these letters in your own objectives. Following each set of examples is a discussion that should also aid your analysis.

Verbal Information

The verbal information subordinate skills included in Table 6.1 are taken from Figure 4.5, which illustrated the instructional goal analysis on composition writing. The left column contains the subskills, and the right column includes a matching performance objective.

In these example verbal information objectives, notice that the conditions specify key terms that must be used in the test items presented to learners.

TABLE 6.1

VERBAL INFORMATION SUBSKILLS AND MATCHING PERFORMANCE OBJECTIVES

5.1 Define subject	5.1 Given the term *subject* (CN), define the term (B). The definition must include that the subject names a topic (CR).
5.2 Define predicate	5.2 Given the term *predicate* (CN), define the term (B). The definition must include that the predicate says something about the topic or subject (CR).
5.4 State that a complete statement includes both a subject and a predicate	5.4 Given the terms *complete sentence* (CN), define the concept (B). The definition must name both the subject and the predicate (CR).
5.6 State the purpose of a declarative sentence.	5.6 Given the terms *declarative sentence* and *purpose* (CN), state the purpose of a declarative sentence (B). The purpose should include to convey/tell information (CR).
5.8 State that periods are used to close declarative sentences.	5.8 Given the terms *declarative sentence* and *closing punctuation* (CN), name the period as the closing punctuation (B). The term *period* must be spelled correctly (CR).

These key terms will function as cues the learner will use to locate related information in memory. Although there are many different ways that corresponding test items could be formatted (e.g., as complete questions or statements or as a list of terms to define), these key terms must be presented to the learner. Notice also that the behaviors used in the subskill and objective are congruent. While the terms used to describe the behaviors in statements 5.4 and 5.8 change from the subskill to the objective, the skill measured does not change. Only the manner in which the student responds to demonstrate the covert skill is changed.

Finally, consider the criteria in each objective. Because definitions generated by students will vary, objectives 5.1, 5.2, 5.4, and 5.6 include information that must be present in a response for it to be considered correct. Objective 5.8 is different in that only one term, *period*, could be considered correct. The only manner in which the responses could be correct and still vary is spelling. If the term must be spelled correctly, then this criterion should be added. If spelling is not an issue for the designer, then this particular objective has an implied criterion in that only one word is acceptable.

Intellectual Skills

The intellectual skills objectives in Table 6.2 are also derived from the subordinate skills analysis on composition writing in Figure 4.5.

In these intellectual subskill examples, notice that the conditions part of the objectives is more complex than those used in the verbal information examples. Here they identify the cues that will be given to learners and limit the complexity of the tasks. Limiting factors include simple sentences only and, when a variety of sentence types is presented as incorrect examples, imperative sentences purposefully are omitted. The instruction is obviously intended for beginners who, at this point in the unit, would be unable to make the fine distinctions required to discriminate between imperative and declarative sentences (e.g., both convey information and both close with periods). This distinction should be left until after instruction on imperative sentences.

The criterion for each objective besides 5.9 and 5.11 is selecting *all* appropriate examples presented. For objective 5.9, only one correct response is possible; thus, the criterion is implied. Notice in objective 5.11 that correctly spelling all words is not required, and producing simple sentences is also not named. The designer has decided to accept any complete declarative sentence as correct.

The performance objectives for the remaining three strands of subskills are omitted from the example, but they would need to be written before proceeding with the design process. An example objective has been included for the instructional goal. Students who could demonstrate accomplishment of each of the subskills would not necessarily be able to accomplish the instructional goal. The designer could also include an objective that required writing a story on a topic that the students choose.

Although such sentence-type restrictions on the terminal objective for story writing might at this point appear unnatural, it is important to recall the initial problem the instruction is designed to address. Remember from Chapter 2 that this particular goal was selected to remedy a specific writing problem identified by teachers. The problem was that, "Students only use one type of sentence, namely declarative, simple sentences, to communicate their thoughts rather than varying their sentence types by purpose and complexity." This particular goal addresses only one part of the problem: vary-

TABLE 6.2

SAMPLE INTELLECTUAL SKILLS AND PERFORMANCE OBJECTIVES

Subordinate Skills	Matching Performance Objectives
5.3 Classify subjects and predicates in complete sentences	5.3 Given several complete, simple declarative sentences (CN), identify (all (CR)) the subjects and predicates (B).
5.5 Classify complete and incomplete sentences	5.5.1 Given several complete and incomplete simple declarative sentences (CN), identify (all (CR)) those that are complete (B).
	5.5.2 Given several complete and incomplete simple declarative sentences (CN), identify (all (CR)) those missing subjects and (all (CR)) those missing predicates (B).
5.7 Classify a complete sentence as a declarative sentence	5.7 Given several complete simple sentences that include declarative, interrogative, and exclamatory sentences (CN), identify (all (CR)) those that are declarative (B).
5.9 Select the punctuation used to close a declarative sentence	5.9 Given illustrations of periods, commas, exclamation points, and question marks; the terms *declarative sentence* and closing *punctuation* (CN), select the period (B). (CR Implied)
5.10 Recognize a declarative sentence with correct closing punctuation	5.10 Given several simple declarative, interrogative, and exclamatory sentences with correct and incorrect closing punctuation (CN), select (all (CR)) the declarative sentences with closing periods (B).
5.11 Write declarative sentences with correct closing punctuation	5.11 Write declarative sentences (B) on: (1) selected topics, and (2) topics of student choice (CN). Sentences must be complete and closed with a period (CR).
Goal: In writing short stories, use a variety of sentence types based on the sentence purpose and the idea or mood being communicated.	T.O. Given a topic, (CN,) write a 300-word short story that includes at least two of each of the following types of sentences: declarative, interrogative, exclamatory, and imperative (B). Each of these sentences must logically "fit" the story as it unfolds (CR).

ing sentence types. The other, varying sentence complexity (e.g., simple, complex, compound, compound-complex), would require a different unit. For this sample unit, being required to vary sentence types based on purpose and mood will cause students to consider their sentence type options and to practice writing sentences using a variety of types. Whether students use a variety of sentence types when they are not required to do so remains to be seen.

Psychomotor Skills

Analyze the behavioral objectives in Table 6.3 that are based on the tire-changing example in Figure 4.11.

As noted previously, writing performance objectives for psychomotor skills is more complex than writing objectives for verbal information and

TABLE 6.3

SAMPLE PSYCHOMOTOR SKILLS AND MATCHING PERFORMANCE OBJECTIVES

Steps	Matching Behavioral Objectives
2.1 Determine how to operate jack	2.1 Given a standard scissors jack and detached jack handle (that is not placed beneath a car) (CN), operate the jack (B). Attach the handle securely, pump the handle so the jack lifts, release the safety catch, and lower the jack to its closed position (CR).
2.2 Determine how to attach jack to car	2.2 Given an unattached scissors jack and a car to be lifted that is perched precariously on the brim of the road (CN), prepare for attaching the jack (B). Relocate the car to a flat, stable location; locate the best place on the frame of the car in proximity to the wheel to be removed; then position the jack squarely beneath the frame at that location (CR).
2.3 Attach jack to car	2.3 Given a scissors jack placed squarely beneath the frame at the appropriate spot (CN), attach the handle and raise the jack (B). Jack is squarely beneath frame at appropriate spot and raised just to meet car frame. Contact between jack and car is evaluated for balance and adjusted if necessary. Car is NOT lifted and lug nuts are NOT loosened (CR).
2.4 Place blocks behind and before wheels to remain on ground	2.4 Without being given blocks and without being told to locate appropriate blocks (CN), locate blocks and place behind wheels to remain on ground (B). Locates enough brick-size blocks of a sturdy composition and places one before and behind each wheel that is away from jack (CR).
Goal: Change tire on an automobile	T.O. Given an automobile with a flat tire, all tools required to change the tire secured in their normal positions in the trunk, and an inflated spare tire secured normally in the wheel well (CN), replace the flat tire with the spare tire (B). Each step in the procedure will be performed in sequence and according to criteria specified for each step (CR).

for many intellectual skills. In this abbreviated list of examples from Table 4.11, notice the increased specificity in the conditions. Any special circumstances must be prescribed. Notice in objective 2.4 that the designer does not want the learner to be given blocks or to be reminded to obtain them. Obviously part of the demonstration will be for the learner to recall as well as to perform this step.

The verbs are also important and may require some translation to ensure that the behaviors are observable. Notice the shifts in 2.1 and 2.2 from "determine how to" to "operate the" and "prepare for." To measure whether the learner has "determined how to," observable behaviors needed to be identified, thus the shift in verbs.

Notice also how the criteria differ from those in the previous examples. Specifying the criteria for steps in a procedure typically requires listing the substeps that must be accomplished. The criteria for each of these objectives contain such a list.

Another interesting feature about procedural performance objectives should be noted. Although each objective has its own conditions, the conditions, behaviors, and criteria in preceding examples are often conditions for performing any given step. For example, an implied condition for objective 2.2 is the successful completion of objective 2.1. Similarly, an implied condition for objective 2.3 is the successful completion of objective 2.2.

Finally, notice the criteria listed for the terminal objective. Actually listing all the criteria for performing this objective would require a relisting of all the specific criteria for each step in the process, because completing all the steps constitutes performing the terminal objective. Thus, the criteria listed for each objective should be placed on a checklist that could be used to guide the evaluation of the learner's performance.

Attitudes

Developing objectives for the acquisition of attitudes can also be complex in terms of the conditions, behaviors, and criteria. The examples listed in Table 6.4 are taken from the attitudinal goal on hotel safety included in Fig-

TABLE 6.4

EXAMPLE ATTITUDES AND MATCHING PERFORMANCE OBJECTIVES

Attitudes	Matching Behavioral Objectives
1. Chooses to maximize safety from fires while registered in a hotel	1.1 Unaware that they are being observed during hotel check-in (CN), employees (always (CR)): (1) request a room on a lower floor, and (2) inquire about safety features in and near their assigned room such as smoke alarms, sprinkler systems, and stairwells (B).
2. Chooses to maximize safety from intrusion while registered in a hotel	2.1 Unaware they are being observed as they prepare to leave the hotel room for a time (CN), employees (always (CR)): (1) leave radio or television playing audibly and lights burning, and (2) they check to ensure the door locks securely as it closes behind them (B).
	2.2 Unaware that they are being observed upon reentering their hotel rooms (CN), employees (always (CR)) check to see that the room is as they left it and that no one is in the room. They also keep the door bolted and chained (B) at all times (CR).
3. Chooses to maximize the safety of valuables while staying in a hotel room	3.1 Unaware that they are being observed during check-in (CN), employees (always (CR)) inquire about lockboxes and insurance for valuables. They place valuable documents, extra cash, and unworn jewelry in a secured lockbox (B).
	3.2 Unaware that they are being observed upon leaving the room for a time (CN), employees do not leave jewelry or money lying about on hotel furniture (B).

ure 4.10, and they serve as good illustrations of problems the designer could encounter.

The first thing you should notice about the conditions in these objectives is that they would be very difficult to implement for several reasons. Individual rights and privacy are two problems, and gaining access to rooms to observe whether doors were bolted and jewelry and money were put away are others. In such instances the designer would undoubtedly need to compromise. The best compromise would probably be to ensure that employees know what to do should they choose to maximize their personal safety while in a hotel. Thus a pencil and paper test on related verbal information may be the best the designer can do.

Consider another attitude example that is more manageable. Recall the courteous, friendly bank tellers in chapter 2. The attitude goal and objectives included in Table 6.5 for teller attitudes appear to be observable and measurable. This particular example will enable us to illustrate some important points. First, the conditions are exactly the same for all four of the selected behaviors. Thus, they are written once before the behaviors to avoid redundancy. Recall that the measurement of attitudes requires that the tellers know how to act while greeting a customer and why they should act in this manner. They also must believe they are free to act in the manner they choose, which means that they cannot know that they are being observed. Another condition is that they choose to be courteous even when they are very busy. The designer could infer that a teller who chooses to greet customers in a friendly manner under these conditions possesses the desired attitude.

The criterion for acceptable performance (always) is also the same for all four objectives, so it too is placed preceding the list of behaviors.

The expected behaviors are listed separately beneath the conditions and criteria. This brief list of behaviors could be expanded to include those behaviors that tellers are never (CR) to exhibit while greeting a customer (e.g., wait for the customer to speak first and fail to look up or acknowledge a customer until ready).

TABLE 6.5

MANAGEABLE ATTITUDE AND MATCHING PERFORMANCE OBJECTIVES

Attitude	Matching Performance Objective
Tellers will choose to treat customers in a friendly, courteous manner	Unaware they are being observed during transactions with customers on busy day (CN), tellers will always (CR): 1. Initiate a transaction with a customer by: (a) smiling, (b) initiating a verbal greeting, (c) saying something to make the service appear personalized, (d) verbally excusing themselves if they must complete a prior transaction, and (e) inquiring how they can be of service (B). 2. Conduct a customer's transaction by: (a) listening attentively to the customer's explanation, (b) requesting any clarifying information required, (c) providing any additional forms required, (d) completing or amending forms as needed, (e) explaining any changes made to the customer, and (f) explaining all materials returned to the customer (B). 3. Conclude each transaction by: (a) inquiring about any other services needed, (b) verbally saying, "Thank you," (c) responding to any comments made by the customer, and (d) ending with a verbal wish (e.g., "Have a nice day," "Hurry back," or "See you soon").

With these objectives a supervisor could develop a checklist for tallying the frequency with which each behavior occurs. From such tallies, the supervisor could infer whether the teller possessed the prescribed attitude.

SUMMARY

Before beginning to write performance objectives, you should have a completed instructional analysis. You should also have completed your analysis of entry behaviors and your description of the target population. With these products as a foundation, you are ready to write performance objectives for each entry behavior and enabling skill and a terminal objective for the instructional goal.

To create each objective, you should begin with the behaviors that are described in the subordinate skills. You will need to add both conditions and criteria to each subordinate skill to transform it into a performance objective. In selecting appropriate conditions, you should consider: (1) appropriate stimuli and cues to aid the learners' search of their memories for associated information, (2) appropriate characteristics for any required resource materials, and (3) appropriate levels of task complexity for the target population. For attitudinal objectives, you will also need to consider circumstances in which the learners are free to make choices without reprisal.

The final task is to specify a criterion or criteria appropriate for the conditions and behavior described, and appropriate for the developmental level of the target group. When there is only one correct response possible, many designers omit criteria as they are clearly implied, whereas other designers choose to insert the term *correctly*. When the learners' responses can vary, as they can for tasks in all four domains, criteria that set the limits for an acceptable response must be added. Deriving criteria for psychomotor skills and attitudes typically is more complex in that several observable behaviors generally need to be listed. These behaviors, however, are very useful for developing required checklists or rating scales.

Your complete list of performance objectives becomes the foundation for the next phase of the design process. The next step is to develop criterion-referenced test items for each objective, and the required information and procedures are described in chapter 7.

═══ PRACTICE ═══

I. Read each of the objectives listed below. Determine if each objective includes conditions, behaviors and criterion, and indicate what, if anything, is missing.

1. Given a list of activities carried on by the early settlers of North America, students should understand what goods they produced, what product resources they used, and what trading they did. The following is missing from the objective:
   a. important conditions and criterion
   b. observable behavior and important conditions

    c. observable behavior and criterion
    d. nothing

2. "Given a mimeographed list of states and capitals, the student matches at least 35 of the 50 states with their capitals without the use of maps, charts, or lists." What is missing from this objective?
    a. observable response
    b. important conditions
    c. criterion performance
    d. nothing

3. Given a list of 50 state capitals, students will know the respective states with 100 percent accuracy. Which of the following is missing from this objective?
    a. observable behavior
    b. important conditions
    c. criterion performance
    d. nothing

4. Students will be able to play the piano. Which of the following is missing from this objective?
    a. important conditions
    b. important conditions and criterion performance
    c. observable behavior and criterion performance
    d. nothing

5. Given daily access to music in the media, students will choose to listen to classical music at least half the time. Which of the following is missing from this objective?
    a. important conditions
    b. observable behavior
    c. criterion performance
    d. nothing

II. Write a performance objective for each of the following subskills. They were selected from the previous instructional analyses. Compare your objectives with those included in the feedback section.

Word processing example (Figure 4.9, Subskill 3.1.1)
    Subskill from Instructional Analysis:
1. Name commands used to move cursor one character to the right:
    a. ∧ D
    b. Spacebar
    Matching Performance Objective:

Banking example (Figure 4.7, Subskill 2.2)
    Subskill from Instructional Analysis:
2. Complete information on deposit slip to identify depositor and date.
    Matching Performance Objective:

Map reading example (Figure 4.12, Step 2)
    Subskill from Instructional Analysis:
3. Use index to find name of street/place and locator block (e.g., A1).
    Matching Performance Objective:

Hotel safety example (Figure 4.10, Subskill 1.1)
    Subskill from Instructional Analysis:
4. At check-in, inquires about the hotel's safety precautions, rules, and procedures.
    Matching Performance Objective:

Egg Separation example (Figure 3.10, Subskill 4)
Subskill from Instructional Analysis:
5. Tilt egg so that half the shell traps the yolk while the white escapes.
Matching Performance Objective:

FEEDBACK

I. 1. c
    2. d
    3. a
    4. b
    5. d

II. Compare your performance objectives with the list of matching performance objectives that follows:

1. Given the cursor direction, "one space to the right," name the appropriate command keys: ∧D and Spacebar.

2. Given a sample, generic deposit slip, correctly enter: (a) name and address, (b) checking account number, and (c) date deposit made.

3. Given a city map and a specified street, correctly locate the name of a street in the map index and name the locator block (e.g., A1).

4. A. While checking into a hotel, guest inquires about fire safety precautions (observe behavior).
    B. Given a scenario about being a hotel guest desiring to maintain personal safety, learners indicate they should inquire about fire safety procedures while checking into the hotel (report of intended behavior).

5. Given an egg that has been cracked and split apart, tilt egg so that half the shell traps all of the yolk while the white escapes.

References and Recommended Readings

Briggs, L. J., & Wager, W. W. (1981). *Handbook of procedures for the design of instruction.* (2nd ed.) Englewood Cliffs, NJ: Educational Technology Publications. The authors provide an extensive number of examples of objectives from Gagné's five domains of learning.

Gagné, R. M., Briggs, L. J., & Wager, W. W. (1988). *Principles of instructional design.* (3rd ed.). New York: Holt, Rinehart, and Winston. The authors describe a five-component behavioral objective, and relate objectives to the various domains of learning.

Kibler, R. J., Cegala, D. J., Barker, L. L., & Miles, D. T. (1974). *Objectives for instruction and evaluation.* Boston, MA: Allyn and Bacon, 29–64. Kibler et al. propose a five-component model for behavioral objectives. Attention is given to common difficulties which arise when writing objectives.

Mager, R. F. (1975). *Preparing instructional objectives.* Palo Alto, CA: Fearon Publishers. This is the original text of Mager's 1962 book on objectives. Mager's humor is well served by the branching programmed-instruction format.

Mager, R. F. (1988). *Making instruction work.* Belmont, CA: David S. Lake Publishers. Current description of Mager's position on objectives.

Roberts, W. K. (1982). Preparing instructional objectives: usefulness revisited. *Educational Technology,* 22 (7), 15–19. The varied approaches to writing objectives are presented and evaluated in this article.

7

DEVELOPING CRITERION-REFERENCED TEST ITEMS

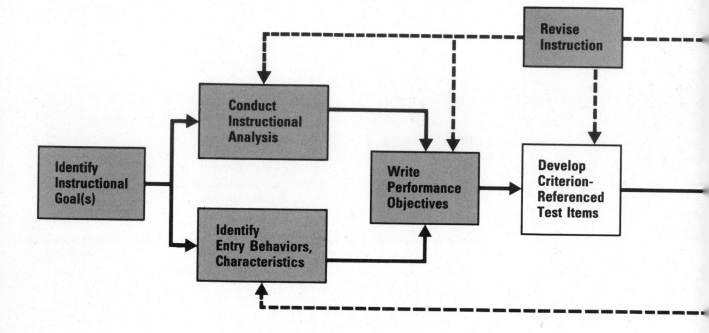

OBJECTIVES

- Identify the characteristics of a criterion-referenced test.
- Describe the characteristics of pretests, embedded tests, and posttests.
- Given a variety of objectives, write appropriate criterion-referenced test items that reflect the behaviors required of learners as stated in the objectives.

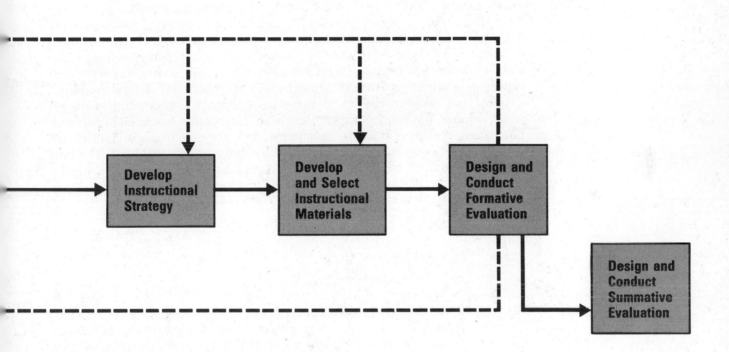

BACKGROUND

We have been testing the general and specific abilities of people for many years. General ability tests such as the Stanford-Binet as well as tests designed for specific courses are widely used. You are perhaps most familiar with instructor-made tests that are used to obtain data to assign grades to students. Quite often these tests are written after instruction has been provided, and are made more or less difficult depending upon the ability of the learners in the class or the perception of the instructor of how well certain topics were taught. The format of this type of test is sometimes determined by the interests and ability of the instructor rather than by the nature of the content that has been taught.

There are also full-time professional test writers. They usually build tests by sampling from a domain of content to select those items for a test that will result in a wide range of student scores. In order to develop this type of test, writers must discard items that are answered either correctly or incorrectly by nearly all students. Although this process tends to increase the reliability of the test, its effect on the validity of the test may be questioned.

In recent years, classroom testing has taken a very different turn. Much of this change can be attributed to the impact of behavioral objectives. As more and more emphasis has been placed on statements of explicit behaviors that students must demonstrate, it has been increasingly obvious that a fair and equitable evaluation system is one that measures those specific behaviors. After students have been told what they have to do to be successful on a learning unit, they should be tested accordingly.

Tests designed to measure an explicit set of objectives are called *criterion-referenced tests*. This type of testing is important to (1) test and evaluate students' progress, and (2) to provide information about the effectiveness of the instruction. The results of criterion-referenced tests indicate to the instructor exactly how well students were able to achieve each instructional objective, and they indicate to the designer exactly what components of the instruction worked well, and which need revision. Thus, criterion-referenced testing is a critical feature of almost every instructional design model.

You may wonder why test development appears at this point in the instructional design process rather than after instruction has been developed. The major reason is that the test items that are constructed should correspond one-to-one with the objectives that have been developed. The performance required in the objective must match the performance required in the test item. Likewise, the nature of the test items given to students serves as a key to the development of the instructional strategy.

CONCEPTS

The major concept in this chapter is criterion-referenced testing. A criterion-referenced test is composed of items that directly measure the behaviors described in a given set of behavioral objectives. The term *criterion* is used because test items serve as a benchmark to determine the adequacy of a student's performance in meeting the objectives; that is, success on these items determines whether a student has achieved the objectives in the instructional unit. However, more and more often the term *objective-referenced* is being used rather than *criterion-referenced*. The purpose is to be more explicit in indicating the relationship between test items and behavioral objectives. Test items are referenced directly to the performance described in the objectives for the instructional materials. Therefore, you may consider these two terms essentially synonymous.

There are at least two ways the term *criterion* is used when referring to criterion-referenced test items. The first refers to the relationship between the performance objective and the test items. If students adequately perform the behavior stated in the objective, then they have reached criterion or mastery on that objective, as mastery on the objective was the criterion for moving ahead.

The second use of the word *criterion* relates to the specification of the adequacy of performance required for mastery. Examples of this second type of criterion include such benchmarks as "the student will answer all the items correctly," "the student will add all punctuation omitted," and "the student will make a cut with 5-degree accuracy." This type of criterion specification may be established for one test item written for one behavioral objective, several test items written for one objective, or several test items written for many objectives. Clarity in specifying objectives and criteria for adequate performance is necessary as a guide to adequate test construction. Based on a particular behavioral objective and established criteria, a posttest may require only one test item or it may require many.

Therefore, in order to determine whether a test item is truly criterion-referenced, the instructor should first determine whether the performance required in a test item or items matches or is parallel to behavior stated in the behavioral objective, and, second, whether criteria have been established to specify how well a student must perform the skill in order to master the objective.

Three Types of Criterion-Referenced Tests and Their Uses

There are basically three types of tests the instructor may use. The first is a pretest. This is a criterion-referenced test designed to measure those skills that have been identified as being critical to beginning instruction and those that the designer intends to teach. Therefore, in considering a hierarchical instructional analysis, a pretest measures all the skills that appear below the line, as well as those that appear above the line.

The second most common test used by the instructor is the posttest. This criterion-referenced test is parallel to the pretest, except it does not include items on entry behaviors. Like the pretest, it measures the objectives taught in the instructional program.

The third type of test is an embedded test. This may consist of a single item that tests a single objective, or may be a test consisting of a large number of items for a number of objectives. These items are included as part of the instructional strategy, and may appear every few pages, or after a major sequence of instruction. They serve two important functions. The first is the testing of learners after instruction on an objective and prior to the posttest. This provides valuable data for the formative evaluation and revision of the instruction. The second purpose is associated with the eventual implementation of the instruction. It may be advantageous for an instructor to have embedded tests to check the progress of students, and to provide an indication of whether remedial activities are needed prior to a more formal posttest.

Let's look at each type of test from the viewpoint of the person who is designing instruction. What purposes do they serve? Eventually tests will probably be used to assign grades to students. But that very real problem is of little concern to the designer at this point. The three types of tests all have important functions within the instructional design process.

PRETEST The pretest may consist of items that measure entry behaviors (prerequisite skills) and items that test skills that will be taught in the instruction. The entry behavior items for the pretest are based upon the objectives for those skills that appear "below the line" on any instructional analysis chart. These are skills, derived directly from the skills to be taught, which students must have to begin instruction. If there are entry behaviors for an instructional unit, test items should be developed and used with students during the formative evaluation. It may be found that, as the theory suggests, students lacking these skills will have great difficulty with the instruction. Or, it may be found that for some reason the entry behaviors aren't critical to success in the instruction. It should be noted that if there are no significant entry behaviors identified during the instructional analysis, there would be no corresponding test items on the pretest.

The pretest also measures those skills that are going to be taught in the instruction. Typically it includes one or more items for each skill identified in the instructional analysis, including the instructional goal.

The function of this part of the pretest is to determine how much prior knowledge learners have of what is to be taught. Do they know none of it, or a great deal? The purpose of testing these skills is not necessarily to show a gain in learning after instruction by comparison with a posttest, but rather to profile the students with regard to the instructional analysis. It may be found, for example, that on the pretest all the students in the formative evaluation are able to answer some of the questions on the lower level skills that will be taught. This suggests that instruction for those topics may be eliminated from the unit.

Do you always administer a pretest over the skills to be taught? Sometimes it is not necessary. If you are teaching a topic that you know is new to your target population, and if their performance on a pretest would only be the result of random guessing, it is probably not advisable to have a pretest. A pretest is valuable only when it is likely that some of the students will have partial knowledge of the content. If time for testing is a problem, it is possible to design an abbreviated pretest that assesses the terminal objective and several key subordinate objectives. The designer must use his or her judgment as to which objectives will be most important to test.

EMBEDDED TESTS An embedded test item is like a practice item with no feedback. This item is only for the benefit of the designer. It is used to answer the question "Did the student know how to do this skill immediately after it was taught"? Embedded items apply almost exclusively to intellectual skills, because the designer should be able to use an item that is new to the student—that is, an unencountered instance of the application of the skill. If embedded items are used with verbal information, they will require the student either to recall the information or refer back to the instruction to answer a question. This is not entirely undesirable, because it may facilitate retention of the information. The problem is that the designer does not know if the student simply looked up the answer and wrote it down, or if the student did, in fact, recall it. Embedded items usually are not used with psychomotor skills, but it may be important in certain types of instruction to have the student stop at one or more points to have the instructor verify that they are following a procedure correctly. This applies particularly to any potentially injurious situations. Embedded items will be discussed in more detail as part of the instructional strategy and formative evaluation.

POSTTEST It can be said with great certainty that the designer will have a posttest (or post-assessment of some sort) for the instruction. The posttest should assess all of the objectives, and especially focus on the terminal objective. Again, as with the pretest, the posttest may be quite long if it measures all the subordinate skills. However, the purpose of the posttest is to help the designer identify the areas of the instruction that are not working. If a student fails to perform the terminal objective, the designer should be able to identify where in the learning process the student began to fail to understand the instruction. By sorting through the items on the subordinate skills on the posttest, the designer should be able to do exactly that.

If time is a factor and a briefer test must be developed, then the terminal objective and important subskills should be tested. Items that test those subskills most likely to give students problems on the terminal objective should be used. On this test, as for all the other tests that have been described, the designer should be able to indicate what skill (or skills) is (are) being tested with any given test item.

All three types of tests are intended for use during the design process. After formative evaluation of the instruction has been completed, it may be desirable to convert the embedded test items to practice-with-feedback items (this is discussed in more detail in the next chapter), to drop part or all of the pretest and modify the posttest only to measure the terminal objective. In essence, much less time would be spent on testing when the instruction becomes operational.

Type of Test	Objectives Usually Tested
Pretest	Entry Behaviors and Selected Instructional Objectives
Embedded	Selected Instructional Objectives
Posttest	All Instructional Objectives

Designing a Test

How does one go about designing and developing a criterion-referenced test? The designer writes one or more test items for each of the behavioral objectives. The important factor is that there are questions on the test that correspond directly to each performance objective.

Objectives in the intellectual skills domain generally require paper-and-pencil items, or items that require a specific product or performance. It is relatively easy to determine achievement of an intellectual skills objective; either students "know" the appropriate response or they do not. At higher levels of intellectual skills, it is more difficult to judge the adequacy of a response. For example, if an objective requires the learner to create a unique solution or product, it is necessary to establish a set of criteria that can be converted to a checklist or rating scale that can be used to assess student products.

Assessment in the attitudinal domain is also difficult. Affective objectives are generally concerned with the learner's attitudes or preferences. Usually there is no direct way to measure students' attitudes (e.g., whether they enjoy baseball); items for attitudinal objectives generally require that either the students state their preferences or that the instructor observes the students' behavior and infers their attitudes. For example, if students voluntarily engaged in baseball games on three different occasions, the instructor may infer that they enjoy baseball. From these stated preferences or observed behaviors, inferences about attitudes can be made.

"Items" for objectives in the psychomotor domain are not the same as those for verbal information or intellectual skills. Typically the student is asked to perform a sequence of steps that collectively represents the instructional goal. Therefore, the "test" often consists of a checklist that the instructor uses to indicate whether each step has been executed properly. The checklist can be developed directly from the skills identified in the instructional analysis. The designer may also wish to test subordinate skills in the procedural analysis. Often these are intellectual skills or verbal information that should be tested using a paper-and-pencil format before having the student perform the psychomotor skill. On occasion the performance of a psychomotor skill results in the creation of a product. It is possible to develop a list of criteria for judging the adequacy of this product.

Determining Mastery Levels

For each behavioral objective you write there must be a criterion level specified, which indicates how well the student must perform the skill described in the objective on the test items you provide. In essence, the criterion indicates the mastery level required of the student. The concept of mastery level, as opposed to criterion level, is more often applied to a test for an entire unit of instruction or an entire course. An instructor may state that, in order for students to "master" this unit, they must achieve a certain level of performance, but the question remains: how do you determine what the mastery level should be?

Researchers who have worked with mastery learning systems have suggested that mastery is equivalent to the level of performance normally expected from the best students. This method of defining mastery is clearly norm-referenced, but it may be the only standard that can reasonably be used.

A second approach to mastery is one that is primarily statistical. If designers want to make sure that students "really know" a skill before they go on to the next instructional unit, then sufficient opportunities should be provided to perform the skill so that it is nearly impossible for correct performance to be the result of chance alone. When multiple-choice test items are used, it is fairly simple to compute the probability that any given number of correct answers to a set of items could be due to chance. With other types of test items it is more difficult to compute the probability of chance performance, but easier to convince others that performance is not just a matter of chance. However, simply *exceeding* the chance level of performance may not be a very demanding mastery level. Setting it higher than chance often is a rather arbitrary decision.

An ideal situation in which to set a mastery level is one in which there is an exact, explicit level of performance that defines mastery. It might be argued that in order for a soldier to learn to send teletype messages, he or she must know how to spell the standard military terms. Therefore, a mastery level of 100 percent on a unit on spelling military terms is not entirely arbitrary. It is based on the criticalness of the skill in question to the learning of subsequent skills. The greater the relationship between the two, the higher the mastery level should be set. As a general principle, mastery level for any performance should be considered with respect to both evaluating the performance at that point in time and enhancing the learning of subsequent, related skills in the unit or in the rest of the course.

Writing Test Items

Regardless of the type of learning involved in the objective, appropriate test-item writing techniques should be applied to the development of criterion-referenced tests. There are several things the instructor should remember while writing criterion-referenced test items. The items should match the behavior and the conditions specified in the objective, and the items should provide students with the opportunity to meet the criteria necessary to demonstrate mastery of an objective.

To match the response required in a test item to the behavior specified in the objective, the instructor should consider the learning task or verb prescribed in the objective. Objectives that ask the student to *state* or *define*, *perform with guidance*, or *perform independently* will all require a different format for questions and responses.

It is critical that test items measure the exact behavior described in the objective. For example, if an objective indicates that a student will be able to match descriptions of certain concepts with certain labels, then the test items must include descriptions of concepts and a set of labels, which the student will be asked to match.

Let's look at an example. Given a scale marked off in tenths and asked to identify designated points on the scale in tenths, label the designated points in decimal form in units of tenths. Corresponding test items for this objective follow:

_____ 1. In tenths of units, what point on the scale is indicated at the letter A?

_____ 2. In tenths of units, what point on the scale is indicated at the letter B?

You can see in this example that the objective requires the student to read exact points on a scale that is divided into units of one tenth. The test item provides the student with such a scale and two letters that lie at specified points on the scale. The student must indicate the value of each point in tenths.

You will encounter more illustrations similar to this in the Examples and Practice sections. It is important to note carefully the behavior described by the verb of the objective. If the verb is *to match, to list, to select,* or *to describe*, then you must provide a test that allows a student to match, list, select, or describe. The objective will determine the nature of the item. You do not arbitrarily decide to use a particular item format such as multiple choice. Format will depend upon the wording of your objectives.

The test item must take into account the conditions under which a skill is to be performed. An open-book examination differs greatly from an examination from which reference material is forbidden. The expected conditions of performance included in the performance objective serve as a guide to the test-item writer. The conditions specify whether the student is to use references or have certain equipment available.

Sometimes the classroom fails to provide the environment or contain the equipment necessary to reproduce exact performance conditions. Instructors must sometimes be creative in their attempts to provide conditions as close to reality as possible. The more realistic the testing conditions are, the more valid the students' responses will be. For example, if the behavior is to be performed in front of an audience, then an audience should be present for the exam.

The behavioral objective also includes the criteria used to judge mastery of a skill. No absolute rule states that performance criteria should or should not be provided to students. Sometimes it is necessary for students to know performance criteria and sometimes it is not. Students usually assume that, in order to receive credit for a question, they must answer it correctly.

A major question that always arises is, "What is the proper number of items needed to determine mastery of an objective?" How many items do students need to answer correctly to be judged successful on a particular objective? If students answer one item correctly, can you assume they have achieved the objective? Or, if they miss a single item, are you sure they have not mastered the concept? Perhaps if you gave the learners ten items per objective and they answered them all correctly or missed them all, you would have more confidence in your assessment. There are some practical suggestions that may help you determine how many test items an objective will require. If the item or test requires a response format that will enable the student to guess the answer correctly, then you may want to include several parallel test items for the same objective. If the likelihood of guessing the correct answer is slim, however, then you may decide that one or two items are sufficient to determine the student's ability to perform the skill.

If you examine this question in terms of the learning domain of the objective, it is easier to be more specific. To assess intellectual skills it is usually necessary to provide three or more opportunities to demonstrate the skill. However, with verbal information, only one item is needed to retrieve the specific information from memory. If the information objective covers a wide range of knowledge (e.g., identify state capitals), then the designer must select a random sample of the instances, and assume that student performance represents the proportion of the verbal information objective that has been mastered. In the case of psychomotor skills, there also is typically only one way to test the skill, namely, to ask the student to perform the skill for the evaluator. The goal may require the student to perform the skill under several different circumstances. These should be represented in repeated performances of the psychomotor skill.

Another important question to consider is, "What type of test item will best assess students' performance?" There are many different test-item formats. Several common ones are true/false, completion, fill-in-the-blank, matching, multiple-choice, and definitions.

The behavior specified in the objective provides clues to the type of item that can be used to test the behavior. In Table 7.1 the column on the far left lists the type of behavior prescribed in the behavioral objective. Across the top are the types of test items that can be used to evaluate student performance for each type of behavior. The table includes only suggestions. The "sense" of the objective should suggest what type of assessment is most appropriate.

As the chart indicates, certain types of behavior can be tested in several different ways. However, some test items can assess specified behavior better than others. For example, if it is important for students to remember a fact, asking them to state that fact is better than requesting reactions to multiple-choice questions. Using the objective as a guide, select the type of

TABLE 7.1

TYPE OF BEHAVIOR AND RELATED ITEM TYPES

Types of Test Items

Type of Behavior Stated in Objective	Essay	Fill-in-the-Blank	Completion	Multiple-Choice	Matching	Product Instructions	Live Performance Instructions
State	X	X	X				
Identify		X	X	X	X		
Discuss	X		X				
Define	X	X	X				
Select				X	X		
Discriminate				X	X		
Solve	X	X	X	X		X	
Develop	X		X			X	
Locate	X	X	X	X	X	X	
Construct	X	X	X			X	X
Generate	X		X			X	X
Operate/Perform							X
Choose (attitude)	X			X			X

test item that gives students the best opportunity to demonstrate the performance specified in the objective. In constructing multiple-choice test items, for example, it is often hard to think of adequate distractor items that are not tricky. Another disadvantage of this type of format is that students can use some cue within the item to guess the correct answer.

There are other factors to consider when selecting the test-item format to use. Each type of test item has its benefits and its weaknesses. To select the best type of item from among those that are adequate, consider such factors as the response time required by students, the scoring time required to grade and analyze answers, the testing environment, and the probability of guessing the correct answer.

The time required for students to complete a test is an important factor. If a behavioral objective requires students to define terms, and limited testing time is available, you may want to construct test items that require students to supply key words in the definition, rather than the type that requires a complete statement of the definition. However, such questions must be written very carefully if they are to be understood by the students.

Certain item formats would be inappropriate even when they speed up the testing process. It would be inappropriate to use a true/false question to determine whether a student knows the correct definition of a term. Given such a choice, the student does not define, but discriminates between the definition presented in the test item and the one learned during instruction. In addition to being an inappropriate response format for the behavior specified in the objective, the true/false question provides students with a fifty-fifty chance of guessing the correct response.

Test items can be altered from the "best possible" response format to one that will save testing time or scoring time, but the alternate type of question used should still provide students with a reasonable opportunity to demonstrate the behavior prescribed in the objective. When the instruction is implemented, it is imperative that teachers be able to use the evaluation procedures. Therefore, the designer might use one type of item during the development of the instruction, and then offer a wider range of item formats when the instruction is ready for wide-scale use. This is often difficult and challenges the designer's creativity.

The testing environment is also an important factor in item format selection. What equipment and facilities are available for the test situation? Can students actually perform a skill given the conditions specified in an objective? If not, can realistic simulations, either paper and pencil or others, be constructed? If simulations are not possible, will such questions as "List the steps you would take to _____" be appropriate or adequate for your situation? The farther removed the behavior in the test item is from the behavior specified in the objective, the less accurate is the prediction that students either can or cannot perform the behavior specified. Sometimes the exact performance as described in the objective is impossible to assess, and thus other, less desirable ways may be used. This will also be an important consideration when the instructional strategy is developed.

The probability of guessing the correct answer is another factor that should be considered when writing test items. Some response methods enable pupils to guess the correct answer more often than others. Multiple-choice questions with three, four, or more responses give students the opportunity to guess the right answer, though the odds of doing so are slim. By giving extra thought to the responses being requested, designers can reduce the likelihood that students will guess correctly. Whenever time permits, construct test items to minimize guessing (e.g., fill-in-the-blank, state the definition, explain the phrase, locate the position, describe the features, construct the object, etc.). Response formats of these types of items increase both assessment time and scoring time, but they provide more reliable estimates of the student's ability to perform tasks specified by objectives.

Once you have decided on the best test-item format, the next step involves the actual writing of "good" test items. You will have to consider such things as vocabulary, the "setting" of the item, the clarity of the item, and the difficulty of items.

The vocabulary used in the directions for completing a question and in the question itself should be appropriate for the intended students. Test items should not be written at the vocabulary level of the instructor unless that level is the same as that expected for the target learners. Students should not miss questions because of unfamiliar terms. If the definition of certain terms is a prerequisite for performing the skill, then such definitions should have been included in the instruction. The omission of necessary terms and definitions is a common error made by many instructors.

The "setting" of the item is another important consideration. Items can be made unnecessarily difficult by placing the desired performance in an unfamiliar setting. When this is done, the instructor is not only testing the desired behavior, but is also testing additional, unrelated behaviors as well. Though this is a common practice, it is an inappropriate item-writing technique. The more unfamiliar the examples, question types, response formats and test-administration procedures, the more difficult successful completion of the test becomes. One example of this "staged" difficulty is creating verbal arithmetic problems using contrived, unfamiliar situations. The setting of the problem, whether at the beach, at the store, or at school, should be familiar to the target group. In another example, students could be required to write a paragraph about an unfamiliar topic when the real object of the test item is to discover whether they can write a paragraph that includes a topic sentence, supporting descriptive sentences, and a summary sentence. Students could demonstrate this skill better using a familiar topic rather than an unfamiliar one. If the item is made unnecessarily difficult, it may hamper accurate assessment of the behavior in question.

The clarity of an item is also important. To help ensure clarity and to minimize examinees' test anxiety, examinees should be given all the necessary information to answer a question before they are asked to respond. Ideally, the examinee should read a question, mentally formulate the answer, and then either supply the answer or select it from a given set of alternatives. A fill-in-the-blank and a multiple-choice item will be used to illustrate this point.

Incorrect Examples	*Improved Examples*
1. A ＿＿＿ is administered to students prior to instruction.	1. The test administered to students prior to instruction is called a ＿＿＿.

2. Pretests are:
  a. administered before instruction
  b. administered during instruction
  c. administered following instruction
	2. When are pretests administered?
	  a. before instruction
	  b. during instruction
	  c. following instruction

In the incorrect fill-in-the-blank example, the only information provided prior to encountering the blank is the letter A; thus, the blank is premature. Considering the complete statement, it does not indicate that the term sought is a type of test. In the improved example, all information required to respond is presented before the learner encounters the blank, and information is added indicating that the name of a type of test is sought. In the incorrect multiple-choice example, the stem, "Pretests are," is not a complete thought. In the improved example, all information required to formulate the answer is included in the stem. In constructing your test items, regardless of format, always ensure that all stimuli or cues that should be provided are contained in the item. Although omitting important information may increase the complexity of the item, it also decreases the quality of the test.

Items written to "trick" students often result in the testing of behaviors other than the one specified in the objective. Instructors would be well advised to spend their time constructing good simulation items rather than inventing tricky questions. If the object is to determine how well students can perform a skill, then a series of questions ranging from very easy to extremely difficult would provide a better indication of students' performance levels than one or two tricky questions (e.g., double negatives, misleading information, compound questions, incomplete information, etc.). If instructors wish to challenge or evaluate advanced students, they should construct test items at a higher level of difficulty.

Sequencing Items

There are no hard and fast rules that guide the order of item placement on a test of intellectual skills or verbal information, but there are suggestions that can guide placement. Final decisions are usually based on the specific testing situation and the performance to be tested.

The traditional method of sequencing items on a test is to cluster items based on item format. Using this strategy, completion items are placed together, multiple-choice items are together, essay items are clustered together, and so forth. Within each group of questions, the content can vary across the content included in the objectives. This method results in an attractive test that appears well organized and requires a minimum amount of directions. In spite of its attractiveness, this formatting strategy has a major flaw for designers who must analyze students' mastery of the objectives measured. After scoring each item and before determining students' mastery of the objectives, the data must be rearranged by objectives for the analysis. This is a very time-consuming and unnecessary step. Individuals who advocate a format-alike sequencing strategy either have their items rearranged and scored by machine or they do not separately analyze performance on objectives within the test.

A superior sequencing strategy for designers, who need to hand-score constructed responses and to analyze responses within objectives, would be to cluster items for one objective together, regardless of item format. The only type of item that would be an exception to this strategy is the lengthy essay question. Such questions typically are located at the end of a test to aid learners in managing their time during the test. A test organized in this fashion is not as attractive as one organized by item format, but it is far more functional for both the learner and the instructor. It enables the learner to concentrate on one area of information and skill at a time, and it enables the instructor to analyze individual and group performance by objective without first resequencing the data.

WRITING DIRECTIONS Tests should include clear, concise directions. Beginning a test usually causes anxiety among students who will be judged according to their performance on the test. There should be no doubt in their minds about what they are to do to perform correctly on the test. There are usually introductory directions to an entire test and subsection directions when the item format changes.

The nature of test directions changes according to the testing situation, but the following kinds of information are usually found in test directions: a test title that suggests the content to be covered rather than simply pretest or "Test I"; a brief statement of the objectives or performance to be demonstrated; the amount of credit that will be given for a partially correct answer; whether students should guess if they are unsure of the answer; whether words must be spelled correctly to receive full credit; whether students should use their names or simply identify themselves as members of a group; whether there is a time limit, a word limit, or a space limit for responses; and whether they need anything special to respond to the test such as number 2 pencils, machine-scored answer sheets, a special text, or special equipment such as calculators or maps.

It is difficult to write clear and concise test directions. What is clear to you may be confusing to others. Write and review directions carefully to ensure that students have all the information they need to respond correctly to the test.

Evaluating Tests and Test Items

Test directions and test items for objective tests should undergo formative evaluation tryout before they are actually used to assess student performance. A test item may seem perfectly clear to the person who wrote it but thoroughly confusing to the individual required to respond to it. Many things can go wrong with a test. The instructor should ensure that (1) test directions are clear, simple, and easy to follow; (2) each test item is clear and conveys to students the intended information or stimulus; (3) conditions under which responses are made are realistic; (4) the response methods are clear to students; and (5) appropriate space, time, and equipment are available for students to respond appropriately.

After writing a test, the instructor should administer it to a student or individual (not one from the actual target group) who will read and explain aloud what is meant by both the directions and questions, and respond to each question in the intended response format. In constructing a test, the instructor can unknowingly make errors, and this preliminary evaluation of the test can prevent many anxious moments for students, wasted time for students and teachers, or even invalid test results. Incorrectly numbered items will result in scrambled answers on response sheets. The same applies to unclear directions, confusing examples or questions, and vocabulary which is too advanced for the students being tested. A preliminary evaluation of the test with at least one person, and preferably several persons, will help pinpoint weaknesses in the test or individual test items that can be corrected prior to exam time.

Even after an exam is actually given, the instructor should assess the results for item clarity. Test items that are missed by most of the students should be analyzed. Instead of measuring the performance of the students, such questions might point to some inadequacy in the test items, the directions for completing the items, or the instruction. Items that are suspect should be analyzed and possibly revised before the test is administered again.

A practical testing problem exists for instructors who must test several different groups of students on the same objectives at the same time or within a short time span of a day or week. To guarantee the integrity of students' answers, instructors may need to construct several different versions of a posttest. Thus, in addition to the pretest and the embedded test items, as many as five or six versions of a posttest may be required.

In this situation, the instructor may want to construct several different test items, or a pool of items, for each performance objective. When this is done, the instructor will need to ensure that all items constructed for one objective are parallel and at about the same level of difficulty. By setting a question in an unfamiliar situation or using more difficult terminology, the difficulty of items can be increased. This can cause the item to assess behavior other than that intended. When many different items are used, the instructor should confirm that items are parallel in assessing performance and at the same level of difficulty.

When constructing test items—and tests in general—the instructor should keep in mind that tests measure the adequacy of (1) the test itself, (2) the response form, (3) the instructional materials, (4) the instructional environment and situation, and (5) the achievement of students.

All the suggestions included in this discussion should be helpful in the development of criterion-referenced tests. If you are an inexperienced test writer, you may wish to consult additional references on test construction. Several references on testing techniques are included at the end of this chapter.

Developing Instruments to Measure
Performances, Products, and Behaviors (Attitudes)

Developing instruments used to measure psychomotor skills, products, or behaviors does not involve writing test items per se. Instead, it requires writing directions to guide the learners' activities or behaviors and constructing an instrument to guide your evaluation of the performances, products, or behaviors.

WRITING DIRECTIONS Directions to learners for performances and products should clearly describe what is to be done and how. Any special conditions such as resources or time limits should be described. In writing your directions, you also need to consider the amount of guidance that should be provided. One one hand, it may be desirable to remind learners to perform certain steps and to inform them of the criteria that will be used in evaluating their work. In such instances (e.g., developing a research paper or making an oral report), examinees can be given a copy of the evaluation checklist or rating scale that will be used to judge their work as a part of the directions. In other circumstances (e.g., answering an essay question or changing a tire), providing such guidance would defeat the purpose of the test. Factors you can use in determining the appropriate amount of guidance are the nature of the skill tested, including its complexity, the sophistication level of the target students, and the natural situations to which learners are to transfer the skills.

Instructions to examinees related to the measurement of attitudes differ from those given for measuring performances and products. For accurate evaluation of attitudes, it is important for examinees to feel free to "choose" to behave according to their attitudes. Examinees who are aware that they are being observed by a supervisor or instructor may not exhibit behaviors that reflect their true attitudes.

Covertly observing employees, however, can be problematic in many work settings. Agreements are often made between employees and employers about who can be evaluated, who can conduct the evaluation, what can be evaluated, whether the employee is informed in advance, and how the data can be used. Even with these understandable limitations, it is sometimes possible through planning and prior agreements to create a situation where reasonable assessment of attitudes can occur.

DEVELOPING THE INSTRUMENT In addition to writing instructions for learners, you will need to develop an instrument to guide your evaluation of performances, products, or behaviors. The steps in developing the instrument are:

1. to identify the elements to be evaluated,
2. to paraphrase each one,
3. to sequence the elements on the instrument,
4. to select the type of judgment to be made by the rater, and
5. to determine how the instrument will be scored.

THE ELEMENTS Similar to test items, the elements to be judged are taken directly from the behaviors included in the behavioral objectives. You should ensure that the elements selected can actually be observed during the performance or in the product.

Each element should be paraphrased for inclusion on the instrument. The time available for observing and rating, especially for an active performance, is limited, and lengthy descriptions such as those included in the objectives will hamper the process. Often only one or two words are necessary to communicate the step or facet of a product or performance to the rater. In paraphrasing, it is also important to word each item such that a "yes" response from the rater reflects a positive outcome and a "no" response reflects a negative outcome. Consider the following examples for an oral speech:

Incorrect	*Yes*	*No*	*Correct*	*Yes*	*No*
1. Maintains eye contact	___	___	1. Maintains eye contact	___	___
2. Pauses with "and, uh"	___	___	2. Avoids "and, uh" pauses	___	___
3. Loses thought, idea	___	___	3. Maintains thought, idea	___	___

In the incorrect example the paraphrased list of behaviors mixes positive and negative outcomes that would be very difficult to score. In the correctly paraphrased list, items are phrased such that a "yes" response is a positive judgment and a "no" response is a negative one. This consistency will enable you to sum the "yes" ratings to obtain an overall score that indicates the quality of the performance or product.

After elements are paraphrased, they should be sequenced on the instrument. The order in which they are included should be congruent with the natural order by events, if there is one. For example, an essay or paragraph evaluation checklist would include features related to the introduction first, to the supporting ideas second, and to the conclusions last. The chronological steps required to change a tire should guide the order of steps on the checklist. The most efficient order for tellers' behaviors would undoubtedly be greeting the customer, conducting the business, and concluding the transaction.

When no natural order of events or components can be identified, other sequencing strategies must be used. Examples might include the importance of the action or component or the frequency with which a particular behavior might occur. If no logical order for listing features is obvious, you should examine sample products or observe several performances to determine the most efficient sequence for the events or components. You may find that the only logical sequence is alphabetical order. The order chosen should enable the rater to locate each element quickly during the evaluation.

DEVELOP THE RESPONSE FORMAT The fourth activity in developing an instrument to measure performances, products, or behaviors is to determine how the rater will make and record the judgments. There are at least three evaluator response formats including a checklist (e.g., yes or no); a rating scale that requires levels of quality differentiation (e.g., poor, adequate, and good); a frequency count of the occurrence of each element considered; or some combination of these formats. The best rater response mode depends on several factors including the nature and complexity of the elements observed; the time available for observing, making the judgment, and recording the judgment; the accuracy or consistency with which the rater can make the judgments, and the quality of feedback provided for the examinee.

THE CHECKLIST The most basic of the three judgment formats is the checklist. If you choose the checklist, you can easily complete your instrument by including two columns beside each of the paraphrased, sequenced elements to be observed. One column is for checking "yes" to indicate that each element was present. The other is for checking "no" to indicate either the absence or inadequacy of an element. Benefits of the checklist include the number of different elements that can be observed in a given amount of time, the speed with which it can be completed by the evaluator, the consistency or reliability with which judgments can be made, and the ease with which an overall performance score can be obtained. One limitation of the checklist is the absence of information provided to examinees about why a "no" judgment was assigned.

THE RATING SCALE A checklist can be converted to a rating scale by expanding the number of quality level judgments for each element where quality differentiation is possible. Instead of using two columns for rating an element, at least three are used. These three columns can include either not present (0), present (1), and good (2); or poor (1), adequate (2), and good (3). Including either a (0) or a (1) as the lowest rating depends on whether the element judged can be completely missing from a product or a performance. For example, some level of eye contact will be present in an oral report; thus, the lowest rating should be a 1. A paragraph, however, may have no concluding sentence at all; thus a score of 0 would be most appropriate in this instance. The particular ratings selected depend on the nature of the element to be judged.

Similar to checklists, rating scales have both positive and negative features. On the positive side, they enable analytical evaluation of the subcomponents of a performance or product, and they provide better feedback to the examinee about the quality of a performance than can be provided through a checklist. On the negative side, they require more time to use, because finer distinctions must be made about the quality of each element evaluated. They also can yield less reliable scores than checklists, especially when more quality levels are included than can be differentiated in the time available or than can be consistently rated. Imagine a rating scale that contains 10 different quality levels on each element scale. What precisely are the differences between a rating of 3 and 4 or a rating of 6 and 7? Too much latitude in making the evaluations will lead to inconsistencies both within and across evaluators.

Two developmental strategies can help ensure more reliable ratings. The first is to provide a clear verbal description of each quality level. Instead of simply using number categories and general terms such as (1) inadequate,

(2) adequate, and (3) good, you should use more exact verbal descriptors that represent specific criteria for each quality level. Consider the following example related to topic sentences in a paragraph.

	General			
	Missing	*Poor*	*Adequate*	*Good*
1. Topic sentence . . .	0	1	2	3

	Improved			
	Missing	*Too broad/ specific*	*Correct specificity*	*Correct specificity & interest value*
1. Topic sentence . . .	0	1	2	3

Both response scales have four decision levels. The example on the top contains verbal descriptors for each rating, but the question of what constitutes a poor, adequate, and good topic sentence remains unclear. In the response format on the bottom, the criterion for selecting each quality is more clearly defined. The more specific you can be in naming the criterion that corresponds to each quality level, the more reliable you can be in quantifying the quality of the element judged.

The second developmental strategy you can use is to limit the number of quality levels included in each scale. There is no rule stating that all elements judged should have the same number of quality levels, say a 4 or 5 point scale. The number of levels included should be determined by the complexity of the element judged and the time available for judging it. Consider the following two elements from a paragraph example.

	Yes (1)	*No (0)*					
1. Indented	____	____	1. Indented	0	1	2	3
2. Topic sentence	____	____	2. Topic sentence	0	1	2	3

In the checklist on the left, the elements could each reliably be judged using this list. Considering the rating scales on the right, you can see an immediate problem. Indenting a paragraph and writing a topic sentence differ drastically in skill complexity. Imagine trying to differentiate consistently four different levels of how well a paragraph is indented! Yet, as indicated in the preceding example, four different levels of the quality of a topic sentence would be reasonable.

A good rule for determining the size of the scale for each element is to ensure that each number or level included corresponds to a specific criterion for making the judgment. When you exhaust the criteria, you have all the levels that you can consistently judge.

THE FREQUENCY COUNT The third response format the evaluator can use in rating products, performances, and behaviors is the frequency count. A frequency count is needed when an element to be observed, whether positive or negative, can be repeated several times by the examinee during the performance or in the product. For example, in a product such as a written report, the same type of outstanding feature or error can occur several times. During a performance such as a tennis match, the service is repeated many times, sometimes effectively and sometimes not. In rating behaviors such as those exhibited by bank tellers, the teller can be observed during transactions with many different customers and on different days. The instances of positive and negative behaviors exhibited by the teller should be tallied across customers and days.

A frequency count instrument can be created by simply providing adequate space beside each element in order to tally the number of instances that occur. Similar to the checklist, the most difficult part of constructing a frequency count instrument is in identifying and sequencing the elements to be observed.

THE SCORING PROCEDURE The final activity in creating an instrument to measure products, performances, and behaviors is to determine how the instrument will be scored. Just as with a paper-and-pencil test, you will undoubtedly need objective-level scores as well as overall performance scores. The checklist is the easiest of the three instrument formats to score. "Yes" responses for all elements related to one objective can be summed to obtain an objective-level score, and "yes" responses can be summed across the total instrument to obtain an overall rating for the examinee on the goal.

Objective-level scores can be obtained from a rating scale by adding together the numbers assigned for each element rated within an objective. A score indicating the examinee's overall performance on the goals can be obtained by summing the individual ratings across all elements included in the instrument.

Unlike objective tests, checklists, and rating scales, determining an appropriate scoring procedure for a frequency count instrument can be challenging. The best procedure to use must be determined on a situation-specific basis, and it depends on the nature of the skills or attitudes measured and on the setting. For example, when rating the interactive performance of classroom teachers or sales personnel, some instances of the behaviors you want to observe will occur during the evaluation, whereas others will not. In such cases you must consider whether a lack of occurrence is a negative or neutral outcome. In another situation such as tennis, you will have many opportunities to observe an element such as the service and to readily count the number of strategically placed first serves, foot faults, or let serves. It is quite easy to tally the total number of serves made by a player and to calculate the proportion of overall serves that were strategically placed first serves, foot faults, let services, and so forth. Yet, once these calculations are made, you must still decide how to combine this information to create a score on the instructional goal related to serving.

Regardless of how you decide to score a frequency count instrument, it is important that you consider during the developmental process how it will be done and compare the consequences of scoring it one way versus an alternative way. The manner in which you need to score an instrument may require modifications to the list of elements you wish to observe; therefore, scoring procedures should be planned prior to beginning to rate learner performances. When no feasible scoring procedure can be found for a frequency count instrument, you might reconsider using either a checklist, a rating scale, or a combination format instead.

EVALUATE THE INSTRUMENT Test directions and instruments to evaluate performances, products, and behaviors should also be formatively evaluated before they are actually used to evaluate examinees' work. Just as with paper-and-pencil tests, you must ensure that the directions are clear to the learner and that learners can follow the instructions to produce the anticipated performance or product.

You must also evaluate the utility of the evaluation instrument. Particular criteria to use in evaluating the elements included in the instrument are: (1) the observability of each of the elements to be judged, (2) the clarity of the manner in which they are paraphrased, and (3) the efficiency of the sequencing order. Related to the evaluator's responding format, you should check whether the response categories and criteria are reasonable in terms of the number and type of judgments you need to make and the time available for you to observe, judge, and mark the judgment. If you are unable to "keep-up" with the performer, the accuracy of your judgments will be affected.

The reliability of the judgments made should be evaluated. This can be done by rating the same performance or product two or more times with an intervening time interval. It can also be checked by having two or more evaluators use the instrument to judge the same performance or product. When the multiple ratings obtained from a single evaluator on a single product differ or the ratings of multiple evaluators differ for a single product, the instrument should be revised. Instrument areas to reconsider are the number of elements to be judged, the number of levels of judgments to be made, and the clarity of the criteria for each level. The number of elements to be observed and the number of judgment categories should be reduced to a point where consistency is obtained. This implies that several iterations of instrument evaluation are necessary to verify the utility of the instrument and the consistency of judgments made using it.

Finally, you should evaluate your scoring strategy. Using the data you gather during the formative evaluation of the instrument, combine or summarize element-level scores as planned. Review these combined scores in terms of objective-level and overall performance. Are the scores logical and interpretable? Can they be used to evaluate particular parts of the instruction and performance? If not, modify the rating and/or scoring procedure until usable data are obtained.

Criterion-Referenced Tests and Norm-Referenced Tests

The major difference between criterion-referenced tests and norm-referenced tests lies in how student performance on the test is interpreted. In criterion-referenced tests, the performance of all students in the group is compared to the number of subordinate skills or objectives passed. For example, if answering 80 percent of the items correctly is established as the criterion for passing, then each student's performance is reviewed in light of the *criterion*, 80 percent. It is possible for all students in the group to exceed the criterion; it is also possible that no student will surpass the criterion specified.

Norm-referenced interpretation, on the other hand, compares the performance of students with each other. The student's rank or position in the group is the reference point for determining the quality of performance rather than a specified proportion of the objectives passed.

Student test performance can be described in both a criterion-referenced and norm-referenced manner. The criterion-referenced comparison would be that a student answered 85 percent of the items correctly while the norm-referenced description would be that this performance, 85 percent correct, equalled or surpassed 90 percent of the members of the class. One method compares student performance against the content of the test whereas the other compares student performance with that of other students in the group.

Tests that are developed using *only* the instructional analysis to select relevant items to include on the test can be interpreted using either a norm-referenced or criterion-referenced focus. However, when items are selected for inclusion on a test by using *prior* information about the statistical properties of the items, then the basic structure of the test as it relates to an underlying instructional analysis or discipline framework may have been compromised. Selecting items to include on a test based upon difficulty and discrimination factors, even though these items originally were taken from a justifiable instructional analysis or domain specification framework, changes the nature of the test and renders it uninterpretable as a criterion-referenced test to accurately reflect student performance on subordinate skills in a carefully constructed analysis.

The practice of selecting items based not only on the domain, but also on item statistical properties designed to automatically create variability (maximize the range of scores on the item and thereby the test) in student performance on the test is a strategy commonly applied in constructing many standardized tests. Even though many standardized test companies report criterion-referenced, or mastery level, scores for their tests, the designer and teacher should keep in mind that this score is an approximation of the instructor's true content and skill domain and not necessarily a reflection of students' knowledge and skill on the whole instructional analysis. Therefore, the justifiability of interpreting standardized test scores as criterion-referenced scores even though they are reported as such by test companies may be questioned.

To determine whether a standardized test is a true criterion-referenced test or an abstraction, you need only to read the administrator's manual to obtain information about whether item difficulty and discrimination factors were used as criteria for selecting items for the test and about the set of objectives that was used to write the items.

Today in education, criterion-referenced tests are designed to assess student performance on specified objectives. It is becoming common practice to use these same criterion-referenced tests not only to assess the progress of individuals, but also to compare the relative performance of students on a set of behavioral objectives. There are many reasons for doing this. Sometimes the comparative results are used to determine which students work faster, to determine which go beyond minimum criteria or standards, to identify the placement of the group on any of the skills in a continuum, or to select outstanding, average, or poor learners for special programs.

Although criterion-referenced tests are now being used for normative comparisons within or among groups, and although the performance of a group at any one time may resemble a normal curve on a set of objectives, the method in which the items for a criterion-referenced test are constructed and selected differs from that used to construct what is traditionally called a norm-referenced test.

EXAMPLES

Test items should be consistent with the behavioral objectives they have been written to measure. The performance required in the test item should match the performance indicated in the objective. The example items in this section are based on the verbal information objectives in Table 6.1, the intellectual skill objectives in Table 6.2, the psychomotor skills in Table 6.3, and the attitudinal objectives in Table 6.5.

Test Items for Verbal Information

Two or more test items are included in Table 7.2 for each of the objectives in Table 6.1. Notice how the condition and behavior parts of the objectives

TABLE 7.2

PARALLEL TEST ITEMS FOR THE VERBAL INFORMATION OBJECTIVES IN TABLE 6.1

Performance Objectives	Parallel Test Items
5.1 Given the term *subject*, define the term. The definition must include that the subject names a topic.	1. Define the *subject* part of a sentence. 2. What does the *subject* part of a sentence do? 3. The *subject* part of a sentence names the _____.
5.2 Given the term *predicate*, define the term. The definition must include that the predicate says something about the subject or topic.	1. Define the *predicate* part of a sentence. 2. What does the *predicate* part of a sentence do? 3. The *predicate* part of a sentence tells something about the _____.
5.4 Given the term *complete sentence*, define the concept. The definition must name both the subject and the predicate.	1. Define a *complete sentence*. 2. What elements does a *complete sentence* contain? 3. A complete sentence contains both a(n) _____ and a(n) _____.
5.6 Given the terms *declarative sentence* and *purpose*, state the purpose of a declarative sentence. The purpose should include to convey/tell information.	1. What *purpose* does a *declarative sentence* serve? 2. The *purpose* for a *declarative sentence* is to _____.
5.8 Given the terms *declarative sentence* and *closing punctuation*, name the period as the closing punctuation. The term *period* must be spelled correctly.	1. The closing punctuation used with a declarative sentence is called a _____. 2. Declarative sentences are closed using what punctuation mark?

are used to guide the construction of the items. Key stimuli or cues prescribed in the conditions appear in each statement or question. The behaviors prescribed in the objective match the behaviors required in the items. Since the objectives clearly prescribe the features of these items, any items you would construct for these same objectives would be similar to the ones we have developed. Notice that only short answer, completion, or fill-in-the-blank items are used. Based on the conditions and behaviors prescribed, alternative response items such as multiple-choice and matching items are not the most appropriate, although they would be relatively easy to construct.

Test Items for Intellectual Skills

Table 7.3 contains test items that are parallel to the intellectual skills objectives contained in Table 6.2. In analyzing these item examples, check to see whether students are: (1) given the materials that are specified in the conditions part of the objective and (2) required to respond in the manner specified or implied by the verb in the objective. Check also to see whether ample items are included to measure the skill. Several test items are needed for some objectives, whereas only one or two items are needed for others.

Consider objective 5.5.2 and the matching test items in Table 7.3. The objective states that students are to be given both complete and incomplete declarative sentences. For the incomplete sentences, some are to be missing subjects, and others are to be missing predicates. Six items are provided to measure this objective: two items, one and three, are complete; four items are incomplete. Items two and five contain only subjects, whereas items four and six contain only predicates. More items could be included to measure this objective, but six items appears to be the minimum practical number that should be presented.

Notice that for most of the examples, the directions are separate from the items. To help ensure that directions are clear, the intellectual skill to be performed is stated first. This statement is followed by instructions about how to respond to demonstrate the skill. Look at the directions for answering items related to objectives 5.3 through 5.7 and 5.10. The first bit of information provided specifies the actual intellectual skill. All the remaining information provides direction on how to mark the items to demonstrate the skill. Although this appears to be an obvious distinction, test directions that focus first on responding methods and later (if at all) on the skill measured can be very confusing to the learners.

A Checklist for Evaluating Motor Skills

In measuring the performance of motor skills, you will need instructions for the performance and an instrument that you can use to record your evaluations of the performance. The examples provided are based on the automobile tire changing instructional goal in Figure 5.5 and the matching performance objectives included in Table 6.3.

The directions for the examinee are contained in Table 7.4. The directions differ slightly from the terminal objective in Table 6.3. For the examination, the car will not have the specified flat tire. Instead, the learner is to replace any tire designated by the examiner. Imagine the logistical problems of having to evaluate 15 or 20 students on these skills and having to begin each test with a flat tire on the car. Other information included in the instructions also is based on the practicality of administering the test. Notice

TABLE 7.3

PARALLEL TEST ITEMS FOR THE INTELLECTUAL SKILLS OBJECTIVES IN TABLE 6.2

Performance Objectives	Parallel Test Items
5.3 Given several complete, simple declarative sentences, locate all the subjects and predicates.	Directions: Locate the *subjects* and the *predicates* in the following sentences. Draw *one* line under the *subject* and *two* lines under the predicate in each sentence. 1. The carnival was a roaring success. 2. The soccer team was victorious this season. 3. Susan got an after-school job weeding flower beds. 4. George's father was pleased with his report card.
5.5.1 Given several complete and incomplete declarative sentences, locate all those that are complete.	Directions: Locate complete sentences. Place an X in the space before each complete sentence. _____ 1. John closely followed the directions. _____ 2. The team that was most excited. _____ 3. The dogsled jolted and bumped over the frozen land. _____ 4. Found the lost friends happy to see her. _____ 5. The plants in the garden.
5.5.2 Given several complete and incomplete declarative sentences, locate all those missing subjects and all those missing predicates.	Directions: Locate missing subjects and predicates. Place a P before all of the items that are *missing a predicate*. Place an S before all items that are *missing a subject*. _____ 1. John closely followed the directions. _____ 2. The team that was most excited. _____ 3. The dogsled jolted and bumped over the frozen land. _____ 4. Found the lost friends happy to see her. _____ 5. The plants in the garden. _____ 6. Played on the beach all day.
5.7 Given several complete simple sentences that include declarative, interrogative and exclamatory sentences that are correctly or incorrectly closed using a period, locate all those that are declarative.	Directions: Locate declarative sentences. Place the letter D in the space before the sentences that are *declarative*. _____ 1. Place the stamp in the upper right corner of the envelope. _____ 2. Are you hungry. _____ 3. Sarah selected a mystery book. _____ 4. The woods looked quiet and peaceful. _____ 5. Wow, look at that fire. _____ 6. Some birds do not migrate. _____ 7. Which of the birds migrate.
5.9 Given illustrations of a period, comma, exclamation point, and a question mark, the terms *declarative sentence* and *closing punctuation*, select the period.	Circle the closing punctuation used to end a declarative sentence. _____ 1. , _____ 2. ! _____ 3. . _____ 4. ?
5.10 Given several simple declarative sentences with correct and incorrect punctuation, select all the declarative sentences with correct closing punctuation.	Directions: Locate correct punctuation for a declarative sentence. Place the letter D in the space before all the *declarative sentences* that *end* with the *correct punctuation* mark. _____ 1. John likes to read space stories? _____ 2. I ride two miles to school on the bus.

TABLE 7.3 *continued*

Performance Objectives	Parallel Test Items
	_____ 3. I got an A on the spelling test!
	_____ 4. Juanita is traveling with her parents.
5.11 Write declarative sentences on: (1) selected topics and (2) topics of student choice. Sentences must be complete and closed with a period.	1. Directions: Write five declarative sentences that describe today's assembly.
	2. Directions: Write five declarative sentences on topics of your own choice.

that the student is required to return and secure all tools, equipment, and parts to their proper place. While helping to ensure that the examinee knows how to perform these tasks, it also ensures that the equipment and car are ready for the next examinee.

Information is also provided for the examinee about how the performance will be judged. These instructions tell examinees that in order to receive credit, they must: (1) recall each step, (2) perform it using the appropriate tool, (3) use each tool properly, and (4) always be safety conscious in performing each step. Given this information, they will understand that failure to comply with any one of these four criteria will mean a loss of credit for that step. They are also told that they can be stopped at any point during the test. Knowing that this can happen, why it can happen, and the consequences of it happening will lessen their anxiety if they are stopped during the exam.

A partial checklist that can be used to evaluate performance is included in Table 7.5. Only main step two, lifts car, is illustrated. Notice that the main headings within step 2 are numbered consistently with the steps in the procedural analysis (Figure 5.5) and the behavioral objectives in Table 6.3. The criteria listed in each objective in Table 6.3 are paraphrased and assigned letters (e.g., a, b, c, etc.) for the checklist.

Related to the evaluator's response format, two columns are provided. An alternative format that was considered was to put four criteria columns beside each step as illustrated:

	Done?	Tool?	Proper: Use?	Safety?
a. Attaches jack handle securely	X	X	X	X
b. Pumps handle to lift jack	X	?	?	?
c. Releases and lowers jack	X	?	?	X

An X in any column would indicate that the criterion was met. It quickly became obvious that all of the criteria named were not appropriate for each of the steps. This formatting strategy also resulted in a very cumbersome instrument. For these reasons, the checklist format was chosen. This means, however, that the evaluator must recall the appropriate set of criteria and holistically judge each step. The feasibility of doing this accurately would need to be checked during a formative trial of the instrument.

TABLE 7.4

DIRECTIONS FOR A PSYCHOMOTOR SKILL TEST (CHANGING A TIRE)

Using the equipment provided in the trunk of the car, remove from the car any one of the tires designated by the instructor. Replace that tire with the spare tire secured in the trunk. The test will be complete when you have: (1) returned the car to a safe-driving condition, (2) secured all tools in their proper place in the trunk, (3) secured the removed tire in the spare tire compartment in the trunk, and (4) replaced any lids or coverings on the wheel or in the trunk that were disturbed during the test.

Your performance on each step will be judged using three basic criteria. The first is that you remember to perform each step. The second is that you execute each one using the *appropriate* tools in the *proper* manner. The third is that you perform each step with safety in mind. For safety reasons, the examiner may stop you at any point in the exam and request that you: (1) perform a step that you have forgotten, (2) change the manner in which you are using a tool or ask that you change to another tool, or (3) repeat a step that was not performed safely. If this occurs, you will not receive credit for that step. However, you will receive credit for correctly executed steps performed after that point.

TABLE 7.5

PARTIAL CHECKLIST FOR EVALUATING A PSYCHOMOTOR SKILL (CHANGING A TIRE)

Name _Karen Haeuser_ _____ Date __6-12__ ____ Score _____
                                                        (   )

_____ 1. Obtains Spare and Tools
     (   )

_____//_____ 2. Lifts Car   Yes   No
     (13)

	2.1 Checks jack operation		
	a. Attaches jack handle securely	X	
	b. Pumps handle to lift jack	X	
	c. Releases and lowers jack	X	
	2.2 Positions jack		
	a. Checks car location, stability	X	
	b. Relocates car if needed	X	
	c. Locates spot on frame to attach jack	X	
	d. Positions jack in appropriate spot	X	
	2.3 Attaches jack to car		
	a. Raises jack to meet frame	X	
	b. Evaluates contact between jack/car		X
	c. Adjusts jack location, if needed		X
	2.4 Places blocks beside wheels		
	a. Locates appropriate blocks	X	
	b. Places block before wheels	X	
	c. Places blocks behind wheels	X	

_____ 3. Removes Tire
     (   )

_____ 4. Replaces Tire
     (   )

          Etc.

The next step in developing the instrument was to determine how students' scores would be summarized. It was decided to obtain both main step scores (e.g., lifts car) as well as a total score for the test. To facilitate this scoring plan, blanks are placed to the left of each main step. The total number of points possible in step 2 are recorded in parentheses beneath the space. The number of points earned by each student can be determined by counting the number of X's in the "Yes" column. This value can be recorded in the blank beside main step 2. In the example, you can see that the examinee earned 11 of the possible 13 points. Summing the points recorded for each main step in the left-hand column will yield a total score for the test. This score can be recorded at the top of the form beside the name. The total possible points for the test can be recorded in the parentheses beneath the total earned score.

One final observation should be made. The evaluator needs to determine how to score items 2.2.b and 2.3.c when no adjustment to the car or jack is needed. One strategy would be to place an X in the column for each of these steps even when they are not needed. Simply leaving them blank or checking the "No" column would indicate that the student committed an error, which is not the case.

An Instrument for Evaluating Behaviors Related to Attitudes

For rating behaviors from which attitudes can be inferred, you will need either a checklist, rating scale, or frequency count. The example is based on the courteous teller illustrations in Chapter 2 and Table 6.5. Because a teller should be evaluated using several example transactions with a customer, a frequency count response format will undoubtedly work best. A sample instrument is contained in Table 7.6.

Notice that at the top of the instrument there is space for identifying the teller and the date or dates of the observations. There is also space for tallying the number of transactions observed. This information will be needed later to interpret the data. There is also space to record the total number of positive and negative behaviors exhibited by the teller during the observations.

The particular behaviors sought are paraphrased in the far left column. Similar to the checklist, there are two response columns for the evaluator. The only difference is that space is provided in this example for tallying many behaviors during several different transactions.

In determining how to score the instrument the number of behaviors perceived as positive (186) were tallied, and the number perceived as negative (19) were also tallied.

Reviewing the summary of this simulated data, it appears that the teller behaved in a courteous manner toward customers in the vast majority of the instances. This information can be interpreted in two ways, depending on the teller's knowledge of the observations. If the teller was unaware of the observations and chose to behave in this manner, then the evaluator could infer that the teller indeed displayed a positive attitude in providing courteous, friendly service. Conversely, if the teller was aware of the examination, then the evaluator could infer that the teller knew how to behave courteously during transactions with customers and chose to do so while under observation.

SUMMARY

In order to develop criterion-referenced tests, you will need the list of behavioral objectives, which are based on the instructional analysis. The conditions, behavior, and criteria contained in each objective will help you determine the best format for the test or for the items.

TABLE 7.6

A FREQUENCY COUNT INSTRUMENT FOR EVALUATING BEHAVIORS FROM WHICH ATTITUDES WILL BE INFERRED (COURTEOUS SERVICE)

Name _Robert Jones_   Date(s) _4-10,17,24_

Total Transactions Observed ~~HHT~~ ~~HHT~~ ~~HHT~~ Total + _186_   Total − _19_

A. Customer Approaches and Teller:

	Yes	No
1. Smiles	HHT HHT	HHT
2. Initiates verbal greeting	HHT HHT HHT	
3. Personalizes comments	HHT HHT HHT	
4. Excuses self when delayed	IIII	II
5. Inquires about services	HHT HHT IIII	I
6. Attends to all in line	HHT HHT	III
7. Other:		

B. During Transaction, Teller:

1. Listens attentively	HHT HHT HHT	
2. Requests clarifying information	HHT IIII	
3. Provides forms required	HHT IIII	
4. Completes/amends forms	HHT IIII	
5. Explains changes made	HHT IIII	
6. Explains materials returned	HHT HHT II	III
7. Other:		

C. Concluding Work, Teller:

1. Inquires about other services	HHT HHT HHT	
2. Says, "Thank you"	HHT HHT HHT	
3. Responds to customer comments	HHT HHT	HHT
4. Makes concluding wish	HHT HHT HHT	
5. Other:		

An objective test format will be best for many of the verbal information and intellectual skill objectives. However, you still must decide what objective item format would be most congruent with the prescribed conditions and behaviors. Objective items should be written to minimize the possibility of correctly guessing the answer, and they should be clearly written so that all stimuli or cues prescribed in the objective are present in the item or instructions. You must also decide how many items you will need to measure performance adequately on each objective. In determining the number of items to produce, you need to consider how many times the information or skill will be tested. Enough items to support the construction of pretests, embedded tests, and posttests should be produced. Whenever possible, students should be presented with a different item each time an objective is measured.

Some intellectual skills cannot be measured using objective test items. Examples include writing a paragraph, making a persuasive speech, and analyzing and contrasting certain features. Intellectual skills that result in a product or a performance, psychomotor skills, and behaviors related to attitudes should be measured using tests that consist of instructions for the learner and an observation instrument for the evaluator. In creating these instruments you must identify, paraphrase, and sequence the observable elements of the product, performance, or behavior. You will also need to select a reasonable judgment format for the evaluator and determine how the instrument will be scored.

It is important to evaluate and refine your objective test items, directions to learners, and instruments for judging products, performances, or behaviors before they are actually used to evaluate the progress of learners or the quality of instructional materials. Test items and evaluation instruments seem to be governed by Murphy's Law: If anything can go wrong, it will. The most important criterion for judging the quality of an item or instrument is its congruence with the conditions, behaviors, and criteria prescribed in the objective. This judgment relates to the content validity of the item. Does the item measure what it is supposed to measure? The second most important criterion is the appropriateness of the language, context, conditions, and criteria used for the ability level of the target students. Another important criterion is the feasibility of administering the test in the given environment and the time available. If you do not have items or instruments that yield valid, reliable test scores, you cannot use them to judge students' mastery of the objectives or instructional quality.

Of course, the quality of your items and instruments depends on the quality of your objectives, which in turn depends on the quality of your instructional analysis and goal statement. Following the Practice and Feedback sections of this chapter is a Design Evaluation section. After reviewing the items you have developed for your objectives, you should stop forward progress in the design process and evaluate your overall design to this point.

Following this overall design evaluation, you can proceed to the next chapter on instructional strategies. During this phase of the design process, you will determine what tests to include in your instructional package and how they will be used. In the subsequent chapter on developing instructional materials, you will use your sample objective items and test plan to construct the objective tests you will need. If you have developed rating instruments instead of objective items, you will plan how and when to use these instruments related to the instructional strategy and materials.

═══ PRACTICE ═══

I. Judge whether each of the following statements about criterion-referenced tests is correct. If it is, place a C in the space before the item. If it is incorrect, state briefly why it is incorrect. Check your answers in section I of the Feedback.

_____ 1. A criterion-referenced test is composed of items that measure behavior.

_____ 2. A criterion-referenced test is the same as an objective-referenced test.

_____ 3. Test items in criterion-referenced tests need not measure the exact type of behavior described in a behavioral objective.

_____ 4. Test items for criterion-referenced tests are developed directly from subtasks identified in the instructional analysis.

_____ 5. Embedded tests are used mainly to give students practice and feedback on their performance during instruction.

_____ 6. It is always a good idea to construct entry behavior test items for the pretest.

_____ 7. Entry behavior test items are developed to measure skills students should possess before beginning instruction.

_____ 8. Pretests are used prior to instruction to indicate students' prior knowledge about what is to be taught as well as their knowledge of prerequisite entry skills.

_____ 9. Some pretest items are developed from behaviorally stated objectives in the entry behavior section of an instructional analysis.

_____ 10. Criterion-referenced test items are written directly from behavioral objectives, which in turn are written directly from the subskills in an instructional analysis.

II. Using the instructional analysis diagram that follows, indicate by box number(s) the behavioral objectives that should be used to develop test items for:

1. Pretest: Entry Behaviors: _____ Instructional Objectives: _____
2. Embedded test _____
3. Posttest _____

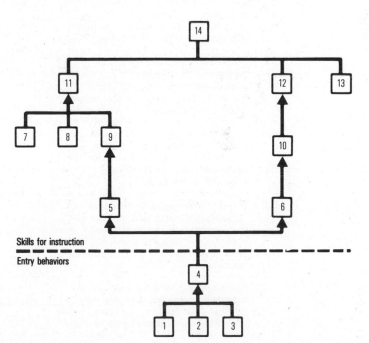

III. Write objective test items for verbal information and intellectual skills performance objectives. Table 7.7 includes behavioral objectives based upon the imperative sentences strand of the instructional analysis for the story-writing goal (Figure 4.5). For each performance objective, write corresponding test items that could be used to measure the objectives on either a pretest or posttest. Compare the items you develop with those provided in Table 7.8 of the Feedback section. Your items will differ from the ones we have provided; ours simply demonstrate a few of an infinite number of items that could be developed.

IV. Develop a test that includes instructions for the learner and evaluation forms for the psychomotor skill of putting a golf ball. The following behavioral objectives are based on the instructional analysis in Figure 4.6. The test should have two parts, including putting form and putting accuracy. Compare the instructions you design with the ones included in

TABLE 7.7

VERBAL INFORMATION AND INTELLECTUAL SKILL OBJECTIVES FOR WRITING PARALLEL TEST ITEMS

Performance Objective	Test Items
5.18 Given an incomplete statement calling for the three purposes of an imperative sentence, state all three purposes. Answers must include to request, command, and instruct.	
5.19 Given simple declarative, exclamatory, and imperative sentences, identify all those that are imperative.	
5.20 Given the imperative sentence purposes, ''to request'' or ''to instruct,'' name the period as the appropriate closing punctuation.	
5.21 Given the imperative sentence purposes, ''to command'' or ''to provide strong emphasis,'' name the exclamation mark as the appropriate closing punctuation.	
5.22 Given imperative sentences that request, instruct, and command and that have no ending punctuation, supply the appropriate closing punctuation for each.	
5.23 Given imperative sentences that request, command, and instruct and that correctly or incorrectly end with a period or exclamation point, identify the sentences that have correct ending punctuation.	
5.24 Given prescriptions for whether an imperative sentence is to request, command, or instruct, write imperative sentences using correct ending punctuation.	

section IV of the Feedback. Compare the evaluation form you design with the one contained in Table 7.9 of the Feedback.

Objectives: On a putting green and using a regulation ball and putter:

5.1 Demonstrate good form while putting the golf ball. The body must be relaxed and aligned with the target, and the club must be comfortably gripped at the correct height. The stroke must be the appropriate height, speed, and direction for the target and smoothly executed. The clubface should be square throughout the stroke.

6.1 Putt uphill, downhill, and across hill on a sloped putting green; from distances of 10, 15, and 25 feet; putt accurately enough for the balls to reach a distance of no less than 3 feet from the cup.

FEEDBACK

I. 1. C
    2. C
    3. They must measure the behavior in the objective.
    4. They are derived from objectives.
    5. They are used by designers for formative evaluation.
    6. There may be no entry behaviors that require testing.
    7. C
    8. C
    9. C
    10. C

II. Generally speaking, behavioral objectives that should have test items included on:

   1. pretests are: entry behaviors 1 through 4, instructional objectives 5 through 14
   2. embedded tests: 5 through 14
   3. posttests: 5 through 14

III. Table 7.8 includes the performance objectives and sample test items for the indicated verbal information and intellectual skills objectives in the story-writing goal (Figure 4.5).

IV. Instructions to students for the putting exam.

The putting exam will consist of two parts: putting form and putting accuracy. You will be required to execute 27 putts for the exam. Your putting form will be judged throughout the test using the top part of the attached rating sheet. The aspects of your form that will be rated are listed in columns A and B. Your score depends on the number of OK's circled in the column labeled (1). You can receive a total score of 10 on putting form if you do not consistently commit any of the mistakes named in the errors column. In the example, the student received a total score of 7. The errors consistently committed were all related to the swing: low backswing and follow-through and slow swing speed.

Your putting accuracy will also be judged on the 27 putts. Nine of the putts will be uphill, nine will be downhill, and nine will be across the hill to the cup. From each area, three putts will be from 10 feet, three from 15 feet, and three from 25 feet.

TABLE 7.8

SAMPLE OBJECTIVE TEST FOR VERBAL INFORMATION AND INTELLECTUAL SKILLS

Performance Objective	Test Items
5.18 Given an incomplete statement calling for the three purposes of an imperative sentence, state all three purposes. Answers must include to request, command, and instruct.	The three purposes of an imperative sentence are to _____, to _____, and to _____.
5.19 Given simple declarative, exclamatory, and imperative sentences, identify all those that are imperative.	Directions: Locate imperative sentences. Place the letter I in the space before all sentences that are imperative. _____ 1. Place the small box into the large box. _____ 2. Use a mild soap to wash your face. _____ 3. It was sunny all day. _____ 4. Go to the end of the line! _____ 5. I am so happy! _____ 6. Please take this book to your brother. _____ 7. This is your brother's favorite book.
5.20 Given the imperative sentence purposes, ''to request'' or ''to instruct,'' name the period as the appropriate closing punctuation.	1. The punctuation mark used to close an imperative sentence that makes *a polite request* is called a(an) _____. 2. The punctuation mark used to close an imperative sentence that *instructs the reader* is called a(an) _____.
5.21 Given the imperative sentence purposes, ''to command'' or ''to provide strong emphasis,'' name the exclamation mark as the appropriate closing punctuation.	1. The punctuation mark used to close an imperative sentence that is a *strong command* is called a(an) _____. 2. The punctuation mark used to close an imperative sentence that needs to *convey strong emphasis* is called a(an) _____.
5.22 Given imperative sentences that request, instruct, and command and that have no ending punctuation, supply the appropriate closing punctuation for each.	Directions: Supply the closing punctuation for each of the following sentences. 1. Come here right now 2. Please close the door 3. You need to make the kite tail a little longer 4. Count the number present 5. Stop, you're hurting me 6. Bring me a fork please
5.23 Given imperative sentences that request, command, and instruct and that correctly or incorrectly end with a period or exclamation point, identify the sentences that have correct ending punctuation.	Directions: Judge whether these imperative sentences have the correct closing punctuation. Place an X before each sentence that ends correctly. _____ 1. Please sit beside me! _____ 2. The last step is to tie the knot. _____ 3. Come over here immediately! _____ 4. Stop or I will shoot. _____ 5. Stir the soup until the lumps are gone! _____ 6. Say please when you want someone to do something for you.
5.24 Given prescriptions for whether an imperative sentence is to request, command, or instruct, write imperative sentences using correct ending punctuation.	1. Write three imperative sentences that make polite *requests*. 2. Write three imperative sentences that make *strong commands*. 3. Write three imperative sentences that *provide instructions* for doing something.

Your accuracy score will depend on the proximity of each putt to the cup. Three rings will be painted on the green at 1-foot intervals from the cup to make a target area. The following points will be awarded for each area:

In cup = 4 points   Within 2' = 2 points   Outside 3' = 0

Within 1' = 3 points   Within 3' = 1 point

Balls that land on a ring will be assigned the higher point value. For example, if a ball lands on the one foot ring, you will receive three points.

Each of your 27 putts will be tallied on the form at the bottom of the sheet. The example is completed to show you how it will be done. Putting uphill from 10 feet, the student putted two balls in the cup and another within the one foot ring. Thus, eleven points (4+4+3) were earned for putting uphill from 10 feet. Look at the 15' × across hill section. One putt was within a foot, one was within three feet, and one was outside three feet for a total of four points (3+1+0). In summing the student's scores, all putts from each distance and from each area are added. For example, the student has a 10' score of 27 and an uphill score of 25. The student's overall score is 56.

TABLE 7.9

CHECKLIST AND TALLY FOR EVALUATING PUTTING FORM AND ACCURACY

Name _Mary Jones_   Date _3/26_

A	B	(1)	Type of Errors		
1. Body	Comfort	(OK)	TNS		
	Aligned	(OK)	RT	LFT	
2. Grip	Pressure	(OK)	TNS		
	Height	(OK)	HI	LOW	
3. Backswing	Height	OK	HI	(LOW)	
	Direction	(OK)	RT	LFT	
4. Follow-through	Height	OK	HI	(LOW)	
	Direction	(OK)	RT	LFT	
5. Speed		OK	FST	(SLW)	JKY
6. Club face		(OK)	OPN	CLS	
	Total	7			
		(10)			

Putting Accuracy Score

Area:	Uphill					Downhill					Across Hill					Totals
Points:	4	3	2	1	0	4	3	2	1	0	4	3	2	1	0	Totals
10'	//	/				/	/	/			/		/	/		27
15'		//	/				/	/	/			/		/	/	18
25'	/		/		/			/	/	/			/		//	11
Totals	25					18					13					56

Total

The following score levels will be used to evaluate your overall putting performance on the test:

Acceptable = 27$^+$ (27×1)   Excellent = 54$^+$ (27×2)
Good = 41$^+$ (27×1.5)   Perfect! = 108 (27×4)

Before reporting for your test, be sure to warm up by putting for at least 15 minutes or 30 putts. Remain on the practice greens until you are called for the exam.

DESIGN EVALUATION

It is important at this point in the process of designing instruction to evaluate the design you have created. The material you have at this stage makes up the framework for the development of your materials. By determining whether flaws exist, many hours of less-than-satisfying developmental work may be saved.

Exactly what is to be evaluated? The materials that should be evaluated are (1) the goal statement, (2) the complete instructional analysis including the goal analysis and the subordinate skills analysis, (3) the performance objectives, (4) the criterion-referenced test items, and (5) the description of the target population.

Who should evaluate your design? There are several options here, and the nature of your materials and time you have available for the evaluation will be major factors in selecting the evaluators. Some persons you might want to consider are content experts, colleagues, and target students.

CONTENT EXPERTS Consult people who are considered content experts or instructional designers who can validate (1) the need for such instruction, (2) the importance of the behaviors stated in the instructional goal, (3) the accurateness of subskills that were identified in the instructional analysis, (4) the accurateness of the sequencing of subskills in the instructional analysis, (5) parallelism between subskills in the instructional analysis and behavioral objectives, (6) the clarity of performance desired and criteria established for the behavioral objectives, (7) the parallelism between behavioral objectives and test items, and (8) the equality of multiple test items constructed to measure performance on the same objective.

COLLEAGUES Peers could be asked to evaluate whether: (1) there is a need for the instruction, (2) it is an area in which their students often experience learning difficulties, (3) such instruction would be feasible in their classroom (equipment, space, etc.), (4) any subskills have been omitted from the instructional analysis, and (5) there is any deviation from the required parallelism among the instructional goal, instructional analysis, behavioral objectives, and test items.

TARGET STUDENTS Target students could react to whether (1) they would find learning the material interesting, (2) they perceive a need for the behavior identified in the instructional goal, and (3) they experience any difficulty understanding vocabulary and required procedures when explained. Given time, the designer may also choose to administer a sample pretest to provide an early sign of whether the appropriate target students have been selected. If they can already perform most of the skills, or if they lack the entry behaviors, they may be the wrong group.

How can you best organize and present your materials so that you can evaluate them? One criterion is that each component builds upon the product from the previous one and, therefore, the materials should be presented in a way that enables comparison among the various components of your design. The designer should, at a glance, be able to see whether the components are parallel and adequate. One way to achieve this is to organize the materials such that related components are together. Consider the structure in Table 7.10. Each segment of the table contains all three elements. The last line should contain the instructional goal, the terminal objective, and the test item(s) for the terminal objective. The evaluator(s) can, at a glance, determine if test items have been included that will enable students to demonstrate whether they have mastered the objective.

Table 7.11 contains an example of the type of material that would be included in each section of Table 7.10. Note that there is only one test item for the first subskill and behavioral objective. That item would appear on any test given—whether it be pretest, posttest, or embedded test—because there is basically only one way to ask the question. However, objective number 2 provides the opportunity for many questions and answers. Also, there is no criterion level specified in objective 1 since the formula cannot be considered correct if it is written incorrectly.

Check the performance required in all three components in Table 7.11 to ensure each is parallel. In addition, check the criteria stated in the objective to determine whether the number of test items or the nature of a test enables students to meet the criteria.

The sequence of subskills presentation on your chart is important. If you place them in the order you believe they should be taught, then you will be able to receive additional feedback from your evaluator concerning the logic you have used for sequencing skills and presenting instruction. This additional feedback may save steps in rewriting or reorganizing your materials at a later point. The topic of sequencing skills will be addressed in greater detail in the next chapter.

TABLE 7.10

STRUCTURE OF THE DESIGN EVALUATION CHART

Subskill	Behavioral Objective	Test Item(s)
Subskill 1	Performance Objective 1	Test item Test item Test item
Subskill 2	Performance Objective 2	Test item Test item Test item
Subskill 3	Performance Objective 3	Test item Test item Test item
Instructional Goal	Terminal Objective	Test item Test item Test item

TABLE 7.11

EXAMPLE OF A DESIGN EVALUATION CHART

Subskill	Behavioral Objective	Test Item(s)
1. Write the formula for converting yards to meters	1. From memory, correctly write the formula for converting yards to meters	1. In the space provided below, write the formula used to convert yards to meters.
2. Convert measures in yards to comparable meters	2. Given different lengths in yards, convert the yards to meters, correct to one decimal place.	2. 5 yds = _____ meters 7.5 yds = _____ meters 15 yds = _____ meters 4 yds = _____ meters 65 yds = _____ meters 10 yds = _____ meters 3 yds = _____ meters 8.25 yds = _____ meters 12 yds = _____ meters

One additional way to show content experts and other evaluators the relationship among subskills that you have identified is to provide them with a copy of the instructional analysis chart. All items should be keyed to the number of the subskills in the analysis chart. This diagram can be used with your design evaluation table to present a clearer representation of your content analysis and design.

After you have received feedback concerning the adequacy of your design and made appropriate revisions in your framework, you will have the input required to begin work on the next component of the model, namely developing an instructional strategy. Having a good, carefully analyzed design at this point will facilitate your work on the remaining steps in the process.

References and Recommended Readings

Carey, L. M. (1988). *Measuring and evaluating school learning.* Boston: Allyn and Bacon. Excellent source on deriving and writing test items. Terminology is consistent with this text.

Dick, W. (1986). The function of the pretest in the instructional design process. *Performance and Instruction,* 25 (4), 6–7. Discusses various issues related to the design and use of a pretest as part of the instructional design process.

Gagné, R. M., Briggs, L. J., & Wager, W. W. (1988). *Principles of instructional design* (3rd ed.). New York: Holt, Rinehart and Winston. The chapter on assessing student performance includes not only the development of objective-referenced assignments, but also the concept of "mastery" and norm-referenced measures.

Gronlund, N. E. (1981). *Measurement and evaluation in teaching.* New York: Macmillan. Principles of item and test construction as well as methods for evaluating items are described.

Haladyna, T. M., & Roid, G. H. (1983). Reviewing criterion-referenced test items. *Educational Technology,* 23 (8), 35–39. The authors provide a data-based procedure for reviewing criterion-referenced test items.

Hopkins, C. D., & Antes, R. L. (1978). *Classroom measurement and evaluation.* Itasca, IL: F. E. Peacock. Presents principles of item and test construction as well as methods for item and test analysis.

Kibler, R. J., Cegala, D. J., Barker, L. L., & Miles, D. T. (1974). *Objectives for instruction and evaluation.* Boston: Allyn and Bacon, 114–142. Kibler et al. include a discussion of norm versus criterion-referenced assessment and the use of mastery learning strategies.

Lathrop, R. L. (1983). The number of performance assessments necessary to determine competence. *Journal of Instructional Development*, 6, 3, 26–31. Lathrop presents a statistical methodology for determining which students are "masters" and which are not through the use of sequential testing procedures.

Millman, J. (1974). Criterion-referenced measurement. In **Popham, W. J. (Ed.)** *Evaluation in education: Current application*. Berkeley, CA: McCutchan Publishing, 309–398. The discussion of the criterion-referenced and domain-referenced testing is extensive and includes some of the quantitative, as well as qualitative, issues associated with them.

Payne, D. A. (1974). *The assessment of learning: Cognitive and affective*. Lexington, MA: D. C. Heath. This is an excellent text that relates various types of test items to the varieties of instructional objectives. It emphasizes techniques for writing effective test items.

8

DEVELOPING AN INSTRUCTIONAL STRATEGY

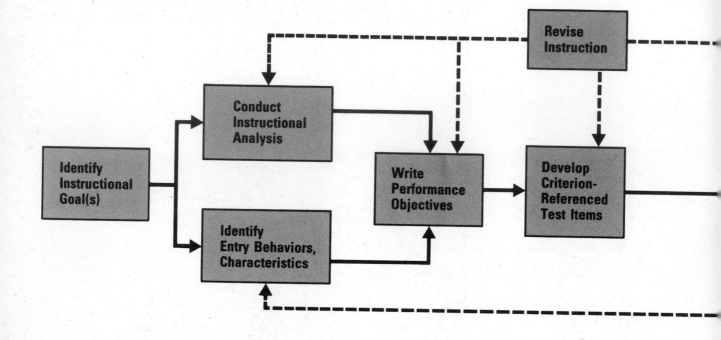

OBJECTIVES

- Identify and describe the major components of an instructional strategy.
- Develop an instructional strategy for a set of objectives for a particular group of learners.

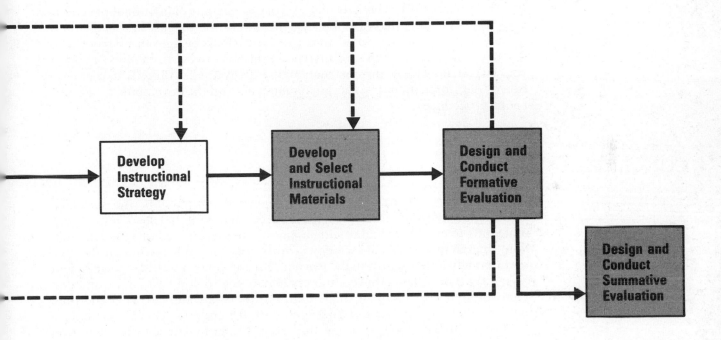

BACKGROUND

If you have a textbook nearby, pick it up and look it over. In what ways is the book structured to facilitate learning by the reader? The typical text, particularly for adults, usually has an introduction, a body of information, references, and an index. Sometimes test items have been prepared and appear at the end of the chapters or in a teacher's manual. In essence a textbook serves primarily as a source of information. The instructional strategy that will be employed to bring learners into a state of full knowledge must be generated by the reader or an instructor. Usually, an instructor must do nearly everything to bring about learning: define the objectives, write the lesson plan and tests, motivate the students, present the information, and administer and score the tests.

A well-designed set of instructional materials contains many of the strategies or procedures that a teacher might normally use with a group of students. Therefore, it is necessary to develop an instructional strategy that employs, to the degree possible, that knowledge we have about facilitating the learning process.

Educational psychologists have conducted much research over the past fifty years to determine appropriate relationships between particular types of stimuli and responses by learners. They have also studied the use of reinforcement, punishment and behavior modification by teachers. If you have read any of this research you may feel that it often seems esoteric and generally removed from real-life learning situations. Psychologists have been successful, however, in identifying several major components in the learning process which, when present, almost always will facilitate learning. These three components are those dealing with motivation, prerequisite and subordinate skills, and pratice and feedback.

This chapter relies heavily on the work of various educational psychologists and especially that of Robert Gagné and Leslie Briggs. In this chapter, procedures will be described that can be used to design an instructional strategy for different types of instructional objectives. In the next chapter you will be shown how this instructional strategy applies directly to the selection or development of instructional materials and the development of classroom procedures.

CONCEPTS

An instructional strategy describes the general components of a set of instructional materials and the procedures that will be used with those materials to elicit particular learning outcomes from students. You should note that an instructional strategy is more than a simple outline of the content that will be presented to the learner. For example, it would be insufficient to say that, in order to have students learn how to add two-digit numbers, you would first teach them single-digit numbers without carrying and then present the main concept of adding two-digit numbers. This is certainly a part of an instructional strategy and refers to the sequence of presentation of information, but this says nothing about what you will do before you present that information, what students will do with that information, or how it will be tested.

There are five major components to an instructional strategy:

1. Preinstructional activities
2. Information presentation
3. Student participation
4. Testing
5. Follow-through

We will look at each of these components in some detail, because the instructional designer must plan an approach to each of these steps.

Preinstructional Activities

Prior to beginning formal instruction, there are three factors that you should consider. These factors include motivating the learners, informing them of what they will learn, and ensuring that they have the prerequisite knowledge to begin the instruction.

MOTIVATION The first factor is the motivation level of the learners who will use your instructional materials. You might assume that students will be assigned this instruction or that you will be dealing with highly motivated adults. If so, you could assume that no effort is required on your part to establish a high motivation level. Or you may wish to use special techniques such as an attractive color scheme, a cartoon, a human-interest story, or some other approach to gain the attention of the learners and "hook" them into your instruction. In order to do this properly, a great deal of knowledge is necessary about what will interest the learners and what will turn them off.

INFORMING THE LEARNER OF THE OBJECTIVES The second component of the preinstructional activities is to inform the learners of the objectives for the instruction. Have you ever studied a text and wondered how much you should be memorizing? If you had been informed of the objectives, you would have known what to memorize, to solve, or to interpret.

By providing learners with the objectives, you help them focus their study strategies on these outcomes. They should not feel they are responsible for "knowing everything," but rather for being able to do certain specific things. Not only does this information help learners to use more efficient study strategies, it also helps them determine the relevance of the instruction.

INFORMING THE LEARNER OF PREREQUISITE SKILLS The third component of the preinstructional activities is informing learners of the prerequisite skills required to begin your instruction, if there are any significant ones. This can be done in either of two ways: (1) provide the students with a brief test of the entry behaviors and inform them that they must demonstrate mastery of these skills to continue, or (2) provide the learners with a brief description of the required entry behaviors and tell them that the instruction will proceed with the assumption that they can perform these skills. The purpose of this activity is to prepare the learners for the instruction that is to follow, to provide information (if the test is used) for the designer on the variability of students' entry behaviors, and to determine if that variability is related to differences in the students' ability to learn from the instruction.

Information Presentation

INSTRUCTIONAL SEQUENCE What sequence should you follow in presenting information to the student? The most useful tool in determining the answer to this question is your instructional analysis. If you have done a hierarchical analysis, then you would begin with the lower-level skills, that is, those just above the line that separates the entry behaviors from the skills to be taught, and then progress up through the hierarchy. At no point would you present information on a particular skill prior to having done so for all related subordinate skills.

The instructional sequence for a task that is a procedure would, of course, logically be sequenced from the left, or the beginning point, and proceed to the right. If there are subordinate capabilities for any of the major steps in the procedure, they would be taught prior to going on to the next major component.

Because the goal analysis indicates each step that must be performed and the subordinate skills analysis indicates the skills that must be acquired prior to learning the major steps in the goal, the instructional sequence tends to be a combination of bottom to top and left to right. That is, the subordinate skills for step 1 are taught first, then step 1. Next the subordinate skills for step 2 are taught, then step 2 itself. This sequence is continued until all the steps are taught. Finally, there is instruction on integrating and practicing all the steps in the instructional goal.

There are two exceptions to this general approach to sequencing. The first occurs when two or more steps in a goal are the same and/or have the same subordinate skills. In this situation, it is not necessary to teach these skills again. The learner can simply be informed that a skill that has been previously learned will be used again at this point in the procedure.

A second exception to the general sequencing approach is when the instruction includes the use of a number of pieces of equipment, or the parts of a single piece of equipment. The instructional analysis may indicate that the student will be required, for example, to be able to identify and locate various pieces of equipment at various points in the instruction. To avoid having to go back and forth to make identifications, it is usually both possible and desirable to present all of this instruction at the beginning of your units. Similarly, it is sometimes desirable to present all the lower level verbal information objectives, such as definitions, at one time at the beginning of the instruction. Use caution when doing this because you may be removing the context required to make the definitions meaningful. It may also make it more difficult for learners to store the information in memory and to retrieve it using contextual cues.

COMBINING OBJECTIVES FOR INSTRUCTION The next question in your instructional strategy deals with the size of the chunk of material you will provide in your instruction. At one extreme of the continuum is the linear programmed-instruction approach, which tends to break all the information down into very small units and requires constant responding by the student. At the other extreme of the continuum is the conventional textbook in which a chapter is usually the unit of information. You may decide that you will present your information on an objective-by-objective basis with intervening activities, or you may wish to present the information on several objectives prior to any kind of student activity.

Five factors that should be taken into consideration when determining the amount of information to be presented (or the size of "chunk") are the age level of your learners, the complexity of the material, the type of learning taking place, and whether the activity can be varied, thereby focusing attention on the task. A fifth factor is the amount of time required to include all the events in the instructional strategy for each chunk of information presented. For example, how much time will be required for informing learners of the prerequisites, presenting material, and providing practice? For younger children it is almost always advisable to keep the instruction, and the chunks within it, relatively small. More mature learners will be able to handle larger chunks of information. Regardless of the age of the learners, when information is varied with performance and feedback activities, the learners do not seem to tire of the activity as quickly.

INFORMATION AND EXAMPLES The next step is to determine exactly what information, concepts, rules, and principles need to be presented to the student. This is the basic explanation of what the unit is all about. The primary error in this step is to present too much information, especially if much of it is unrelated to the objective. It is important not only to define any new concepts, but to explain their interrelationships with other concepts. You will also need to determine the types and number of examples you will provide with each of the concepts. Many research studies have investigated how we learn concepts and how we use examples and nonexamples to accomplish that task. A nonexample is a deliberate attempt by the designer to point out why a particular example is wrong. We know that learning is facilitated by the use of examples and nonexamples, so, generally, they should be included in your instructional strategy. In a later section we will consider, in more detail, what should be included in this part of the strategy, as well as student participation, for objectives in different domains of learning.

Student Participation

One of the most powerful components in the learning process is that of practice with feedback. You can enhance the learning process greatly by providing the student with activities that are directly relevant to the objectives. Students should be provided an opportunity to practice what you want them to be able to do. Not only should they be able to practice, but they should be provided feedback or information about their performance. Feedback is sometimes referred to as "knowledge of results." That is, students are told whether their answer is right or wrong, or are shown a copy of the right answer or an example from which they must infer whether their answer is correct. Feedback may also be provided in the form of reinforcement. Reinforcement for adult learners is typically in terms of statements like "Great, you are correct." Young children often respond favorably to forms of reinforcement such as an approving look from the instructor or even the opportunity to do some other activity.

Testing

CRITERION-REFERENCED Three basic criterion-referenced tests have been described: pretests, embedded tests, and posttests. The general function of each has been described as well as how to develop them. At this point you must decide exactly what your strategy will be for testing. This strategy may differ significantly from that which would eventually be used by an instructor who uses your completed instruction.

Your decisions are:

- Will I test entry behaviors on a pretest? When will it be administered?
- Will I have a pretest over the skills to be taught? When will it be administered? Exactly what skills will it cover?
- Will I have embedded test items? Where in the instruction will they be located? What will they test?
- When and how will I administer the posttest?

ATTITUDE In addition to the formal testing that has been described, the designer may want to consider using embedded attitude questions. These questions serve essentially the same function as the embedded test items in that they indicate what learners thought of the instruction at the time they encountered it. The idea is not to wait until the end of the unit of instruction to ask general questions about, for example, the quality of the illustrations, but to ask questions directly in the instruction about the illustrations that have just been presented. These attitude or opinion questions can be physically located directly after embedded test items and refer to the same section of the instruction.

What types of items are most helpful? Items that are as specific as possible will provide the most information to the designer when the time comes to do the formative evaluation. The questions could refer to such aspects of the instruction as the clarity of a specific example or illustration, the sufficiency of a set of practice problems, the fairness of an embedded test item, or the general interest level of the content.

Sometimes there will be parts of the instruction in which the designer uses a special procedure or approach—either from a content or a pedagogical point of view. At these locations in the instruction, the designer can insert very specific questions about the students' reactions to what has been done. This approach, as reported by Nathenson and Henderson (1980), does not seem to be disruptive to the learners, and seems to provide the kind of on-the-spot specific reaction to the instruction rather than the general reactions that are often received on a questionnaire that is administered at the end of an instructional unit. The end-of-unit questions can help the designer obtain an overall reaction to the instruction, but the embedded attitude questions will provide more precise, targeted information.

Follow-Through Activities

As a part of your instruction, you will want to have materials, or at least recommendations, about what students should do as a result of a particular level of performance on the posttest. Will you have separate remediation materials available for them? If so, what type of strategy will be involved with them? Will you have certain enrichment materials or proposed instructional activities that students who are successful with the instruction might participate in while other students are reaching mastery? These decisions have implications not only for helping with the learning process, but also for the directions necessary to implement your instruction in the classroom.

These follow-through activities are part of the instructional strategy, but typically no detailed plans are made for enrichment or remediation activities until the formative evaluation is nearly completed and there is a clearly identified need for particular activities. All the components of a complete instructional strategy are summarized below in their typical chronological sequence.

A. Preinstructional activities
   1. Motivation
   2. Objectives
   3. Entry behaviors
B. Information presentation
   1. Instructional sequence
   2. Size of instructional unit
   3. Information
   4. Examples
C. Student participation
   1. Practice
   2. Feedback

  D. Testing
   1. Pretest
   2. Embedded tests
   3. Posttest
  E. Follow-through activities
   1. Remediation
   2. Enrichment
Components B3, B4, C1, C2, and D2 are repeated for each instructional chunk.

Instructional Strategies for Various Learning Outcomes

The basic components of an instructional strategy are the same regardless of whether you are designing instruction for an intellectual skill, verbal information, a motor skill, or an attitude. Thus, they can be used as an organizing structure for your design. Within each component, however, there are distinctions you should consider related to each type of learning outcome. These are noted in the sections that follow. Developing strategies to help ensure that material is motivational is omitted from this discussion and addressed separately in a later section.

INTELLECTUAL SKILLS The designer should be aware of both the way in which learners may have organized their entry knowledge in memory and the limits of their ability to remember new information. The strategy should provide ways in which the learner can link new information to existing prerequisite knowledge in memory. When the links may not be obvious to the learner, direct instruction about the links and the relationships between existing knowledge and new skills should be provided. The strategy should provide the learner with ways of organizing new skills so they can be stored along with relevant existing knowledge and thus be recalled more easily. When no prerequisite knowledge is present, mnemonics to recall attributes and steps should be considered.

  In presenting information about intellectual skills, it is important to recall the hierarchical nature of intellectual skills in determining the sequence for presentation. Subordinate skills should always come first. It is also important to point out the distinguishing characteristics of concepts that make up rules. These distinguishing characteristics may include physical characteristics or role and relationship characteristics. It is also important to focus learners' attention on irrelevant characteristics that may be present as well as common errors that learners make in distinguishing among concepts or in applying rules.

  In selecting examples and nonexamples of a concept, the designer should select both clear examples and nonexamples. Direct information about why the examples fit or do not fit the definition may need to be provided. You should also ensure that the examples and illustrations selected are familiar to the learner. Teaching an unknown using an unfamiliar example unnecessarily increases the complexity of the skill for the learner. Thus, you should select instances and examples likely to be contained in the learner's memory. To enhance transfer, you could progress from familiar examples to less familiar ones and to new instances.

  There are several important things to consider when designing practice exercises for intellectual skills. One is the congruence of the practice to the conditions and behaviors prescribed in the objectives and covered in the instruction. This criterion helps separate relevant practice from busy work. Others are ensuring the link between prerequisite knowledge and new skills and progressing from less difficult to more complex problems. Yet another is providing a familiar context within which the skill can be rehearsed. Imagine having to practice analyzing an instructional goal in an unfamiliar skill area or having to write a paragraph on a topic you know nothing about. When you are skilled in performing the instructional goal, you are able to focus on the goal analysis process; when you are familiar with the paragraph topic, you are able to concentrate on the structure of the paragraph and the design of the message. As with designing the presentation strategy, structuring practice exercises using unfamiliar contexts unnecessarily increases the complexity of the skill for the learner.

The nature of feedback to learners is also important. It should be balanced in that it focuses on both the successes and failures in the rehearsal. Focusing only on errors may cause learners to perceive that nothing they did was meritorious, which is seldom the case. When errors are committed, learners should be provided with information about why their response was inadequate. Learners tend to perceive corrective feedback as informative rather than critical, especially when they can use the feedback to improve their performance.

The instructional strategy related to testing learners' performance of intellectual skills involves determining when and how to test the skills. In order to make these decisions, the designer should consider how the test results will be used by both the designer and the learner. Premature testing, or tests administered prior to learners' readiness for them, can be more damaging than beneficial, because they tend to discourage learners and to provide incorrect information about the adequacy of presentations. In designing tests for complex intellectual skills, it is often desirable to test whether students understand concepts and relationships and know the correct steps for performing a procedure prior to asking them to perform the procedure. For example, you might want to test whether students know the characteristics of a good paragraph and the criteria for judging paragraph quality prior to asking them to write paragraphs. Practicing incorrect constructions will not improve students' ability to write. Testing their writing skills prior to their mastery of subordinate skills will yield paragraphs that require a great amount of feedback from the instructor and frustration for the students.

Just as damaging as premature testing is applying inappropriate standards for judging the quality of intellectual skill products and performances. You should carefully consider levels of performance that reflect outstanding work, acceptable work, and unacceptable work for a given target group. Setting these standards is somewhat arbitrary, but they must be based on a realistic conception of what is possible for a particular age group in a given situation.

Follow-through considerations are important for hierarchically related skills, especially when the skills from one instructional unit are subordinate to those in a subsequent one. You must consider whether corrective feedback following the posttest will suffice or whether additional instruction with practice and feedback will be required. You should also use data from the posttest to target additional instruction on specific subordinate skills where it is needed. A shotgun design for follow-through activities will be insufficient for maintaining students' motivation and for time constraints.

VERBAL INFORMATION Designing preinstructional activities is important for verbal information outcomes. In informing learners of the objectives, you should consider ways in which the objectives can be summarized using organizational structures. You should also consider informing learners about how they can use the information besides possibly winning a trivia game several years hence.

In presenting verbal information, the context for storing information and recalling it when needed is extremely important. Strategies that link new information to knowledge currently stored in memory will improve the effectiveness of the instruction. Gagné (1985) referred to this linking process as elaboration. The more detailed the elaboration or linking procedure, the greater likelihood that learners will store new information in a logical place and recall it later. She also suggests elaboration strategies such as providing analogies or asking learners to imagine something or to provide an example from their own experience for facilitating storage and recall of new information. These contextual links form the cues learners will use to recall the information.

Another strategy recommended for presenting verbal information is to present like information in subsets and to provide direct instruction on the relationship among items in the subset and among different subsets. This is referred to as organization. Procedures recommended by Gagné for aiding students in organizing new information is to provide them with an outline or table that summarizes information by related subsets.

When information is entirely new and unrelated to prior learning, then the strategy should include a memory device, or mnemonic, to aid the student in recalling the information. In developing mnemonics, however, those logically related to the material to be recalled are recommended. Cuing letters that form a familiar word and that are logically related to the information to be remembered can work well. Illogical mnemonics, however, can be as difficult to recall as the information they are designed to help retrieve.

What does it mean to "practice" verbal information? Rote repetition of unrelated facts is not effective for recalling information over time. Designing practice activities that strengthen elaborations and cues and that better establish an organizational structure are believed to be better. Practice in generating new examples, in forming images that cue recall, and in refining the organizational structure should also help. Focusing the exercise on meaningful contexts and relevant cues is another consideration for the strategy.

Just as with intellectual skills, feedback about the accuracy of verbal information recalled should be provided. Whenever possible the feedback should include the correct response and information about why a given response is incorrect.

In testing verbal information you will want to be sure to provide appropriate cues for recalling the information. You may also want to sequence verbal information items near related intellectual skills, motor skills, or attitudes to provide a relevant context for recalling the information. As noted previously, such a sequencing strategy for tests would negate placing all items related to definitions and facts in a separate section at the beginning or end of the test.

Follow-through activities for remediating verbal information can be problematic. Although they will involve additional elaboration and organization strategies, they may also require a better motivational strategy. You may need to create something for learners to "do" with the information to hook them into learning it. Your strategy might include such activities as crossword puzzle contests for teams of learners that aid each other in recalling the information. A team approach to recall may provide them with practice in recalling for themselves and in coaching their teammates to recall. Although such an activity may seem like fun to learners, it can enrich elaborations and help ensure that the additional cues provided by teammates are based on their prior knowledge and are meaningful to them.

MOTOR SKILLS The learning of a motor skill usually involves several phases. Initial learning concerns the development of an "executive routine," which consists of the "directions" that the learner is to follow. The mental statement of each step in the routine is followed by the performance of that step. With repeated practice and appropriate feedback, the steps in the routine begin to smooth out, there is less hesitation between each step, and the skill begins to assume its final form. The last phase is often represented by the reduction of the dependency on the executive routine and a more automated execution of the skill.

What are the implications of this description of a typical motor skill for the presentation of information, examples, practice, and feedback? One very apparent implication is the requirement of some form of visual presentation of the skill. Obviously video or films can be used to capture movement, but often photos or drawings can be used, at least at the initial stages of learning a motor skill. The categories of information and examples in a strategy usually take the form of a verbal description of the skill followed by an illustration.

It is important to determine an effective way to group information on a motor skill. It is not unusual to cluster meaningful parts of the skill, which can later be integrated into the complete skill. In our earlier example of learning how to putt a golf ball, we showed that this skill can be broken down into lining up the ball with the cup, the backswing, hitting the ball, and follow-through.

Practice and feedback are the hallmarks of psychomotor skills. Research has shown that learners can benefit from mentally practicing a skill before they physically engage in it. Actual practice of a skill should be repetitious. Immediate feedback on the correctness of the execution of the skill is very important, since incorrect rehearsal will not promote skill improvement.

A special problem that occurs when a motor skill involves the use of a piece of equipment is deciding at what points the learner should interact with the equipment. At one extreme all instruction is received before the learner practices on the actual equipment. Logistically this is the easiest approach, but it puts a great burden on the student to remember all the details of the instruction. The other extreme is to have the learner interact with the equipment at each step in the instruction. While there is less of a memory problem, this approach requires one piece of equipment per learner.

One solution to this instructional problem, which may later become a performance problem, is to provide the learner with a job-aid. A job-aid is a device that the learner can use to reduce the memory requirements while performing a skill. For example, if the learner must enter a coded number into a piece of equipment to make it operate in a particular way, there may be no reason to require the learner to memorize all the possible codes when they could be listed on a plate on the equipment or on a card that the learner could easily review. Job-aids can also include lists of steps to be executed or criteria to be used to evaluate a product or performance. If the designer chooses to incorporate a job-aid into the training, it is obvious that the learner must be taught how to use it.

The ultimate question in testing any motor skill is, "Can the learner execute the skill that has been taught?" The question of transfer of learning, which was raised with regard to intellectual skills, must also be addressed with motor skills. What are the conditions under which this skill must be performed? Any requirements should be present as the skill is practiced in the instructional setting and present for the exam.

ATTITUDES Researchers believe that our attitudes consist of three components: feelings, behaviors, and cognitive understandings. Feelings, in this case, can be described as pleasures or displeasures that are expressed through our tendency to approach or avoid a situation. This tendency is thought to depend upon our success or failure in prior, similar situations or our observation of others in these situations. This is the key to a successful instructional strategy for an attitude. The information and example portion of the strategy should be delivered by someone or by an imaginary character who is respected and admired by the learners. This "human model" should display the behaviors involved in the attitude and indicate why this is an appropriate attitude. If possible, it should be obvious to the learner that the model is being rewarded for displaying this attitude.

The substance of the instruction for an attitude consists of teaching the behavior that is to be demonstrated by the learner, such as personal cleanliness, as well as the supporting information about why this is important. The behaviors should be demonstrated under the conditions described in the behavioral objectives.

You may also need to consider in your strategy whether you are developing an attitude or reshaping one. For existing negative behaviors (and attitudes) such as the learner becoming emotional or angry in a meeting when reactions do not occur as anticipated, you may need to focus instruction on self-awareness and teach alternative ways of behaving in the circumstance. Creating simulations that evoke emotions that lead to damaging behaviors may be required. Guiding the learner to more positive behaviors that they can associate with the same emotions can be difficult. You may wish to consider strategies such as videotaping them as they respond in context and then working with them as they analyze how they felt and reacted. You may want them to hear how others in the situation judged their reactions. You may want them to observe someone they admire react positively in a similar circumstance and, through remaining calm, direct the conclusion of the meeting to the anticipated outcome.

Undoubtedly the strategy you choose for instruction related to an attitude hinges on multiple factors. In addition to attempting to develop or reshape an attitude, several questions should be considered. Are the learners volunteers for the program because they perceive a need for it and wish to change? Are they satisfied with themselves but have been directed or "sentenced" to the program by a supervisor, school administrator, or judge? Are the attitude and behaviors ones the learners care little about, or do they represent strong convictions or sensitive feelings? How free can you be in delivering instruction, creating simulations, and providing feedback? Will group instruction suffice or will individualized instruction be required? The answers to all such questions should be considered in designing an instructional strategy for attitudes.

How can the learner practice an attitude? Making inappropriate or ineffective choices that are followed by ineffective or even positive feedback will not help the learner make better choices. Practice, therefore, must incorporate opportunities to choose followed by consistent feedback (rewards/consequences) to help ensure that a given behavior becomes associated with a given response. The feedback should include information about what the learner did right and what the learner did wrong. Related to inappropriate responses, information about more appropriate responses should be provided.

Since attitudes can be learned vicariously, mental rehearsals may prove beneficial for practicing them. Such rehearsals might include dramatic scenes that present respected models who are faced with alternatives. Following the presentation of alternatives, the learners can observe the model reacting in positive ways and can observe the model receiving rewards considered positive and relevant by the learners. Additionally, other models could be observed reacting in negative ways and receiving negative consequences. These story simulations are especially useful because characters affected by the negative model's attitudes and behaviors can be observed by learners. When respected characters are injured, insulted, or angered by the "bad" model, the learner can associate or empathize with these reactions. This empathy will help the learner rehearse associating the attitude and behavior with the unpleasant consequences. These reactions of the respected characters constitute feedback to the learner. Reactors can be seen discussing the behavior of the negative model, and they can provide informative feedback by describing alternative ways the model should have behaved.

Attitudes might also be practiced vicariously by using discussion groups. A scenario or story can be read by learners or a dramatization can be viewed. Following the presentation, the instructor can ask members of the group to analyze the characters' behaviors related to the observed consequences. They might be asked to generate consequences for observed stories without endings. They might be asked to describe their feelings about circumstances they observed or read. Members of the discussion group can learn vicariously from their peers' reactions to the fictitious characters. Such vicarious practice may be less painful than when learners are actually confronted by unpleasant consequences from their peers for their own behaviors.

As discussed previously, an important consideration when designing tests for attitudes is whether learners will know they are being observed. Other considerations include tests of verbal information related to knowledge of the expected behaviors and the potential rewards and consequences for behaving in certain ways. The testing strategy should also encompass any intellectual or motor skills required for exhibiting the required behaviors. For example, it would be difficult to demonstrate positive attitudes toward safe driving if one could not drive a car, did not know rules of the road, and could not solve safety problems encountered while driving. Although this is an extreme example, it illustrates the point.

You may need to design questionnaires with hypothetical situations and questions for the learners about how they would react in the described circumstance. If this is your strategy, you should be aware that research demonstrates there is little relationship between what we say about our attitudes in a written situation and what we do when confronted with a similar situation in real life. Therefore, to the extent possible, the designer should create hypothetical situations that simulate those in which the attitude would influence the learners' choices and behaviors.

Follow-through activities may also be required for learners who do not succeed following an instructional program for an attitude. Such activities will challenge designers, since they will need to decide whether additional instruction is required, whether rewards need to be more direct and relevant, or whether unpleasant consequences are effective. Finding the right combination for additional instruction and motivation is the problem to be solved through the strategy. The next section describes instructional strategy considerations related to motivating learners, gaining and holding their attention throughout the components of the strategy.

Motivating Learners

One of the major criticisms of instructional materials is their lack of interest and appeal to the learner. Simon and Garfunkel summarized popular sentiment about school learning in the first line of one of their lyrics: "When I think back on all the crap I learned in high school, it's a wonder that I can think at all."

One instructional designer who attempts to deal with this problem in a systematic way is John Keller (1987), who developed the ARCS model based upon his review of the psychological literature on motivation. The four parts of his model are *Attention*, *Relevance*, *Confidence*, and *Satisfaction*. In order to produce instruction that motivates the learner, these four attributes of the instruction must be considered throughout the design of the instructional strategy.

The first aspect of motivation is to gain the attention of learners and subsequently sustain it throughout the instruction. Students must attend to a task in order to learn to perform it. Their initial attention can be gained by using emotional or personal information, asking questions, creating mental challenges, and perhaps the best method of all, using human interest examples.

According to Keller, the second aspect of motivation is relevance. While you may be able to gain learners' attention for a short period of time, it will be difficult to sustain when they do not perceive the subsequent instruction as relevant to them. When instruction is thought irrelevant, learners ask, "Why do we have to study this?," and employees question the relationship between training and their job. If learners understand the relevance of the skills included in instruction, you will have their attention; if not, you undoubtedly will lose them. In other words, instruction must be related to important goals in the learner's life.

The third major component of the ARCS model is confidence. For learners to be highly motivated, they must be confident that they can master the objectives for the instruction. If they lack confidence, they will be less motivated. Learners who are overconfident are also problematic; they see no need to attend to the instruction because they already know it all. The challenge with under- and overconfident learners is to create the appropriate level of expectation for success. Learners who lack confidence must be convinced that they have the skills and knowledge to be successful, whereas the overconfident learner must be convinced that there are important details in the instruction that remain to be learned. However, if students have, in fact, already mastered the instruction, they should be given more advanced instruction that more nearly meets the four aspects of the ARCS model.

The final component of Keller's model is satisfaction. High motivation depends on whether the learner derives satisfaction from the learning experience. Some would refer to this as reinforcement. Sometimes satisfaction is sustained through the use of rewards for successful performance such as free time, a high grade, a promotion in the workplace, or some other form of recognition. Of equal or greater importance is the intrinsic satisfaction a learner can gain by mastering a new skill and being able to use it successfully. Self-esteem can be greatly enhanced through meaningful learning experiences.

When taken alone, any of the four aspects of Keller's model may not be sufficient to keep a learner on task in a learning situation. If you can incorporate all four—attention, relevance, confidence and satisfaction—into your strategy, however, the likelihood of maintaining the learners' interest is greatly increased.

THE INSTRUCTIONAL STRATEGY AND MOTIVATION There is a direct relationship between the five main components of the instructional strategy and the four aspects of motivation included in Keller's ARCS model. This relationship is illustrated in Figure 8.1. Following exposure to each component of the instruction, the learners ask themselves three questions. The first question relates to the relevance of the information presented or activity performed. If the materials are perceived as relevant to personal needs and interests, then attention is gained and maintained. The second relates to how confident they are that they can be successful. If they understand the material and are confident that they will be successful, then attention is sustained. The third question relates to how satisfied they are that the information presented and activities provided meet their needs. If they are satisfied with each component, then attention is maintained.

In designing the instructional strategy, we must devise ways to present each component to help ensure that learners continue to answer the three questions affirmatively. In order to do this, we must understand the target learners' characteristics. We must also understand their needs, interests, and performance levels well enough to infer how *they* will perceive the information and activities. In designing each component of the instructional strategy for the goal, we should ask ourselves, "How does this relate to the learners' needs and interests and to their feelings of confidence and satisfaction?"

FIGURE 8.1

THE RELATIONSHIP BETWEEN EACH MAJOR COMPONENT OF INSTRUCTION AND ARCS

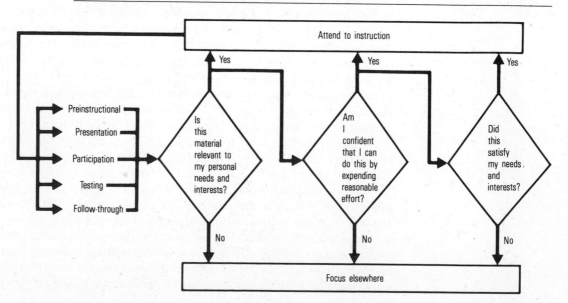

Related to the issue of perceived relevance, the most important criterion appears to be the congruence between the learners' expectations and the materials they encounter. For example, the initial motivating material must be congruent with the learners' perceptions of their needs and interests. What material would best meet learners' initial expectations and hook them into the instruction? Should you judge that the congruence of the material in any component would not be immediately obvious to the learner, you must devise ways to illustrate the congruence so that they will perceive it as relevant. Problems will result if learners fail to see the relationships among their initial expectations, the information presented, the examples described, the practice activities provided, and the test questions administered.

You must also consider how to design each activity to build and sustain the learners' confidence. You will need to present the objectives so that the learners perceive them as achievable instead of overwhelming. A list of 30 or 40 technically worded objectives would be likely to shatter the learners' confidence. A list of three or four global objectives written in the learners' language would tend to build confidence. Learners who are sure that they have previously mastered all prerequisites will be more confident than those who doubt their skill and knowledge.

Related to the volume of material presented initially, are learners more likely to feel comfortable and confident or overwhelmed with the amount of material you have chosen? Considering practice exercises, are learners likely to succeed on those you have provided and thus gain confidence in themselves? Has enough instruction preceded the practice for learners to be successful? You must also consider how students will perceive pretests in deciding whether it is advisable to administer one. Will pretests demonstrate the manageability of skills to be learned or create doubt and insecurity instead?

Learner satisfaction is the third general area of consideration. Will learners be rewarded for learning the skills? Will they consider the proposed rewards as adequate for the amount of effort required? Should you provide additional information to point out potential rewards? On your practice exercises, are they likely to succeed and thus gain intrinsic feelings of satisfaction and accomplishment? Are they likely to perceive the feedback you have designed as verification of their success or as criticism? After they complete your posttest, are they likely to be satisfied with their progress? Will they perceive the effort they had to expend as justified by the reward? Will they believe that the promises you made in the preinstructional materials were realized? Will they feel that they can do something better? If they believed that the rewards would be forthcoming, yet the rewards failed to materialize, your task in motivating them for a subsequent unit undoubtedly will be more difficult.

Developing an Instructional Strategy

It would be inappropriate to go directly from a list of behavioral objectives to developing a set of instructional materials without first planning and writing out your instructional strategy. The instructional strategy is an actual product that can be used (1) as a prescription to develop instructional materials, (2) as a set of criteria to evaluate existing materials, (3) as a set of criteria and a prescription to revise existing materials, or (4) as a framework from which class lecture notes, interactive group exercises, and homework assignments can be planned. Regardless of the availability of existing instructional materials, the instructor should develop an instructional strategy for a set of behavioral objectives before selecting, adapting, or developing instruction.

What is needed to develop an instructional strategy? The instructor should begin with an instructional design that includes: (1) an instructional goal and goal analysis, (2) subskills identified through an instructional analysis, (3) a statement of behavioral objectives, and (4) test items.

Having completed all these steps, you are ready to develop your instructional strategy. At this point you should realize that you have already completed some of the work needed to develop an instructional strategy. You have already (1) identified objectives, (2) identified prerequisite knowledge (through your analysis of the relationship among subskills in the instructional analysis), (3) identified the sequence for presenting instruction (when you completed your design evaluation table and your analysis diagram), (4) identified the content required (when you analyzed the knowledge and skills during the instructional analysis), and (5) identified appropriate test items for each objective. All this information, already included in your design evaluation table, can serve as input for the development of the instructional strategy.

Even though we recommend that instructional events occur in the order presented in the previous section (preinstructional activities, presentation of information, student participation, testing, and follow-through), we do not recommend that you try to develop your instructional strategy in this order. The developmental sequence differs from the suggested order in which students encounter instructional events during a lesson.

Your instructional strategy can best be described in the following way:

1. Indicate the sequence of objectives and how you will cluster them for instruction. To do this, consider both the sequence and the size chunks that are appropriate for the attention span of students and the time available for each session. In designing the sequence, remember to include review or synthesizing activities when needed. The decisions you make about sequence and chunks can be summarized using a form such as that shown in Table 8.3. Later, this prescription will help you assign objectives to lessons.

2. Indicate *what* you will do with regard to preinstructional activities and testing. The relevant issues are listed in Table 8.1. These can be answered in narrative form with reference to each of the side headings in the table. Note that these components of the instructional strategy apply to all of your objectives; that is, they apply to your total lesson. The next section will apply to individual objectives, or clusters of objectives.

3. Indicate the content to be presented and the student participation activities for each objective. To do this, you may wish to use a form similar to the one included in Table 8.2. The objective number from your list of performance objectives could be identified at the top of the form. Your form should include two main sections: information to be presented and student participation. The presentation section should briefly describe the required information and typical examples. In selecting your examples, remember to choose congruent ones that are most likely to be familiar and interesting to the target group. The participation section should illustrate sample practice exercises and the type of feedback that will be provided in the instruction. Table 8.2 will be used as part of in-

TABLE 8.1

**PREINSTRUCTIONAL, TESTING, AND FOLLOW-UP ACTIVITIES COMPONENTS
OF AN INSTRUCTIONAL STRATEGY**

Preinstructional Activities:

MOTIVATION: Explain how you will gain the learners' attention and maintain it throughout the instruction.
OBJECTIVES: Explain how you will inform the learners about what they will be able to do when they finish your lesson. Explain why doing this is important to the learners.
PREREQUISITE SKILLS: Explain how you will treat prerequisite skills required to begin your instruction.

Testing:

PRETEST: Explain if you will test for entry behaviors and what you will do if a learner does not have them. Explain also if you will test for skills you will teach.
EMBEDDED ITEMS: Explain if you will use embedded items and where they will be located.
POSTTEST: Explain when and how the posttest will be administered.

Follow-up Activities:

REMEDIATION: Explain what instruction or procedure you would design for the student who does not master your instructional goal.
ENRICHMENT: Explain what instruction or procedure you would design for the student who does very well on your posttest.

formation required for assigning objectives to lessons and for developing or selecting instructional materials.

4. Review your sequence and clusters of objectives, preinstructional activities, testing, information presentation, and student participation strategies. Using this information coupled with the amount of time available for each lesson and the predicted attention span of target learners, assign objectives to lessons. The first session will undoubtedly contain preinstructional activities, and the last will include the posttest or feed-

TABLE 8.2

**FORMAT FOR INSTRUCTIONAL STRATEGY FOR INFORMATION PRESENTATION
AND STUDENT PARTICIPATION**

Objective #

Information Presentation:

INFORMATION:

EXAMPLES:

Student Participation:

PRACTICE ITEMS:

FEEDBACK:

back from the posttest. Intervening lessons should include time for any needed review, presentation, and participation.

5. Reserve your decision about the follow-through activities until you have a good sense of the effectiveness of the instruction. The data from the field evaluation can be used to pinpoint exactly what types of remediation and enrichment will be required. Table 8.1 lists the basic questions about the follow-through activities.

Several things should be noted about developing an instructional strategy as outlined here. First of all, certain instructional components must be considered in terms of the entire sequence of instruction; that is, preinstructional, testing, and follow-up activities apply to the whole lesson. On the other hand, the information presentation, practice, and feedback sections must be completed for each objective or cluster of objectives, including your terminal objective. It is not intended that you write the whole lesson in the strategy. If you do, you have written too much. The purpose of the written strategy is to require you to think through the entire lesson before you start developing or selecting any instruction.

After completing your instructional strategy, it is wise to evaluate it before spending hours developing the prescribed instruction. Subject matter specialists and individuals familiar with the needs, interests, and attention spans of target learners can be asked to review all three of your strategy tables and to pinpoint potential problems. Spending a short time with selected evaluators now may save hours during later stages of the instructional development process. You may need to provide evaluators with additional information such as a description of your instructional goal, a list of your objectives, and a description of the characteristics of your target group. This information will help them judge the quality of the information included in your strategy.

EXAMPLES

The four phases to planning the instructional strategy for a unit of instruction are as follows: (1) sequence and cluster objectives; (2) plan preinstructional, testing, and follow-up activities for the unit; (3) plan the information presentations and student participation sections of each lesson; (4) assign activities to lessons and estimate the time required for each. We will consider each of these in turn with an example drawn from the composition instructional analyses in chapter 4.

Sequence and Cluster Objectives

The subskills and instructional goal from Figure 4.5, varying sentence types, are included in Table 8.3. Notice that subskills have been clustered by topic area, with clusters 1 through 4 on the table. The content and nature of each subskill within a cluster were analyzed to ensure it represented a logical set of information. Each of the first four sections was estimated to require about one hour. Lesson 5 in Table 8.3 repeats subskills 5.11, 5.24, and 5.31 in one section. Obviously, additional presentations and practice in these four subskills are planned. Lesson 6 requires students to select the best type of sentence to convey a specified mood or emphasis.

TABLE 8.3

OBJECTIVES FROM FIGURE 4.5 SEQUENCED AND CLUSTERED

Subskill Number	Learning Time	Subskill Number	Learning Time
Cluster 1		**Cluster 4**	
Objectives 5.6 5.7 5.8 5.9 5.10 5.11	1 hour	Objectives 5.25 5.26 5.27 5.28 5.29 5.30 5.31	1 hour
Cluster 2		**Cluster 5**	
Objectives 5.12 5.13 5.14 5.15 5.16 5.17	1 hour	Objectives 5.11 5.17 5.24 5.31	1 hour
Cluster 3		**Cluster 6**	
Objectives 5.18 5.19 5.20 5.21 5.22 5.23 5.24	1 hour	Objective 5.32	1 hour

The clusters of subskills planned and the amount of time assigned may need to be revised as you continue to develop the strategy. However, this initial structure will help you focus on lessons rather than on individual objectives. In this example, we have planned for six clusters.

Plan Preinstructional, Testing, and Follow-up Activities

These components of the instructional strategy relate to the overall lesson or lessons and do not refer to individual instructional objectives within a lesson. First, how will you design the preinstructional activities? Remember, this area contains three separate sections: motivation, objectives, and entry behaviors. Table 8.4 shows the instructional strategy plans for these components. Notice that the stories that will be used in the lessons are not included in the table, the objectives are not written out, and the entry behaviors are not listed. Instead, what you will need to do for the lesson is briefly described.

Let's focus now on the second phase of the instructional strategy, namely plans for testing students. How would you plan testing activities for the unit on sentence types? Would you administer a pretest, a posttest, as well as embedded tests? We have outlined example test activities in Table 8.5 for this unit. We plan to test entry behaviors that cover subskills 5.1 through 5.5, since this was prescribed in the previous section on preinstructional activities. We plan two other pretests: one written story and one objective pretest on subordinate skills in the unit. Embedded test items to provide interim

TABLE 8.4

PREINSTRUCTIONAL ACTIVITIES FOR UNIT ON WRITING COMPOSITIONS

Preinstructional Activities:

MOTIVATION: A brief story will be used as an introduction. It will be on a topic of *high interest* to sixth graders, and it will contain all four sentence types to illustrate the point of variety and increased interest through varying sentence type.

OBJECTIVES: Each of the four types of sentences in the sample story will be highlighted and described in the introduction. The purpose of the unit, learning to write stories that contain a variety of sentence types, will be included.

ENTRY BEHAVIORS: Since there are several entry behaviors noted in the instructional analysis, a test including entry behaviors will be developed and administered to determine whether students have the required prerequisite skills.

information about student performance are also planned. Finally, we prescribe two different types of posttests, one that covers subskills individually to facilitate diagnosis and one that requires students to write a story.

With the testing strategy complete, we see that the next activity prescribed is to plan enrichment and remediation activities. However, this is not the time to complete this since you have no data to use to decide whether any remediation will be needed, or, if needed, for what objectives. The same is true for enrichment materials. This portion of the strategy is not completed until after the materials are field tested and student performance data on each objective are analyzed. Then, based upon evidence of student performance, the strategy for remediation and/or enrichment can be planned for objectives requiring such support.

Information Presentation and Student Participation

Information presentation and student participation sections make up the interactive part of the lesson. They are considered the exchange or interface point. The presentation section has two parts, namely the information and examples. The examples section often includes nonexamples to illustrate common errors students can be expected to make or to further illustrate the point you want to emphasize. The student participation component has two areas: sample practice items and the planned feedback strategy.

Table 8.6 includes selected objectives from the composition unit as an illustration of how this format is used to sketch out the strategy. These objectives were taken from the Examples section in chapter 5. Notice that the information conveyed to students for several of the objectives is the same:

TABLE 8.5

TESTING ACTIVITIES FOR UNIT ON WRITING COMPOSITIONS

Testing:

PRETESTS: Administer a brief test of entry behaviors for subskills 5.1, 5.2, 5.3, 5.4, and 5.5. The test will be a short, paper-and-pencil test. If learners do not have prerequisites, then a lesson covering these subskills will be inserted as the first lesson in the unit. Two pretests will be administered after the first lesson, which will be used to motivate learners, inform them of the objectives, and provide example stories. For the pretests, students will be asked to write a brief story using all four sentence types as well as to complete objective questions on subordinate skills.

EMBEDDED ITEMS: Embedded items will be used in instructional materials to test each set of subskills included in the unit.

POSTTESTS: Two different types of posttests will be administered. An objective test will be administered following instruction on objective 5 to facilitate diagnosis of problems students may be having with these subordinate skills. A second posttest, story writing, will be administered following all instruction in the unit.

TABLE 8.6

INSTRUCTIONAL STRATEGY FOR THE INFORMATION PRESENTATION AND STUDENT PARTICIPATION COMPONENTS OF THE COMPOSITION UNIT—*(continued)*

Objective 5.6 State purpose of declarative sentence	Objective 5.7 Classify a complete sentence as declarative
Information Presentation	Information Presentation
INFORMATION: Declarative sentences are used to convey information, to tell the reader something.	INFORMATION: Declarative sentences are used to convey information, to tell the reader something.
EXAMPLES: Joan likes to roller skate. It rained the day of the picnic. Fire drills are important. The roller coaster makes my stomach flutter.	EXAMPLES: 1. Tom enjoys space stories. 2. The kittens are all sold. 3. Mr. Jones is very tall. NONEXAMPLES: (Point out why each is not an example.) 1. What does Tom like to read? 2. Are the kittens still for sale? 3. How does Mr. Jones look?
Student Participation	Student Participation
PRACTICE ITEMS: What does a declarative sentence do? What does Joan like to do? How does a roller coaster make me feel? FEEDBACK: State that a declarative sentence is used to convey information. Point out what each sentence tells us.	PRACTICE ITEMS: Choose the declarative sentences: 1. How did the flowers smell? 2. Where was Julie going? 3. The traffic is noisy. 4. The sailboat is fun to ride. 5. This dog is very, very thin. FEEDBACK: State why 3, 4, and 5 are declarative sentences, and 1 and 2 are not.

Objective 5.8 State periods used to close declarative sentence	Objective 5.9 Select punctuation to close declarative sentence
Information Presentation	Information Presentation
INFORMATION: Periods are used to close declarative sentences. EXAMPLES: The story is exciting. The bear slinked through the campground.	INFORMATION: Periods are used to close declarative sentences. EXAMPLES: The windows had cobwebs in them. The zebra sounded like a horse. NONEXAMPLES: The poppies were red and orange? The sunset was red and orange!
Student Participation	Student Participation
PRACTICE ITEMS: What punctuation mark is used to close declarative sentences? FEEDBACK: Restate that the period is used to close declarative sentences.	PRACTICE ITEMS: Select the punctuation mark—period (.), question mark (?), or exclamation mark (!)—to close these declarative sentences: 1. The frost covered the ground 2. Snow was piled along the road 3. The pond was covered with ice FEEDBACK: State that periods should be used to close all the declarative sentences.

Objective 5.10 Recognize declarative sentence with correct punctuation	Objective 5.11 Write a declarative sentence with correct punctuation
Information Presentation	Information Presentation
INFORMATION: Only periods are used to close declarative sentences. EXAMPLES: 1. The store had many different bicycles. 2. The store had several types of trains.	INFORMATION: Declarative sentences convey information and are closed using a period. EXAMPLES: 1. The classroom was sunny and bright. 2. Everyone came to the party.

TABLE 8.6 *continued*

Objective 5.10 Recognize declarative sentence with correct punctuation	Objective 5.11 Write a declarative sentence with correct punctuation
Information Presentation	Information Presentation
NONEXAMPLES: What types of trains did the store have? Put your trains away! I feel so happy!	NONEXAMPLES: 1. Did John come to the party? 2. John, look out!
Student Participation	Student Participation
PRACTICE ITEMS: Which of the followng are declarative sentences with correct punctuation? 1. Place your hands on the desk! 2. Begin on page one! 3. Where should we stop? 4. Camping can be fun. 5. Surfing is good exercise. FEEDBACK: Indicate why 4 and 5 are declarative, and 1, 2, and 3 are not.	PRACTICE ITEMS: 1. Write five declarative sentences. 2. Change the following sentences to declarative. a. How did John look? b. Where did Billie go? c. The sky was very dark! FEEDBACK: Provide students with list of criteria they can use to evaluate their sentences, e.g., has subject, has predicate, conveys information, and is closed with a period. Give examples of how 2a, b, and c could be rewritten as declarative sentences.

either "declarative sentences convey information," "periods are used to close them," or both. The examples and practice items for each objective clarify the specific intentions for the increasingly complex discriminations students are expected to make during the lesson. Both examples and nonexamples are used for some of the objectives to help illustrate the desired discriminations. Notice also that the context of the examples and vocabulary selected are geared for sixth graders.

At this point, we have completed examples of how to design the instructional strategy related to the following: (1) sequencing and clustering objectives; (2) planning preinstructional, testing, and follow-up activities; and (3) identifying presentation and student participation materials.

Allocate Activities to Sessions

With this information complete, we should review it and allocate prescribed activities to lessons. Lesson prescriptions are included in Table 8.7.

Compare the strategy for individual sessions in Table 8.7 with the initial sequence and cluster of objectives in Table 8.3. Notice that in Table 8.3 we predicted a total of six hours for instructional time. The time estimate for instruction increased to nine hours when requirements for preinstructional, student participation, and testing strategies were considered along with the information presentation. The original sequence and clusters of objectives did not change, however. Do not be surprised if, after considering all the components of your instructional strategy, you need to break a cluster of objectives into two sessions. In fact, it is not uncommon to find that student participation and feedback activities can require an entire session. The designer should be aware that the time allocations prescribed at this point in the design process remain tenuous.

TABLE 8.7

LESSON ALLOCATION BASED UPON INSTRUCTIONAL STRATEGY

Activity	Time Planned	Activity	Time Planned
Session 1		Session 5	
1. Introductory, motivational materials	1 hour	1. Pretest on objectives 5.18–5.24	15 min.
2. Entry behaviors pretest		2. Instruction on objectives 5.18–5.24	40 min.
Session 2		Session 6	
1. Theme writing pretest	1 hour	1. Pretest on objectives 5.25–5.31	15 min.
		2. Instruction on objectives 5.25–5.31	40 min.
Session 3		Session 7	
1. Pretest on objectives 5.6–5.11	15 min.	1. Review of objectives 5.11, 5.17, 5.24 and 5.31	1 hour
2. Instruction on objectives 5.6–5.11	40 min.		
Session 4		Session 8	
1. Pretest on objectives 5.12–5.17	15 min.	1. Pretest on objective 5.32	15 min.
2. Instruction on objectives 5.12–5.17	40 min.	2. Instruction on objective 5.32	40 min.
		Session 9	
		1. Posttest on objectives 5.6–5.32	1 hour

Notice that one session was reserved for introductory materials and the first pretest on entry behaviors. Another was reserved for writing a pretest story since time must be allocated for testing as well as for instruction. Pretests for each separate cluster of skills were planned as the first activity in a session. This will help keep objective pretests short in order to minimize the amount of time spent on pretests in any one day as well as keep tests in close proximity to the content of related sessions.

The instructional strategy is now complete, and we have the prescriptions necessary to begin developing materials for the subordinate skills related to objectives 5 and 6 in the instructional goal.

SUMMARY

Materials you will need in order to design your instructional strategy include the instructional goal, a description of the target group, the instructional analysis, the performance objectives, and the criterion-referenced test items. You will need to reference these materials several times as you design your strategy.

The instructional strategy is a design that will be used for developing or selecting instructional materials. Four of the five components in the instructional strategy are based on the work of educational psychologists, and these components represent the events of instruction believed to facilitate all kinds of school learning. These four components include preinstructional activities, information presentation, student participation with feedback, and follow-through activities. The testing component is included in the strategy to facilitate instructional management. Testing enables us to tailor instruction to the needs of learners, to evaluate the quality of instructional materials, and to evaluate the progress of learners. While the major function of testing in the strategy is management, it also can support learning when corrective feedback about performance is provided to learners.

Instruction is presented to students in the sequence of the named components in the strategy; however, the strategy is not designed in this order. The first step in designing the strategy is to sequence and cluster objectives for presentation. The second is to prescribe the preinstructional activities and testing strategies. The third is to prescribe the information presentation and student participation strategies for each objective. The final step is to assign objectives to lessons.

The type of instructional goal desired is an important consideration when designing your strategy. Whether intellectual skills, verbal information, motor skills, or attitudes, all five of the components of the strategy are important. Each type of goal, however, may require unique designs for each of the instructional strategy components.

In creating each component of your strategy, you should also consider the characteristics of your target students; their needs, interests, and experiences; and the information about how to gain and maintain their attention throughout the five events of instruction. Keller's ARCS model provides a handy structure for considering how to design materials that motivate students to learn.

With your strategy complete, you can begin to develop instruction based on the prescriptions in the strategy. Before proceeding, however, you should request an evaluation of your materials from content experts as well as from individuals familiar with the characteristics of your target learners.

=== PRACTICE ===

To provide practice in developing an instructional strategy for a unit of instructional materials, we have selected the checking account example from Figures 4.7 and 4.8, because most readers probably have a checking account and are familiar with the information, skills, and procedures required to open and maintain one.

Assume that your target group consists of college-bound, high school seniors, all of whom have the required arithmetic entry behaviors for beginning your unit.

To complete this activity, follow the steps outlined below:

1. Sequence and cluster objectives for lessons. Assume that each class period is 50 minutes long. Remember that at this point, you are simply predicting how many of the tasks can be accomplished during a 50-minute period and clustering similar content together. (Refer to Figure 4.7 and concentrate only on the main steps in the goal, or 1.0 through 5.0.)
2. Develop a table that describes preinstructional and testing activities for only the objectives included in step 2.0, deposit money into a checking account. The steps are illustrated in Figure 4.8, and the behavior objectives and test items you will need for this exercise are included in Table 8.8.
3. Develop presentation and practice components of an instructional strategy for the depositing money cluster of procedures, step 2. To aid you with this activity, a sample bank deposit slip for a checking account is provided in Figure 8.2 as a reference for your work.

TABLE 8.8

BEHAVIORAL OBJECTIVES AND TEST ITEMS FOR STEPS 2.1 THROUGH 2.10 IN THE CHECKING ACCOUNT UNIT. THIS INFORMATION WILL PROVIDE YOU WITH THE FRAMEWORK YOU NEED FOR THE INSTRUCTIONAL STRATEGY.

Step	Objective	Test Items
2.1 Indicate where to obtain a deposit slip.	Name two sources for obtaining deposit slips.	List two sources where you can obtain deposit slips. 1. _____ 2. _____
2.2 Complete information to identify depositor and date.	Given a sample generic deposit slip, enter: name, address, account number, date.	Review the sample deposit slip. Enter the information required to identify you as the depositor.
2.3.1 Determine where currency and coins are entered on deposit slip.	Given a sample deposit slip, locate spaces where currency and coins are recorded.	Look at the sample deposit slip. 1. Place a B for bills beside the space where bills should be recorded. 2. Place a C for coins beside the space where coins should be entered.
2.3.2 Count money and enter the amount in the appropriate spaces on deposit slip.	Given specified amounts of bills and coins, count money and enter the totals on the deposit slip.	Sum the following amounts of money and enter the total on your deposit slip. Coins Bills 3 quarters 4 20-dollar bills 4 dimes 5 10-dollar bills 2 nickels 3 1-dollar bills 3 pennies
2.4.1 Sign checks and record account number on each.	Given a set of sample checks, sign each as name appears on account and enter account number beneath name.	Review the sample checks provided for deposit. Prepare each check for deposit into your checking account.
2.4.2 Identify where checks are entered on front and back of deposit slip.	Given a sample deposit slip, locate spaces where checks should be entered including space provided for bank number and for amount of check.	1. Locate the spaces on the front of the deposit slip where checks can be entered. 2. Locate the spaces on the back of the deposit slip where checks can be entered. 3. Locate spaces where bank number should be recorded.
2.4.3 Record each check, including the bank number and amount, on the deposit slip.	Given sample checks, locate bank number on check. Given sample checks, enter the checks on the deposit slip. The entry will include both the bank number and the amount of the check.	Review the sample checks below. Circle the bank number that should be recorded on the deposit slip. Record each of the sample checks on the deposit slip.
2.4.4 Sum the checks recorded on the back of the deposit slip to obtain the total amount.	Given the back side of the deposit slip with checks entered, total the amount to be deposited.	For the checks you have entered on the back side of your deposit slip, total them and record the total in the space provided.
2.4.5 Record subtotal of checks from back onto front of deposit slip.	Given a total of checks to be deposited from the back side of the deposit slip, record the total on the front side on the appropriate line.	Record the total amount of checks recorded on the back side of the deposit slip in the appropriate space on the front side of the deposit slip.
2.5.1 Total all checks to be deposited.	Given a deposit slip with currency, individual checks listed on the front as well as a subtotal of checks from the back, total the checks to be deposited.	Total the checks recorded on the sample deposit slip.

TABLE 8.8 *continued*

Step	Objective	Test Items
2.5.2 Enter on deposit slip amount of cash to be returned.	Given a specified amount of cash to be returned from deposit, enter amount on slip.	From the deposit, indicate that x amount of cash is to be returned.
2.5.3 Subtract cash to be returned from checks deposited to determine deposit total.	Given a specified amount of checks to be deposited and a specified amount of cash to be returned, calculate amount of total deposit.	Given that x amount of cash is to be returned, calculate the total amount of the deposit.
2.5.4 Sign deposit slip indicating cash to be returned.	Given a deposit slip with cash to be returned, place signature on deposit slip.	Sign deposit slip in appropriate space indicating cash to be returned.
2.6 Record total amount of deposit on slip.	Given a deposit slip, determine the total amount to be deposited.	Sum the deposit slip indicating the total amount of the deposit.
2.7 Give deposit slip, checks, and/or money to teller.	Identify where to submit the deposit.	To whom should you give the deposit slip and money? _____
2.8 State that one should verify total deposit on receipt, and 2.9 Place deposit receipt in bank records.	State that: (1) deposit receipts should be verified and (2) placed with bank records.	When a deposit receipt is returned by the teller, what should you do? 1. _____ 2. _____
2.10 State that amount of cash returned should be verified.	State that the amount of cash returned by the teller should be counted before leaving the window.	What should you do before leaving the teller window with cash returned from a deposit by the teller? _____

FEEDBACK

1. Possible sequence and cluster of objectives for unit on opening and maintaining a checking account.

   Lesson 1
   Introduction, pretest over all main steps in goal (1.0–5.0)
   Lesson 2
   Step 1 and all related objectives
   Lesson 3
   Step 2 and all related objectives
   Lesson 4
   Step 3 and all related objectives
   Lesson 5
   Step 4 and all related objectives
   Lesson 6
   Step 5 and all related objectives
   Lesson 7
   Posttest over all main steps in goal (1.0–5.0)

2. Instructional strategy: preinstructional, testing and follow-up activities for the checking account unit.

Preinstructional Activities: (Entire unit)

MOTIVATION: Introductory material will be included regarding: (1) why students should have a checking account while in college, (2) the benefits of paying bills using checks, (3) who can legally have

FIGURE 8.2

SAMPLE BANK DEPOSIT SLIP, FRONT AND BACK

Front Side of Slip

	Dollars	Cents
Currency		
Coins		
C		
H		
E		
C		
K		
S		
Total from other side		
TOTAL		

Back Side of Slip

Bank Number	Dollars	Cents
TOTAL CHECKS		

a checking account, (4) and legal penalties for purposefully misusing checking accounts. Several types of sample checks will be used as illustrations in the materials.

OBJECTIVES: A list of the overall objectives that includes only the five major steps in the checking account procedure will be provided.

PREREQUISITE SKILLS: It will be assumed that the entry behaviors of adding and subtracting decimal numbers will be present in college-bound high school seniors.

Testing: (Entire unit)

PRETEST: There will be no entry behaviors tested. A pretest will be given since some students may already have their own checking accounts. The test will cover all major objectives in the unit.

EMBEDDED TEST: Items will be given for each of the major steps in the procedure.

POSTTEST: A posttest will be administered only at the conclusion of instruction. The test will be paper-and-pencil simulation and cover the following main objectives:

1. Given simulated signature cards and application to open a checking account, complete forms.
2. Given a specified amount of money and checks, complete a deposit form.
3. Given simulated checks and specified amounts of money, write checks to persons or organizations prescribed.
4. Given receipts for deposits and withdrawals, make specified entries in a simulated check register.
5. Given a simulated bank statement, sample checks, and a check register, balance the checking account.

Follow-Up Activities:

REMEDIATION: To be planned after initial field trial.

ENRICHMENT: To be planned after initial field trial.

3. Information presentation and sample practice and feedback activities for only step 2, deposit money into a checking account.

Objective 2.1   Name two sources for obtaining a deposit slip

Information Presentation

INFORMATION: Deposit slips are located in (1) back of checkbook, (2) from bank.

EXAMPLE:
1. Show preprinted form from back of checkbook with identifying information.
2. Show generic deposit slip from bank.

Student Participation

PRACTICE ITEM
1. List two places where you can obtain a deposit slip to deposit money into your checking account.
   1. _____
   2. _____

FEEDBACK
1. Back of checkbook
2. From bank

Objective 2.2   Complete information to identify depositor and date

Information Presentation

INFORMATION:
1. To identify the depositor, the user must add name, address, account number, and date on generic deposit slip.
2. Must add date to preprinted deposit slip.

EXAMPLE:
Sample preprinted and generic deposit slips will be illustrated with arrows pointing to where information should be placed.

Student Participation

PRACTICE ITEM:
1. List information that should be provided on a generic deposit slip.
   1. _____
   2. _____
   3. _____
   4. _____
2. Complete the sample generic deposit slip to indicate the depositor and account.

FEEDBACK:
1. 1. Name
   2. Address
   3. Date
   4. Account number
2. Show generic deposit slip completed with information.

Objective 2.3.1 Determine where currency and coins are entered on deposit slip

Information Presentation

INFORMATION:
1. The top line of this deposit slip is reserved for dollar bills. The word *currency* is used to indicate where to place the amount of money. Have students note the division for dollars and cents.
2. Show completed currency line:

Currency _____

Coin _____

Student Participation

PRACTICE ITEMS:
1. Given an illustration of a blank deposit slip, place an X beside the line where the amount of dollar bills to be deposited should be written.
2. Select the currency line that is correctly completed.

	Dollars	Cents
A. Currency	400	00
B. Currency		400
C. Currency	400	20

FEEDBACK:
1. Illustrate where amount of dollar bills should be inserted.
2. A is correct; B has the currency listed in the coin space; C has coins included in the currency line.

Objective 2.3.2 Count money and enter the totals in the appropriate spaces on the deposit slip

Information Presentation

INFORMATION:
1. Count all dollar bills, total the amount, and enter the total on the currency line of the deposit slip.
2. Count all coins and record the total on the line marked "coins."

EXAMPLE:

1. *Dollars*

   4 10 dollar bills = $40.00
   3   5 dollar bills = $15.00
   4   1 dollar bills = $ 4.00
                             $59.00

2. *Coins*

   6 quarters   =   1.50
   3 dimes   =   .30
   4 nickels   =   .20
   3 pennies   =   .03
                      $ 2.03

	Dollars	Cents
Currency	59	00
Coin	2	03

Student Participation

PRACTICE ITEMS:

1. Total the money described below and enter the total amount in the appropriate lines in the deposit slip.

Dollars		*Coins*	
#	Value	#	Value
1	50.00	4	.50
3	20.00	3	.25
6	10.00	7	.10
2	5.00	2	.05
7	1.00	3	.01

	Dollars	Cents
Currency		
Coins		
Checks		
Total		

Feedback:
Dollars = $187.00
Coins =   3.58

	Dollars	Cents
Currency	187	00
Coins	3	58
Checks		
Total		

Objective 2.4.1   Sign checks and enter account number on each

Information Presentation

INFORMATION:

Sign checks and record account number of depositor on each.

EXAMPLE:

Illustrate back of check with account number and signature included.

Student Participation:

PRACTICE ITEMS:

1. Sign your name as it appears on the signature card of your account and record your account number beneath it.

FEEDBACK:
Show illustration of back of check with signature and account number complete.

Objective 2.4.2   Identify where checks are entered on front and back of deposit slip

Information Presentation

INFORMATION:
Checks are listed one at a time on the deposit slip. Record the bank number for each check, which is located in the upper right corner of the check and total amount of the check in the money column. The bank number is recorded to the left.

EXAMPLES:

Back side of deposit slip

		Dollars	Cents

Show sample check including bank number and value of check	C	Bank Number		
	H			
	E			
	C			
	K			
	S			

Student Participation

PRACTICE ITEMS:
1. Besides the amount of the check, what other identifying information about the check should you write on the deposit slip? _____
2. Circle the bank number on this sample check.

Sara Jones	400
402 Shadow Lane	63-656
	631

Date _____

Pay to the order of _____ $ _____

_____ Dollars

_____

4023010201

3. Where on the deposit slip should you write the bank number of checks being deposited?

FEEDBACK:
1. Bank number
2. Show check with bank number circled. Explain other numbers on check as check number and account number.
3. To the left of the amount of money on the same line.

Objective 2.4.3   Record each check including the bank number and amount

Information Presentation

INFORMATION: Record each check deposited including the amount and the bank number on the deposit slip.

EXAMPLE: Provide students with several example checks of varying sizes and amounts from several different banks and a deposit slip. Point out on the deposit slip where to record the information for each check included.

	Bank number	Dollars	Cents
C			
H			
E			
C			
K			
S			
	Total Checks		

Student Participation

PRACTICE ITEMS: Provide students with a variety of checks and a deposit slip. Have students record relevant data from checks onto deposit slip.

FEEDBACK: Provide a sample deposit slip correctly completed for sample checks used. Point out where each type of information is recorded on the deposit slip.

Objective 2.4.4   Sum the checks recorded on the back of the deposit slip

Information Presentation

INFORMATION: Add together the total amount of checks listed on the back of the deposit slip and record the total at the bottom of the form.

EXAMPLE:

	Bank number	Dollars	Cents
C			
H	36-142	100	00
E	14-426	32	50
C	18-421	45	00
K	1-402	1000	00
S			
	Total Checks	1177	50

Student Participation

TEST ITEMS: Sum the amount of checks listed and record the total at the bottom of the form in the space marked "Total."

	Bank number	Dollars	Cents
C			
H	12-143	15	30
E	19-125	5	20
C	3-402	103	50
K	12-143	2000	75
S			
Total Checks			

FEEDBACK: $2124.75

Objective 2.4.5   Record total amount of checks listed onto front of deposit slip

Information Presentation

INFORMATION: The total amount of checks listed on the back side of the deposit slip should be transferred to the front and placed in the line marked "total from other side."

EXAMPLE: Deposit Slip Front Side

Currency		100	00
Coin		4	32
C	90-425	32	50
H	36-102	150	00
E	15-432	630	15
C			
K			
S			
Total from other side		2124	75

Deposit Slip Back Side

C	Bank number	Dollars	Cents
H	12-143	15	30
E	19-125	5	20
C	3-402	103	50
K	12-143	2000	75
S			
	Total Checks	2124	75

Student Participation

TEST ITEMS: Locate the total amount of checks listed on the back of the deposit slip and transfer the total to the front of the deposit slip in the correct space.

Back side of slip

	12-264	200	00
	32-105	50	10
	32-105	2	20
	12-143	150	00
Total		402	30

Front side of slip

Currency		
Coin		
Total from other side		

FEEDBACK:

Front side of slip

Total from other side	402	30

Objective 2.5.1   Total all checks to be deposited

Information Presentation

INFORMATION:
Total all checks to be deposited.

EXAMPLE:
Illustrate deposit slip with two or three checks on front side, and sum in "total from other side" line. Add amounts together and highlight total.

Student Participation

PRACTICE ITEM:
Sum the total amount of checks recorded on the deposit slip and enter the total in the appropriate space.

FEEDBACK:
Correct total located on total line highlighted by arrow.

Objective 2.5.2   Enter on deposit slip amount of cash to be returned

Information Presentation

INFORMATION:
Can have cash returned during transaction by indicating amount on "less cash received" line.

EXAMPLE:
Illustrate deposit slip with __X__ amount of cash to be returned entered on "less cash received" line.

Student Participation

PRACTICE ITEM:
Indicate on deposit slip that __X__ dollars are to be returned in cash during the transaction.

FEEDBACK:
Correct dollars entered on "less cash received" line and highlighted with arrow.

Objective 2.5.3   Subtract cash to be returned from checks deposited to determine total deposit

Information Presentation

INFORMATION:
Subtract cash to be returned from checks deposited to determine deposit total.

EXAMPLE:
Provide illustration of correct deposit total after cash subtracted and highlight with arrow.

Student Participation

PRACTICE ITEM:
What is the total deposit after cash to be returned is subtracted?

FEEDBACK:
Provide correct answer of total deposit.

Objective 2.5.4   Sign deposit slip indicating cash to be returned

Information Presentation

INFORMATION:
Sign deposit slip indicating cash to be returned during transaction.

EXAMPLE:
Provide illustration of deposit slip with signature in place and highlight with arrow.

Student Participation

PRACTICE ITEM:
Sign deposit slip in appropriate place indicating cash to be received.

FEEDBACK:
Provide illustration of signature and highlight.

Objective 2.6   Record total amount of deposit on slip

Information Presentation

INFORMATION:
Record total amount of deposit (cash and checks) on slip.

EXAMPLE:
Provide illustration with correct total entered.

Student Participation

PRACTICE ITEM:
Sum the sample deposit slip and enter the total in the correct line.

FEEDBACK:
Provide illustration with correct total entered and highlighted.

Objective 2.7   Give deposit slip checks and/or money to teller

Information Presentation

INFORMATION:
Give deposit slip, checks, and/or money to teller.

EXAMPLE:
Illustrate complete deposit slip, money, and checks, and illustrate a teller at the window.

Student Participation

PRACTICE ITEM:
To whom should you give the deposit slip and money?

FEEDBACK:
Teller

Objective 2.8/2.9   Verify total deposit on receipt   Place deposit receipt in bank records

Information Presentation

INFORMATION:
You will receive a receipt from the deposit.
1. Verify that the amount recorded as a deposit is correct.
2. Place the receipt with bank records.

EXAMPLE:
Show illustration of deposit receipt with amount of deposit highlighted.

Student Participation

PRACTICE ITEM:
When a deposit receipt is returned by the teller, what should you do?

FEEDBACK:
1. Verify amount.
2. Place in bank records.

Objective 2.10   Verify amount of cash returned

Information Presentation

INFORMATION:
When receiving cash from a deposit, verify that the sum is correct *before* leaving the window.

EXAMPLE:
Provide scenario of student returning later to explain that cash received was not correct and consequences of being late with this information.

Student Participation

PRACTICE ITEM:
What should you do with cash returned by the teller when making a deposit?

FEEDBACK:
Immediately verify that the amount of cash is correct.

References and Recommended Readings

Ali, A. M. (1981). The use of positive and negative examples during instruction. *Journal of Instructional Development*, 5 (1), 2–7. A number of suggestions are provided on the selection and use of examples and nonexamples in instruction.

Beaudin, B. P. (1987). Enhancing the transfer of job-related learning from the learning environment to the workplace. *Performance and Instruction*, 26 (9 & 10), 19–21. Tips on how to analyze the work site to plan instruction that results in the learning of skills that get used on the job.

Briggs, L. J. (1970). *Handbook of procedures for the design of instruction.* Pittsburgh, PA: American Institutes for Research. Briggs provides an in-depth approach for designing an instructional strategy based upon the type of learning involved.

Carey, L. M. (1988). *Measuring and evaluating school learning.* Boston, MA: Allyn and Bacon, 29–70. Includes several different approaches to analyze goals and identify content.

Gagné, E. D. (1985). *The cognitive psychology of school learning.* Boston, MA: Little, Brown. Gagné describes different types of school learning and suggests strategies for teaching them.

Gagné, R. M. (1985). *Conditions of learning* (4th ed.). New York: Holt, Rinehart and Winston. Gagné describes in detail the factors that should be present to stimulate learning in each of the learning domains.

Gagné, R. M., Briggs, L. J., & Wager, W. W. (1988). *Principles of instructional design* (3rd ed.). New York: Holt, Rinehart and Winston. The chapter on the events of instruction in this book will provide additional background on the major concepts that have been included.

Gagné, R. M., & Driscoll, M. P. (1988). *Essentials of learning for instruction.* Englewood Cliffs, NJ: Prentice-Hall. This book includes a description of the events of instruction as they are incorporated into an instructional strategy.

Journal of Educational Psychology includes a variety of research articles about the effectiveness of various instructional strategies that might be incorporated in instructional materials.

Keller, J. M. (1987). Strategies for stimulating the motivation to learn. *Performance and Instruction*, 26, (8), pp. 1–7.

Keller, J. M. (1987). The systematic process of motivational design. *Performance and Instruction*, 26, (9), 1–8.

Keller, J. M., & Kopp, T. W. (1987). Application of the ARCS model of motivational design. In C. M. Reigeluth (Ed.), *Instructional Theories in Action: Lessons illustrating selected theories and models.* Hillside, NJ: Lawrence Erlbaum Associates. These three publications describe the theory, research background, and application of Keller's ARCS model.

Markle, S. M. (1978). *Designs for instructional designers.* Champaign, IL: Stipes Publishing Co. This text includes suggestions for many areas of the instructional design process, but is particularly useful in determining instructional strategies.

Nathenson, M. B., & Henderson, E. S. (1980). *Using student feedback to improve learning materials.* London: Croom Helm. This general text on formative evaluation details the use of embedded student attitude items.

9

DEVELOPING INSTRUCTIONAL MATERIALS

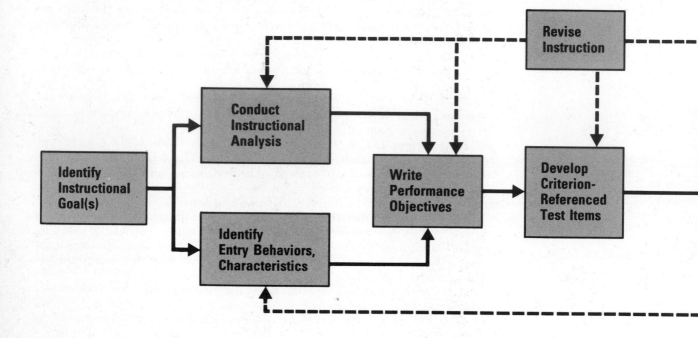

OBJECTIVES

- Given an instructional strategy, describe the procedures for developing instructional materials.
- Develop instructional materials based on a given instructional strategy.

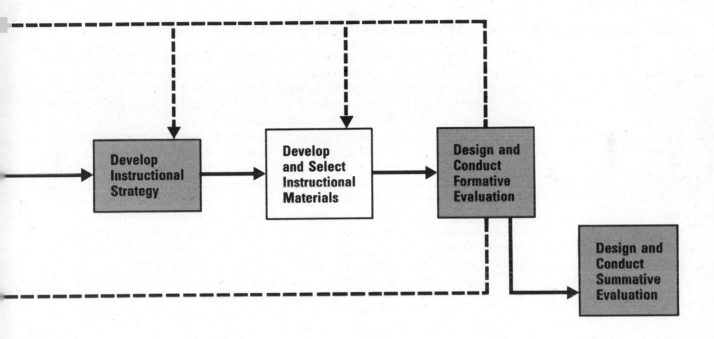

BACKGROUND

In a typical classroom setting the instructor does many of the things we described as being components of an instructional strategy. The instructor is often the motivator, the information presenter, the leader of practice activities, and the tester. The instructor makes decisions that affect the whole group as well as individual students. Instructors are usually locked into a strategy and must move the whole class forward or retain the whole class at a particular point until they feel that sufficient understanding has developed within the group.

The hallmark of individualized instruction is that many of the instructional events typically carried out by the instructor with a group of students are now presented to the individual student through instructional materials. As we have said elsewhere, this does not mean that the instructor is removed from the instructional setting. The instructor's role is even more important than that in lock-step instruction. The instructor is still a motivator as well as a counselor, evaluator, and decision maker.

We recommend that your first attempt at instructional design involves producing self-instructional materials. That is, the materials should permit the student to learn the criterion behaviors without any intervention from an instructor or fellow students. Once having performed this feat as a designer you can very easily move back to the point of using the instructor or other students. But, as a first effort, components like motivation and decision making should be built into the instructional materials. If you were to start your development with the instructor built into the instructional process, it would be very easy to begin to use him or her as a crutch in order to deliver the instruction.

CONCEPTS

The Instructor's Role in Instructional Development and Delivery

The instructor may be involved at three different levels in the design and delivery of instruction. The differences between the three levels lie in the role the instructor plays in developing the instruction and in the actual delivery of instruction to target students. Table 9.1 includes a description of the instructor's role in the design and the delivery process.

When instructors design and develop individualized materials, or materials that can be delivered independent of an instructor, their role in instructional delivery is passive. In this case, their task during instruction is to monitor and guide the progress of students through the materials. Students can progress at their own speed through the instruction, with the instructor providing additional help for those who seem to need it.

Except for the pretests and posttests, all instructional events are included within the materials. In some materials, even these tests are included and submitted to the teacher only when students complete them.

In the second case, in which instructors select and adapt materials to suit their instructional strategy, it is probable that the instructor will have an increased role in delivering instruction. Some available materials may

TABLE 9.1

THE METHOD OF DELIVERING INSTRUCTION FOR VARIOUS INSTRUCTIONAL APPROACHES

The Instructor's Role in Designing Materials	Instructional Strategy Components				
	Preinstructional Activities	Presenting Information	Student Participation	Follow Through Activities	Pretest/Posttest and Unit Motivation
I Instructor designs individualized instructional materials	Materials	Materials	Materials	Materials	Instructor/ Materials
II Instructor selects and adapts existing materials to suit the instructional strategy	Materials and/ or Instructor	Materials and/ or Instructor	Materials and/ or Instructor	Materials and/ or Instructor	Instructor/ Materials
III Instructor uses no material but delivers instruction to suit the instructional strategy	Instructor	Instructor	Instructor	Instructor	Instructor/ Materials

be instructor independent, but when they are not, the instructor must provide any instruction specified in the strategy, but not found in the materials.

When an instructor uses a variety of instructional resources, he or she plays a greater role in materials management. By providing a student guide for available materials, instructors may be able to increase the independence of the materials and free themselves to provide additional guidance and consultation for students who need it.

The third type of instruction illustrated in Table 9.1 is heavily dependent on the instructor. The instructor delivers all the instruction according to the instructional strategy that has been developed. This commonly occurs in public schools or in other settings in which there is a small budget for materials or in which the content to be taught changes rapidly.

The instructor uses the instructional strategy as a guide in producing outlines for lecture notes and directions for group exercises and activities. Most often, the pretest and posttest are the only materials that are typed and duplicated for student use.

This type of instruction has both advantages and disadvantages. A major advantage is that the instructor can constantly update and improve instruction as changes occur in the content. But, instructors spend the majority of their time lecturing and delivering information to a group, leaving little time to help individual learners with problems. Progress through a lesson is difficult because when the teacher stops to answer a question for one student, the progress of the entire group is halted.

The intended delivery mode for instruction is a very important consideration in the development of materials based on the planned instructional strategy. If instruction is intended to be instructor-independent, then the materials will have to include all the instructional events in the strategy. The instructor is not expected to play a role in delivering instruction.

If the instructor plans to combine available materials, then instructional delivery will combine materials and instructor presentation. The instructor may not be required to develop any new materials in this mode, but may be required to deliver some of the needed instruction. The amount of original materials developed for this type of instruction will depend upon available time, budget, and secretarial support.

If instructors plan to deliver all the instruction with materials such as lecture notes, an overhead projector, and a chalkboard, then they may need to develop little besides lecture outlines, practice worksheets, and formal tests.

Your decision about the intended development and delivery mode should be made prior to materials development. These decisions will affect developmental activities as well as the required budget and staff.

Selecting Appropriate Instructional Materials

The next step following the development of the instructional strategy is to determine if there are already existing materials that fit your objectives. In some situations you will find an abundance of materials available, either superficial or greatly detailed, which are not really directed to the target population in which you are interested. On the other hand, occasionally it is possible to identify materials that will serve at least part of your needs. When you consider the cost of developing a videotape or a slide/tape presentation, it is clearly worth the effort to spend several hours examining existing materials to determine if they meet your needs.

Your instructional strategy can be used to determine whether existing materials are adequate as is, or whether they need to be adapted or enhanced prior to use. Materials can be evaluated to determine whether (1) motivational concerns are addressed, (2) the appropriate content is included, (3) the sequence is correct, (4) all the required information is available, (5) practice exercises exist, (6) adequate feedback is included, (7) appropriate tests are available, (8) adequate follow-up directions are included for remediation, advanced work, or general progress, and (9) adequate learner guidance is provided to move students from one event or activity to the next.

The instructional strategy should be used to evaluate each selected reference. It may be possible to combine references to improve the materials. When materials lack one or more of the necessary instructional activities—such as motivation, prerequisite skills, and so on—they can be adapted so that the missing components are made available for use by students.

If no appropriate materials exist, you are in the materials writing business, and you must make an additional decision with regard to your instructional strategy. What type of medium will you use to deliver the materials?

Media Selection

One of the most interesting and challenging decisions in the instructional design process is the selection of the medium or media that will be used to deliver the instruction. The decision is dependent upon a thorough knowledge of what is being taught, how it is to be taught, how it will be tested, and who will be the learners. Unfortunately, the decision is sometimes made at the beginning of the design process, for example, "Since we have a new microcomputer, we should develop some new instruction for it," or, "It has been decided that this will be a TV project." If this is the case, just hope that what you are trying to do will fit the medium that has been preselected. Most readers will be able to recall situations in which the medium did not seem to fit the learning situation. The results are often very unfortunate, but it is sometimes too late to reverse decisions that were made in advance.

Assuming that the media selection decision is to take place at the time development is to begin, how is the choice made? Certainly there are practical considerations one immediately thinks of in terms of availability of resources and personnel. But there are prior decisions that should be made that relate to the selection of the appropriate media for the various types of learning activities. For example, some media are more effective for teaching verbal information while others are more effective for psychomotor skills.

Reiser and Gagné (1983) have published a model showing how to select the best medium for instruction. The designer uses the model by answering questions about the skill to be taught, and then follows a flow diagram to the point that *several* media are suggested. The designer can then look at the practical aspects associated with the use of what are referred to as the *candidate media.*

The Reiser and Gagné technique is based upon a complete review of the research on the use of media in instruction. While it sometimes appears that you can teach almost anything with any medium, it is advisable to consider the special conditions that foster various types of learning and to try to include media that offer these conditions to the learner.

Consider for example the analysis of the type of media that might be used to teach intellectual skills. Research suggests that students should be provided precise corrective feedback to responses made during the learning process. Often there is more than one "correct answer." In order to provide responsive feedback, there is a need for such interactive media as computer-based instruction or programmed instruction—that is, print instruction that requires responses from learners and provides the correct answer. If broadcast radio or TV is to be used, then supplemental student packages that require responses and provide feedback could be developed.

If the instructional goal is in the domain of verbal information, there is still the requirement of eliciting responses from learners, but there is less need for specific, diagnostic feedback. Because the student can easily compare his or her own response to the correct answer, there is less need for interactive media with verbal information goals.

The other two domains of goals that we have considered are motor skills and attitudes. If the learning of a motor skill begins with the learning of an executive routine (which is a description of what the learner will do and how it will be done under various circumstances), then this first phase can be treated as if it were an intellectual skill. However, as the learner masters the executive routine, it is necessary to practice in the real physical environment or with the equipment described in the instructional goal. Therefore, simulators or real objects should be used for teaching psychomotor skills.

Research about how we learn attitudes suggests that one of the most powerful methods is to observe a person we highly regard doing something for which they are rewarded or have received approval. It is then likely that we will tend to make the same choice when we are in a similar situation. Thus, for teaching attitudes, the visual media, such as television, are often suggested.

When the Reiser and Gagné method is used to select media, it is assumed that the objectives are all in the same domain. For a short lesson, it is not unlikely that all of the objectives might be intellectual skills or verbal information. However, as the unit of instruction increases—for example, to a forty-hour course—then there would probably be a mixture of domains represented in the objectives. Therefore, it is necessary to select a medium for a cluster of similar objectives, and attempt to mix compatible media for a variety of objectives.

The purpose of this review has been to suggest that the differences in learning outcomes are reflected in the media used to deliver instruction. The flow diagram of Reiser and Gagné makes the media selection process relatively easy. A portion of the actual diagram appears in Figure 9.1. For example, if you were developing self-instructional materials for an attitude objective for learners who have adequate reading skills, you would quickly find through the use of the flow chart that the suggested media are motion pictures, TV cassette, slides or tapes. Having narrowed the selection to these media, it is possible to consider other factors such as those described below, to make the final decision.

An important factor in media selection is the projected availability of various media in the environment in which the instructional package will be used. If the materials will be used in the learning resource center of a public school, community college, or university, then a whole array of media devices would probably be available to the learner and thus to you as the instructor. However, if the package is designed for home study or use in a community center where this equipment is not likely to be available, then you must either develop a means of making that equipment available or limit yourself to paper-and-pencil types of instructional materials. A

FIGURE 9.1

REISER AND GAGNÉ MEDIA SELECTION DIAGRAM FOR SELF-INSTRUCTIONAL DELIVERY SYSTEMS

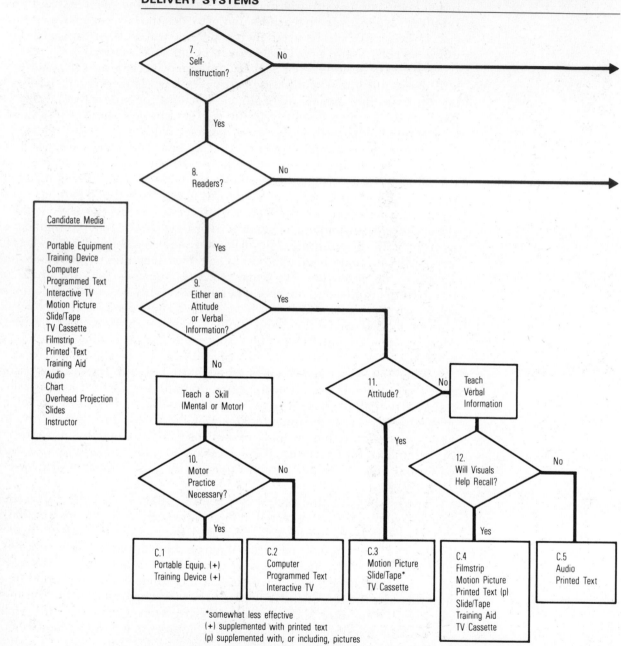

*somewhat less effective
(+) supplemented with printed text
(p) supplemented with, or including, pictures

Explanation of Questions

7. Self-Instruction? Are students expected to learn by self-instruction, without an instructor?
8. Readers? Can the students, with reasonable efficiency, gain information from printed text?
9. Either an Attitude or Verbal Information? Is the aim either to influence the student's values (attitudes) or to have the student learn to 'state' (rather than 'do') something?
10. Motor Practice Necessary? Does the skill to be learned require smooth timing of muscular movements (a "motor skill")?
11. Attitude? Does instruction aim to influence the student's values or opinions?
12. Will Visuals Help Recall? Is it likely that the use of visuals will help the student establish images that will aid recall of verbal information?

related concern is the ability of the teacher and the student to manage the media that you incorporate in the instructional package. If you use a videotape, a slide tape, an audio tape, and a programmed instruction text in combination, the variety of media could create logistical problems. This is a practical consideration you must not overlook.

Another factor in media selection is the ability of the designer or an available expert to produce materials in a particular media format. For example, you may find that computer-assisted instruction would be an ideal medium for a particular instructional objective, but because you do not already have the skills to develop instruction using computers or the time to learn them, or because there is no staff available to do it, another choice must be made. On the other hand, if such resources are available or you have these skills, then certainly they should be used.

The flexibility, durability, and convenience of the materials within a specified medium are other factors. If the materials are designed so that they require equipment found only in a learning center, is there a learning center available? Is it open during hours when students can participate in independent study? Are the materials in a form that students can handle alone without destroying either the materials or equipment required for the materials? Should the materials be portable and, if so, how portable can they be with the media you have chosen?

The final factor is the cost-effectiveness, over the long run, of one medium compared to others. Some materials may be initially cheaper to produce in one medium than another, but these costs may be equalized when one considers costs in other areas such as lecturers, evaluators, and feedback personnel. It might be cheaper to videotape a lecture for a large group of students to view again and again as needed, which frees the lecturer or specialist to work with small groups of students or to help individuals solve problems.

All the factors discussed here present both theoretical and practical criteria that must be met. These criteria illustrate the extreme importance of your medium selection in the instructional development process.

Components of an Instructional Package

With your completed instructional strategy in hand, and the medium of your choice selected, you are, at last, ready to start developing instruction. As you begin you should be aware of the several components that usually make up an instructional package.

STUDENT MANUAL The student manual contains the directions on how to use all the resources included in the package. The manual contains the master strategy for students; it tells them what to do first, second, third, and so on. It may also include some of the instructional materials, examples of test items, statements of objectives, and practice tests.

INSTRUCTIONAL MATERIALS The instructional materials contain the information, either written or mediated, that a student will use to achieve the objectives. This includes materials for the major objectives, and any remedial or enrichment materials. Instructional materials refer to any pre-existing materials that are being incorporated as well as those materials that will need to be specifically written for the objectives.

TESTS All instructional materials should be accompanied by tests. These may include a pretest and a posttest. (Embedded test items would be found in the instructional materials.) You may decide that you do not wish to have the tests as a separate component in the materials, but prefer to have them appear as part of one of the other components. You may, for example, want to have the pretest and posttest printed in the instructor's guide so they are not available to the students. The package will be incomplete, however, unless you have included at least a posttest and the other tests that are necessary for using the instructional package.

INSTRUCTOR'S MANUAL There should be a general description of the total package that provides the instructor with an overview of the materials and shows how they might be incorporated into an overall learning sequence for students. It might also include the tests and other information that you judge to be important for the instructor. Special attention should be paid to the ease with which the manual can be used by the instructor. It should undergo the same type of formative evaluation as would tests and instruction.

BEFORE BEGINNING THE DEVELOPMENT PROCESS Before describing the steps in the development process, it is important to note two important concerns: the characteristics of the students for whom the instruction is being written, and how you write the first draft of your instruction for the medium you have chosen. First let's consider the learners.

A common problem in the instructional design process is the relationship, or lack thereof, between the designer and the learners. At times the designer will also be serving as the teacher of a given set of students. The teacher/designer has a good understanding of the interests and motivations of the students, of their preferences and expectations, and their general and specific knowledge of the content area.

However, it is much more often the case that the designer is unfamiliar with the students for whom the instruction is intended and may have little or no direct contact with them. When this situation exists, the designer often depends on his or her own stereotypes of what the learners are like, which may result in more problems than if the designer had no knowledge of the learners at all.

If possible, the designer should observe the learners for whom the instruction is being designed—observing not just school children, but military recruits, adult volunteer learners, middle-management trainees, and any others for whom instruction is to be designed. Based on these observations, the designer can determine the size of chunks of instruction, how to use illustrations, and what types of models should be used to shape attitudes. Although it is impossible to indicate all the characteristics of a learner population that might be important to the design of new instruction, the instructional designer must become as knowledgeable as possible about the target population.

It is also impossible to describe in this text how the designer prepares the first draft of instruction for every possible medium. There are relatively traditional ways of preparing a story board for a television production, for example, but standard ways for communicating between the designer and the programmer who prepares computer-assisted instruction are only now being developed. This is the point of interaction between those whose expertise lies in the production of instruction in various media and the instructional designer. The individual who is skilled in both areas is quite fortunate!

For the purposes of this text, it will be assumed that a printed text version of the instruction will be developed. For the novice designer, this is a very natural starting point because it avoids the problem of being required to have complex media development skills—but it doesn't avoid them entirely. It is not unusual for a printed text to require illustrations. The acquisition and reproduction of those illustrations can become a media production problem.

For the designer who is preparing instruction for media other than print, the techniques described in this and succeeding chapters still apply. In other words, the instructional strategy must be developed before preparing the first draft of the instruction, regardless of the medium; and once that first draft of the instruction is prepared, then the formative evaluation process should begin.

We will show in our examples how the instructional strategy is used as a guide for developing the first draft of your instruction. The strategy should keep you on track as you write your materials to motivate and inform the learners, present each objective, provide practice and feedback, and implement your testing and follow-up strategies. Listed below are the general steps you will follow from the development of the instructional strategy to the completion of the first draft of the instruction and support materials.

Steps in the Development of Instruction

1. Review the instructional strategy for each objective in each lesson.
2. Survey the literature and ask subject-matter experts to determine what instructional materials are already available.
3. Consider how you might adapt available materials.
4. Determine whether new materials need to be designed. If so, proceed to step 5. If not, begin organizing and adapting available materials, using the instructional strategy as a guide.
5. For each lesson, consider the best medium to present the materials, to monitor practice and feedback, to evaluate, and to guide students to the next instructional activity, whether enrichment, remediation, or the next activity in the sequence.
6. Determine the format and presentation procedures for each objective or cluster of objectives. Plan any general format or presentation pattern you believe is necessary or would be effective. Plan the actual script and illustrations for the instructional strategy.
7. Write the instructional materials based on the instructional strategy in rough form. You will be amazed at how stick figures and rough illustrations can bring your ideas to life for a first trial. Printed, visual, or auditory materials in this rough form will allow you to check your sequence, flow of ideas, accuracy of illustration of ideas, completeness, pace, and so on. Make a rough set of materials as complete as possible for each instructional activity.
8. Consider each completed lesson or class session for clarity and flow of ideas.
9. Using one complete instructional unit (complete instructional program), write the student's manual or accompanying instructions to the students for that activity. A course or program syllabus is often used to guide students through the materials. Directions could include the objectives, motivational materials, and assignments.

10. Using the materials developed in this first inexpensive, rough draft, you are ready to begin evaluation activities. Chapter 10 introduces and discusses procedures and activities for evaluating and revising instructional materials.

11. You may either develop materials for the instructor's manual as you go along or you can take notes as you develop and revise the instructional presentations and activities. Using the notes, you can later write the instructor's guide.

EXAMPLES

Selected parts of the instructional strategy for the story-writing unit will be used to illustrate materials development. Materials will be produced for sessions 1, 2, and 3 as described in the lesson allocation plans in Table 8.7. Session 1 prescribes preinstructional information that should contain information to (1) motivate the learners, (2) inform them of the objectives, and (3) assess their knowledge of entry behaviors. The prescriptions for these three activities are described in Table 8.4. Session 2 is composed of writing a story that will be used as a pretest to evaluate students' skills on the instructional goal before beginning the unit. Session 3 includes a pretest over subordinate skills 5.6 through 5.11 as well as instruction on these same skills.

A special format for the materials was used to enable you to compare the materials developed to the strategy in Tables 8.4, 8.5, and 8.6. The left column identifies the component, the next column the related subskill, and the text column contains information the students will read. Please note that this is not a format that you would want to use with your materials. Columns 1 and 2 would not appear in your instruction, nor is it likely that you would use the headings that have been inserted in the instruction. These have been placed there so you can trace the relationship between the strategy and the instructional materials.

SESSION 1

PLAN FOR DECLARATIVE SENTENCES: MOTIVATIONAL MATERIAL, UNIT OBJECTIVES, AND ASSESSMENT OF ENTRY BEHAVIORS

Component	Subskill	Text
Introduction/ Motivation (Strategy Table 8.4)		We can make stories we write more interesting by using different types of sentences when we write them. Using different types of sentences in our stories does not change the message, it only changes the way we tell it. Different kinds of sentences help the readers know exactly what we want to say and how we feel about what we have said. It involves them in what they are reading because it helps the story come alive.
		To show you how using several different kinds of sentences makes a story more interesting, we have written the same story two ways. Story A has all the same kind of sentences in it, whereas Story B has four different kinds of sentences in it. Read both stories and compare them.

Story A	*Story B*
(1) Yesterday, my Uncle Frank bought a present for me. (2) It	(1) Yesterday, my Uncle Frank bought a present for me! (2) It

Component	*Subskill*	*Text*
		was large, wrapped in fancy blue paper, and it had model cars on the ribbon. (3) The card said not to open it until my birthday. (4) I wondered what was inside the box. (5) I held the package, shook it, and turned it upside down. (6) My mother told me to stop playing with the package. (7) Later when she saw me holding the present, she took it and put it away. (8) I would like to find it.
		was large, wrapped in fancy blue paper, and had model cars on the ribbon. (3) "Do not open until your birthday!" was written on the card. (4) What could be inside the box? (5) I held the package, shook it, and turned it upside down. (6) "Stop playing with your package," said Mother. (7) Later, when she saw me holding the present, she took it and put it away. (8) Where could she have hidden it?
		Story B simply tells the same story in a more interesting way. When we write our own stories, we should remember that using several different kinds of sentences in them will make any story more interesting.
Objectives (Strategy Table 8.4)		During this unit you are going to learn to write stories that have different kinds of sentences in them. You will focus on four different kinds of sentences including: 1. Declarative sentences that tell the reader something 2. Interrogative sentences that ask questions 3. Imperative sentences that command, direct or request something 4. Exclamatory sentences that show emotion or excitement. Of course, writing stories that have all four kinds of sentences will require some instruction and lots of practice. The lessons that follow will teach you about each of the sentences and allow you to practice writing each one. After learning to write all four sentence types, you will use them together to create interesting short stories.
Prerequisites (Strategy Table 8.4)		Before learning to write different types of sentences, it is important for you to remember facts about complete and incomplete sentences. To help you remember these facts, answer the questions on the short quiz that follows. When you have finished the quiz, close your booklet and read quietly at your desk until your teacher tells you what to do next. *REMEMBER TO PUT YOUR NAME ON YOUR QUIZ PAPER*
		Define the following terms related to sentences.
Pretest on Entry Behaviors (Strategy Tables 8.4 and 8.5)	5.1	1. A subject ________________ 2. A predicate ________________
		Locate subjects and predicates. In the following statements, draw one line under the subjects and two lines under the predicates.
	5.3	3. The carnival was a roaring success. 4. The soccer team was victorious this season.

Component	Subskill	Text
	5.4	5. Susan got an after-school job weeding flower beds.
		6. Define a complete sentence. _____
		_____
	5.5	Locate complete and incomplete sentences. Place a C before all the following sentences that are *complete*. If the sentence is not complete, write an S to indicate that the *subject* is missing. Write a P to indicate that the *predicate* is missing.
		____ 7. John closely following the directions.
		____ 8. The team that was most excited.
		____ 9. The dogsled jolted and bumped over the frozen land.
		____ 10. Found the lost friends happy to see her.

SESSION 2

PRETEST THEME

Component	Subskill	Text
Pretest Theme (Strategy Table 8.5)	Instructional Goal	Write a short, one-page story using a variety of sentence types to hold the interest of the reader and to strengthen the idea or mood of your story. In your story you should:
		1. Use at least *two* of each of the following types of sentences: declarative, interrogative, imperative, and exclamatory.
		2. Use only *complete* sentences.
		3. Use the *correct punctuation* based upon sentence *type* and *mood*.
		4. Select the best type of sentence to convey the idea you wish.
		Select one of the following titles for your theme.*
		1. I Really Didn't Expect That!
		2. He/She/You Shouldn't Have Done It!
		3. I Will Think Twice Before I Do That Again!
		*The title does not count as one of your exclamatory sentences.

SESSION 3

PRETEST AND INSTRUCTION IN SUBORDINATE SKILLS 5.6 THROUGH 5.11

Component	Subskill	Text
Objective Pretest (Strategy Table 8.5)		The following short quiz has questions about declarative sentences on it. Put your name and the date on the top before you begin. Answer each question. If you are not sure of the answer, guess what the answer might be. Do not be upset if you do not know some of the answers since you may not have had instruction on declarative sentences yet. When you finish the quiz, raise your hand and it will be collected. You may begin the lesson when you finish the quiz.
Instructions	5.6–5.11	

Component	Subskill	Text
	5.6	1. The purpose of a declarative sentence is to _____.
	5.7	Determine whether the following sentences are declarative. If a sentence is declarative, mark a *D* in the space before the sentence.
		2. ____ Wow look at that fire 3. ____ Sarah selected a mystery book 4. ____ Did Sarah select a mystery book 5. ____ The woods look quiet and peaceful 6. ____ Are you hungry
	5.8	7. The punctuation mark used to close a declarative sentence is called a(an) _____.
	5.9	Place the punctuation mark that should follow these sentences in the blank to the left of the sentence.
		8. ____ Gina did not get a bike for her birthday 9. ____ Sam worked in the yard after school
	5.10	Identify declarative sentences with correct ending punctuation. Place a D beside each correct sentence.
		10. ____ Did George get many presents. 11. ____ The air was warm and balmy? 12. ____ Jenny was late for class. 13. ____ Ken was happy when they arrived. 14. ____ What is the first day of winter.
	5.11	Write two declarative sentences with correct punctuation that describe today's class.
		15. 16.
	5.11	Write two declarative sentences, with correct punctuation, on topics of your choice.
		17. 18.
		Declarative Sentences
Information Presentation (Table 8.6)	5.6	A declarative sentence is used to convey information, to tell the reader something or describe something. When you want to state a fact or describe something in a direct manner, you write a declarative sentence.

Component	Subskill	Text
Examples		Here are some declarative sentences used to state facts. 1. Joan likes to roller skate. 2. Fire drills are important. The first sentence tells us what Joan likes to do. The second sentence tells us that fire drills are an important activity.
Information		Declarative sentences can also be used to describe something. The following sentences are descriptions.
Examples		1. It rained the day of the picnic. 2. The roller coaster makes my stomach flutter. The first sentence describes the day as rainy and the second one describes how a roller coaster makes the writer's stomach feel. Look at the next two sentences. One is a declarative sentence and one is not.
	5.7	
Nonexamples		1. Tom enjoys reading space stories. 2. What does Tom want to read? The first sentence is declarative since it tells us what kind of stories Tom likes to read. The second sentence is not declarative. After reading this sentence, we do not know what Tom likes to read. Since the second sentence cannot give the reader information, it is *not* a declarative sentence.
Practice	5.6 5.7	Read the following pairs of sentences. Which of the sentences are declarative and why? Are the kittens still for sale? The kittens are all sold. Mr. Jones is very tall. How did Mr. Jones look?
Feedback		In the first pair of sentences the declarative sentence tells us that the kittens are all sold. The other sentence does not tell us whether they are sold or not. Likewise, the declarative sentence tells us that Mr. Jones is very tall, but the other sentence does not provide any clues about how Mr. Jones looks.
Embedded Questions	5.6 5.7	1. What does a declarative sentence do? _____ _____ 2. Which of the following sentences are declarative? Place a *D* beside the declarative ones. _____ a. How did the flowers smell _____ b. Where was Julie going _____ c. The traffic is noisy _____ d. How do you do it _____ e. The sailboat is fun to ride
Information Presentation (Table 8.6)	5.8	Punctuation marks are used to close complete sentences. The period (.) is the punctuation mark that is always used to close a declarative sentence. When you see a period at the end of a sentence, it is a clue that the sentence *may be* a declarative one. Other types of sentences may use a period, but a sentence that (1) conveys information and (2) is closed with a period is always a declarative sentence.

Component	Subskill	Text
Information Presentation	5.9	Here are some declarative sentences that are correctly punctuated. 1. The story is exciting. 2. The bear slinked through the campground. We know the first sentence is declarative because it describes the story and is closed using a period. The second sentence is declarative because it tells what the bear did, and it is closed with a period. If a sentence appears to be declarative because it tells something or describes something, yet the punctuation mark at the end of the sentence is not a period, then the sentence is not a declarative one. Some sentences tell the reader something, and this is a clue that they might be declarative. However, a period is not used to close the sentence. This means that they are *not* declarative. Look at these examples.
Nonexamples		1. He is huge! 2. My shoes are gone! Neither of these sentences is declarative because periods are not used to close them.
Practice	5.8 5.9	Remember, to be a declarative sentence, it must tell the reader something, and it must close with a period. Consider these sentences. Which are declarative? _____ 1. The frost covered the ground! _____ 2. The frost covered the ground. _____ 3. What covered the ground?
Feedback		The first sentence is *not* declarative. Although it tells about frost on the ground, it does not end with a *period*. The second sentence is declarative. It tells about frost on the ground and it ends with a period. The third sentence is *not* declarative because it does not convey information and it does not end with a period.
Embedded Questions	5.8	3. What punctuation mark is used to close a declarative sentence? _____
	5.9	4. Place the *correct punctuation mark* at the end of these sentences. a. The sunset is red and orange _____ b. The snow was piled along the road _____ c. The pond is covered with ice _____
	5.10	5. Which of the following sentences are declarative? Place a *D* beside the declarative ones. _____ a. The poppies were red and orange. _____ b. Did the zebra sound like a horse? _____ c. The zebra sounded like a horse! _____ d. The windows had cobwebs in them. _____ e. I lost my key!

Component	Subskill	Text
Information Presentation	5.11	You can write your own declarative sentences. To write correct declarative sentences, you should write them *to tell or describe something*, and you should always *close them with periods*.
		For each of the topics listed below, a declarative sentence has been written. Write a sentence of your own on each topic that is different from the one shown.
		Topic *Sentence*
Examples and Embedded Test	5.11	Oranges 1. Oranges grow on trees. 2.
		Mother 1. My mother is a teacher. 2.
		School 1. I like to go to school. 2.
		Friends 1. My friends come to my house to play. 2.
		The Ocean 1. Fish live in the ocean. 2.
Embedded Test	5.11	Write four declarative sentences on topics of your own choice. 1. 2. 3. 4.

Answers to embedded questions 5.6, 5.7, 5.8, 5.10, 5.9, and 5.11 (These are not for students during field trials, but may be inserted later in instruction for use as feedback.)		1. A declarative sentence tells us something or conveys information.
		
		 2. ____ a. How did the flowers smell
		    ____ b. Where was Julie going
		    _D_ c. The traffic is noisy
		    ____ d. How do you do it
		    _D_ e. The sailboat is fun to ride
		
		 3. Period
		
		 4. a. The sunset is red and orange.
		    b. The snow was piled along the road.
		    c. The pond is covered with ice.
		
		 5. _D_ a. The poppies were red and orange.
		    ____ b. Did the zebra sound like a horse?
		    ____ c. The zebra sounded like a horse!
		    _D_ d. The windows had cobwebs in them.
		    ____ e. I lost my key!

		Topic *Sentence*

		Oranges 1. Oranges grow on trees.
		            2. Oranges grow in Florida and California.
		 Mother 3. My mother is a teacher.
		          4. Mother goes to practice with me.

Component	Subskill	Text
	School	5. I like to go to school. 6. School can be fun and boring.
	Friends	7. My friends come to my house to play. 8. I play games with my friends.
	The Ocean	9. Fish live in the ocean. 10. The ocean is very deep.

A brief explanation of the sample presentation materials will help illustrate some decisions we made about what information to include and exclude in the first draft. All instruction about interrogative sentences was excluded from the material. Questions were only used in the materials as nonexample declarative sentences in that they did not convey information and they did not close with periods. Information about the purpose and uses for questions will be introduced in the next lesson.

There were no imperative sentences used as nonexamples in the lesson because it would have been impossible to use them without explaining exactly how they were different. This would have involved mixing the third lesson into the first one. The fine distinction between a request closed with a period and a declarative sentence could be taught best in the subsequent lesson on imperative sentences—after students already know about declarative ones.

The only exclamatory sentences used as nonexamples of declarative sentences were those with exclamation points. The differences between declarative and exclamatory sentences in mood and intent will be postponed until the lesson on exclamatory sentences. It would be impossible to teach these distinctions before students have learned about exclamatory sentences as well as declarative ones.

The first lesson on declarative sentences will serve as a building block for subsequent lessons on the other sentence types. The only nonexamples used in the first lesson were those that required gross discriminations.

These examples should illustrate the close relationship between the instructional strategy and the materials to be developed. When a pretest was prescribed, one was developed and placed in the materials at the point predetermined in the lesson activities sequence and cluster. The strategy also called for a pretest theme to evaluate students' skill on the instructional goal at the outset of the unit, so one was developed and inserted into the sequence prior to the first instruction on declarative sentences. Embedded tests were prescribed as well, so they were developed and inserted in the instruction.

You would continue to develop lessons 4, 5, and so forth in the same manner as the first three provided in the example. You might enliven the text portion with humorous stories or illustrations if they fit the context and situation and do not detract from the lesson. For the first three sessions, humor seemed inappropriate and it was difficult to imagine logical, necessary illustrations for these materials. Therefore, they are absent.

We also developed feedback answers for the embedded questions in the instruction. This information would not be used during the field testing phase of the materials development project, but might be useful to students for additional practice and feedback when the materials are converted from the field test to the final versions.

One final component related to the theme pretest should be provided. Table 9.2 contains a rating form that could be used to evaluate either pre-

TABLE 9.2

CHECKLIST TO EVALUATE STORIES

NAME_____

PERIOD_____ DATE_____

TOTAL ERRORS

_____ I. Declarative Sentences
    _____ 1. Number of declarative sentences
    _____ 2. Sentences complete
        _____ a. number of subjects incomplete
        _____ b. number of predicates incomplete
    _____ 3. Number of periods used to close sentences
    _____ 4. Sentence type appropriate for idea/mood conveyed
        _____ a. number appropriate
        _____ b. number inappropriate
    _____ 5. Transition smooth

TOTAL ERRORS

_____ II. Interrogative Sentences
    _____ 1. Number of interrogative sentences
    _____ 2. Sentences complete
        _____ a. number of subjects incomplete
        _____ b. number of predicates incomplete
    _____ 3. Question marks used to close sentences
    _____ 4. Number of questions appropriate to lead reader
    _____ 5. Number of questions appropriate to seek information
    _____ 6. Sentence type appropriate for idea/mood conveyed
        _____ a. number appropriate
        _____ b. number inappropriate
    _____ 7. Transition smooth

TOTAL ERRORS

_____ III. Imperative Sentences
    _____ 1. Number of imperative sentences
    _____ 2. Sentences complete
        _____ a. number of subjects incomplete
        _____ b. number of predicates incomplete
    _____ 3. Number of exclamation points used for strong requests, instructions
    _____ 4. Number of periods used for mild directions, requests
    _____ 5. Sentence type appropriate for idea/mood conveyed
        _____ a. number appropriate
        _____ b. number inappropriate
    _____ 6. Transition smooth

TOTAL ERRORS

_____ IV. Exclamatory Sentences
    _____ 1. Number of exclamatory sentences
    _____ 2. Sentences complete
        _____ a. number of subjects incomplete
        _____ b. number of predicates incomplete
    _____ 3. Number of exclamation points used to close sentences
    _____ 4. Sentence type appropriate for idea/mood conveyed
        _____ a. number appropriate
        _____ b. number inappropriate
    _____ 5. Transition smooth

test or posttest themes. Notice that it is a combination checklist and frequency tally. When student performance is complex, we often need reminders to help us focus on the objectives of the test during grading. This rating form has four separate sections, one for each type of sentence. Although using a performance rating scale is a complex task, the time spent is worthwhile since it helps us eliminate other behaviors that, while important, are not the focus of this unit. If the materials you develop require complex performance, the development of a rating scale, based upon the instructional analysis, will provide you with a valuable guide to assess the performance.

SUMMARY

Resource materials you have for developing your package includes the design of your instruction which is made up of the following:

- Instructional goal
- Instructional analysis

- Behavioral objectives
- Sample test items
- Characteristics of the target students
- Instructional strategy that includes prescriptions for:
  - Cluster and sequence of objectives
  - Preinstructional activities
  - Tests to be used
  - Follow-up activities
  - Information presentation and examples
  - Student practice and feedback
  - Activities from strategy assigned to individual lessons

Begin the development process by first considering the available media for the materials. Review resources, time, experience, durability, and convenience in making the final media selection for your materials.

It is a good idea to keep two of your resources close at hand while writing the materials. The first is the tables that include each subskill, a complete behavioral objective which includes the conditions, and several sample test items. The other critical resource is the instructional strategy documents. Constant reference to these documents while you work will keep your efforts targeted and help avoid introducing interesting—but extraneous—material. Focus carefully on the conditions specified in the objectives.

When you complete this phase of the instructional design, you should have a draft set of instructional materials, draft tests, and draft student manual and/or an instructor's manual.

We need to caution you on one important point: Do not feel that any of the materials you develop on the first attempt will stand for all time. It is extremely important that you consider the materials you develop as draft copies. They will be reviewed and revised based upon feedback from students, instructors, and subject-matter experts. You should not begin engaging in elaborate and expensive production procedures. You should be considering the use of five-by-seven inch cards instead of finely printed materials or slides, the use of crude pictures instead of filmstrips; the use of videotapes instead of films. Delay the development of any mediated materials, particularly ones that will be expensive, until you have completed at least one revision of your materials.

You can be assured that no matter how humble your materials may be at this point, there will be costs associated with them. Try to minimize the costs now in order to gather the data that you will need to make the correct decisions about the final version. We will have more to say about this in succeeding chapters.

PRACTICE

I. Developmental Considerations
  1. List below the four major components of an instructional package.
      a. _____
      b. _____
      c. _____
      d. _____
  2. In question 1, which of the components are intended primarily for the instructor and which are intended primarily for the students?

Instructor:_____

Students:_____

3. What types of information would you be likely to include in an instructional guide intended for students?

    a. _____
    b. _____
    c. _____
    d. _____
    e. _____

4. What types of information would you be likely to include in the instructional materials?

    a. _____
    b. _____
    c. _____
    d. _____
    e. _____

5. What types of materials would you be likely to include in an instructor's guide?

    a. _____
    b. _____
    c. _____
    d. _____

6. What factors are of major importance in deciding the most appropriate media for your lesson?

    a. _____
    b. _____
    c. _____
    d. _____
    e. _____

7. Number from 1 to 4 the following materials to show the order in which you believe you would develop them: ( ) student guide, ( ) instructional materials, ( ) tests, and ( ) instructor's guide. (There is no set answer to this question, but with your developmental project in mind, it is time to give the developmental procedure some thought. This will enable you to collect pertinent information at the proper time.)

II. Developing Instructional Materials

For this exercise, you should practice developing materials based upon the instructional strategy you developed for depositing money into a checking account. The entire instructional strategy appears in the Feedback section of the previous chapter. Because this task is complex, select only the following components to develop:

1. A pretest for objectives 2.1 through 2.10 (III in the Feedback section of Chapter 8).
2. Actual information and presentation materials for objectives 2.1 through 2.10 (III in Feedback section of Chapter 8). Embedded test items are prescribed in the strategy.

You may like the instructional strategy that you developed for depositing money better than the example we provided in the last chapter. If this is the case, use your original strategy rather than ours to develop materials.

It may help you to use the script format we used earlier to develop your material. Simply divide a sheet of paper into three sections and label each component and objective as you work.

Component	Subskills	Text

This format will help keep you on track. Of course you would not use this format when field testing your own instruction. The first two columns would be omitted. Compare your materials with our examples in the Feedback section that follows.

FEEDBACK

I. Developmental Considerations
   1. The four major components of an instructional package are:
      - Student guide or syllabus
      - Instructional materials
      - Tests
      - Instructor's guide
   2. Components intended for students are the student guide and the instructional materials. The component intended for instructors is the instructor's guide. The tests may be intended for use in evaluating students' performance or for students' use if included in a self-instructional, self-evaluation program. They fit into the category of being intended for both instructors and students.
   3. The contents of the student guide will vary according to your instructional materials, your purpose, your needs, and your target population. Information you may want to consider includes:
      - Behaviorally stated objectives
      - Overview
      - Motivational materials (historical, why do this anyway, overall goals, etc.)
      - Directions on how to use the instructional materials, any equipment needed, tests to be taken, and self-scoring procedures
      - Other references for remediation and enrichment
      - Work schedules (what should be completed at what time)
      - Elaborations on any products or projects to be completed by students
   4. Types of information you are likely to include in the instructional materials are:
      - Information that must be presented to students to enable them to achieve your objectives. This may include objectives and review materials as well as motivational materials and activities.
      - Examples and nonexamples of information, concepts, or skills that need to be learned.
      - Performance activities that enable students to practice or to try out the concept or skills for themselves.
      - Feedback on students' performance that enables them to reconsider their ideas or adjust their techniques.
      - Follow-through instructions telling students what to do next.
   5. Types of materials you may want to include in an instructor's guide are:
      - Information about the target population for the materials.

- Suggestions on how to adapt materials for older, younger, brighter, or slower students.
- Overview of the content.
- Intended learning outcomes of the instruction.
- Suggestions for using the materials in a certain context or sequence.
- Suggestions for materials management for individualized learning, small-group learning, learning-center activities, or classroom activities.
- Enrichment or remedial activities.
- Tests that can be used to evaluate students' performance on terminal objectives.
- Evidence of the effectiveness of the materials when used as suggested with the intended target populations.
- Suggestions for evaluating students' work and reporting progress.
- Estimation of time required to use the materials properly.
- Equipment or additional facilities needed for the materials.

6. Major factors for deciding the most appropriate medium for an instructional module or unit are:
   - Type of learning expressed in the objective.
   - Availability of equipment and facilities for certain media.
   - Technical skills of the designer in designing materials for a specified medium.
   - Flexibility, durability, and convenience of the materials using a specified medium.
   - Cost-effectiveness of a particular medium over the long run. It may be more expensive to develop some media than others (computer-managed instruction or videotape), but the costs of instruction using some other media over a period of time may defray developmental expenses and make it cheaper in the long run. In addition, a person on a videotape can repeat a lesson enthusiastically twenty-five times in one day. Few teachers could match that enthusiasm or energy.

7. A rigid pattern of development for the four components of the instruction—the student guide, instructional materials, tests, and instructor's guide—does not exist. The following order of events may serve as an example of how you might proceed. Constraints on your time, materials, and resources may cause you to deviate. The suggested order of development remains the same whether developing an instructional strategy, a unit of instruction, or a whole course:
   - Tests
   - Instructional materials
   - Students' guide
   - Instructor's guide

II. Materials for checking account unit

Component	Subskill	Text
Pretest		Score_____ Name_____ Date _____ Period_____
		Depositing Money in a Checking Account
	2.1	1. List the places where you can obtain a deposit slip to deposit money into a checking account.

Component	Subskill	Text
		a. _____ b. _____
	2.2	2. If the deposit slip you use is not printed specifically for your checking account, what information should you add to it so that banks can identify it as yours? a. _____ b. _____ c. _____
Pretest	2.3.1 2.3.2 2.4.2 2.4.3 2.4.4 2.4.5 2.6	3. Use the descriptions of money and checks in Table 1 to complete the sample deposit slip provided in Table 2. Both sides of the deposit form are illustrated. Place the correct information in the appropriate space on the deposit slip. No money is to be returned during the transaction.

TABLE 1

COINS		BILLS		CHECKS	
Number	Coin	Number	Bill	Bank #	Amount
5	50¢	14	$100.	63-656	$145.20
8	25¢	12	50.	12-402	235.00
9	10¢	8	20.	13-320	500.00
3	5¢	4	10.	63-656	25.00
6	1¢	3	0.	17-402	650.00
				19-200	892.00
				16-420	200.00
Your account number is 4023161020.				13-920	100.00

TABLE 2
Front Side of Deposit Slip

	CURRENCY		
	COIN		
Name	C ___		
	H ___		
	E ___		
	C ___		
Address	K ___		
	S		
Date ___	Total from other side		
	TOTAL		
	Less Cash Received		
Sign here only if cash received from deposit	Total Deposit		

Component	Subskill	Text
Pretest		*Back Side of Deposit Slip*

Please list each check separately by Financial Institution Number		Dollars	Cents
Checks by Financial Institution			
TOTAL Enter on front side			

Component	Subskill	Text
	2.7	4. To whom should you give a deposit slip, checks, and/or money?
	2.8 2.9	5. When a deposit receipt is returned to you, what should you do with it? a. ___ b. ___
	2.10	6. What should you do with cash returned by the teller during a deposit transaction?

Component	Subskill	Text
Information Presentation	2.1	After you have opened a checking account, you will want to continue to deposit money in it. Banks have specially printed forms you should use to deposit your money. One type of deposit form is provided along with your checks. It has your name, your address, and your account number printed on it. It is wise to use these printed slips because it helps insure that your money is credited to the appropriate account.
Information Presentation	2.2	Sometimes you may need to deposit money into your account when you do not have your personalized deposit forms with you.

Component	Subskill	Text
Example	2.1 2.2	For this purpose, banks have general deposit slips that can be used by any of their customers. These forms may be obtained in the bank lobby or in the automatic teller machine. Before using these deposit slips, you should always print your name as it appears on your account in the appropriate space. You should also print the number of your checking account in the boxes provided for the account number. Failure to provide this identifying information on general deposit slips will result in delays and possibly errors because the bank will not know where to put the money you have deposited. The following form is a personalized checking account deposit slip. Notice the name of the customer is printed in the upper left corner (A), and the checking account number is located in the bottom center of the form (B). There is also a line provided where you can write the date when the money is deposited (C). It is a good idea to always put the date on your deposit tickets to help identify them.

(A) Sara Jones		63-656
302 Shadow Lane		631
Tampa, Florida 33617		

(C) Date_____	Currency	
	Coins	
	C	
	H	
	E	
	C	
	K	
	S	
	Total from other side	
_____	TOTAL	
Sign here only if cash	Less cash received	
received from deposit	Total Deposit	

(B) 6401121010

Component	Subskill	Text
Information	2.3.1	After obtaining a deposit slip and ensuring that your name, your account number, and the date are recorded, you are ready to enter the amount of money you wish to deposit into your account. Three different forms of money can be deposited into your account: dollar bills, coins, and checks. There is a separate space on the deposit slip for each. It is a good idea to separate the kinds of money you wish to deposit. Make one pile of bills, one pile of coins, and another pile of checks.
Example	2.3.1	Locate on the deposit slip where you are to record each type of money. Dollar bills are recorded on the line marked "currency," and coins are entered on the line marked "coins."

Component	Subskill	Text

* Currency		
* Coins		
C		
H		
E		
C		
K		
S		
Total from other side		
TOTAL		

Information   **2.3.2**

Add together all the bills you wish to deposit, and record the total amount on the "currency" line. For example, if you have two fifty-dollar bills and three ten-dollar bills, what would you enter? Since these bills total $130, you would write this amount on the currency line.

The second step is to record the total amount of coins you wish to deposit. Sum the coins you have, locate the line marked "coins" and enter the total on that line. If you have two half dollars, two quarters, and five nickels, what would you write on the coin line?

Example

$$
\begin{aligned}
2 \times .50 &= 1.00 \\
2 \times .25 &= .50 \\
5 = .05 &= .25 \\
\hline
&\$1.75
\end{aligned}
$$

→ Currency	130	00
→ Coins	1	75

Information   **2.4.1**

You should prepare the checks you wish to deposit into your account. Each check to be deposited should be signed on the back using the *name* and signature you have registered on your signature card. After signing your name, you should record your *account number* beneath your name. This will help if your checks become separated from your deposit slip during bookkeeping.

Back Side of Check

Example

For deposit only
Ann Jones
402316 1020

Component	Subskill	Text
Information	2.4.2	You are now ready to enter the checks on the deposit slip. Each check should be listed separately in spaces provided for checks, and the amount of the check as well as the bank number should be written on the deposit slip. The bank number should be recorded on the left side of the line, and the amount of the check should be written on the right side. The first step is to locate the bank number on the check. It is usually located on the upper right corner of the check, above the date. The bank number is the top one in a set of two numbers. The sample check illustrates the bank number and its location.

Sara Jones
402 Shadow Lane

400 ◄── check number

$\frac{63\text{-}656}{631}$ ◄── bank number

Date _____

Pay to the order of __*Mary Jones*__ $ *40.⁰⁰*

Forty and no/100 _____ Dollars

Sara Jones

4023010201 ──► account number

Notice the number $\frac{63\text{-}656}{631}$ on the sample check. The top number of this set identifies the bank. The amount of the check and the identifying bank number would be recorded on the deposit slip.

Each check you wish to deposit should have the identifying number of the issuing bank and the total amount of the check recorded.

			Dollars	Cents
		Currency	130	00
		Coin	1	75
	C H E C K S	63-656	40	00
		____		
		____		
		____		

| Information | 2.4.4 | If you have more checks to deposit than will fit on the front side, then turn over the deposit slip. There is room on the reverse side of the slip to list additional checks you wish to deposit. To complete this side of the deposit form, simply list the identifying number of the issuing bank and the amount of each check. The |

(Component column entries: Information 2.4.2, Example 2.4.2, Example 2.4.3, Information 2.4.3, Information 2.4.4)

Component	Subskill	Text
Example	2.4.4	checks included on the back side of a deposit slip are totaled and the sum is written on the "total" line provided at the bottom of the list. This total is then entered on the front side of the slip. The sample reverse-side of a deposit ticket illustrates how it should be completed.

Please list each check separately by financial institution

Financial Institution	Dollars	Cents
42-301	100	00
24-206	5	00
13-925	43	00
63-402	50	00
Total (enter on front side)	198	00

Component	Subskill	Text
Information	2.4.5	With all the cash and the checks you wish to deposit entered on the deposit ticket, you are ready to total the deposit. Remember to write the total amount of checks listed on the back side of the deposit slip on the front in the space labeled "Total from other side." Add together the amount of money listed on the front of the form, and record the sum on the line marked "TOTAL." The following illustration shows a deposit slip completed to this point.

Sara Jones
402 Shadow Lane

Date _____

_____

	Dollars	Cents
Currency	130	00
Coin	1	75
CHECKS 63-656	40	00
42-301	300	25
12-924	402	16
Total from other side	198	00
TOTAL	1072	16
Less Cash Received		
Total Deposit		

6401121010

Component	Subskill	Text
Embedded Test	2.3.1 2.3.2 2.4.1	Given the following dollars, coins, and checks in column A, fill out the sample deposit slip in column B. Use both sides of the deposit slip.

Component	Subskill	Text

	2.4.2	
	2.4.3	
	2.4.4	
	2.4.5	

A

Bills:

  3 × $100.00 =
  2 × $ 20.00 =
  1 × $ 5.00 = _____

Coins:

  4 × $.25 =
  3 × $.10 =
  2 × $.05 =
  7 × $.01 = _____

Checks:

  24-102 $32.00
  16-904 12.00
  52-129   5.00
  32-926 15.00
  40-524 26.00
  13-240 80.00
  52-160 95.00

B

FRONT SIDE OF SLIP

	Dollars	Cents
Currency		
Coins		
C		
H		
E		
C		
K		
S		
Total from other side		
TOTAL		

BACK SIDE OF SLIP

Bank Number	Dollars	Cents
TOTAL CHECKS		

Component	Subskill	Text
Information	2.5.1	

Sometimes you only have checks to deposit rather than a combination of cash and checks. When this is the case, you simply

Component	Subskill	Text
Information	2.5.2	sum the checks and enter the amount in the total column as you did previously when cash was involved.
		It is possible to receive cash from a transaction when only checks are deposited. For example, you may have $100 worth of checks; you want to deposit $80 and have $20 returned to you in cash. You do not need to deposit the check and then write a personal check to obtain $20 in cash. On the front of the deposit slip there is a line marked "less cash received." You simply write the amount of cash you wish to receive back from the checks on that line.
	2.5.3 2.6	After you have entered the amount of cash you wish returned to you on the line, you simply subtract that amount from the total amount of checks you have listed on the deposit slip. This operation is illustrated in the following example. The remainder is the total amount of the deposit, and it should be recorded on the "total deposit" line.
Example	2.5.1 2.5.2 2.5.3 2.6	

			Dollars	Cents
Mary Jones 302 Shadow Lane				
Date _____	Currency			
	Coins			
	C H	42-134	100	00
	E C			
	K			
	S			
	Total from other side			
_____	TOTAL		100	00
Sign here only if cash received from deposit	Less cash received		20	00
	TOTAL DEPOSIT		80	00

5049061432

Component	Subskill	Text
Information	2.5.4	When you have cash returned from a deposit transaction, you must sign the deposit slip to verify that you have received cash. This signature provides the bank with your acknowledgment that you did not deposit the total amount of checks, but rather, you received the indicated amount of cash. There is a special space on the deposit slip for your signature. In the sample deposit slip it is identified by an arrow.

Component	Subskill	Text

Example — 2.5.4

Name _____		Dollars	Cents
_____			
Date _____	Currency		
	Coins		
C H E C K S 42-134		100	00
Sign here only if cash received from deposit	Total from other side		
	TOTAL	100	00
	Less cash received	20	00
	TOTAL DEPOSIT	80	00

4029614041

Information — 2.7

After you have prepared your deposit slip and checks for deposit, you are ready to give them to the teller. This can be done either in the bank lobby, at a drive-through window at the bank, or by using an automatic teller at the bank or at a remote site in a grocery store or shopping plaza. Some remote sites cannot return cash as part of the deposit transaction. It is also possible to deposit by mail using a special envelope provided by the bank. Again, you cannot receive money back from the deposit transaction if you choose to use the mail service.

Information — 2.8, 2.9

As a result of the deposit transaction, you will receive a deposit receipt from the bank. Immediately upon receiving it, you should check to see that the amount recorded on the receipt by the bank corresponds to the total amount of your deposit. After you have determined that the totals match, you should place the receipt in your bank records for future reference.

Example — 2.8

Sunshine State Bank
Deposit Receipt

May 4 1985 $80.00
Account: 5049061432

Component	Subskill	Text
Information	2.10	If you receive cash as part of the deposit transaction, you should immediately count the cash before leaving the teller's window. If you leave the window, or the bank, and return later to report the amount of cash is incorrect, there is room for doubt about whether you actually received the cash. Therefore, before fiddling with your purse or wallet, count the cash immediately. If you find an error, the teller will be more likely to believe that it occurred during the transaction.
Embedded Test	2.5.1 2.5.2 2.5.3 2.5.4 2.6	Complete the sample deposit slip to correspond to the transaction described below.

1. Deposit the following checks:

42-341	$50.00
39-243	25.00
36-192	10.00

2. Obtain $5.00 in cash during the transaction. Your account number is 4392061050

Name_____		Dollars	Cents
Date_____	Currency		
	Coins		
	C		
	H		
	E		
	C		
	K		
	S		
_____ Sign here only if cash received from deposit	Total from other side		
	TOTAL		
	Less cash received		
	TOTAL DEPOSIT		

References and Recommended Readings

Briggs, L. J. (1970). *Handbook of procedures for the design of instruction.* Pittsburgh, PA: American Institutes for Research, 93–162. The author provides a detailed procedure, with examples, for selecting appropriate media for learning outcomes.

Gagné, R. M., & Driscoll, M. P. (1988). *Essentials of learning for instruction.* (2nd ed.) Hinsdale, IL: Dryden Press, 71–96. The conditions of learning are related to the types of learning outcomes desired.

Gagné, R. M., Wager, W., & Rojas, A. (1981). Planning and authoring computer-assisted instruction lessons. *Educational Technology,* 21 (9), 17–26. In this article the authors provide specific examples of procedures which could be employed with CAI to present the events of instruction for various types of learning outcomes.

Johnson, S. R., & Johnson, R. B. (1970). *Developing individualized instructional material.* Palo Alto, CA: Westinghouse Learning Press.

Reiser, R. A., & Gagné, R. M. (1983). *Selecting media for instruction.* Englewood Cliffs, N.J.: Educational Technology Publications. This book describes an easy-to-use media selection method which is based upon the domains of learning.

Russell, J. D. (1974). *Modular instruction.* Minneapolis: Burgess Publishing Co. This volume, and the one by Johnson and Johnson, outline procedures which should be used in the systematic design of instruction. They present an orientation that differs somewhat from ours.

10
DESIGNING AND CONDUCTING FORMATIVE EVALUATIONS

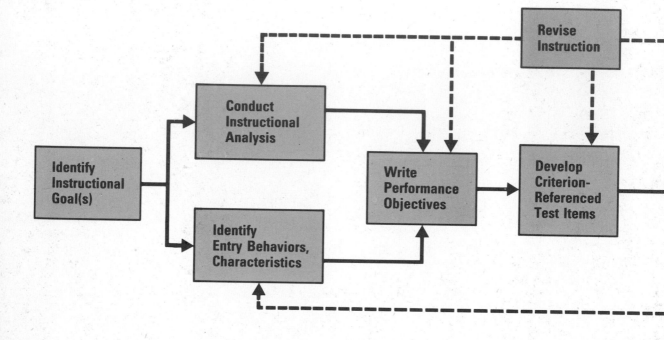

OBJECTIVES

- Describe the purposes for and various stages of formative evaluation of instructor-developed materials, instructor-selected materials, and instructor-presented instruction.
- Describe the instruments used in a formative evaluation.
- Develop an appropriate formative evaluation plan and construct instruments for a set of instructional materials or an instructor presentation.
- Collect data according to a formative evaluation plan for a given set of instructional materials or instructor presentation.

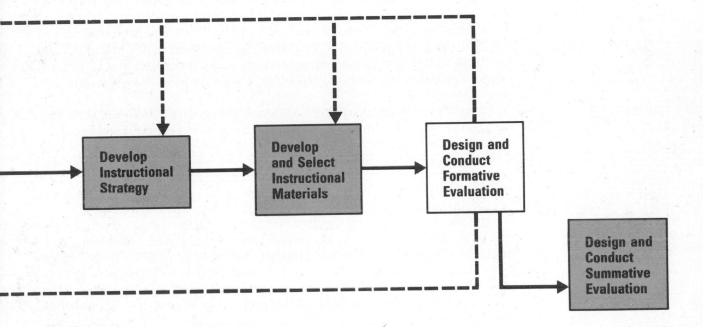

BACKGROUND

If you had been developing instructional materials twenty years ago, it is likely that your initial draft of those materials would have been put into final production and distributed to the target population. As a consequence, it was almost certain that many problems would occur in the classroom due to the limited effectiveness of first draft instructional materials. Too often instructors have been blamed for poor teaching and students for poor learning when, in fact, the materials were not sufficient to support the instructional effort.

The problem of untested materials was magnified in the 1960s with the advent of large curriculum development projects. At that time the concept of "evaluation" tended to be defined as the determination of the effectiveness of an innovation as compared with other existing products. When such studies were carried out, researchers often found a relatively low level of student achievement with the new curriculum materials. In reviewing this situation, Cronbach and Scriven concluded that we must expand our concept of evaluation. They proposed that developers conduct what has come to be called *formative evaluation*—the collection of data and information during the development of instruction which can be used to improve the effectiveness of the instruction.

Recent studies have shown that thousands of the instructional products sold in the United States each year have not been evaluated with students and revised prior to distribution. Other studies have demonstrated that simply trying out materials with a single-learner and revising the materials on the basis of that data can make a significant difference in the effectiveness of materials. Therefore, this component of the instructional design model emphasizes the necessity of gathering data from members of the target population about the effectiveness of materials and using that information to make the materials even more effective.

You should note that all of the design and development steps in the instructional design process are based upon theory, research, and some common sense. At this point, you are about to become an evaluator as you collect data about the effectiveness of your own instructional materials. By following the instructional design model, you have, in essence, generated instructional materials that will produce learning gains for students who initially cannot perform your terminal objective. You are now at the point of testing that assumption.

A rather arbitrary division of content has been made between this chapter and the next. We typically think about formative evaluation and revision of instructional materials as one major step. However, for the sake of clarity and to emphasize the importance of re-examining the whole instructional design process when instructional materials are to be revised, we have separated the design and conduct of the formative evaluation study from the process of revising the instructional materials.

In this chapter we will discuss how to apply formative evaluation techniques to newly-developed materials, to selected and adapted materials, to instructor-delivered instruction, and to combinations of these three presentation modes. We will also show how to apply these techniques to instructional procedures as well as to instructional materials to ensure that instruction, regardless of the presentation mode, is properly implemented and managed.

CONCEPTS

The major concept underlying this chapter is formative evaluation. Formative evaluation is the process instructors use to obtain data in order to revise their instruction to make it more efficient and effective. The emphasis in formative evaluation is on the collection and analysis of data and the revision of the instructional materials. When a final version of the instruction is produced, other evaluators may collect data to determine its effectiveness. This latter type of evaluation is often referred to as *summative evaluation*. It is summative in that this instruction is now in its final form, and it is appropriate to compare it with other similar forms of instruction.

There are three basic phases of formative evaluation. The first is one-to-one or clinical evaluation. In this initial phase the designer works with individual students to obtain data to revise the materials. The second stage of formative evaluation is a small-group evaluation. A group of eight to twenty students who are representative of the target population study the materials on their own and are tested to collect the required data. The third stage of formative evaluation is usually a field trial. The number of students is not of particular consequence; often thirty are sufficient. The emphasis in the field trial is on the testing of the procedures required for the installation of the instruction in a situation as close to the "real world" as possible.

The three phases of formative evaluation are typically preceded by the review of instruction by interested specialists who are not directly involved in the instructional development project, but have relevant expertise. The role of these reviewers is described, followed by descriptions of the three student-oriented phases of formative evaluation.

Role of Subject Matter and Learner Specialists in Formative Evaluation

While the focus of the formative evaluation process is on the acquisition of data from learners, it is also important to have the instruction reviewed by specialists. It is assumed that the designer is knowledgeable about the content area or is working with a content specialist, and is also knowledgeable about the target population. Still, there are several good reasons to have the instruction reviewed by outside specialists.

When the first draft of the instruction has been written, there tends to be the old "forest and trees" problem. The designer has seen so much that he or she cannot see anything. It is invaluable to the designer to get others to review what has been developed. One type of reviewer is usually a person outside the project who has special expertise in the content area of the instruction. This subject matter expert (SME) should comment on the accuracy and currency of the instruction. Although many suggestions for improvement may be received, the designer should give considerable thought to making any changes that are counter to the instructional strategy already developed. Another type of reviewer is a specialist in the type of learning outcome involved. This evaluator should comment on your instructional strategy related to what is known about enhancing that particular type of learning. Because these specialists are rare, a colleague familiar with the suggestions for instruction related to the type of learning may be able to provide useful insights about your materials.

It is also helpful to share the first draft of the instruction with a person who is familiar with the target population—a person who can look at the instruction through the target population's eyes and react.

The designer is not obligated to incorporate the suggestions of these specialists into the instruction. There may be some recommendations that the designer may want to consider after data from students have been collected and summarized. At least the designer is sensitized to potential problems before students become involved in the formative evaluation process.

One-to-One Evaluation

In our discussion of the three phases of formative evaluation, we will assume that the designer has developed original instruction. In subsequent sections we will discuss the differences in procedures when existing materials are used, or when instructor-led instruction has been created.

The purpose of the first stage of formative evaluation, the one-to-one stage, is to identify and remove the most obvious errors in the instruction, and to obtain initial reactions to the content from learners. This is accomplished through direct interaction between the designer and individual learners. During this stage, the designer works individually with three or more learners who are representative of the target population.

Both the tests and the instructional materials are used with the learners. The designer picks at least one learner from the target population who is slightly above average in ability, one who is average, and at least one learner who is below average, and works on an individual basis with each. After these evaluations the designer may wish to select more learners from the target population to work in a one-to-one mode, although three is the usual number of learners to use.

The typical procedure in a one-to-one evaluation is to explain to the learner that a new set of instructional materials has been designed and that you would like his or her reaction to them. You should say that any mistakes that learners might make are probably due to deficiencies in the material and not theirs. Encourage the learners to be relaxed and to talk about the materials. You should not only have the learners go through the materials, but also have them take the test(s) provided with the materials. You might also note the amount of time it takes a learner to complete the material.

Instructional designers have found this process invaluable in the preparation of materials. When learners use the materials in this manner, they find typographical errors, omissions of content, missing pages, graphs that are improperly labeled, and other kinds of mechanical difficulties that inevitably occur. Learners often are able to describe difficulties that they have with the learning sequence and the concepts being taught. They can critique the tests in terms of whether they think they measure your objectives. You can use all of this information to revise your materials and tests and correct relatively gross problems as well as small errors.

In contrast to the earlier stages of instructional design, which emphasize the analytical skills of the designer, the one-to-one formative evaluation is almost totally dependent upon the ability of the designer to establish rapport with the learner and then to interact effectively. The learner has typically never been asked to critique instruction; the assumption is made that if learning does not occur, it is the student's fault. This is a real role reversal, and the learners must be convinced that it is legitimate to be critical of what is presented to them. This is sometimes particularly difficult for the young person who is being asked to criticize an authority figure. Therefore, the designer must establish an atmosphere of acceptance and support for any negative comments from the learner.

The second critical hallmark of the one-to-one approach is that it is an *interactive* process. The power of the process is greatly diminished if the designer hands the instruction to the learner and says, "Here, read this and let me know if you have any problems." Instead, the designer should read along with the learner and, at predetermined points, discuss with the learner what has been presented in the text. The dialogue may focus on the answers to practice questions or to embedded test items, or may be a consideration of special points made in the information presentation. Before each one-to-one session, the designer should formulate a strategy about how the interaction will take place, and how the learner will know when it is appropriate to talk with the evaluator.

It is clear that a one-to-one session can take place with only one learner at a time. Doing it with two or more reduces the effectiveness of the process. As the designer proceeds with the evaluation, it is necessary to note the comments and suggestions made by the learner as well as any alternative explanations made by the designer that seem effective. These can be noted on one copy of the instruction, or a tape recorder can be used during the session, which students seem to adapt to quite readily.

After the students in the one-to-one trials have completed the instruction, they should review the posttest and attitude questionnaire in the same fashion. After each item or step in the assessment, ask the learners why they made the particular responses that they did. This will help you spot not only mistakes, but the reasons for the mistakes. This information can be quite helpful during the revision process. You will also find that there will be test items that appeared to be perfectly clear to you but are totally misinterpreted by the learner. If these faulty items remain in the assessment for the small-group evaluation, there will be major problems in determining if only those items or the entire instruction was defective. Exert as much care in evaluating your assessment instruments as you do the instruction itself.

One of the interests of the designer during the one-to-one evaluation is to determine the amount of time required for learners to complete their instruction. Only a very rough estimate can be obtained from the one-to-one evaluation because of the inclusion of the interaction between the learner and the designer. You can attempt to subtract a certain percentage of the time from the total time, but experience has indicated that such estimates can be quite inaccurate.

One final comment about the one-to-one evaluation process is in order. Rarely are learners placed in such a vulnerable position and required to expose their ignorance. Even with adults, there will be occasions when they must admit that they do not know the meaning of a fairly common word — they always meant to look it up in the dictionary, but forgot. In the one-to-one stage, the designer is in control and thus has the responsibility for providing a comfortable working situation. What the learners may reveal about their current state of knowledge may be deplorable to the evaluator, but it may also be a fact that some of the instruction is deplorable to the learner. Every possible effort should be made to be both objective about the instruction and supportive of the learner. Without the learner, there is no formative evaluation.

Small-Group Evaluation

There are two primary purposes for the small-group evaluation. The first is to determine the effectiveness of changes made following the one-to-one evaluation and to identify any remaining learning problems that students may have. The second purpose is to determine if learners can use the instruction without interaction with the instructor.

After you have revised the materials on the basis of information obtained from the one-to-one evaluation, you should next select a group of approximately eight to twenty learners from the small-group evaluation. If the number of learners is fewer than eight, then the data you obtain will probably not be representative of the target population. On the other hand, if you obtain data on many more than twenty learners, you will find that you have more information than you need, and that the data from additional learners does not provide you with a great deal of additional information.

The selection of learners to participate in your small-group trial is a very important procedure. The learners who evaluate the materials should be as representative of your target population as possible. In an ideal research setting, you would select the learners randomly, which would enable you to apply your findings generally to the entire target population. In typical school, industrial, and adult education settings, however, true randomization is often impossible, and perhaps not even desirable.

When you cannot select your learners at random, or when the group you have available to draw from is relatively small, you want to ensure that you include in your sample at least one representative of each type of subgroup that exists in your population. Examples of such subgroups might include the following:

- Low, average, and high achieving students
- Learners with various native languages
- Learners who are familiar with a particular procedure, such as computerized instruction, and learners who are not
- Males and females
- Younger or inexperienced learners as well as more mature learners

When your target group is homogeneous, these subgroups are not a problem. When the target population is made up of persons with varied skills and backgrounds, the designer should consider including representatives of each group in the small-group sample. For example, it is almost impossible to predict how a low-achieving learner will perform on your materials based on the observed efforts of a high achieving learner. By selecting a representative sample, you will be able to be more insightful about changes you may need to make in your instruction.

Small-group participants are sometimes a biased sample because they consist of people who willingly participate in the group instead of being people who truly are a representative group. The instructor must be aware of this problem and obtain the most representative group possible, considering all the constraints usually present in obtaining participants for small-group trials.

It is also important to note that while this stage is referred to as *small-group evaluation*, the term refers to the number of learners and not the setting in which the learners actually use the materials. For example, if your materials are intended for individual use at home or on the job, then you would attempt to obtain eight to twenty learners who would use your materials in these settings. It is not necessary to get all the learners together in one room at one time to conduct a small-group evaluation.

The basic procedures used in a small-group evaluation differ sharply from those used in a one-to-one. The evaluator (or the instructor) begins by explaining that the materials are in the formative stage of development and that it is necessary to obtain feedback on how they may be improved. Having said this, the instructor then administers the materials in the manner in which they are intended to be used when they are in final form. If a pretest is to be used, it should also be given. The instructor should intervene as little as possible in the process. Only in those cases when equipment fails, or when a learner becomes bogged down in the learning process and cannot continue, should the instructor intervene. Each learner's difficulty and the solution should certainly be noted as part of the revision data.

Additional steps in small-group evaluation are the administration of an attitude questionnaire and, if possible, in-depth debriefings with some of the learners in the group. The primary purpose for obtaining learner reactions to the instruction, in addition to those obtained from the embedded attitude questions, is to identify, from their perceptions, weaknesses and strengths in the implementation of the instructional strategy. Therefore, the questions should reflect various components of the strategy. The following questions would usually be appropriate:

- Was the instruction interesting?
- Did you understand what you were supposed to learn?
- Were the materials directly related to the objectives?
- Were sufficient practice exercises included?
- Were the practice exercises relevant?
- Did the tests really measure your performance on the objectives?
- Did you receive sufficient feedback on your practice exercises?
- Did you receive sufficient feedback on your test results?
- Did you feel confident when answering questions on the tests?

These questions might be included in an attitude questionnaire, and then pursued at some depth in a discussion with learners. By using questions directed at components of the instructional strategy, such as those described above, it is possible to relate the learners' responses directly to particular components of the instructional materials or procedures. In the discussion with the learners after the materials have been completed, the instructor can ask questions about such features as the pacing, interest, and difficulty of the materials.

All data from these various sources are summarized and decisions are made as to how to revise the materials. In the next chapter, we will show you how to summarize these data and determine the implications they have for the revision process. In this chapter, we have focused our concern on the formative evaluation study and the collection of data.

Field Trial

In the final stage of formative evaluation the instructor attempts to use a learning situation that closely resembles that intended for the ultimate use of the instructional materials. The purpose of this final stage of formative evaluation is to determine if the changes in the instruction made after the small-group stage were effective, and if the instruction can be used in the environment for which it was intended—that is, is it administratively possible to use the instruction in its intended setting?

In order to answer these questions, all materials, including the tests and the instructor's manual, should be revised and ready to go. If an instructor is involved in implementing the instruction, the designer should not play this role.

In picking the site for a field evaluation, you are likely to encounter one of two situations. First, if the material is tried out in a class that is presently using large-group, lockstep pacing, then using self-instructional materials may be a very new and different experience for the learners. It will be important to lay the groundwork for the new procedure by explaining to the learners how the materials are to be used and how they differ from their usual instruction. In all likelihood you will obtain an increase in interest, if not in performance, simply because of the break in the typical classroom instructional pattern. Second, if the materials are tried out in an individualized class, it may be quite difficult to find a large enough group of learners who are ready for your instructional materials because learners will be "spread out" in the materials they are studying.

You should identify a group of about thirty individuals to participate in your field trial. Again, the group should be selected to ensure that it is representative of the target population for which the materials are intended. Because a "typical" group is sometimes hard to locate, designers often select several different groups to participate in the field trial. This ensures that data will be collected under all intended conditions such as an open classroom, traditional instruction, and learning centers.

There is a second aspect to the selection of the site of the field trial that is especially important. Proximity to the work site where the skills are ultimately to be performed is desirable. If possible, the formative evaluation should be extended beyond the classroom and into the setting where the skills and knowledge will be used. It is then possible to determine if the skills are being used, how well, and with what impact. While this situation would not be typical for public school or collegiate instruction, it is vitally important to vocational or business training. The designer should take the responsibility for observing on-site use of the skills that were taught, and use this information when necessary to revise the training program.

FORMATIVE EVALUATION OF SELECTED MATERIALS

The three phases of formative evaluation previously described are not totally applicable when the instructor has selected existing materials to try with a group of learners. The kinds of editorial and content changes that are made as a result of one-to-one and small-group evaluations are typically not used when one uses existing materials. These procedures are avoided not because they would be unproductive in improving the instruction, but because in reality the instructor who selects existing materials seldom has the time or resources to conduct these phases. Therefore, the instructor should proceed directly to a field trial with a group of learners. The primary purpose of formative evaluation with existing materials is to determine whether they are effective with a particular population or in a specific setting, and to identify ways in which additions to and/or deletions from the materials or changes in instructional procedures might be made to improve the effectiveness of the materials. Therefore, the formative evaluation procedures for selected materials most nearly resemble those in a field trial.

Preparations for the field trial of existing materials should be made as they would be for a field trial of original materials. An analysis should be made of existing documentation on the development of the materials, the effectiveness of the materials with defined groups, and particularly any description of procedures used during field evaluations. Descriptions of how materials are to be used should be studied, any test instruments that accompany the materials should be examined for their relationship to the performance objectives, and the need for any additional evaluations or attitude questionnaires determined.

In the field trial study, the regular instructor should administer the pretest unless he or she knows that learners already have the entry behaviors and lack knowledge of what is to be taught. A posttest and an attitude questionnaire should certainly be available to evaluate students' performance and their opinions of the materials.

The instructor who conducts a field trial is able to observe the progress and attitudes of learners using a set of adopted or adapted materials. It is even possible to examine the performance of different groups of learners using modified or unmodified materials to determine whether the changes increased the effectiveness of the materials. The instructor should certainly take the time following the field evaluation to thoroughly debrief the learners on their reactions to the instruction because additional insights about the materials or procedures can be gained during such debriefing sessions. After completing a field trial of selected materials, the instructor should have collected approximately the same types of data that would have been collected if original materials were being formatively evaluated.

FORMATIVE EVALUATION OF INSTRUCTOR-PRESENTED INSTRUCTION

If the instructor plans to deliver the instruction to a group of students according to an instructional strategy and a set of lecture notes, the purposes of formative evaluations are much the same as they are for the formative evaluation of independent instructional materials: to determine whether the instruction is effective and how to improve it. Once again, the formative evaluation of an instructional plan most nearly approximates that of the field trial phase for instructional materials. In all likelihood, there will be little time for a one-to-one or even a small-group evaluation of a total lesson plan.

In preparing for a field trial of instructor-presented instruction, the instructor should be concerned with the entry behaviors and prior knowledge, the posttest knowledge, and the attitudes of learners. In addition, the instructor is in a unique position to provide interactive practice and feedback. Interactive practice and feedback should be included in the instructional plan, because it will provide students with the opportunity to demonstrate specific skills they have acquired. These sessions also serve to identify those skills not yet acquired. This form of in-progress practice and assessment may be administered in one of two formats. The instructor may deliver it orally to a variety of learners and keep notes on learners' performance, or the instructor may periodically distribute various printed practice and feedback exercises during the lesson. This latter approach provides concrete evidence of the learners' learning progress.

The instructor can also use the field trial as an opportunity to evaluate the instructional procedures. Observation of the instructional process should indicate the suitability of grouping patterns, time allocations, and learner interest in various class activities.

Many instructors already use these types of formative evaluation in their instruction. Our point is to stress the thorough and systematic use of these techniques to collect and analyze data in order to revise the lesson plan. To identify weak points in the lesson plan, and to provide clues to their correction, in-progress data can be compared to results obtained with the posttest, attitude questionnaire, and students' comments during debriefing sessions.

Very often, the field testing of selected materials and the field testing of instructor-presented instruction are interwoven. Frequently the use of selected materials will require an interactive role for the instructor and, likewise, the implementation of an instructional strategy may well involve the use of some prepared instructional materials. Therefore, under either of these circumstances, approximately the same types of field evaluation procedures should be employed and similar types of revisions carried out.

DATA COLLECTION

What frame of reference can you use to design the formative evaluation? Keeping in mind that the purpose for the formative evaluation is to pinpoint specific errors in the materials in order to correct them, the evaluation design—including instruments, procedures, and evaluators—needs to yield information about the location of and the reasons for any mistakes. Focusing the design only on the goals and objectives of the instruction would be too limited. Data on learners' achievement of the goals and objectives would be insufficient, though important, because these data will only provide information about where errors occur, not why they occur. Similarly, a shotgun approach to the collection of data would also be inappropriate. While collecting data on everything you can imagine will produce a variety of information, it may yield some data that are irrelevant and incomplete.

Perhaps the best anchor or framework for the design of the formative evaluation is the instructional strategy. Since the strategy was the foundation for creating the materials, it is likely to hold the key to the nature of errors you made in producing them. Using the instructional strategy as the frame of reference for developing evaluation instruments and procedures should help you avoid designing a formative evaluation that is either too narrowly focused or too patchy.

How can the instructional strategy be used to aid the design of the formative evaluation? One way would be to create a matrix that lists the components of the instructional strategy along one side and the major areas of questions about the instruction along the other. In the intersecting boxes of the component by question matrix, you can generate questions that should be answered in the evaluation related to each area and component. Using these questions, you can then plan the appropriate instruments and procedures to use and the appropriate audiences to provide the information.

The different components of the strategy should be quite familiar to you by now. What general areas of questions should be asked about each component of the materials? Although undoubtedly there are questions that would be unique for a given set of materials, the five following areas of questions would be appropriate for all materials. These areas are directly related to the decisions you made while developing the materials.

1. Are the materials appropriate for the type of learning outcome? Specific prescriptions for the development of materials were made based on whether the objectives were intellectual or motor skills, attitudes, or verbal information. You should be concerned about whether the materials you produced are indeed congruent with suggestions for learning each type of capability. The best evaluator of this aspect of the materials would undoubtedly be an expert in the type of learning involved.
2. Do the materials include adequate instruction on the subordinate skills, and are these skills sequenced and clustered logically? The best evaluator for this area of questions would be an expert in the content area.
3. Are the materials clear and readily understood by representative members of the target group? Obviously, only members of the target group

can answer these questions. Instructors familiar with target learners may provide you with preliminary information, but only learners can ultimately judge the clarity of the materials.

4. What is the motivational value of the materials? Do learners find the materials relevant to their needs and interests? Are they confident as they work through the materials? Are they satisfied with what they have learned? Again, the most appropriate judges of these aspects of the materials are representative members of the target group.

5. Can the materials be managed efficiently in the manner they are mediated? Both target learners and instructors would be appropriate to answer these questions.

Table 10.1 contains an example of the suggested framework for designing the formative evaluation. Using such a framework will help ensure that you include relevant questions about different components of the materials and that appropriate groups and individuals are included.

Notice the two rows at the bottom of the matrix. The first indicates those individuals or groups most appropriate for evaluating each aspect of the materials. The second provides a reminder that you must consider how to gather each type of information needed from the evaluators. You may want to create a checklist or list of questions to accompany the materials for solicit-

TABLE 10.1

EXAMPLE FRAMEWORK FOR DESIGNING A FORMATIVE EVALUATION

Main Components of Materials	Main Areas of Questions about Materials				
	Type of Learning	Content	Clarity	Motivation	Management
Preinstructional Initial motivation Objectives Entry behaviors					
Presentation Sequence Size of unit Content Examples					
Participation Practice Feedback					
Testing Pretests Embedded Tests Posttests					
Who Judges?	Learning Specialist	Content Expert	Target Learners	Target Learners	Target Learners/ Instructors
How Is Data Gathered?	Checklist Interview	Checklist Interview	Observations Interviews Tests Materials	Observations Interviews Tests	Observations Interviews

ing information from the specialists you choose. You may also want to interview them to determine why they believe particular parts of the material are inadequate and to obtain their suggestions about how the materials might be improved.

In designing instrumentation for gathering information from learners, you must consider the setting (i.e., one-to-one, small-group, and field trial) and the nature of the information you are gathering. In the one-to-one evaluations, one instrument is the materials themselves. You will want learners to circle words or sentences and to write comments directly in the materials. The questions included in the intersecting blocks of the matrix should help you develop other instruments such as checklists to guide your observations and questions to include in your interviews and questionnaires. It is important to note that although different areas of questions about the materials are described separately here, it does not mean to imply that they must be on separate instruments. The instruments you produce should be efficient in gathering information from evaluators.

At a minimum, the types of data you will probably want to collect include the following:

- Test data collected on entry behaviors, skills to be taught, posttests, and embedded tests.
- Comments or notations made by learners to you or marked on the instructional materials about difficulties encountered at particular points in the materials.
- Data collected on attitude questionnaires and/or debriefing comments in which learners reveal their overall reactions to the instruction and their perceptions of where difficulties lie with the materials and the instructional procedures in general.
- The time required for learners to complete various components of the instruction.
- Reactions of a subject matter specialist. It is the responsibility of this person to verify that the content of the module is accurate and current.

CONCERNS INFLUENCING THE FORMATIVE EVALUATION

The formative evaluation component distinguishes the instructional design process from a philosophical or theoretical approach. Rather than speculating about the instructional effectiveness of your materials, you will be testing them with learners. Therefore, you will want to do the best possible job of collecting data that truly reflect the effectiveness of your materials. There are several concerns the designer should keep in mind when planning and implementing data collection procedures.

One concern in any evaluation of your materials is to ensure that any technical equipment is operating effectively. More than one instructor has been discouraged because a new set of instructional materials was tried with a particular piece of equipment and the equipment failed to operate correctly. Therefore, the data from learners were invalid, and the instructor learned little more than that the equipment must operate effectively to try out materials.

It is also important in the early stages of formative evaluation, especially in the one-to-one trials, that you work with students in a quiet setting—one in which you can command their full attention. At this point you are concerned about how the materials will work under the best possible conditions. As you move to the small-group sessions and field trial you are increasingly concerned with how the materials will work in more typical settings. If the typical setting is an individualized classroom that has a relatively high noise level, then you will want to know if the materials work in that situation. But you should not begin the formative evaluation under these conditions.

Another caution with regard to the selection of learners for participation in field studies is to avoid depending entirely upon the instructor to assess entry knowledge of the learners. Whenever possible, administer entry-behavior tests to learners to verify that they are actually members of the target population for whom the materials are intended. Experience has shown that instructors, for whatever reason, sometimes make poor estimates of the readiness of learners who are recommended for participation in formative evaluation studies. Do what you can to verify the entry knowledge of the learners.

When you get the information on entry knowledge of learners, you sometimes encounter the problem of what to do with those learners who have already mastered some or all of the skills to be taught, or learners who do not have the required entry behaviors. Do you drop them from the formative evaluation?

It is preferable to include some of these learners who do not exactly match the skill profile of the real target population. Those who already know some of the content can serve as "subject matter sophisticates" who can infer how other students, who do not know the content, will respond. You can also determine whether your instruction can bring these learners up to approximately 100 percent peformance. If it does not work for these learners, it is unlikely that it will be effective with learners who have less entering knowledge.

Learners who do not have the entry behaviors should also be included in a formative evaluation. The entry behaviors have been theoretically derived and therefore are in need of validation. If the learners who cannot demonstrate the entry behaviors do, in fact, struggle through the instruction with little success, while those with the entry behaviors are successful, it suggests that you have identified skills that learners must have to begin the instruction. If, on the other hand, learners without the entry behaviors are successful with the instruction, you must seriously reconsider the validity of the entry behaviors you have identified.

It has been suggested that in the one-to-one formative evaluation, the designer should use at least three learners—one high, one average, and one low in ability. This is a vague recommendation that can be made more specific by identifying a high-ability learner as one who already knows some of the content to be taught, the average learner as one who has the entry behaviors, but no knowledge of the skills to be taught, and the low-ability learner as one who does not have some or all of the entry behaviors. By using these definintions the designer can be much more sure of getting the desired range of abilities. Research indicates that these three types of learners will provide different but useful information to the designer, and thus all three should be included in the formative evaluation.

The designer should be aware of student characteristics, other than ability, that may be highly related to performance, and therefore should be systematically represented in the formative evaluation. As noted in this chapter, attitudes and previous experience can be very important. Thus, the designer may wish to select one learner with a very positive attitude toward that which is being taught, one who is neutral, and one who is negative, to participate in a one-to-one formative evaluation. Or, if experience on the job is an important factor, select someone who has been on the job ten or more years, one who has been there two to five years, and someone who has been working for less than a year. The point is that ability may not be the critical factor in selecting learners for a formative evaluation. The designer will have to make this decision for each particular instructional design situation.

A final word of caution: Be prepared to obtain information that indicates that your materials are not as effective as you thought they would be after going through such an extensive instructional design process. It is common to become tremendously involved when putting a great deal of time and effort into any kind of project. It is just as common to be sharply disappointed when you find that your efforts have not been entirely satisfactory.

However, you should note that in the formative evaluation process, positive feedback from students provides you with little information about how you might proceed to change anything. Positive feedback only indicates that what you have is effective with the students who used the materials. You can then only make the limited inference that the materials would be effective with learners who are of similar ability and motivation.

As you move through the formative evaluation process, it might be helpful to pretend that the materials were developed by another instructor and that you are merely carrying out the formative evaluation for that person. We do not suggest that you mislead the learners about it, but rather that you adopt this noninvolved psychological set in order to listen to what learners, instructors, and subject matter experts might say. These kinds of feedback must be integrated into an objective assessment of the extent to which your materials are meeting the objectives you have set for them, and how they can be improved.

Data Collection for Selected Materials and Instructor-Presented Instruction

Much of the information dealing with the collection of data in a field trial of original instructional materials applies equally well to the data collection procedures used in the evaluation of selected materials and instructional procedures. For example, it is critically important that any equipment to be used during instruction is in good running order, and that the environment in which the field trial is conducted be conducive to learning.

When an instructor evaluates original materials, selected materials, or instructor-presented instruction, existing rapport with learners can be a great advantage. It is important during the evaluation of materials and lessons that students understand the critical nature of their participation in, and contributions to, the study. The instructor, in working with familiar learners, also has knowledge of the learners' entry behaviors and, quite possibly, is able to predict accurately the pretest performance of students. However, the instructor should avoid relying entirely on such predictions. If there is any doubt at all concerning the learners' performances, the students should be tested to verify the need for instruction in specified skills.

When the instructor selects materials to implement an instructional strategy, a number of unique concerns arise. Information can be gathered about these concerns by observation and the use of questionnaires. The major question will be, "Did the instruction have unity?" To answer this question, the instructor should determine the adequacy of the learner guide in directing students to various resources. Redundancy and gaps in the instructional materials should be noted. Was sufficient repetition and review built into the strategy? If the instructor is presenting the instruction, events that reflect the same types of problems should be noted as the presentation progresses. The types of questions raised by learners will provide a key to the strategy's inadequacies.

RELATIONSHIP OF RESEARCH AND EVALUATION

In the instructional design process the designer is often faced with questions that can be answered with data from students. It is interesting to find how often it is possible to settle a design argument by saying, "Let's have the students tell us the answer to that." The whole formative evaluation process is one of gathering data from learners to answer questions you may (or may not) have had about your instruction.

You may not think of doing formative evaluation as doing research, and by most definitions, it is not. Evaluations are conducted to get answers to specific problems at specific times and in specific places. Research is a process used to identify knowledge that is generalizable to many situations at various times. The difference between research and evaluation is sometimes blurred because similar techniques are often employed in each. For example, it is possible to use research techniques during formative evaluation to obtain information to make a decision.

Assume that following a series of one-to-one evaluations, it becomes clear that there is a question about the use of illustrations in your instruction. Several students liked and used them, while several others said they were of no use. Since it is expensive to use illustrations in instruction, a significant question must be answered: Should illustrations be used in your instruction?

In order to answer this question, the designer might develop two versions of the instruction for use in the small-group evaluation. Ten randomly selected learners might receive the instruction with illustrations, while ten receive it with no illustrations. Then the performance and attitudes of both groups could be compared. How did they do on the posttest? How did they do on those items directly related to the illustrations? What did they say on the attitude questions about their use of (or the absence of) the illustrations? How did the learning times of the two groups compare?

Is this research? Not really. The purpose is to make a decision about what to do with a particular unit of instruction, not to determine the benefits of using illustrations in instruction. If we were trying to determine the latter, different procedures and materials would be used. Nevertheless, the designer could collect enough data about the illustrations to make at least a tentative decision about their continued use in this instruction. This same methodology can be used by the designer to answer a wide array of questions that will inevitably arise during the design process.

EXAMPLES

The following list includes information that you can use for planning a one-to-one, a small-group, and a field trial evaluation. While looking through these suggested procedures, assume that you know your intended target population, but are unsure whether they possess the required entry behaviors. The examples below are not offered as the only activities you should pursue in formative evaluation, but as a list of suggestions you can use to begin thinking about your own project. You may be able to identify other activities for your project.

Formative Evaluation Activities

I. One-to-One Evaluation
  A. Participation by students from the target population
    1. Identify students who are typical of those you believe will be found in the target population. (Include each major type of student that can be found in the target population.)
    2. Arrange for the student(s) to participate.
    3. Discuss the process of a one-to-one test of the materials with each student separately.
    4. Evaluate the pretest you have constructed to measure entry behaviors.
      a. Can the student read the directions?
      b. Does the student understand the problems?
      c. Does the student have the required prerequisite skills?
    5. Sit with the student while he or she goes through the materials.
      a. Instruct the student to write on the materials to indicate where difficulty is encountered or to discuss ideas and problems.
      b. If the student fails to understand an example, try another verbal example. Does this clarify the issue? Note in writing the changes and suggestions you make as you go through the materials.
      c. If the student fails to understand an explanation, elaborate by adding information or changing the order of presentation. Does this clarify the issue? Note the changes you make in writing.
      d. If the student appears to be bored or confused while going through the materials, you may want to change the presentation to include larger or smaller bits of information before practice and feedback. Record your ideas concerning the regrouping of materials as you go along.
      e. Keep notes on examples, illustrations, information you add, and changes in sequence during the evaluation process. Otherwise, you may forget an important decision or idea. Note taking should be quick and in rough form so the student is not distracted from the materials.
    6. You may choose to test another student from the target population before you make any changes or revisions in your materials in order to verify that the changes are necessary. If errors pointed out by your student "consultant" are obvious, you may want to make revisions before testing the next student, both to save testing time and to enable the next student to concentrate on other problems that may exist in the materials.
  B. Participation by subject matter experts
    1. You should provide the expert with the:
      a. Instructional analysis
      b. Behaviorally stated objectives
      c. Instruction
      d. Tests
      These materials should be in rough form because major revisions could well be the outcome of this one-to-one testing. You may want to present your materials in the order described above.
    2. You should be looking for verification of the:
      a. Objective statements

       b. Instructional analysis

       c. Accuracy and currency of the content

       d. Appropriateness of the instructional materials in vocabulary, interest, sequence, chunk size, and student-participation activities

       e. Clarity and appropriateness of test items and test situations

       f. Placement of this piece of instruction relative to prior and subsequent instruction.

    3. The number of subject matter experts you should approach for assistance will vary with the complexity of the information and skills covered in your materials. For some instruction one expert will be sufficient, while for others four may still seem inadequate. The nature of the teaching task will dictate the number and type of expert consultants you will need.

  C. Outcomes of one-to-one formative evaluation

    1. Consider again the types of information you are looking for in the one-to-one testing. They include:

       a. Errors in judgment about entry behaviors of students in the target population

       b. Faulty instructional analysis

       c. Faulty wording or unclear passages

       d. Inadequate information presentation

          1. Unclear examples

          2. Examples, graphs, or illustrations that are too abstract

          3. Too much or too little information at one time

          4. Wrong sequence of information presented

       e. Unclear test questions, test situations, or test directions

       f. Unclear or inappropriate objectives and expected outcomes

II. Small-Group Evaluation

  A. Participation by students from the target population

    1. Identify a group of students that typifies your target population.

    2. Arrange for a group to participate.

       a. Adequate time should be arranged for required testing as well as instructional activities.

       b. Learners should be motivated to participate.

       c. Learners should be selected to represent the types of people expected in the target population. You may want to include several students from each expected major category in your target population.

    3. During the pretest, instruction, and posttest, you may want to make notes about suggestions for instructors who will use the materials or about changes you want to make in the instruction or procedures as a result of your observation of students interacting with the materials.

    4. Administer the pretest of required entry behaviors if one is appropriate.

       a. Check the directions, response patterns, and questions to ensure the wording is clear.

       b. Instruct learners to circle words they do not understand and place a check beside questions or directions that are unclear.

       c. Do not stop and discuss unclear items with learners during the test unless students become bogged down or stop.

       d. Record the time required for students to complete the entry test.

5. Administer the pretest of skills to be taught during instruction. This test and the test of required entry behaviors could be combined into one pretest if desirable.
   a. Have learners circle any vocabulary that is unclear to them.
   b. Have learners place a check beside any directions, questions, or response requirements that are unclear to them.
   c. Have learners write additional comments in the test if they desire.
   d. Do not discuss problems with students during the test.

6. Administer the instructional materials. Have the instructional setting as close to reality as possible with all required equipment and materials present. Any instructional assistance required should also be available during the trial.
   a. Instruct students that you will need their help in evaluating the materials.
   b. Have learners sign their work so you can compare their performance on the lesson with your expectations of their performance based on their entry behaviors.
   c. Instruct learners to circle any unclear words and place a check beside any illustrations, examples, or explanations that are unclear in the instruction. Learners should keep working through the materials to the end without stopping for discussion.
   d. Record the time required for learners to complete the instructional materials. Time required may be more than anticipated if students need instruction on unfamiliar equipment or procedures.

7. Administer the posttest.
   a. Have learners sign their posttest to enable comparisons with the pretest and embedded tests.
   b. Have learners circle any unclear vocabulary and place a check beside any unclear directions, questions, or response requirements.
   c. Have learners respond to as many items as they can whether they are sure of the answer or whether they are just guessing. Often incorrect guesses can provide clues to inadequate instruction. You may want them to indicate which answers elicited guessing.
   d. Record the time required for learners to complete the posttest.

8. Administer an attitude questionnaire to learners.
   a. You may want to ask questions like:
      - Did the instruction hold your attention?
      - Was the instruction too long or too short?
      - Was the instruction too difficult or too easy?
      - Did you have problems with any parts of the instruction?
      - Were the cartoons or illustrations appropriate or distracting?
      - Was the use of color appealing or distracting?
      - What did you like most?
      - What did you like least?
      - How would you change the instruction if you could?
      - Did the tests measure the material that was presented?
      - Would you prefer another instructional medium?

9. Arrange for students to discuss the pretest, instruction, and/or

posttest with you or their instructor after they have completed all the work.

   a. You may want to structure the discussion with planned questions.

   b. You may want to ask questions like, "Would you change the exercises in section X?" or "Did you like the example in section X?"

III. Field Trial

   A. Select an appropriate sample from the target population.

      1. Arrange for the selected group to try the materials.

         a. Ensure that there is an adequate number of learners in the group. Thirty is an often-suggested number of learners to participate in a field trial.

         b. Ensure that selected learners reflect the range of abilities and skills of learners in the target population.

         c. Ensure that there are adequate personnel, facilities, and equipment available for the trial.

      2. Distribute the instructional materials as well as the instructor's guide, if it is available, to the instructor conducting the field test.

      3. Discuss any instructions or special considerations that may be needed if the instruction is out of context.

      4. Personally play a minimal role in the field trials.

      5. Summarize the data you have collected. Summarized data may include the following:

         a. Report on the entry-behavior part of the pretest

         b. Report on pretest and posttest scores on skills taught

         c. Report on the time required for students to complete each test used

         d. Report on the time required for students to complete the instruction

         e. Remediation or enrichment needs that become apparent

         f. Report on the attitude survey for learners as well as participating instructors.

IV. Formative Evaluation of Selected Materials and Instructor-Delivered Instruction

   A. Selected materials

   In addition to the formative suggestions for originally developed instruction, you should determine whether:

      1. All parts of the instructional strategy are accounted for in the selected materials or provided by the instructor.

      2. The transitions between sources are smooth.

      3. The flow of content in the various instructional resources is consistent and logical.

      4. The learners' manual or instructor adequately presents objectives.

      5. Directions for locating instruction within each source are adequate.

      6. Sections of the instructional strategy that must be supplied by the instructor are adequate.

      7. The vocabulary used in all the sources is appropriate.

      8. The illustrations and examples used are appropriate for the target group.

   B. Instructor-Delivered Instruction

   A major factor in evaluating instruction that is delivered by instructors is that they are an interactive part of the instruction. Therefore, in addition to all the considerations we have mentioned previously, several important evaluation considerations are unique to this type of instruction. You should determine if the instructor:

1. Is convincing, enthusiastic, helpful, and knowledgeable.
2. Is able to avoid digressions to keep instruction and discussions on relevant topics and on schedule.
3. Makes presentations in an interesting, clear manner.
4. Uses the chalkboard and other visual aids to help with examples and illustrations.
5. Provides good feedback to learners' questions.
6. Provides adequate practice exercises with appropriate feedback.

You should record events that occur during instruction so that you can study them for what they imply about the effectiveness of the instruction.

SUMMARY

Formative evaluation of instructional materials is conducted to determine the effectiveness of the materials and to revise them in areas where they are ineffective. Formative evaluations should be conducted on newly developed materials as well as existing materials that are selected based on the instructional strategy. Evaluations are necessary for both mediated and instructor presented materials. The evaluations should be designed to produce data to pinpoint specific areas where the instruction is faulty.

An iterative process of formative evaluation containing at least three cycles of data collection, analysis, and revision is recommended. Each cycle focuses on different aspects of quality. The first cycle, one-to-one evaluation, is conducted to pinpoint gross errors in the materials. These errors typically relate to both the clarity of vocabulary, contexts, and examples used and the motivational value of all five components of the instructional materials. Evaluations can be conducted with content experts and individuals familiar with the characteristics of target learners. One-to-ones must be conducted with individuals who are representative of the target population. An interactive, interview process is used so the evaluator can learn not only what was wrong with the materials but also why it was wrong.

The second cycle, small-group evaluations, follows correction of gross errors contained in the materials. The group typically consists of from eight to twenty representative members of the target population. The purpose of the small-group evaluation is to locate additional errors in the instructional materials and management procedures. The elements of the instructional strategy are again the anchor for the evaluation instruments and procedures. During this cycle the evaluator plays a less interactive role, performance and attitude data are collected, and in-depth debriefings are conducted to obtain both quantitative and qualitative data.

The final cycle, a field trial, is conducted following refinement of the materials based on the small-group evaluation. The purpose of this evaluation is to pinpoint errors in the materials when they are used as prescribed in the intended setting. Similar to the first two cycles, evaluation instrumentation and procedures should be anchored in the five components of the instructional strategy. Instruments to gather data on learner performance and attitudes are important. The gathering of management data such as the time required to use the materials and the feasibility of the management plan is also important. During the trial, the evaluator does not interfere as data are gathered from the learners and perhaps the instructor, although observation while materials are used can provide insights for the interpretation of data gathered.

This chapter has focused on the design of the formative evaluation and the data-gathering procedures. The next chapter describes data analysis and materials revision based on the data.

═══ PRACTICE ═══

The following exercises are based on the instructional analysis and strategy of writing themes using a variety of sentence types presented in chapter 8. Again, the target population is sixth-grade students of varying levels of knowledge and skills. For each type of formative evaluation (one-to-one, small-group, and field trial), you are to consider the questions and determine decisions you would make based on the purposes of the evaluation, the nature of the instruction, and the target population.

I. One-to-One Evaluation
1. Describe how many sixth-grade students you would select for a one-to-one evaluation of the composition instruction and explain why you would include each student in your sample.
2. Describe the kinds of information you would be seeking during the one-to-one evaluation with sixth graders.
3. Describe the appearance (typed, rough copy, polished copy, etc.) of your materials for one-to-one evaluation.

II. Small-Group Evaluation
1. Describe the number and achievement level of students that you would include in your small group trial
2. Describe how you would determine whether one small-group evaluation session was sufficient.
3. Describe the materials (level of completeness, rough copy, polished copy, etc.) you would use for a small-group evaluation session.
4. Describe the information you would record to help evaluate the instruction on sentence types for sixth-grade students with varying backgrounds and levels of achievement.

III. Field Trial
1. Why would you be interested in a field trial of the materials?
2. What information would you collect during the field trial that you would not have collected during the small-group evaluation session?
3. Describe an appropriate sample group and instructional setting that could be used to evaluate the materials on writing different types of sentences.
4. What materials would you include in the field trial?

IV. Formative Evaluation of Selected Materials and Instructor-Presented Instruction
1. How would your procedures differ if you were conducting a field trial of adapted or adopted materials, rather than a set of "original" materials?
2. Describe the major procedural differences between the field trial of selected materials and the field trial of instructor-delivered instruction.

V. Develop an attitude questionnaire to use with students when conducting the small-group and field trials for lessons one, two, and three from the unit on using a variety of sentence types.

═══ FEEDBACK ═══

I. One-to-One Evaluation

1. The exact number of students selected for one-to-one evaluation is arbitrary. The sample should include students from different levels of achievement in the sixth grade. If there are three or four levels, then there should be at least one student from each of the levels. Should you discover that the instruction is inappropriate for the lowest achievers, you will need to decide whether to adapt the instruction to include these students, or to be more specific about required entry skills rather than revising entry skills.

    Students of average achievement should be included to check vocabulary, reading difficulty level, pacing, entry skills, clarity of examples, exercises, and feedback.

    You should also include high achieving students to determine whether
    a. Some sections can be skipped
    b. Examples are clear and exercises are challenging but clear
    c. Exercises and feedback are appropriate
    d. Use of enrichment materials is advisable. These students could help determine whether selected practice or enrichment activities appear to students to be interesting or busywork.

2. Types of information you should obtain during the one-to-one evaluation are:
    a. Does the initial motivation material interest the student?
    b. Are the objectives clear and interesting as well as relevant to the student?
    c. Can the student perform all the skills identified in the entry-behaviors analysis?
    d. What review is necessary for entry behaviors?
    e. What instruction is necessary for entry behaviors?
    f. What skills from the instruction do the students already possess?
    g. Do the instructional materials provide adequate:
        • Vocabulary
        • Pacing
        • Chunk size
        • Clarity of descriptions
        • Clarity of examples
        • Adequacy of sequence of content and activities
        • Interest level of exercises
        • Student performance on embedded exercises
        • Clarity of feedback information
        • Motivation
    h. Are the test instructions, vocabulary, questions, and response expectations clear to the students?

3. The appearance of materials is again arbitrary and rests on the judgment of the instructor. A set of materials to teach the objectives may consist of loose pages of instruction with directions typed and illustrations hand drawn. Each new idea and any required student

responses should be placed on one page, and feedback on a separate page. This way sequences can be changed easily. Another benefit of grouping instruction and student performances for one concept together is that it will help pinpoint concepts, which have been inadequately explained or examples, illustrations, and feedback that confuse rather than clarify an idea.

Illustrations, graphs, and figures should be "roughed in" because students will "see" the idea whether you have stick figures or artistically-drawn characters.

Students should be encouraged to write on the materials (embedded questions, practice exercises), to circle unclear words, and to place a check by unclear parts. Therefore, you will need as many copies of materials as students you intend to sample, plus extra copies on which to tally your results and make revisions.

II. Small-Group Evaluation

1. You should include at least three or four students from each expected achievement level. This will help you avoid the error of assuming that all students at a particular achievement level will respond in the same manner. It will give you a basis for comparing students' responses who are at various achievement levels. Information of this type will help you determine the adequacy of remedial, review, and enrichment materials as well as the adequacy of the basic instruction for the entire target population. As a guideline you should have at least eight students, and probably not more than twenty.

2. One session of small-group evaluation may not be enough. A good way to judge is to consider the amount and types of revisions made in the materials as a result of the previous evaluation. If only a few slight revisions are made and you believe that similar students would react the same way to the instruction, then continued small-group evaluation is unnecessary. If, however, you make several revisions as a result of the previous evaluation, you may need another small-group session to evaluate your new version of the materials. Some of your decisions may result in improvements; others may not.

3. Your materials must be developed to the appropriate level of sophistication. Problems resulting from the medium itself cannot be detected unless the instruction appears in that medium. Tests used prior to and after instruction should also be complete and administered in their intended format. If possible, the instructor's guide should be complete and tested at this time and necessary revisions made before the field evaluation. Information from the field evaluation session will probably be included in the information section of the instructor's guide, but it will be necessary to evaluate the clarity of instructions and suggestions for using the materials.

4. After the small-group evaluation, you may want to summarize the various types of information for the following groups:
   a. Divide the sample into low, average, and above-average achieving students.
   b. Record their responses on the pretest:
      • Record performance on each of the required entry behaviors.
      • Record performance on each subskill required to reach the terminal objective.
      • Tally any vocabulary words circled as unclear.
      • Tally any questions checked as unclear.
      • Tally directions marked as unclear.

c. Record their responses in the instructional package:
- Tally any explanations marked unclear.
- Tally any examples and illustrations marked unclear.
- Tally vocabulary words circled or marked unclear.
- Tally students' responses to embedded questions, both correct and incorrect.
- Tally any feedback sections students mark as unclear.
- Tally their performance on embedded tests.

d. Record their responses on the posttest.
- Tally correct and incorrect objective-by-objective answers.
- Tally any questions marked unclear.
- Tally any directions marked unclear.
- Tally any response requirements marked unclear.
- Tally any vocabulary circled or marked unclear.

e. Use the checklist to evaluate their compositions.
- Tally the number of correct and incorrect declarative sentences.
- Tally the number of correct and incorrect interrogative sentences.
- Tally the number of correct and incorrect imperative sentences.
- Tally the number of correct and incorrect exclamatory sentences.
- Tally the number of awkward sentences, e.g., correctly constructed but inappropriate for mood or idea being conveyed.
- Tally the number of missed opportunities, e.g., another type of sentence would have conveyed the idea better.

f. Record time required for pretest, instruction, and posttest activities.

III. Field Trial

1. Materials are field tested to determine their effectiveness with the target population when used under specified conditions. Field trials answer the question, "Do these materials actually work for given students, and are there any improvements that can be made?" It helps to determine the instructional effectiveness of the materials in the absence of coaching by an instructor. It also aids in determining whether the materials are actually ready for use. The materials, tests, and instructions for both students and teachers should be examined during the field trial. Have the materials had enough revision, or is more revision required? Revision at this point can be either in the materials themselves or in suggestions for using the materials.

2. You would probably want to collect the same types of information that were obtained during the small-group evaluation. Other information might include students' attitudes concerning:
   a. Their interest in the instruction.
   b. Whether they thought instruction was too easy, too difficult, or just right.
   c. Whether they thought instruction was too fast, too slow, or just right.
   d. Whether they thought the materials were easy to use or complicated.
      You might also want to include instructors' attitudinal information about whether the materials are easy to use, complicated, or just right, and why the instructors hold these opinions.

3. An appropriate population to field test the instruction on varying sen-

tence types would be a regular sixth-grade class that includes above-average, average, and below-average achievers—a typical class of approximately twenty-five to thirty-five students. This would enable the instructor to use individualized techniques in a regular classroom and evaluate whether enrichment and remedial and review instruction, as well as basic instruction, was effective. It would provide information about both performance and learning time when materials are used under normal classroom conditions.

4. All materials developed should be included and evaluated in the field trial. This may include the student manual, instructional materials, audiovisual equipment required for materials, tests, and the instructor's guide.

IV. Formative Evaluation of Selected Materials and Instructor-Delivered Instruction

1. The major difference between field evaluation of selected materials and original materials is that the instructor is present during the evaluation of selected existing materials. This provides the instructor with the opportunity to observe the use of the materials and to determine the adequacy of the various components of the instructional strategy.

2. With instructor-delivered instruction, the instructor interacts with the learners while delivering the instruction. The instructor controls the practice and feedback components of the instruction. The instructor is more passive when evaluating selected materials.

V. Attitude Questionnaire

The attitude questionnaire (Table 10.2) can be given to students to complete during the small-group and field trials. However, during the one-to-one trials, you should use it as an interview form. You can write responses students make on the form. The one-to-one trials will help you formatively evaluate the attitudinal questionnaire to determine whether the questions you have asked are clear. If you get several "I don't know" responses, rephrase the questions until the student understands the question and expresses an opinion. Note on the questionnaire changes you need to make to clarify what you are asking.

The attitudinal questionnaire can be used as an interview guide during the debriefing session as well. It will help you focus the evaluation on important components in the materials.

References and Recommended Readings

Baker, E. L., & Alkin, M. C. (1973). Formative evaluation of instructional development. *Audio Visual Communication Review,* 21 (4), 389–418. The authors provide an in-depth description of the formative evaluation process and some research on formative evaluation.

Cronbach, L. J. (1975). Course improvement through evaluation. Reprinted in Payne, D. A., & McMorris, R. F. (Eds.), *Education and Psychological Measurement.* Morristown, NJ: General Learning Press, 243–256. This is one of the original articles on the need for formative evaluation of instructional materials.

Komoski, K. P. (1974). An imbalance of product quantity and instructional quality: The imperative of empiricism. *Audio Visual Communication Review,* vol. 4, 357–386. Komoski documents the number of instructional materials being commercially produced and the lack of formative evaluation prior to sale.

Nathenson, M. B., & Henderson, E. S. (1980). *Using student feedback to improve learning materials.* London: Croom Helm. A detailed description of the use of the formative evaluation process with Open University courses in England.

Performance and Instruction Journal, 22 (5), 1983. Special issue on formative evalua-

TABLE 10.2

ATTITUDE QUESTIONNAIRE

Name_____ Date_____ Class_____

Attitude Questionnaire

Please answer the following questions to help us understand what you think about the lessons on writing different kinds of sentences. Your opinions will help us make better lessons for you.

A. Motivation
1. Did you enjoy the story about the birthday present?
   _____ Yes
   _____ No
2. Did you think the version of the story that had all types of sentences included (B) was more interesting than the first (A)?
   _____ Yes
   _____ No
3. Did reading the story make you want to try to write more interesting stories yourself?
   _____ Yes
   _____ No
4. What kinds of stories do you most like to read?
   _____
   _____

B. Objectives
1. Did you understand that you were going to learn to write interesting stories?
   _____ Yes
   _____ No
2. Did you understand that you were going to learn to use four different kinds of sentences in your stories?
   _____ Yes
   _____ No
3. Did you want to write different kinds of sentences?
   _____ Yes
   _____ No

C. Entry Behaviors
1. Were the questions about subjects, predicates, and complete sentences clear to you?
   _____ Yes
   _____ No
2. Did you already know about subjects, predicates, and complete sentences before you started?
   _____ Yes
   _____ No
3. Do you wish information about subjects, predicates, and complete sentences had been included in the lesson?
   _____ Yes
   _____ No

D. Instruction
1. Was the instruction interesting?
   _____ Yes
   _____ No
2. Was the instruction clear?
   _____ Yes
   _____ No
   If not, what wasn't clear?_____
3. Were the example questions helpful?
   _____ Yes
   _____ No
4. Were there too many examples? Too few?
   _____ Yes   _____ Yes
   _____ No   _____ No
5. Did the practice questions in the instruction help you?
   _____ Yes
   _____ No
   If not, why not?_____
   _____

TABLE 10.2

ATTITUDE QUESTIONNAIRE—*(continued)*

    6.   Did the feedback exercises in the instruction help you?
          _____ Yes
          _____ No
          If not, why not?_____
          _____

E.   Tests
    1.   Did you think questions on the pretest were clear?
          _____ Yes
          _____ No
    2.   Did you think you knew most of the answers on the pretest?
          _____ Yes
          _____ No
    3.   Were the questions on the posttest clear or confusing?
          _____ Clear
          _____ Confusing
    4.   Did you think questions within the lesson were clear or confusing?
          _____ Clear
          _____ Confusing

F.   Overall
    1.   Generally, did you like the lesson?
          _____ Yes
          _____ No
    2.   Did you learn to do things you couldn't do before?
          _____ Yes
          _____ No
    3.   What do you think would improve the lesson most?

tion. This issue carries a number of articles of interest to the designer. See especially: Wager, "One-to-One and Small Group Formative Evaluation"; Komoski, "Formative Evaluation;" Lowe, "Clinical Approach to Formative Evaluation;" and Golas, "Formative Evaluation Effectiveness and Cost."

Russell, J. D., & Blake, B. L. (1988). Formative and summative evaluation of instructional products and learners. *Educational Technology*, 28 (9), 22–28. This article distinguishes between the formative evaluation of instruction and the formative evaluation of learners.

Schwier, R. A. (1982). Design and use of student evaluation instruments in institutional development. *Journal of Instructional Development*, 5, 4, 28–34. Practical suggestions are provided for the development of questionnaires which assess student reactions to instruction.

Scott, R. O., & Yelon, S. R. (1969). The student as a coauthor—The first step in formative evaluation. *Educational Technology*, October, 76–78. This is one of the few articles which describes procedures to be used in one-to-one formative evaluation with students.

Scriven, M., Tyler, R., & Gagné, R. (1967). Perspectives of curriculum evaluation. AERA Monograph Series on Curriculum Evaluation. Chicago: Rand McNally. In this monograph the authors made the first functional distinction between formative and summative evaluation.

Zsohar, H., Hegstad, L. N., Sullivan, H. J., & Hug, A. C. (1981). Incorporating experimental research into the instructional development process. *Journal of Instructional Development*, 5, 1, 30–35. This is an example of the use of embedded research studies to make decisions during the formative evaluation of instruction.

11
R EVISING INSTRUCTIONAL MATERIALS

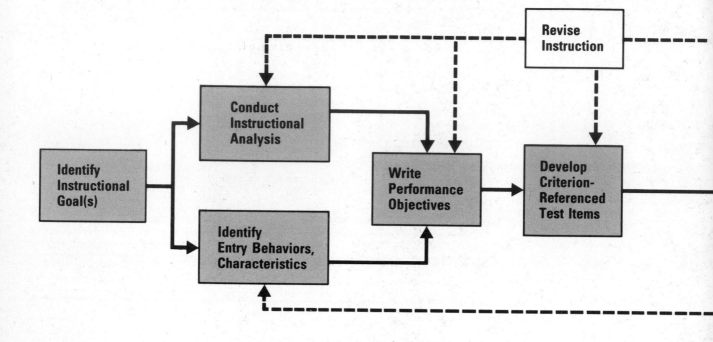

OBJECTIVES

- Describe various methods for summarizing data obtained from formative evaluation studies.
- Summarize data obtained from formative evaluation studies.
- Given summarized formative evaluation data, identify weaknesses in instructional materials and instructor-delivered instruction.
- Given formative evaluation data for a set of instructional materials, identify problems in the materials, and suggest and carry out revisions of the materials.

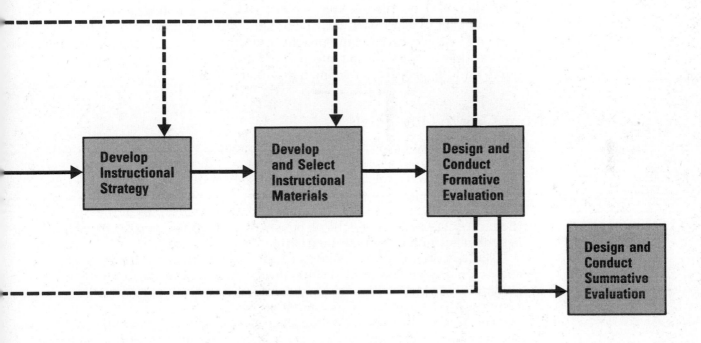

BACKGROUND

If you examine almost any instructional design model, you will find major emphasis on the concept of formative evaluation, that is, on collecting data to identify problems and to revise instructional materials. Models often indicate that after data have been collected and summarized, you should revise the materials "appropriately." Although a number of studies have indicated the benefit of revising instructional materials, few have proposed any theories around which to gather the data. In effect, we interpret the data in the most reasonable way possible and then make changes that seem to be indicated by the data and our understanding of the learning process.

There are two basic types of revisions you will consider with your materials. The first is changes that are made to the content or substance of the materials to make them more accurate or more effective as a learning tool. The second type of change is related to the procedures employed in using your materials.

In this chapter, we will point out how data from various formative evaluation sources can be summarized and used to identify portions of your materials that should be revised. You will note that you will not be concerned about the use of complex statistics in this step of the instructional design process because simple descriptive summaries of the data are sufficient. Elaborate statistical tests are not employed in the formative evaluation and revision process.

CONCEPTS

There are many different ways in which the data collected in the formative evaluation may be summarized to point to areas of student difficulties and possible revisions. The methods we describe here are merely suggestions. As you begin to work with your own data, you may find other techniques that will help you derive more insight from them. We will first look at what you can do with the data and information from a one-to-one formative evaluation, and then consider the small-group and field-trial phases.

Analyzing Data from One-to-One Trials

Following the one-to-one formative evaluation the designer has very little data because information typically is available for only three to five students. Since these learners were selected based on their diversity, the information they provide will, in all likelihood, be very distinct, rather than blending into some type of group average. In other words, the designer must look at the similarities and differences among the responses of the learners, and determine the best changes to make in the instruction.

The designer has four kinds of basic information available: student characteristics and entry behaviors, direct responses to the instruction including embedded test and attitude items, posttest performance, and responses to an attitude questionnaire, if used.

The first step is to describe the learners who participated in the one-to-one evaluation and to indicate their performance on any entry-behavior measures. Next the designer should bring together all the comments and suggestions about the instruction that resulted from going through it with each learner. This can be done by integrating everything on a master copy of the instruction using a color code to indicate which students had which problems, and to indicate student performance on embedded test items. It is also possible to include comments from a subject-matter expert, and any alternative instructional approaches that were used with learners during the one-to-one sessions.

The next set of data to be summarized is that associated with the posttest. One should begin by obtaining individual item performance and then combining item scores for each objective and for a total score. It is often of interest to develop a table that indicates each student's pretest score, posttest score, and total learning time. In addition, student performance on the posttest should be summarized, along with any comments, for each objective. The same type of summary can be used for examining the data on the attitude questionnaire, if one is used at this point in the instruction.

With all this information in hand, the designer is ready to revise the instruction. Of course, certain obvious revisions may have been made before completing the one-to-one sessions. Now the more difficult revisions must be made. Certainly the place to begin is within those sections that resulted in the poorest performance by learners and in those that resulted in the most comments.

First, try to determine, based upon learner performance, whether your test items are faulty. If they are, then changes should be made to make them consistent with the objectives and the intent of the instruction. If the items are satisfactory, and the learners performed poorly, then the instruction must be changed. You have three sources of suggestions for change: learner suggestions, learner performance, and your own informed intuitions. Learners often can suggest sensible changes. In addition, the designer should carefully examine the *mistakes* made by learners in order to identify the kinds of misinterpretations they are making and, therefore, the kinds of changes that might be made. You should not ignore your own insights about what changes will make the instruction more effective. You have used systematic design procedures, so you have made careful descriptions of what is to be learned and have provided examples; you have offered students the opportunity to practice each skill and they have received feedback. The basic components are there! The usual revisions at this stage are ones of clarification of ideas and the addition or deletion of practice activities. Hopefully, the three sources of data will suggest the most appropriate steps to take.

There will be times when it is not obvious what to do to improve instruction. It is sometimes wise simply to leave that part of the instruction as is and see how it works in the small-group formative evaluation, or the designer can develop several alternative approaches to solving the problem and try these out during the small group.

Analyzing Data from Small-Group and Field Trials

The small-group formative evaluation provides the designer with a somewhat different data summary situation. The data from 8 to 20 students are of greater collective interest than individual interest; that is, these data can show what problems and reactions this representative group of students had. The available data typically include: item performance on the pretest, embedded items, and posttest, as well as responses to an attitude questionnaire, learning and testing time, and comments made directly in the materials.

The fundamental unit of analysis for all the assessments is the individual item. Performance on each item must be scored as correct or incorrect. If an item has multiple parts, each part should be scored and reported separately so that the information is not lost. This individual item information is required for three reasons:

1. Item information can be useful in deciding whether there are particular problems with the item or whether it is effectively measuring the performance described in its corresponding objective. The method for doing this will be described in a later section.
2. Individual item information can be used to identify the nature of the difficulties students are having with the instruction. Not only is it important to know that, for example, half the learners missed a particular item, but it is just as important to know that most of those who missed the item picked the same distractor in a multiple-choice item or made the same type of reasoning error on a problem-solving item.
3. Individual item data can be combined to indicate learner performance on an objective, and eventually, on the entire test. Sometimes, the criterion level for an objective is expressed in terms of getting a certain

percentage of items correct on a set of items. The individual item data can be combined not only to show percentage of items correct for an objective, but the number and percent of learners who achieved mastery.

After the item data have been collected and organized into a basic item-by-objective table, it is then possible to construct more comprehensive data tables.

GROUP'S ITEM-BY-OBJECTIVE PERFORMANCE The first data summary table that should be constructed is an item-by-objective table. An example is illustrated in Table 11.1. The objectives are listed across the top of the table, and items are inserted in the second row within the objectives they measure. Students' data are recorded in the rows beneath the items and objectives. An X in the column beneath an item indicates a correct response, and a blank indicates an incorrect response for each student. Although the table contains data for only five students, assume the entire table contains data for 20 students.

With the raw data displayed in this manner, we can use it to create two summaries for analysis: item quality and learner performance. You should analyze item quality first, because faulty items should not be considered when analyzing learner performance. The bottom rows contain the data summaries needed for the item analysis. The first row contains the number of the 20 students who answered each item within an objective correctly. The next row contains the proportion of learners who answered each item correctly. These figures are obtained by dividing the total number of students in the evaluation into the number of students who answered correctly—i.e., for item 1, $18/20 = .90$. The last row contains the percentage of the group that mastered each objective.

The purpose for the item analysis is threefold: to determine the difficulty of each item for the group, to determine the difficulty of each objective for the group, and to determine the consistency with which the set of items within an objective measures learners' performance on the objective.

Item with difficulty values above .80 reflect relatively easy items for the group, whereas lower values reflect more difficult ones. Similarly, consis-

TABLE 11.1

ITEM-BY-OBJECTIVE ANALYSIS TABLE

Objectives:	1		2		3			4			Items		Objectives	
Items:	1	2	3	4	5	6	7	8	9	10	#	%	#	%
Students 1	X	X	X	X	X	X	X	X	X	X	8	100	4	100
2	X	X	X	X	X	X	X	X	X	X	8	100	4	100
3		X	X	X	X	X	X	X	X	X	7	88	3	75
4	X			X	X	X		X		X	4	50	0	0
20	X	X			X	X	X	X			4	50	2	50
# Students Correct	18	19	15	17	17	6	18	18	10	9				
% Students Correct	.90	.95	.75	.85	.85	.30	.90	.90	.50	.45				
% Mastering Objectives	.90		.75		.85			.45						

tently high or low values for items within an objective reflect the difficulty of the objective for the group. For example, the difficulty values for items 1 and 2 in Table 11.1 (.90 and .95) indicate that objective 1 is easy for the group. If these data were from a posttest, we could infer that the instruction related to objective 1 is effective. Conversely, if they are low, they point to instruction that should be considered for revision.

The consistency of item difficulty indices within an objective reflects the quality of the items. If items are measuring the same skill, and if there is no inadvertent complexity or clues in the items, then students' performance on the set of items should be relatively consistent. With small groups, differences of .10 or .20 are not considered large, but differences of .40 or more should cause concern. Notice in Table 11.1 that item data are consistent within objectives 1 and 2. The data, however, are inconsistent within objectives 3 and 4. For objective 3, two items are quite consistent (.85 and .90), while one item, 6, yielded a much lower difficulty index. Such a pattern reflects either inadvertent complexity in the item or a different skill being measured. The pattern in objective 4 illustrates two consistent items (.50 and .45) and one outlier (.90). This type of pattern reflects either a clue in item 8 or a different skill being measured. When inconsistent difficulty indices are observed within an objective, it indicates that the items within the set should be reviewed and revised prior to reusing the set to measure learner performance. If the item is judged sound, it reflects an aspect of instruction that should be reconsidered.

LEARNER'S ITEM-BY-OBJECTIVE PERFORMANCE The second type of analysis that can be conducted using the item-by-objective table is individual learner performance. Before conducting this analysis, you should eliminate any items judged faulty during the item analysis. For illustration purposes, assume that items 6 and 8 in Table 11.1 were removed because of confirmed errors in the items. We have eight items remaining, two for each of the four objectives. The last four columns contain the individual performance data. The first two columns contain the number and percent of items answered correctly by each learner. The last two columns contain the number and percent of objectives mastered by each learner. Answering both items within an objective was set as the criterion for mastery.

Setting the criterion for mastery of an objective is rather subjective. It depends on several factors, including whether students could guess the correct answers, the number of different facets of an objective measured in the set of items, the possibility of inadvertent errors, and the number of items contained in the set. Based on these considerations you may decide that learners must answer all items correctly; you should at least require that they answer the majority of the items correctly.

The hypothetical data for learners in Table 11.1 illustrate that individuals in the group performed quite differently on the test. Two individuals mastered all four objectives, and the scores for the other three learners range from no objectives mastered to 75 percent. Should these data represent performance on entry behaviors or skills to be included in the instruction, they would suggest who was ready for instruction, or whether instruction was needed by some members of the sample. Should they reflect posttest performance, the designer could make inferences about the necessity of enrichment and remediation materials.

Data about learners' performance on items and objectives provide different information. For example, learners 4 and 20 in Table 11.1 both earned raw scores of 4 on the test, or 50 percent correct. These data alone would lead us to conclude that their performances were similar on the test. The data on objectives mastered indicate that this is not true. Learner 4 failed to master any of the objectives, whereas learner 20 mastered half of them. For the formative evaluator, data on objectives mastered are more informative than raw scores.

LEARNER'S PERFORMANCE ACROSS TESTS The item-by-objective table provides the data for creating tables to summarize learners' performance across tests. Table 11.2 illustrates how learner-by-objective mastery can be illustrated across tests administered. The first row identifies the objectives, the second row identifies the tests, and subsequent rows are used to record students' mastery of objectives on each test. The two summary rows at the bottom of the table contain the percentage of students who mastered each objective on each test and the increase or decrease in percentages across tests for each objective. Ideally, the percentages of students who mastered each objective should increase from pretests to embedded tests and from embedded tests to posttests.

Such a pattern is illustrated for objectives 1, 2, and 3. For objective 1, the percentage increase from pretest to embedded test is +60. From the embedded test to the posttest, it is +20. Such differences indicate that the instruction for that objective was effective. A different pattern is observed for objective 4. A 40 percent increase is observed from the embedded test to the posttest, yet a 20 percent decrease is observed from the embedded test to the posttest. This pattern could indicate one of two things: learners are able to copy answers from the text for answering the embedded questions, or their retention of the information and skills is inadequate. Either way, you should review the instruction for objective 4.

You may also want to summarize learners' performance across tests using the percentage of objectives mastered by students on each test administered. Such a summary is illustrated in Table 11.3. The top row identifies the test and the number of objectives measured by each one. Subsequent rows contain the percentage of objectives mastered by each student on each test. The bottom row contains the average percentage of objectives mastered by the group on each test. From these data the designer could infer that: (1) the

TABLE 11.2

STUDENT PERFORMANCE ON THE PRETEST, EMBEDDED TEST, AND POSTTEST BY OBJECTIVE

Objectives:	1			2			3			4		
Test	PR	E	PS	PR	E	PS	PR	E	PS	PR	E	PS
Students 1		X	X		X	X	X	X	X	X	X	X
2		X	X		X	X		X	X		X	X
3	X	X	X			X	X	X	X			
4		X	X		X	X		X	X		X	X
20			X		X	X	X	X	X		X	X
% Mastering	20	80	100	10	80	100	50	100	100	40	80	60
Diff.	+60		+20	+70		+20	+50		0	+40		−20

PR = pretest; E = embedded test; PS = posttest; X = mastered
Note: Table includes data for only 5 of 20 students in the evaluation.

TABLE 11.3

ENTRY-BEHAVIOR, PRETEST, AND POSTTEST DATA SUMMARIZED BY THE PERCENT OF TOTAL POSSIBLE OBJECTIVES

Student Number	3 Entry Behavior Objectives	9 Pretest Instructional Objectives	9 Posttest Objectives
1	100	11	89
2	100	22	89
3	100	22	89
4	100	11	100
5	67	0	67
6	100	11	78
7	67	11	89
8	100	22	100
Mean	92	14	88

group selected was appropriate for the evaluation, (2) the instruction covered skills not previously mastered by the group, and (3) the instruction was effective in improving learners' skills.

GRAPHING LEARNERS' PERFORMANCES Another way to display data is through various graphing techniques. A graph may show the pretest and posttest performance for each objective in the formative evaluation study. You may also want to graph the amount of time required to complete the instructional materials as well as the amount of time required for the pretest and posttest. An example of a pretest/posttest graph appears in Figure 11.1.

FIGURE 11.1

PRETEST/POSTTEST GRAPH SHOWING LEARNER PERFORMANCE

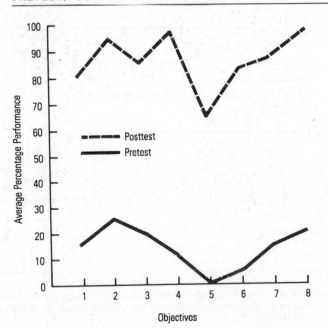

An excellent technique for summarizing formative evaluation data involves the instructional analysis chart. This procedure requires the determination of the average pretest and posttest performance of learners participating in the formative evaluation on each of the skills indicated on the instructional analysis chart. The designer uses a copy of the instructional analysis chart, without the statement of skills. See Figure 11.2 for an example of this technique. The pretest and posttest scores for each objective are entered in the appropriate boxes. This provides an interesting display of the interrelationships of the scores on the various skills in the instructional materials. It will become apparent if learners' performance declines as they approach the top of the hierarchy. You may also find a skill mastered by only a few learners that seems to have little effect on the subsequent mastery of superordinate skills.

OTHER TYPES OF DATA There are other kinds of data to summarize and analyze in addition to learners' performance on objectives. It has been found that a good way to summarize data from an attitude questionnaire is to indicate on a blank copy of the questionnaire the percent of learners who chose each alternative to the various questions. If you also request open-ended, general responses from the learners, you can summarize them for each question.

Another important type of data is the comments obtained from learners, from other instructors involved in the formative evaluation, and from subject-matter experts who react to the materials. It is almost impossible to sum-

FIGURE 11.2

SUMMARY OF PRETEST AND POSTTEST SCORES FOR A HYPOTHETICAL INSTRUCTIONAL ANALYSIS

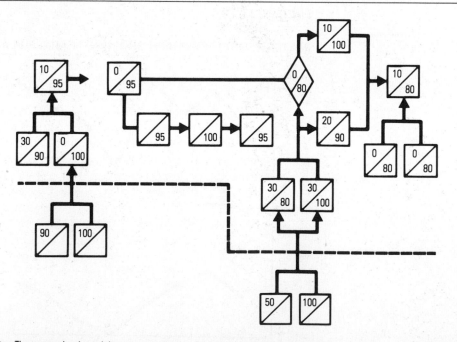

Note: The top number in each box represents the percentage of students who answered items correctly on the pretest. The bottom number represents the percentage who answered correctly on the posttest. Entry behaviors were not tested on the posttest.

marize these comments in tabular or graphic form. It is better to try to relate each of these comments to the instructional materials themselves, or to the objective in the materials to which they refer. These comments can be written directly on a copy of the materials.

The final type of data summary you may wish to prepare is related to any alternative approaches you may have used during either the small-group or field-trial evaluations. These data may be performance on specific test items, responses on an attitude questionnaire, or even an indication of total learning time.

SEQUENCE FOR EXAMINING DATA As you prepare summaries of your data, you will quickly begin to get an overall picture of the general effectiveness of your instructional materials and the extent of revisions you may be required to make. After generally examining the data, we suggest that you examine the data in the sequence described below.

First, after reviewing data for any defective items, you should examine the data with regard to the entry behaviors of students. Did the students in the formative evaluation have the entry behaviors you anticipated? If so, did they succeed with the instructional materials? If they did succeed, but did not have the required entry behaviors, you must question whether you have identified critical entry behaviors.

The second step is to review the pretest and posttest data as displayed on the instructional analysis chart. If you sequenced the materials appropriately and if you identified skills that are hierarchically dependent upon each other, then learner performance should decrease as you move upward through the hierarchy—that is, there should be poorer learner performance on the terminal objective than on the earlier skills. When the instruction is working well, there will, of course, be no decline in learner performance as learners complete the skills at the top of the hierarchy. These data will help you identify exactly where problems exist and perhaps even suggest a change in the instructional sequence for certain skills.

Third, you might examine the pretest scores to determine the extent to which individual learners, and the group as a whole, had already acquired the skills that you were to teach. If they already possess most of the skills, then you will receive relatively little information about the effectiveness of the instruction or how it might be improved. If they lack these skills, you will have more confidence in the analyses that follow.

By comparing pretest with posttest scores objective-by-objective, which is usually what is done when you examine the instructional analysis chart, you can assess learners' performance on each particular objective and begin to focus on specific objectives that appear to need revision.

As you identify objectives on which the students performed poorly, examine the exact wording of the objective and the associated test items. Before revising the instructional materials, refer to your item analysis table to see if poor test items, rather than the materials, indicated poor learner performance. All that may be needed is revised test items rather than a major revision of the instructional materials.

The next step is to examine the instructional strategy associated with the various objectives with which learners had difficulty. Was the planned strategy actually used in the instructional materials? Are there alternative strategies that might be employed? The final step is to examine the materials themselves to evaluate the comments about problem areas made by learners, instructors, and subject-matter experts.

An important concern in any formative evaluation is the amount of time required by students to complete the instructional materials. It may be necessary for you to revise the materials to make them fit within a particular time period. This is an extremely difficult task and it must be done with great care. With individualized materials it is not unusual for the slowest learner to take two or three times longer than the fastest student. Knowing what to remove from the materials or change without interfering with learning is very difficult to determine. Often the decision can be made only after a trial/revise/trial/revise process with target learners.

Data that relate to the implementation of the instructional materials must also be examined. We suggested earlier that you may gather misleading data because of the faulty operations of media equipment. There may also have been disruptions in the classroom, a lunch break, or any one of a variety of other kinds of activities that are common to various instructional settings. Since these disruptions cannot be controlled, they simply must be noted and explained.

On the other hand, there are procedural concerns that can be controlled. Were learners hindered by the logistics required to use the materials? Were there questions about how to proceed from one step to the next? Were there long delays in getting test scores? These are the kinds of implementation procedures' problems that often are identified in questionnaires and debriefing discussions. Solutions to such problems must be found and incorporated into either the instruction or the instructor's manual to make the instructional activity run more smoothly.

We suggest that as you begin the revision process, you summarize your data as suggested in this chapter. We recognize that the needs of instructional designers will differ according to the type of materials with which they are working. However, the strategy suggested here should apply to almost any instructional design effort. For example, if you have taught a psychomotor skill, your posttest performance would be recorded on a checklist of some sort, and summarized on your instructional analysis chart. There might also be a paper-and-pencil test of subordinate skills and knowledge. These scores should be examined in connection with their associated motor skills. The use of attitude responses and learning time would be the same for any type of instruction.

Given all the data from a small-group or field-trial evaluation, the designer must make decisions about how to make the revisions. It is almost always apparent where the problems are, but it is not always apparent what changes should be made. If a comparison of several approaches has been embedded in the formative evaluation, then the results should indicate the type of changes to be made. Otherwise, the strategies suggested for revising instruction following the one-to-one evaluations also apply at this point—namely, use the data, your experience, and sound learning principles as the bases for your revisions.

One caution: Avoid responding too quickly to any single piece of data, whether it is the learners' performance on a particular objective, a comment from an individual learner, or an observation by a subject-matter expert. They are all valuable pieces of information, but you should attempt to corroborate these data with other data. Look for performance as well as observational data that will help you focus on particular deficiencies in the instructional materials.

An additional suggestion: When summarizing data from the field evaluation, you should be careful to summarize it in an accurate and clear fashion.

You will find that these data will be of interest not only to you as the instructional designer, but will also serve as an effective vehicle to show others how learners performed with this mode of instruction. The table and graphs can provide both a general and a detailed description of the overall performance of the learners.

Revising Selected Materials and Instructor-Delivered Instruction

The data summary and revision procedures described above are equally appropriate when the instructor develops original instructional materials, uses a variety of selected materials, or works from lecture notes. The types of data that are collected, the ways in which they are summarized, and the ways in which they are used to direct the revision process are all similar. When working with selected materials, however, there is little opportunity to revise the materials directly, especially if they are commercially produced and copyrighted. Therefore, the instructor can consider the following: In the future, delete portions of the instruction, add other materials, or simply develop supplementary instruction. Procedures for the use of materials and the student guide should also be reconsidered in light of formative evaluation data.

Instructors working from lecture notes or an outline have the same flexibility as the developer for changing instruction. A pretest and a posttest, together with an attitude questionnaire, should provide data for a thorough analysis of the instruction. Summary tables that indicate performance on each objective should be prepared. Examine learner performance on test items and objectives and then relate learner performance by objective to the instructional analysis diagram.

The instructor's class notes should reflect questions raised by learners and responses to those questions. Learners' questions should be examined to determine whether basic misunderstandings have developed. Were the responses to the questions sufficient to provide adequate performance by learners on the related test items?

An instructor who used lecture notes is also likely to obtain a greater "spread" in the scores on tests and reactions on attitude questionnaires. Research data indicate that, by the very nature of group-paced, interactive instruction, some students are unlikely to understand the concepts as rapidly as others during a given class period. Since there are typically no embedded remedial strategies in group instruction, such learners learn progressively less during a series of lessons, and receive progressively poorer scores; their attitudes will likely reflect this situation. In this interactive, group-paced mode, learners' performance is likely to resemble a bell curve distribution (i.e., a few high scores, a few low scores, and mostly average scores).

Identifying learners who are performing poorly and inserting appropriate activities are important components of the revision process for the instructor who is using an interactive instructional approach. Unlike using written instructional materials, the instructor can revise the presentation during its implementation and note the reasons for the change.

One final observation needs to be made. We have stressed that you are working with a systems approach to build an instructional system, and when you change one component of the system, you are changing the whole system. You need to be aware, therefore, that when you make changes through the revision process, you cannot assume that the remaining unchanged instruction will necessarily maintain its initial effectiveness. You may hope your changes are for the better, but you cannot assume that they always are.

EXAMPLES

The theme writing unit will be used to illustrate techniques for summarizing and analyzing data collected during formative evaluation activities. Examples provided in this section are designed to illustrate procedures you might use for either a small-group or field-trial evaluation of materials and procedures. Of course, the types of tables and summary procedures you actually use should be tailored to your instructional materials, tests, and procedures. These examples simply show some ways the information gathered could be summarized for the composition unit.

Fifteen students are used for the sample evaluation: five are below average, five are average, and five are above average in previous language skills achievement. Achievement was used to group students for the trial because we believed previous language skills might affect students' performance on the objectives included in the unit. If you believe that other factors besides achievement might make a difference in your group's performance level or learning speed, then those factors should be used to group learners for the evaluation.

Before beginning a description of each data summary table used, it might be worthwhile to discuss the order in which we have developed and presented tables. We started with item and objective analysis tables and worked toward more general objective and test data summaries. This strategy was followed since detailed item data will be needed as the basis to create the more general, synthesizing types of information.

SUMMARIZING ITEM-BY-OBJECTIVE DATA As you complete the field test, you will have individual tests to score for each student who participated. The item-by-objective table should be created *during* the grading process. Its purpose is to provide a method of summarizing each student's response to each item on the test. These data are valuable in the analysis process because they not only illustrate which items were missed by which students, but also provide a means to analyze their incorrect responses. The items missed will help guide you to areas in which the instruction needs to be revised, and the incorrect answers will provide clues about how instruction might be modified to be made more effective. Item analysis also provides the basis for determining whether objectives have been mastered.

The item-by-objective chart in Table 11.4 is based on the entry behavior items for the story writing materials contained in chapter 9. There were five entry behavior objectives and ten items used in the materials to measure students' performance on them. Item-by-objective data are summarized at the bottom of the table and learner mastery data are summarized in the far right columns.

With the data arranged as in Table 11.4, you will be able to make observations about the items and the learners on the test. First, you can evaluate the quality of the items. The bottom of Table 11.4 indicates the percentage of students who answered multiple items within an objective correctly. The results are consistent for objective 5.3, reflecting that each item is accurately

TABLE 11.4

STUDENT RESPONSES BY ITEM WITHIN OBJECTIVE ON THE ENTRY BEHAVIORS SECTION OF THE PRETEST

Objectives:	5.1	5.2	5.3			5.4	5.5							
Items	1	2	3	4	5	6	7	8	9	10	Score	%	Obj.	%
Students 1							X		X		2	20	0	0
2			X	X	X		X		X		5	50	1	20
3			X	X	X		X		X		5	50	1	20
4	X		X	X	X		X		X		6	60	2	40
5	X	X	X	X	X		X	X	X	X	9	90	4	80
6	X	X	X	X	X	X	X	X	X	X	10	100	5	100
7	X	X	X	X	X	X	X	X	X	X	10	100	5	100
8	X	X	X	X	X	X	X	X	X	X	10	100	5	100
9	X	X	X	X	X	X	X	X	X	X	10	100	5	100
10	X	X	X	X	X	X	X	X	X	X	10	100	5	100
11	X	X	X	X	X	X	X	X	X	X	10	100	5	100
12	X	X	X	X	X	X	X	X	X	X	10	100	5	100
13	X	X	X	X	X	X	X	X	X	X	10	100	5	100
14	X	X	X	X	X	X	X	X	X	X	10	100	5	100
15	X	X	X	X	X	X	X	X	X	X	10	100	5	100
Total Right	12	11	14	14	14	10	15	11	15	11				
% Right	80	73	93	93	93	66	100	73	100	73				
% Object.	80	73	93			66	73							

Note: X = correct response; blank = incorrect response.

measuring students' skills. The inconsistencies observed in the items for objective 5.5 indicate that further investigation is warranted. In this instance, the students selected all four items as correct; thus, they correctly guessed the answers to items 7 and 9.

Next, look at the students' scores on items and objectives in the last four columns. It appears that students one through four will have difficulties while studying the materials. The remaining students all appear to have all the prescribed prerequisite skills.

From our analysis of Table 11.4 we can make two conclusions: one about the entry behavior items and one about the group we have selected. First, the items within the test are functioning well to identify the level of student performance on the prerequisite skills. Second, our instruction may be inappropriate for those students who do not possess the required entry behaviors. We must observe the lessons closely to determine whether the second conclusion is true.

Another objective-by-item table was constructed to summarize performance data for the remainder of the pretest. These data appear in Table 11.5. First, review the data summaries at the bottom of the table. The only objectives mastered by the entire group were 5.8 and 5.9, which are related to the period. The inconsistent performance of students on items within other objectives reflected the fact that individual items could be answered correctly by guessing. This means that raw scores are misleading, and only objective level scores should be considered. When guessing correctly is a factor, you should set a criterion of answering all items within the set correctly for mastery. Examining the students' answers for objective 5.7, we found that students were classifying all items as declarative, which explains their high performance on items 3 and 5. Inspection of their answers for objective 5.10 indicated that inconsistent students were classifying anything with a period as a declarative sentence. The declarative sentence ending with a question mark (item 11) was identified as incorrect by everyone. This alerts us to the fact that students used ending punctuation rather than sentence content to

TABLE 11.5

PRETEST FOR DECLARATIVE SENTENCES: STUDENT PERFORMANCE BY ITEM WITHIN OBJECTIVE

Objective:	5.6	5.7					5.8	5.9		5.10					5.11				#		#	
Student/Item	1	2	3	4	5	6	7	8	9	10	11	12	13	14	15	16	17	18	Score	%	Obj.	%
1			X		X		X	X	X		X	X	X						8	44	2	33
2			X		X		X	X	X		X	X	X						8	44	2	33
3			X		X		X	X	X		X	X	X						8	44	2	33
4			X		X		X	X	X		X	X	X						8	44	2	33
5			X		X		X	X	X		X	X	X			X	X	X	11	61	2	33
6			X		X		X	X	X		X	X	X			X	X	X	11	61	2	33
7			X		X		X	X	X		X	X	X			X	X	X	11	61	2	33
8			X		X		X	X	X		X	X	X			X	X	X	11	61	2	33
9			X		X		X	X	X		X	X	X		X			X	10	55	2	33
10	X		X	X	X	X	X	X	X		X	X	X		X	X	X	X	15	83	4	66
11	X	X	X	X	X	X	X	X	X	X	X	X	X	X	X	X	X	X	18	100	6	100
12	X	X	X	X	X	X	X	X	X	X	X	X	X	X	X	X	X	X	18	100	6	100
13	X	X	X	X	X	X	X	X	X	X	X	X	X	X	X	X	X	X	18	100	6	100
14	X	X	X	X	X	X	X	X	X	X	X	X	X	X	X	X	X	X	18	100	6	100
15	X	X	X	X	X	X	X	X	X	X	X	X	X	X	X	X	X	X	18	100	6	100
# Right	6	5	15	6	15	6	15	15	15	5	15	15	15	5	7	10	10	11				
% Right	40	33	100	40	100	40	100	100	100	33	100	100	100	33	46	66	66	73				
% Mastering	40	26					100	100		33					40							

classify sentences. The inconsistencies in the four sentences (objective 5.11) reflected problems ranging from incomplete sentences to sentences that were not declarative. Some students could not write a declarative sentence, some came close to producing acceptable sentences, while others consistently produced declarative sentences.

Next, consider the last four columns related to individual student's performance. The group was quite heterogeneous in their skill related to declarative sentences. The first four students that we predicted would have difficulty, based on their entry behavior skills, earned lower scores than other students on the test. Another interesting finding was that five students earned perfect scores on the pretest, indicating that they have little to learn from this lesson. The remaining six students' performances fell between these two low and high clusters of students, indicating that they could benefit from the lesson on declarative sentences.

Based on the data from the pretest we can make the following conclusions:

1. Five students (11–15) did not appear to need the instruction.
2. Six students (5–10) appeared to need the instruction and should benefit from it since they possessed the entry behavior skills.
3. The performance of the four students who lacked the entry behavior skills (1–4) was lower than the performance of the other students in the group.
4. The items in objectives 5.7 and 5.10 were individually inadequate in measuring students' performance on these objectives. They were sufficient when mastery was set at answering all items within an objective correctly. Alternative item formats should be considered.
5. Students do not appear to need instruction on objectives 5.8 and 5.9 related to the period.

A third objective-by-item table was developed to summarize performance data for the embedded items; it is contained in Table 11.6. The data are overwhelmingly positive, because all difficulty values are .86 or above, and only one student failed an objective. Our conclusion based on these data was that students understood the instruction provided well enough to answer questions correctly within the text. Data from the subsequent posttest will need to be added before we can make more claims about the effectiveness of the instruction.

Summarizing Data Across Tests

We can use the summary data from these basic, detailed item-by-objective tables to construct objective summary tables that can be used to display our data from different measures administered throughout the instruction. These summaries can help us determine whether students progressed in skill development. Table 11.7 contains a summary of students by objective on the pretest, embedded test, and posttest, and it indicates that instruction was effective. Students who did not have the skills when they entered instruction had acquired them by the time they took the embedded tests. The posttest scores indicate that most students remembered the information and skills beyond immediately reading and practicing them in the instruction. One problem does surface in reviewing these data: Students who did not have the prescribed entry behaviors had difficulty writing declarative sentences on the posttest, which causes us to wonder whether their performance on the entry behaviors items is related to their difficulties on the posttest.

TABLE 11.6

STUDENT PERFORMANCE BY ITEM WITHIN OBJECTIVE ON EMBEDDED QUESTIONS FOR DECLARATIVE SENTENCES

Objective	5.6	5.7					5.8	5.9			5.10					5.11									Raw Score	Percent Correct	# obj	% obj
Item	1	A	B	C	D	E	3	A	B	C	A	B	C	D	E	1	2	3	4	5	6	7	8	9	(24)	Correct	obj	obj
1	X	X	X	X	X	X	X	X	X	X	X		X	X	X		X			X		X	X	X	19	79	4	66
2	X	X	X	X	X	X	X	X	X	X	X	X	X	X	X		X		X	X	X	X	X	X	22	92	5	83
3	X	X	X	X	X	X	X	X	X	X	X	X	X	X	X	X	X	X	X	X	X	X	X	X	24	100	6	100
4	X	X	X	X	X	X	X	X	X	X	X	X	X	X	X	X	X	X	X	X	X	X	X	X	24	100	6	100
5	X	X	X	X	X	X	X	X	X	X	X	X	X	X	X	X	X	X	X	X	X	X	X	X	24	100	6	100
6	X	X	X	X	X	X	X	X	X	X	X	X	X	X	X	X	X	X	X	X	X	X	X	X	24	100	6	100
7	X	X	X	X	X	X	X	X	X	X	X	X	X	X	X	X	X	X	X	X	X	X	X	X	24	100	6	100
8	X	X	X	X	X	X	X	X	X	X	X	X	X	X	X	X	X	X	X	X	X	X	X	X	24	100	6	100
9	X	X	X	X	X	X	X	X	X	X	X	X	X	X	X	X	X	X	X	X	X	X	X	X	24	100	6	100
10	X	X	X	X	X	X	X	X	X	X	X	X	X	X	X	X	X	X	X	X	X	X	X	X	24	100	6	100
11	X	X	X	X	X	X	X	X	X	X	X	X	X	X	X	X	X	X	X	X	X	X	X	X	24	100	6	100
12	X	X	X	X	X	X	X	X	X	X	X	X	X	X	X	X	X	X	X	X	X	X	X	X	24	100	6	100
13	X	X	X	X	X	X	X	X	X	X	X	X	X	X	X	X	X	X	X	X	X	X	X	X	24	100	6	100
14	X	X	X	X	X	X	X	X	X	X	X	X	X	X	X	X	X	X	X	X	X	X	X	X	24	100	6	100
15	X	X	X	X	X	X	X	X	X	X	X	X	X	X	X	X	X	X	X	X	X	X	X	X	24	100	6	100
Number of students	15	15	15	15	15	15	15	15	15	15	15	14	15	15	15	13	15	13	14	15	14	15	15	15	$\bar{x} = 17.8$			
Percent of students correct	100	100	100	100	100	100	100	100	100	100	100	93	100	100	100	86	100	86	93	100	93	100	100	100				

X = Correct
A blank space reflects an incorrect response

TABLE 11.7

STUDENT PERFORMANCE ON OBJECTIVES ON THE PRETEST, EMBEDDED TEST ITEMS, AND POSTTEST

Objective	5.6			5.7			5.8			5.9			5.10			5.11		
Content	Purpose			Identify			Name Punctuation			Punctuate			Recognize			Write		
Test	Pre	Emb	Post	Pre	Emb	Post	Pre	Emb	Post	Pre	Emb	Post	Pre	Emb	Post	Pre	Emb	Post
1		X	X		X	X	X	X	X	X	X	X		X				
2		X	X		X	X	X	X	X	X	X	X		X			X	
3		X	X		X	X	X	X	X	X	X	X		X	X		X	
4		X	X		X	X	X	X	X	X	X	X		X			X	
5		X	X		X	X	X	X	X	X	X	X		X	X		X	
6		X	X		X	X	X	X	X	X	X	X		X	X	X	X	X
7		X	X		X	X	X	X	X	X	X	X		X	X	X	X	X
8		X	X		X	X	X	X	X	X	X	X		X	X	X	X	X
9		X	X		X	X	X	X	X	X	X	X		X	X		X	X
10	X	X	X		X	X	X	X	X	X	X	X		X	X	X	X	X
11	X	X	X	X	X	X	X	X	X	X	X	X	X	X	X	X	X	X
12	X	X	X		X	X	X	X	X	X	X	X	X	X	X		X	X
13	X	X	X	X	X	X	X	X	X	X	X	X	X	X	X	X	X	X
14	X	X	X	X	X	X	X	X	X	X	X	X	X	X	X	X	X	X
15	X	X	X	X	X	X	X	X	X	X	X	X	X	X	X	X	X	X
Number of students passing	6	15	15	4	15	15	15	15	15	15	15	15	5	15	12	8	14	10
Percent of students passing	40	100	100	27	100	100	100	100	100	100	100	100	33	100	80	53	93	66
Differences	+60		0	+73		0	0		0	0		0	+67		−20	+40		−27

X = Objective passed

By reviewing the data at the bottom of the table, however, you can see that the instruction was partially effective for those who did not have the skills prior to instruction: 60 percent more students passed objective 5.6 on the posttest than did on the pretest, objective 5.7 had an increase of 73 percent from pretest to posttest, objective 5.10 had 47 percent more students pass the posttest, and 13 percent more students passed objective 5.11 on the posttest. There was no gain on 5.8 and 5.9 since the students earned 100 percent on both tests.

It would seem that instruction was not needed for objectives 5.8 and 5.9 for any member of the group. However, these two objectives appear to be the only ones in this category.

It is often helpful to review students' overall scores on the various tests. Table 11.8 illustrates the percent of items each student answered correctly

TABLE 11.8

ENTRY BEHAVIOR ITEMS, PRETEST, EMBEDDED TEST, AND POSTTEST BY PERCENTAGE OF POSSIBLE ITEMS AND BY PERCENTAGE OF POSSIBLE OBJECTIVES

	Percentage of Total Items					Percentage of Total Objectives			
Student	Entry behavior	Pretest	Embedded Test	Posttest	Student	Entry behavior	Pretest	Embedded Test	Posttest
1	20	44	79	80	1	0	33	66	66
2	50	44	92	80	2	20	33	83	66
3	50	44	100	85	3	20	33	100	83
4	60	44	100	80	4	40	33	100	66
5	90	61	100	85	5	80	33	100	83
6	100	61	100	100	6	100	33	100	100
7	100	61	100	100	7	100	33	100	100
8	100	61	100	100	8	100	33	100	100
9	100	55	100	100	9	100	33	100	100
10	100	83	100	100	10	100	66	100	100
11	100	100	100	100	11	100	100	100	100
12	100	100	100	100	12	100	100	100	100
13	100	100	100	100	13	100	100	100	100
14	100	100	100	100	14	100	100	100	100
15	100	100	100	100	15	100	100	100	100
# items	10	18	24	24	# obj	5	6	6	6

and the percent of objectives passed for the lesson. This information confirms the information from the previous tables, namely:

1. Students who performed poorly on the entry behaviors items did not progress as well as students who had mastered the entry behaviors.
2. All students' scores progressed from the pretest to the embedded test. However, students who did not have the entry behaviors did not progress as far or maintain their position on the posttest.
3. All students who possessed the entry behaviors mastered the embedded test and maintained their positions on the posttest.

Plotting data together from the three tests directly related to the instruction can help you visualize the impact of instruction. The data from these summary tables are displayed in Figure 11.3. The percent of students in each group was plotted by objective and by test. The groups are made up of students who mastered the pretest (5), who mastered the prerequisite skills but not the skills related to instruction (6), and who failed the prerequisite skills (4). The graph shows no new information; it simply displays what we already know:

1. Students who mastered the pretest did not need the instruction.
2. Students who mastered the prerequisite skills part of the pretest did not need instruction on the punctuation objectives; they benefited from the instruction related to all other objectives.
3. Students who did not have the entry behaviors did not need instruction on the punctuation objectives; they made significant gains on the classification and definition objectives; and they had trouble with the sentence writing objectives.

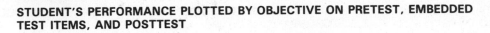

FIGURE 11.3

STUDENT'S PERFORMANCE PLOTTED BY OBJECTIVE ON PRETEST, EMBEDDED TEST ITEMS, AND POSTTEST

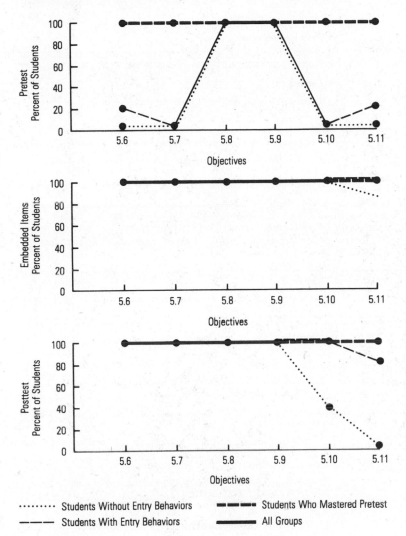

·········· Students Without Entry Behaviors   ▬ ▬ ▬ Students Who Mastered Pretest

─ ─ ─ Students With Entry Behaviors   ▬▬▬ All Groups

Summarizing Attitudinal Data

The data collected on attitude questionnaires and in debriefing sessions can be summarized to provide additional information about the effectiveness of instruction. Students' answers can be tallied on a blank form of the questionnaire. Table 11.9 provides an example of how overall questionnaire data can be summarized. As each questionnaire is read, the responses can be tallied on a blank form and then summarized by the percentage of each subgroup that answered the question in a particular way. Free response comments from the questions and debriefing session are also summarized on the form. This type of information may provide insights into how to improve either your instruction or procedures.

You may want to consider students' attitudes about the instruction by group. In the example, four students did not have the entry behaviors, six students had the entry behaviors but lacked several of the skills to be taught,

TABLE 11.9

SUMMARY OF STUDENTS' RESPONSES ON ATTITUDE QUESTIONNAIRE BY GROUP

Name _____*Summary*_____ Date __*1-16*__ Class __*Small Group*__

Attitude Questionnaire

Please answer the following questions to help us understand what you think about the lessons on writing different kinds of sentences. Your opinions will help us make better lessons for you.

A. Motivation

1. Did you enjoy the story about the birthday present?
   _*15*_ Yes   //// ЦЩ / ЦЩ
   _____ No

2. Did you think the version of the story that had all types of sentences included (B) was more interesting than the first (A)?
   _*15*_ Yes   //// ЦЩ / ЦЩ
   _____ No

3. Did reading the story make you want to try to write more interesting stories yourself?
   _*15*_ Yes   //// ЦЩ / ЦЩ
   _____ No

4. What kinds of stories do you most like to read?
   *horses, pets, space, sports, nature, cars, mysteries*

B. Objectives

1. Did you understand that you were going to learn to write stories that were more interesting?
   _*15*_ Yes   //// ЦЩ / ЦЩ
   _____ No

2. Did you understand that you were going to learn to use four different kinds of sentences in your stories?
   _*15*_ Yes   //// ЦЩ / ЦЩ
   _____ No

3. Did you want to write different kinds of sentences?
   _*15*_ Yes   //// ЦЩ / ЦЩ
   _____ No

C. Entry Behaviors

1. Were the questions about subjects, predicates, and complete sentences clear to you?
   _*15*_ Yes   //// ЦЩ ЦЩ
   _____ No

2. Did you already know about subjects, predicates, and complete sentences before you started?
   _*14*_ Yes   /// ЦЩ / ЦЩ
   _*1*_ No   /

3. Do you wish information about subjects, predicates, and complete sentences had been included in the lesson?
   _____ Yes
   _*15*_ No   //// ЦЩ ЦЩ

D. Tests

1. Did you think questions on the pretest were clear?
   _*8*_ Yes   /// ЦЩ   *Didn't know the answers*
   _*7*_ No   ////   ///   *Vocabulary clear*

2. Did you think you knew most of the answers on the pretest?
   _*9*_ Yes   /   ///   ЦЩ
   _*6*_ No   ///   ///

3. Were the questions on the posttest clear or confusing?
   _*15*_ Clear   //// ЦЩ / ЦЩ
   _____ Confusing

4. Did you think questions within the lesson were clear or confusing?
   _*15*_ Clear   //// ЦЩ / ЦЩ
   _____ Confusing

E. Instruction

1. Was the instruction interesting?
   _*15*_ Yes   //// ЦЩ / ЦЩ
   _____ No

2. Was the instruction clear?
   __15__ Yes //// ₩ / ₩
   _____ No
   If not, what wasn't clear? _____*Where were the stories?*_____

3. Were the example questions helpful?
   __10__ Yes //// ₩ /
   __5__ No   ₩

4. Were there too many examples? Too Few?
   __5__ Yes   __3__ Yes
   __10__ No   __4__ No

5. Did the practice questions in the instruction help you?
   __10__ Yes //// ₩ /
   __5__ No   ₩
   If not, why not? _____
   _____

6. Did the feedback exercises in the instruction help you?
   __10__ Yes //// ₩ /
   __5__ No   ₩
   If not, why not? _____
   _____

F. Overall

1. Generally, did you like the lesson?
   __15__ Yes //// ₩ / ₩
   _____ No

2. Did you learn to do things you couldn't do before?
   __10__ Yes //// ₩ /
   __5__ No   ₩

3. What do you think would improve the lesson most?
   _____*More example stories to see; pick out declarative*_____
   _____*sentences in stories; the lesson wasn't about*_____
   _____*writing stories*_____
   _____
   _____
   _____

and five students had mastered all the skills prior to taking the pretest. It is likely that these differences in skill levels among students in the group influenced their attitudes during instruction; therefore, their responses were tallied on the questionnaire by group. The first cluster of four tallies reflects the lowest level students, the second cluster of six tallies reflects students who possessed the entry behaviors, and the third cluster of five tallies reflects students who had already mastered the skills. The total number of students selecting each response is summarized in the blanks.

Additionally, write-in responses are summarized on the questionnaire. These summaries may provide insights into how to improve either your instruction or procedures. For example, students reported wanting to see more example stories. They also voiced disappointment about the fact that the lesson was not about writing stories. These comments came from students who did and did not possess the entry behavior skills. From these comments we concluded that they did not perceive the lesson as relevant to the objectives and stories in the preinstructional material. Thus, the material should be revised.

An approach to revising the material might be to embed example stories in the text. Declarative sentences within the stories could be illustrated using underlining, and the information presented about declarative sentences could focus on the underlined sentences. For practice in locating declarative sentences, students could be asked to underline other declarative sentences in the story. For practice in writing declarative sentences, students could be asked to write a declarative sentence to introduce or conclude a given story. Perhaps keeping the lesson focused on sentences in stories will correct the error.

Determining How to Revise Instruction

It is premature to make final decisons about all the changes that may need to be made in the materials for one segment of a total unit of instruction. Before actually making some changes, other lessons should be field tested and analyzed. The changes should be made based upon the overall effectiveness of material in the unit. However, we can use data gathered on the first instructional lesson as well as the entry behaviors items to create a materials revision analysis table such as the one in Table 11.10. The table has four parts.

TABLE 11.10

MATERIALS REVISION ANALYSIS FORM

Component	Problem	Change	Evidence and Source
Motivational introductory material	None	Perhaps add another example story to the material	Students reported enjoying illustrative story and understanding the purpose for the unit (attitude questionnaire). All groups reported wanting to read more example stories on the questionnaire and in the debriefing session.
Entry behaviors items	None	None	1. Items did identify students who would have difficulty with first lesson (comparison of entry behavior scores and posttest scores). 2. Test fits time frame. 3. Students understood vocabulary used and question structure.
Pretest on Instructional Objectives	None	None	1. Pretest did separate students who knew the materials from those who did not. 2. Vocabulary level OK. 3. Time frame OK. 4. Question format OK.
Materials content	1. Instruction on punctuation (5.8 and 5.9) not needed by any students	Potential removal of punctuation objectives from lesson	Observe problems with periods used to close imperative and exclamatory

TABLE 11.10 *(continued)*

Component	Problem	Change	Evidence and Source
			sentences in subsequent lessons—may provide foundation here.
	2. Entire lesson not needed by students who mastered pretest	Possibly have high ability students begin with lesson two	Five students did not need lesson (pretest, embedded test, posttest, attitude questionnaire).
	3. Entry behaviors skills and sentence writing skills not mastered by some members of the group	Develop a set of remedial materials for these students to cover entry behaviors as well as provide more practice in writing sentences	1. Four students had difficulty recognizing complete sentences, subjects, and predicates (pretest). 2. Four students had difficulty writing sentences (posttest, objective 5.11).
	4. Students lost focus on story writing in lesson on sentences	Add stories from which students can classify declarative sentences. Have students write declarative sentences for given stories.	Debriefing session and questionnaire.
Embedded Tests	Predictive Validity (embedded items did not indicate eventual problems on posttest for same items)	Insert embedded test items on recognizing complete sentences and writing sentences in materials a distance from instruction and examples.	Embedded test items functioned well in the materials, *but* they did not predict students who would have difficulty on the posttest. This may be related to students' ability to mimic sentences in the embedded tests (embedded and posttest scores).
Posttest	None	None	1. Test did idenfity students having difficulty with objectives 5.10 and 5.11. 2. Time OK. 3. Question format OK. 4. Vocabulary OK (posttest data).
Attitude Questionnaire	None	None	1. Did detect dissatisfaction of high ability students with lesson. 2. Information corroborated correct level of difficulty for students with prerequisite skills. 3. Information from students without the prerequisites (guessing) was corroborated with test data.

The component being evaluated is listed in the left column. Problems identified and potential changes are described in the next two columns. The last column contains the evidence used and source of evidence to justify the change. The resources used to complete the table are: (1) test data and observations of students using the materials, (2) notes and remarks students make in the materials, and (3) information taken from the attitude questionnaire. By reviewing the materials revision prescriptions, you can see the value of the verbal descriptions of each item analysis table made previously.

It is important to remember that changes you make in your materials may have consequences other than the ones you anticipate. If extensive changes are made, such as inserting remedial materials for below average students and excusing above average students from selected lessons, then you should conduct another field trial with these changes in place to see whether the desired impact was realized.

SUMMARY

The data you collect during the formative evaluation should be synthesized and analyzed in order to locate potential problems in the instructional materials. Your data summaries should include learners' remarks in the materials; their performance on the pretest, embedded tests, and posttest; their responses on the attitude questionnaire; and their comments during debriefing sessions. Once you get the data summarized you should perform the following analyses:

1. Examine the summarized data relative to entry behaviors and draw implications about the entry behaviors of students in your target group.
2. Review summarized pretest, embedded test, and posttest data both for total performance and objective-by-objective performance. Superimpose the averages on your instructional analysis chart. Draw inferences about your group's performance on each test and each objective. You may want to compare data obtained from the entry-behavior items with pretest and posttest data as well.
3. Examine the objectives, test items, and instructional strategy for those objectives where student performance failed to meet your established criteria. Check the objectives, test items, vocabulary, sequence, and instructional strategy for those objectives prior to making direct changes in the instructional materials.
4. Check procedures and implementation directions as well as equipment required for instruction for possible guides to revision.
5. Develop a materials revision analysis table that describes problems, changes, evidence that changes are needed, and sources of evidence cited for each component in the materials.
6. Revise instruction based upon your prescriptions in the materials revision analysis table. Delay any revisions that may depend upon information from the field testing of other lessons.

These data synthesis and analysis activities are undertaken following each of the one-to-one, small-group, and field-trial formative evaluations. If you make major revisions in your materials following the field trial, another trial is advisable to check the effectiveness of your revisions.

The final revision of your materials should be effective in bringing about the intended learning with members of your target audience. Therefore, you are ready to reproduce or publish a good, professional set of instructional materials.

=== PRACTICE ===

1. What data would you use to determine whether students in your target group actually possessed the entry behaviors identified and whether those you identified were relevant to your instruction?
2. When should you develop remedial materials?
3. What type of data table should you create to provide the information necessary to determine the exact nature of problems students have with the materials?
4. Why should you construct a narrative explanation from data tables of problems that occurred with each test?
5. Why should you summarize performance by objective across tests administered (pretest, embedded test, posttest)?
6. What materials should you evaluate using an attitude questionnaire?
7. What information should you include in a materials revision analysis table?
8. Table 11.11 contains an incomplete item-by-objective table. Using the raw data included, calculate the following:
   a. Raw score for each student
   b. Percent of items correct for each student
   c. Number of objectives passed by each student
   d. Number of students answering each item correctly

TABLE 11.11

ITEM-BY-OBJECTIVE ANALYSIS TABLE

Objective	1			2			3			4			Raw Score	Percent Correct	Objectives Passed	Percent Objectives Passed
Item	1	2	3	4	5	6	7	8	9	10	11	12				
Student 1	X	X	X		X	X				X	X					
2	X	X	X	X	X	X	X	X	X	X	X					
3				X	X	X				X	X					
4	X			X	X	X	X	X	X	X	X					
5	X	X	X	X	X	X	X	X	X	X	X					
Total students correct																
Percent students correct																
Percent students passing objective																

X = Correct answer
Incorrect answer is left blank
To pass an objective, all items within the objective must be correct since each item was constructed to test a different facet of the objective.

e. Percent of students answering each item correctly
f. Percent of students passing each objective.

Check your answers with those in Table 11.12.

══ FEEDBACK ══

1. You would use item and objective analysis data from the items on the pretest, embedded test items, and posttest. Data from the entry behaviors' pretest would tell you whether students possessed the entry behaviors. Data from tests used with the instructional materials would tell you whether you had actually identified relevant entry behaviors. If students perform poorly on the entry behaviors items yet are successful on subsequent tests, then you need to reexamine the entry behaviors you have identified.

2. You should *not* develop remedial materials prior to at least the one-to-one test of your materials. As you could see in the examples section, data from the field test will tell you whether any remedial materials are needed at all and for what specific objectives they are needed.

3. You should construct an item/objective analysis table. It should be constructed in a manner to enable you to analyze correct answers as well as incorrect answers. Correct-answer analysis tells you whether your in-

TABLE 11.12

ITEM-BY-OBJECTIVE ANALYSIS TABLE

Objective	1			2			3			4			Raw Score	Percent Correct	Objectives Passed	Percent Objectives Passed
Item	1	2	3	4	5	6	7	8	9	10	11	12				
Student 1	X	X	X		X	X				X	X		7	58	1	25
2	X	X	X	X	X	X	X	X	X	X	X		11	91	3	75
3				X	X	X				X	X		5	41	1	25
4	X			X	X	X	X	X	X	X	X		9	75	2	50
5	X	X	X	X	X	X	X	X	X	X	X		11	91	3	75
Total students correct	4	3	3	4	5	5	3	3	3	5	5	0				
Percent students correct	80	60	60	80	100	100	60	60	60	100	100	0				
Percent students passing objective	60			80			60			0						

X = Correct answer
Incorrect answer is left blank
To pass an objective, all items within the objective must be correct since each item was constructed to test a different facet of the objective.

struction was effective; incorrect-answer analysis tells you what went wrong and helps you focus on revisions that might help.

4. You should construct a narrative analysis from the data for each test while the information is fresh in your mind, because this information becomes one basis for the materials revisions analysis table. If you do not do it and have many raw data tables from several tests before you, it is very difficult to focus and pinpoint problems that have occurred.

5. The summary tables highlight trends in performance. If students failed to master an objective on the pretest, was it mastered on the embedded test or on the posttest? If students mastered an objective on the embedded test, did they retain the information until the posttest?

6. All components of the materials should be evaluated on the attitude questionnaire. It is recommended that attitude questionnaires be administered at the same time that materials are used by students. We recommend embedding attitude questions within the lessons so students comment while the material is fresh in their minds. If this approach is used, care must be taken not to disrupt the flow of learning.

7. A materials revision analysis table should contain five types of information: (a) the name of the component, (b) problems identified with the component, (c) changes to be made in the materials, (d) evidence from either test or questionnaire data, remarks in materials and observations of how procedures worked, and (e) the source of evidence cited as the reason(s) for changes.

8. See Table 11.12.

References and Recommended Readings

Baker, E. L. (1974). *Evaluating instruction programs.* National Institute for Education Researcher Training Task Force, University of California, Los Angeles. This book describes the various stages of formative evaluation, the types of data that can be collected, and the types of revisions that may be made.

Performance and Instruction 22 (5), 1983. This is a special issue on formative evaluation.

Wager, W. (1976). The formative evaluation outcomes matrix. *Educational Technology*, 16 (10), 36–38. Wager describes a procedure for determining what revisions should be made in the instruction, based on the pattern of performance of the learners.

Wolf, R. M. (1974). Data analysis and reporting considerations in evaluation. In Popham, W. J. (Ed.), *Evaluation in education, Current applications.* Berkeley, CA: McCutchan Publishing Corp., 205–242. This chapter suggests various ways of setting up evaluation studies, how to analyze data, and how to display data.

12

SUMMATIVE EVALUATION

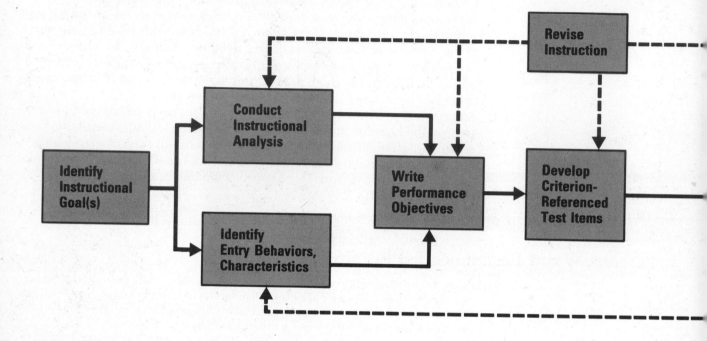

OBJECTIVES

- Describe the purpose of summative evaluation.
- Describe the two phases of summative evaluation and the decisions resulting from each phase.
- Design a summative evaluation for comparing alternative sets of candidate instructional materials.
- Contrast formative and summative evaluation by purpose and design.

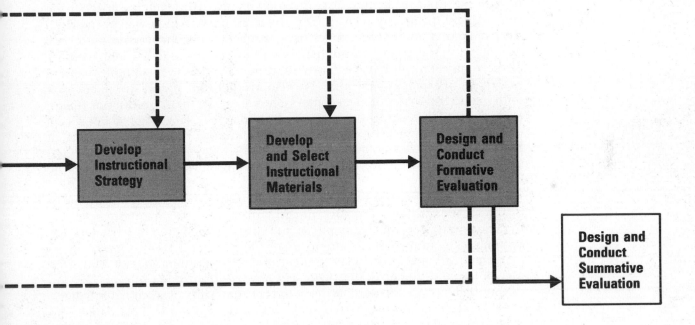

BACKGROUND

At present a technological revolution in the production, packaging, and distribution of instructional materials is occurring. The previous high costs of producing and marketing sophisticated-looking instructional materials meant that those available had been carefully reviewed by commercial publishers. In selecting materials, they employed several content experts who read the manuscripts and recommended whether the quality of the materials justified their production. Instructional materials were typically available from a few publishers, and decisions to adopt materials depended on what was available, the reputation of the publisher for quality materials, and the appearance of the materials. The technological revolution in the production of materials is rapidly changing this system.

Today, individuals have access to high-quality word processors, word processing and graphics programs, and laser printers that enable them to produce instructional materials that rival in appearance those available from long-established publishing firms. There is also a growing national network for marketing these "maverick" materials through copy services. Terms such as *desktop publishing* and *professor publishing services* are now part of our vocabulary. These new materials, just like those produced by established publishers, may or may not be quality materials from a learning standpoint. The new technology means that eventually it will be more difficult to judge the quality of materials "by their cover." It also will make obsolete the old saying, "publish or perish." Today, virtually anyone who wants to can publish instructional materials, and thus the saying is likely to become "publish and publish."

We predict that this revolution will increase the need for summative evaluation and for instructional designers as summative evaluators during the 1990s. In the past two decades, summative evaluation was more a principle than a practice, and its lack of application in the field caused many designers (ourselves included), to question its fate. However, we now believe that we had a concept derived from systems logic, which was premature. We predict that increased competition for marketing instructional materials will mean that established publishers will attend more to the effectiveness of their materials with target learners rather than to the acceptability of the materials to experts in the field. We also predict that successful publishers will include instructional designers as a part of their production team. Designers, unlike content experts, editors, and artists, can judge other aspects of competing manuscripts and can conduct studies to verify the quality of materials from a design perspective with target learners. Such documented evidence will make a dramatic improvement in marketing materials in the future.

Another prediction is that school districts and training organizations in business, the military, and government will need to become more selective in choosing among materials purported to meet their needs. Instructional designers as summative evaluators can help organizations choose those materials that are most likely to meet their instructional needs. Thus, the instructional designer in the 1990s will have a tailor-made role as a liaison for publishers and potential authors and for materials users and publishers.

Considering the present revolution and the demands it will place on go–no go decisions about instructional materials, we have renewed our interest in summative evaluation. This chapter contains some new perspectives and procedures and maintains those ideas that remain relevant from past editions of the text.

CONCEPTS

Summative evaluation is defined as the design of evaluation studies and the collection of data to verify the effectiveness of instructional materials with target learners. Its main purpose is to make go–no go decisions about maintaining currently used instructional materials or about adopting materials that have the potential for meeting an organization's defined instructional needs. The materials evaluated may or may not have undergone formative evaluation and revision. Materials evaluated may come from commercial publishers, a local curriculum team, or an individual. The scope of the materials varies as well. They may be intended for a one-day workshop, a short course of some type, or for a semester or year of instruction. The scope of the materials does not change the basic design of the study; rather, it influences the amount of time required to complete it.

A summative evaluation has two main phases: expert judgment and field trial. The purpose of the expert judgment phase is to determine whether presently used materials or other candidate materials have the potential for meeting an organization's defined instructional needs. The purpose of the field-trial phase is to document the effectiveness of promising materials with target group members in the intended setting. The decisions to be made during each phase and the evaluation activities supporting each one are diagrammed in Figure 12.1.

FIGURE 12.1

THE EXPERT JUDGMENT AND FIELD-TRIAL PHASES OF SUMMATIVE EVALUATION

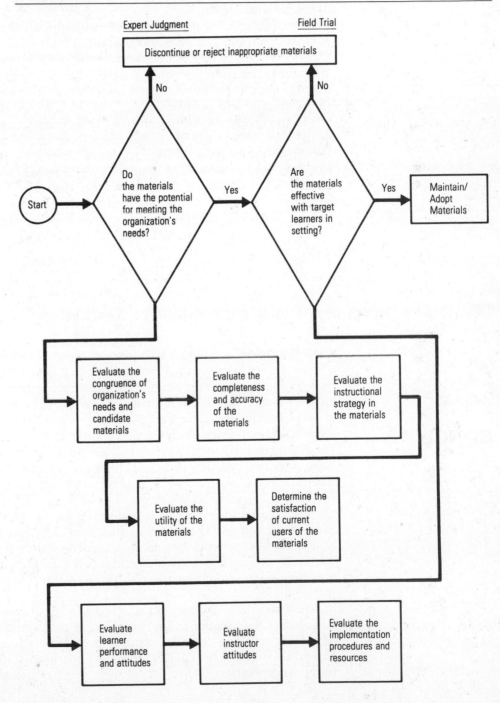

The activities undertaken in the expert judgment phase to decide whether candidate materials are promising include: (1) evaluating the congruence between the organization's instructional needs and candidate materials, (2) evaluating the completeness and accuracy of candidate materials, (3) evaluating the instructional strategy contained in the candidate materials, (4) evaluating the utility of the materials, and (5) determining current users' satisfaction with the materials. When materials have been tailored to the defined needs of the organization, systematically designed and developed, and formatively evaluated prior to the summative evaluation, then the expert judgment phase has been accomplished. The expert judgment phase is imperative when the organization is unfamiliar with the materials and their developmental history.

The field trial for the summative evaluation includes documenting learner performance and attitudes, documenting instructor/implementor attitudes, and documenting procedures and resources required to implement the instruction. The main purpose of the field trial is to locate both the strengths and weaknesses in the materials, to determine their causes, and to document the strengths and problems.

Both the expert judgment and the field trial can be focused on one set of instructional materials or on competing sets of materials. Typically the expert judgment phase is used to choose among available materials in order to select one or two sets of materials that appear most promising for a field trial. Both phases are described in more detail in the following sections. In reading the material on the expert judgment phase, assume that the materials to be evaluated are unfamiliar to you and that you are faced with the decision of whether to recommend expending additional effort and cost for a field trial.

The Expert Judgment Phase of Summative Evaluation

CONGRUENCE ANALYSIS Regardless of whether the summative evaluation involves materials comparisons or is focused on one set of instructional materials, the evaluator must determine the congruence between the organization's needs, the characteristics of their target learners, and the needs and characteristics the candidate materials were designed to address. To perform the congruence analysis, you should first obtain a clear description of the organization's needs, which include an accurate description of the entry behaviors and characteristics of the target learners. After obtaining this information, you should locate instructional materials that have potential for meeting the organization's needs. For each set of candidate materials identified, you should obtain a clear description of the goals and objectives of the instruction and the target audience for which it is intended. This information can sometimes be found in a foreword or preface in the materials themselves or in the instructor's manual. If these descriptions are too general, you may wish to contact the publisher of the materials for more detailed information.

You should also analyze the congruence between the resources the organization has available for purchasing and implementing instructional materials and the costs of obtaining and installing candidate materials. Materials that are too costly, however effective, often cannot be considered by an organization.

Once adequate descriptions are obtained, you should compare: (1) the organization's needs versus needs addressed in the materials, (2) the organization's target groups versus target groups for the materials, and (3) the organization's resources versus requirements for obtaining and implementing the instruction. The information from your congruence analysis should be shared with the organization's administrators. Although you may be asked to make recommendations, final decisions about which of the candidate materials to include in a summative evaluation, or whether to even continue the evaluation, rests with the administrators.

Quality of Materials

Several groups of questions related to the design of quality materials should be addressed for any instruction selected for a summative evaluation. These questions should be answered prior to engaging in any field trials of the materials with learners. The first area relates to the accuracy and completeness of the materials and any accompanying tests. The second relates to the adequacy of the instructional strategy related to the type or types of learning outcomes anticipated, the third relates to the utility of the materials, and the fourth relates to the satisfaction of current users of the materials. If some or all of the candidate materials are judged to be unsound in these important aspects, continuing the summative evaluation would be fruitless. Thus administrators should be informed of your judgments following this phase of the summative evaluation, and again they should be asked whether they wish to continue the summative evaluation.

The manner in which we design and conduct this phase of the summative evaluation is similar to some of the strategies used in the one-to-one formative evaluation, but it has some distinctive features as well. Let's consider each area of questions in turn.

ACCURACY AND COMPLETENESS OF MATERIALS Since you may not be a content expert in the materials you evaluate, it may be necessary to engage a content expert as a consultant. What you must consider is how best to use this expert. One strategy would be to provide the experts with copies of all candidate materials and ask them to judge the accuracy and completeness of the materials for the organization's stated goals. A better, more cost-effective strategy would be to work with the expert(s) to produce an instructional analysis of the stated goal. The document the expert(s) produces should include both the goal analysis and the subordinate skills analysis. A framework that identifies and sequences the main steps and subordinate skills in the goal would be a valuable standard against which you can evaluate the accuracy and completeness of any candidate materials.

How can the framework be used? The skills included in the framework can be converted to a checklist or rating scale the evaluator uses to review and judge the quality of the candidate materials and any accompanying tests.

ADEQUACY OF THE DESIGN Similar to the one-to-one formative evaluation, you need to evaluate the adequacy of the components of the instructional strategy included in the candidate materials. As an external evaluator, you may not know whether particular components of the strategy are present, and if present, whether they have the potential for gaining and maintaining learners' attention. Again, a checklist that can be used for reviewing and comparing candidate materials would be the most thorough and time-saving approach.

In developing this checklist, you should list the components of the instructional strategy in the far left column and use the remaining columns for recording related information about candidate materials. Although the basic components of the strategy do not change, you may want to adopt criteria related to each component based on the type of learning outcome(s) addressed in the materials. The evaluator's response format you use can also be expected to vary based on the nature of the instruction.

UTILITY OF MATERIALS The third area of questions about the instructional materials relates to the utility of the candidate materials. For each set, you should consider such factors as the availability of a learner guide or syllabus and an instructor's manual. Factors related to the durability of the materials are another consideration. Another is any special resources, such as instructor capabilities, equipment, or environments (e.g., learning centers) that are required. A utility concern is whether the materials require group pacing or can be individualized. You may also wish to revisit the issue of the relative costs of obtaining and implementing the materials. In fact, any factors that might enhance or restrict the utility of the materials for the organization should be considered.

To design this part of the summative evaluation, you may need to interview the administrators who requested the evaluation. Through discussions with them you can ensure that you have determined their needs, resources, and constraints. They may help to identify utility questions that you may not have considered.

Using the utility questions you select, you can design a summary form to focus your attention on each question as you reevaluate all the candidate materials. As in the previous examples, the important questions can be listed in the left column of your checklist and a separate response column provided for each set of materials. One possible difference between this checklist and the preceding ones is that you may need to include descriptive information related to each set of materials rather than simply judging the presence or absence of selected criteria. Briefly summarizing the descriptive information in tabular form will assist you in making the appropriate comparisons across materials and in formulating your recommendations.

CURRENT USERS OF MATERIALS There is one other activity in the expert judgment phase of the summative evaluation that you may wish to include in your design. It is to seek additional information about the candidate materials from organizations that are experienced in using them. The names of current users can often be obtained from the publishers of the materials.

What types of information should you seek from the users? One type of information you should request involves data about the target learners in the other settings. For example, what are their entry behaviors and motivations for studying the materials? What are their pretest and posttest performance levels using the instruction? Finally, what are their attitudes about the materials?

Another type of information relates to the instructor's perceptions of the materials. For example, are the materials easy to use? What problems have they experienced in implementing the materials? What resources are required to use them? Do they plan to continue using the materials, and if not, why?

Depending on the logistics involved, you may wish to travel to the other organization, or you may decide to gather the information through questionnaires and telephone interviews. Either way you should plan carefully before obtaining the information.

At this point you have concluded the expert judgment phase of the summative evaluation. Based on the data you have gathered, you should be able to recommend the most promising set or sets of materials for the field-trial phase. The evaluation design and procedures used to conduct this part of the evaluation should be documented in your evaluation report, together with your recommendations and rationale.

The Field-Trial Phase of Summative Evaluation

The second phase of the summative evaluation is the field trial. During the trial the instruction is implemented as intended, within the organization, and with selected target learners. The field trial typically includes the following parts: planning for the evaluation, preparing for the implementation, implementing instruction and collecting data, summarizing and analyzing data, and reporting results.

Table 12.1 contains a matrix that summarizes the activities related to each part of the evaluation. Each column is headed by one of the main parts, and activities related to each are listed beneath. With the exception of the top row, which is the expert judgment phase, all activities in the first column, "Planning," should be completed from top to bottom before beginning the activities in the second column, preparing. Similarly, activities in the second column should be sequenced from top to bottom, and they should be completed prior to moving to the third column, implementing and collecting data. At the point of instruction implementation and data collection, however, this top-to-bottom sequencing pattern within each part ceases. Data related to each area (across rows) should be collected using the most time- and cost-efficient schedule. This is true for the sequence of data summary and report sections as well. The activities in the last three columns are presented in this sequence simply to illustrate their relationship to the activities named in the first two columns. The following paragraphs describe each of these summative field-trial activities in more detail.

PLANNING The first planning activity is the design of your field trial. The exact nature of the design depends on several factors, including the needs assessment, the nature of materials, and whether competing materials are included. You may need to evaluate only one set of materials using one group, one set of materials using several groups with different characteristics or in different settings, or competing sets of materials using comparable groups and settings.

Another design activity is to describe clearly the questions to be answered during the study. Questions will undoubtedly relate to learners' entry-behavior levels, their pretest and posttest performance on the objectives, and their attitudes. They may also relate to any resources, equipment, or facilities needed. They could relate to the skills and attitudes of those responsible for implementing the instruction. Others might relate to the implementation procedures and schedules. The precise areas of questions you include will depend on the nature of and resources for the study.

With the instructional materials and a skeleton of the evaluation design in hand, you can describe the resources, facilities, and equipment appropri-

TABLE 12.1

OVERVIEW OF ACTIVITIES FOR A SUMMATIVE EVALUATION

Planning	Preparing	Implementing/ Collecting Data	Summarizing and Analyzing Data	Reporting Results
Select Material to be evaluated (Expert Judgment)	Obtain materials for study Design instruments	Congruence? Accuracy? Inst. strategy? Utility? User satisfaction? (Checklist, Rating Scale)	Summary tables comparing candidate materials × criteria	Recommendations Rationale
Design evaluation (Field Trial)	Obtain instruments Set schedule for instruction and testing Create/Modify syllabus			Describe limitations of design
Describe resources, facilities, equipment needed	Obtain resources, facilities, equipment	Adequate? (Observation, Interview, Questionnaire)	Describe problems × resources, facilities, and equipment	Recommendations Rationale
Describe ideal entry behaviors/characteristics of target group Describe number of groups and individuals needed	Select sample Verify entry behaviors (data) Schedule learners	Learner performance? (Pre-Posttests) Learner attitudes? (Observation, Interview, Questionnaire)	Item × objective analysis by group and individual Cross-test summary by group and individual by objective Attitude summary	Explanation, Recommendations, Rationale
Describe skills/capabilities of instructors or managers Describe number of instructors needed	Select instructors Verify skills Schedule instructors	Validity of implementation? Modifications? (Observation, Interview)	Describe problems × instructor × objective	Recommendations and Rationale
Plan and develop any training needed for instructors/ managers	Provide training for instructors	Training effective? (Observation, Interview)	Describe implementation problems × objective × activity	Recommendations and Rationale

ate for the study. This activity is included prior to planning for the sample, because any limitations you encounter in this area will undoubtedly influence the nature of the group you can use. Plan initially for the ideal requirements and then negotiate with the administrators to determine the feasibility of these requests.

With the available resources issue settled, you can turn your attention to describing the ideal target learners. Your prescription should include their entry behaviors and any other characteristics that are relevant for the materials (e.g., prior experiences, personal goals). You also need to determine the number of learners you will need (or can afford) and how many groups you will need. In making this determination you should estimate conservatively, because quality and not quantity of data is the criterion. Often 20 to 30 carefully selected individuals who are truly representative of the target group will suffice. The term *group* is not intended to infer group-paced instruction; it refers to the number of individuals from whom data will be collected.

Once you know how many learners will be included in the study, you can decide how many instructors or managers you will need. Besides the ideal number to include, you should describe any skills they will need to implement the instruction. The availability of appropriate instructors may cause you to modify the number of learners in the design. If limiting learners is not feasible, you may need to plan training beyond orientation for the instructors.

The final planning activity is to develop orientation and perhaps training for the instructors. A good summative evaluation will require the cooperation of those who are implementing the instruction. They must feel that they are an important part of the study, that they are informed, and that their opinions count. Developing initial rapport with this group and maintaining a cooperative relationship throughout the study will enhance the quality of the field trial and the data you are able to obtain. One final caution: the instructors must believe that you are *not* evaluating either them or the learners. From the outset the focus must be on evaluating the materials. Building trust and being sensitive to learners' needs will help ensure your access to the setting and to the data. In fact, it may be a good idea to refer to them as implementor/evaluators throughout the study.

PREPARING The activities in the preparation stage flow from the decisions made during the planning stage. They involve obtaining all the materials, instruments, resources, and people prescribed. When trade-offs must be made between what is prescribed and what is available, you may need to note these changes in the limitations section of your report.

IMPLEMENTING/COLLECTING DATA During the implementation of instruction you will need to collect all the types of data prescribed. You might include performance measures, observations, interviews, and questionnaires. The density of your data collection will depend both on your questions and on your resources. At a minimum you will want pretest-posttest data and information about learners' perceptions of the materials and procedures. This information can usually be obtained inexpensively and unobtrusively from the instructors.

SUMMARIZING AND ANALYZING DATA The data summary techniques described for the formative evaluation field trial are appropriate for the summative field trial. At a minimum you will want to produce objective-by-item tables and to summarize learners' performance by group and individual. You will also want to create tables to compare individual and group progress from pretests to posttests.

In analyzing the data, you will want to document areas of the instruction that were ineffective and the potential reasons for the weaknesses. You will also want to document areas of the instruction that were effective. During a summative evaluation field trial, it is important to provide a balanced analysis of both the strengths and weaknesses of the materials. Focusing only on weaknesses will result in a biased report of the worth of the materials.

REPORTING RESULTS The nature of your summative evaluation report depends on your design. If you included both the expert judgment and the field-trial phases, both should be documented in the report. For each one you should describe the general purpose, the specific questions, the design and procedures, the results, and your recommendations and rationale. The rationale for your recommendations should be anchored in the data you present in the results section.

You should always consider the reader as you design and produce your report. After analyzing several program evaluation reports, Worthen and Sanders (1987) concluded that, although the reports were informative, they were also arsenic in print! You may want to follow their formatting suggestion for remedying this problem. They suggest beginning the report with an executive summary or abstract that highlights your final recommendations and rationale. Readers can then selectively read the remainder of the technical documentation to verify the quality of your procedures or the validity of your conclusions.

Comparison of Formative and Summative Evaluation

Formative and summative evaluation differ in several aspects. These differences are summarized in Table 12.2. The first difference is related to the purpose for conducting each type of evaluation. Formative evaluations are undertaken to locate weaknesses and problems in the materials in order to revise them. Summative evaluations are undertaken to locate both strengths and weaknesses in materials and to document the findings for administrators who must make decisions about whether to maintain or adopt the materials.

The second difference involves the stages of the evaluations. The formative evaluation includes three stages—the one-to-one, small group, and field trial—all conducted directly with target learners. During each stage, a great deal of time is spent observing and interviewing learners in order to understand the nature of problems they encounter with the materials. The summative evaluation, conversely, contains only two stages: expert judgment and field trial. The expert judgment stage resembles evaluative decisions made by the designer and content expert during the design and development of materials. Target learners are not involved in this stage of summative evaluation. The field-trial stage is conducted with target learners, but little if any time is spent interviewing learners to determine why they did or did not succeed with particular objectives in the instruction. Data are typically obtained through unobtrusive observations, questionnaires, and criterion-referenced tests.

TABLE 12.2

A COMPARISON OF FORMATIVE AND SUMMATIVE EVALUATION

	Formative Evaluation	Summative Evaluation
Purpose	Locate weaknesses in materials in order to revise them	Document strengths and weaknesses in materials in order to decide whether to maintain or adopt them
Phases or stages	One-to-one Small group Field trial	Expert judgment Field trial
Materials Development History	Systematically designed in-house and tailored to the needs of the organization	Produced in-house or elsewhere not necessarily following a systems approach
Materials	One set of materials	One set of materials or several competing sets
Position of Evaluator	Member of design and development team	External evaluator
Outcomes	A prescription for revising materials and revised materials	A report documenting the design, procedures, results, recommendations, and rationale

The materials subjected to formative and summative evaluations typically have different developmental histories. Those subjected to formative evaluations usually have been systematically designed and developed, and thus hold promise for being effective with target learners. Conversely, materials included in a summative evaluation may or may not have been developed following systematic design procedures. Those for which field trials are conducted, however, should have many of the characteristics of systematically designed instruction and thus should also hold promise for being effective with target learners.

Yet another difference between formative and summative evaluations is the number of materials evaluated. Formative evaluations are conducted on only one set of materials. Summative evaluations may focus on either one set of materials or on competing sets of promising materials. Summative evaluations may involve one set of materials and groups with different characteristics or several sets of materials and groups with similar characteristics.

Another contrast between formative and summative evaluations is the investment of the evaluator in the materials. Typically, formative evaluators have a personal investment in the materials evaluated and thus seek valid judgments about the materials in order to produce the best materials possible. Evaluators with personal investments in the outcome of the evaluation are called internal evaluators. It is wise for summative evaluators not to have a personal investment in the materials evaluated, because such detachment helps them maintain objectivity in designing the evaluation and in describing both the strengths and weaknesses in the materials. Detached evaluators are commonly referred to as external evaluators.

A final difference between formative and summative evaluations is the outcome. The results of a formative evaluation include prescriptions for revising the materials and actual materials revisions between the three stages of the evaluation. The outcome of the summative evaluation is not a prescription for the revisions. Instead it is a report for administrators, which documents the strengths and weaknesses of the materials evaluated.

EXAMPLES

This section contains examples of the evaluation instruments for the expert judgment phase of the summative evaluation. Instrumentation and data analysis procedures required for the field-trial phase were described in detail in the chapter on formative evaluation and will not be repeated here. Basically, the instruments required for the expert judgment stage consist of information summary charts and product evaluation checklists or rating scales to be completed by the evaluator.

Data Summary Form for the Congruence Analysis

Table 12.3 contains an example information summary for completing the congruence analysis. The left-hand column is used to describe the instructional needs of the organization, the entry behaviors and characteristics of the target group in the organization, and the organization's resources for obtaining and implementing the instruction. Additional columns can be included to record related information about sets of potentially promising materials. Summarizing the information in this manner will enable both you and the

TABLE 12.3

CONGRUENCE ANALYSIS INFORMATION SUMMARY FORM

Statements of Organization's Characteristics	Candidate Materials (Set 1)	Candidate Materials (Set 2)	Candidate Materials (Set 3)
Organization's instructional needs (goals and main objectives)	Stated goals and objectives in materials	Etc.	Etc.
Entry behaviors of organization's target group	Stated entry behaviors for learners	Etc.	Etc.
Characteristics of organization's target group	Stated characteristics of learners (age, motivation, etc.)	Etc.	Etc.
Organization's resources available for obtaining and implementing instruction	Costs of purchasing and implementing materials	Etc.	Etc.
Organization's facilities and equipment available for implementing instruction	Facilities required to implement materials (learning centers, equipment, etc.)	Etc.	Etc.

administrators to make judgments about the appropriateness of candidate materials.

Checklist for Evaluating the Completeness and Accuracy of Materials

A hypothetical goal framework and materials checklist are illustrated in Table 12.4. The goal analysis appears in the top portion of the table, and the checklist appears in the lower portion. Using such a checklist, the completeness of the materials and tests as well as the sequence of information in the materials can be evaluated. You could develop any number of response formats to record your judgments. In the example, three response columns are used. The first is for indicating the presence and sequence of subordinate skills in the instruction. The second and third columns are for indicating whether related test items are included in the pretest and posttest.

After evaluating each set of materials for its accuracy and completeness, you can tally the number of positive marks for each one in the bottom row of the table, and then compare the relative value of the candidate materials. In the hypothetical example, candidate instruction 2 appears the most promising, because it includes instruction on all 22 steps and subordinate skills identified by content experts. The accompanying tests also appear to be the most thorough in measuring the prescribed skills. Comprehensiveness, however, is only the second criterion for summatively evaluating instructional materials.

Checklist for Evaluating the Instructional Strategy in Materials

Table 12.5 contains a checklist for evaluating the instructional strategies contained in the candidate materials. The left-hand column contains the parts of the instructional strategy, excluding pretests and posttests. Space is provided for two response columns for each set of materials judged. The first can be used to judge the presence or absence of each strategy component, and the second, marked "Attention," can be used to judge the perceived motivational value of each component for the intended learner. Remember that the motivational value depends on the relevance of the material for the learners' interests and needs, their confidence that they can succeed, and the satisfaction they will gain from learning the skills and knowledge. You may choose to check each criterion separately instead of holistically as formatted in the example. You might also prefer to use a rating scale instead of a yes–no checklist.

A summary row is included at the bottom of the checklist to tally the number of positive responses given for each set of materials. Comparing the candidate materials in this way (Tables 12.3, 12.4, and 12.5), you can begin to make recommendations about which set of materials appears to be most promising for the organization.

Form for Judging the Utility of Materials

Table 12.6 contains a form for summarizing and comparing the utility of the candidate materials. The elements to be judged for each set of materials are listed in the left-hand column, and space for noting the characteristics of each set of materials is included in subsequent columns. The particular ele-

TABLE 12.4

A FRAMEWORK FOR EVALUATING THE ACCURACY AND COMPLETENESS OF CANDIDATE INSTRUCTIONAL MATERIALS AND THE CONTENT VALIDITY OF ACCOMPANYING TESTS

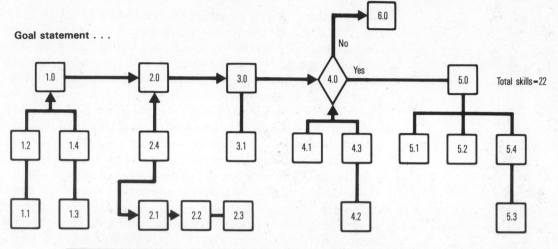

Subordinate Skill Statements	Candidate 1 MAT	PRE	POST	Candidate 2 MAT	PRE	POST	Candidate 3 MAT	PRE	POST
1.0	X	X	X	X	X	X			
1.1	X			X		X			
1.2	X		X	X	X	X			
1.3	X			X		X			
1.4	X		X	X	X	X			
2.0	X	X	X	X	X	X	X	X	X
2.1	X			X		X			
2.2	X			X		X			
2.3	X			X		X			
2.4	X		X	X	X	X	X	X	X
3.0	X	X	X	X	X	X	X	X	X
3.1				X	X	X			
4.0				X	X	X			
4.1				X		X			
4.2				X		X			
4.3				X		X			
5.0	X	X	X	X	X	X	X	X	X
Etc.									
Totals	16	5	11	22	16	22	4	4	4

Note: MAT = Instructional materials contents; PRE & POST = test item contents; X = skill addressed in materials or tests

TABLE 12.5

CHECKLIST FOR EVALUATING THE INSTRUCTIONAL STRATEGIES IN CANDIDATE MATERIALS

Strategy Component

	Candidate 1		Candidate 2		Candidate 3	
	Present	Attention	Present	Attention	Present	Attention
I. Preinstructional A. Initial Motivation	X	X	X	X		
B. Objectives	X	X	X	X		
C. Entry Behaviors 1. Described	X	X	X	X		
2. Sample items	X	X	X	X		
II. Information Presentation A. Organizational Structures 1. Headings	X	X	X	X	X	X
2. Tables and illustrations	X	X	X	X	X	X
B. Elaborations 1. Analogies/synonyms	X	X	X	X		
2. Prompts to imagine/consider	X	X	X	X		
3. Examples and nonexamples	X	X	X	X	X	
4. Relevant characteristics of examples	X	X	X	X		
5. Summaries/reviews	X	X	X	X	X	
III. Learner Participation A. Relevant practice	X	X	X	X	X	X
B. Feedback 1. Answers	X	X	X	X	X	X
2. Example solutions	X	X	X	X		
3. Common errors and mistakes	X	X	X	X		
IV. Follow-up Activities A. Enrichment	X	X	X	X		
B. Remediation	X	X	X	X		
TOTALS	17	17	17	17	6	6

ments you choose to compare across sets of materials will depend on the organization's stated needs and resources. The information you record about each set of materials will tend to be descriptive rather than a check indicating the presence or absence of an element or a rating of the quality of the element.

Form for Summarizing Information from Current Users of the Materials

Information collected about competing materials from current users is similar to that collected during a field trial. The difference is that most of these

TABLE 12.6

FORM FOR DOCUMENTING AND COMPARING THE UTILITY OF COMPETING MATERIALS

	Candidate 1	Candidate 2	Candidate 3
Learner's Guide?			
Instructor's Guide?			
Format of Materials?			
Durability of Materials?			
Portability of Materials?			
Equipment required?			
Environments required?			
Individual vs. group pacing?			
Instructor skills required?			
Etc.			

data are attitudinal rather than performance based. Table 12.7 contains a summary of the types of information you may wish to gather from users.

The factors to consider are again listed in the left-hand column. The evaluator response format you use will differ from the previous ones for this data-gathering activity. You will need space to record the opinions of multiple users for each set of materials. Space for the responses for two users of each set of materials is included on the form in Table 12.7.

SUMMARY

Summative evaluations are conducted to make decisions about whether to maintain or adopt instructional materials. The primary evaluator in a summative evaluation is rarely the designer or developer of the instructional materials; this person is frequently unfamiliar with the materials, the organization requesting the evaluation, or the setting in which the materials are evaluated. Such evaluators are referred to as external evaluators; these evaluators are preferred for summative evaluations because they have no personal investment in the materials and are likely to be more objective about the strengths and weaknesses of the materials evaluated.

Instructional designers make excellent summative evaluators because of their understanding of the instructional design process, the characteristics of well-designed materials, and the criteria for evaluating instruction. These skills provide them with the expertise for designing and conducting the expert judgment as well as the field-trial phases of the summative evaluation.

The design of the expert judgment phase of summative evaluation is anchored in the model for systematically designing instruction. Similar to initially designing instruction, the materials evaluator begins by judging the congruence between the instructional needs of an organization and the goals

TABLE 12.7

INFORMATION GATHERED FROM CURRENT USERS OF THE MATERIALS

	Candidate 1		Candidate 2		Candidate 3	
	User 1	User 2	User 1	User 2	User 1	User 2
1. Instructional needs for which materials are used?						
2. Entry behaviors of target learners?						
3. Characteristics of target learners?						
4. Achievement level of learners on pretests?						
5. Achievement level of learners on posttests?						
6. Attitudes of learners about materials?						
7. Setting in which materials are used?						
8. Current satisfaction with materials?						
9. Plans for continuing use of materials?						

for candidate instructional materials. Inappropriate materials are rejected, and promising materials are further evaluated. Next, the completeness and accuracy of the content presented in the materials are evaluated. The standard for this evaluation is an instructional goal analysis with required subordinate skills. Content experts are involved in either producing or verifying the quality of the skills diagram. Again, inappropriate materials are rejected, and promising materials are further evaluated. These materials are then evaluated for the quality of their instructional strategies, their utility, and their influence on current users. Materials that appear sound following these evaluation activities are then subjected to a field trial.

During the field-trial phase, the materials are evaluated for their effectiveness with the target group in the intended setting. Following the evaluation, both the strengths and the weaknesses of the materials are documented in the areas of learner performance and attitudes, instructor attitudes, and implementation requirements.

The evaluation report should include the expert judgment analysis (if one was conducted), as well as the field-trial phase of the evaluation. It should be designed and written with the reader's needs in mind.

PRACTICE

1. What is the main purpose of a summative evaluation?
2. What are the two main phases of a summative evaluation?
3. Why is the first phase of a summative evaluation often necessary?
4. Name five different types of analyses conducted during the first phase of a summative evaluation and the types of instruments used to collect the information.
5. What is the main decision made following the second phase of a summative evaluation?

6. Name three different types of analyses conducted during the second phase of a summative evaluation and the procedures used to collect information for each type.

7. Contrast the purposes for formative and summative evaluation.

8. Contrast the position of the evaluator in a formative and summative evaluation.

9. Contrast the final products of formative and summative evaluation.

═ FEEDBACK ═

1. Purpose: to document the strengths and weaknesses of instructional materials.

2. Phases: expert judgment and field trial.

3. Expert judgment: to determine the potential of candidate materials for meeting the needs of the organization.

4. Types of analyses conducted during expert judgment phase:
   a. Congruence analysis—information summary form
   b. Completeness and accuracy of materials—product checklist or rating scale
   c. Quality of instructional strategy—product checklist or rating scale
   d. Utility of materials—information summary form, product checklist, or rating scale
   e. Current users' satisfaction—questionnaire or interview

5. Field trial: to document the effectiveness of materials with target learners in the intended setting.

6. Types of data collected during the field trial:
   a. Learner performance and attitudes—criterion-referenced tests and questionnaire
   b. Instructor/implementor attitudes—questionnaire or interview
   c. Effectiveness of implementation procedures—observation or interview

	Formative Evaluation	*Summative Evaluation*
7. Purpose:	To collect data in order to revise instructional materials.	To collect data in order to document the strengths and weaknesses in instructional materials.
8. Evaluator Position	Evaluators are internal evaluators with a personal investment in the improvement of the instructional materials.	Evaluators are external evaluators who can objectively evaluate the quality of materials produced by others.
9. Final Products	Prescriptions for the revision of materials and revised materials.	An evaluation report for administrators that documents the purpose, procedures, results, and recommendations from the study.

References and Recommended Readings

Brinkerhoff, R. O. (1987). *Achieving results from training.* San Francisco, CA: Jossey-Bass. A six-stage evaluation model is presented, which includes assessments in the workplace and impact of training on the organization.

Cronbach, L., & Associates. (1980). *Toward reform of program evaluation.* San Francisco: Jossey-Bass. This book takes the position that the evaluator serves in a supportive role in the instructional design process.

Dick, W. (1977). Summative evaluation. In L. J. Briggs (Ed.), *Instructional design.* Englewood Cliffs, NJ: Educational Technology Publications. The major models of summative evaluation are presented together with a step-by-step description of the process.

Gagné, R. M., & Briggs, L. J. (1979). *Principles of instructional design.* New York: Holt, Rinehart and Winston, 236–238. This text includes a brief description of the summative evaluation process from the instructional designer's point of view.

Stufflebeam, D. (1973). Educational evaluation and decision making. In B. Worthen and J. Sanders (Eds.), *Educational evaluation: Theory and practice.* Belmont, CA: Wadsworth Publishing, 128–150. Stufflebeam's CIPP model is the one now predominantly used in educational evaluation.

Worthen, B. R., & Sanders, J. R. (1987). *Educational evaluation.* White Plains, NY: Longman. Major models of educational program evaluation are presented; however, the focus of the text is not on instructional materials evaluation.

GLOSSARY OF TERMS

A   **Attitude** An internal state that influences an individual's choices or decisions to act under certain circumstances. Attitudes represent a tendency to respond in a particular way.

B   **Behavior** An action that is an overt, observable, measurable performance.
Behavioral objective See Objective.

C   **Candidate media** Those media that can present the desired information, without regard to which may be the most effective. The distinction is from "noncandidate media." A book, for example, cannot present sound, and thus would be an inappropriate choice for delivering instruction for certain objectives.
Chunk of instruction All the instruction required to teach one objective or a combination of two or more objectives.
Cluster analysis A technique used with goals in the verbal information domain to identify the specific information needed to achieve the goal and the ways that information can best be organized or grouped.
Competency-based Instruction or tests based upon predetermined behaviors and criteria or mastery levels for skills, knowledge, and attitudes.
Complex goal A goal that involves more than one domain of learning.
Concept A set of objects, events, symbols, situations, etc., that can be grouped together on the basis of one or more shared characteristics, and given a common identifying label or symbol. Concept learning refers to the capacity to identify members of the concept category.
Congruence analysis Analyzing the congruence between: (1) an organization's stated needs and goals and those addressed in candidate instruction; an organization's target learners' entry behaviors and characteristics and those for which candidate materials are intended; and an organization's resources and those required for obtaining and implementing candidate instruction. Conducted during the expert judgment phase of summative evaluation.
Content stability The degree to which information to be learned is likely to remain current.
Criterion A standard against which a performance or product is measured.
Criterion-referenced test items Items designed to measure performance on an explicit set of objectives; also known as objective-referenced test items.

D   **Design evaluation chart** A method for organizing design information to facilitate its evaluation. The chart relates subskills, objectives, and associated test items, allowing easy comparison among the components of the instructional design.

Discrimination Distinguishing one stimulus from another and responding differently to the various stimuli.

Domain of learning A major type of learning outcome that can be distinguished from other domains by the type of learned performance required, the type of mental processing required, and the relevant conditions of learning.

E **Embedded attitude question** Question asked of learners about the instruction at the time they first encounter it.

Embedded test item A criterion-referenced item designed to test performance on an objective after instruction but prior to a posttest. Used to test student performance and diagnose student progress at that point in the instruction.

Entry behavior test item Criterion-referenced test items designed to measure skills identified as necessary prerequisites to beginning a specific course of instruction. Items are typically included in a pretest.

Entry behaviors Specific competencies or skills a learner must have mastered before entering a given instructional activity.

Evaluation An investigation conducted to obtain specific answers (typically value judgments) to specific questions at specific times and in specific places.

Expert judgment evaluation Judgments of the quality of instructional materials made by content experts, learner specialists, or design specialists. The first phase of summative evaluation.

F **Feedback** Information provided to learners about the correctness of their responses to questions embedded in the instruction.

Field trial The third stage in formative evaluation, referring to the evaluation of the program or product in the setting in which it is intended to be used.

Formative evaluation Evaluation designed to collect data and information that is used to improve a program or product; conducted while the program is still being developed.

Fuzzy A goal that is important, but abstract or intangible.

G **General learner characteristics** The general, relatively stable (not influenced by instruction) traits describing the learners in a given instructional program.

Goal A broad, general statement of an instructional intent, expressed in terms of what learners will be able to do.

Goal analysis The technique used to analyze a performance objective to identify the sequence of operations and decisions required to achieve it.

Group-based instruction The use of learning activities and materials designed to be used in a collective fashion with a group of learners; interactive, group-paced instruction.

H **Hierarchical analysis** A technique used with goals in the intellectual skills domain to identify the critical subordinate skills needed to achieve the goal, and their interrelationships. For each subordinate skill in the analysis, this involves asking, "What must the student know how to do in order to learn the specific subskills being considered?"

I **Individualized instruction** The use, by students, of systematically designed learning activities and materials specifically chosen to suit their individual interests, abilities, and experience. Such instruction is usually self-paced.

Instruction A set of events or activities presented in a structured or planned way, through one or more media, with the goal of teaching prespecified learner behaviors.

Instructional analysis The procedures applied to an instructional goal in order to identify the relevant skills and their subordinate skills and information required for a student to achieve the goal.

Instructional materials Print or other mediated instruction used by a student to achieve the instructional goal.

Instructional package The total collection of instructional materials, which also includes the student manual or syllabus, instructor's manual, and tests.

Instructional strategy An overall plan of activities to achieve an instructional goal. The strategy includes the sequence of intermediate objectives and the learning activities leading to the instructional goal.

Instructor's manual The collection of written materials given to instructors to facilitate their use of the instructional materials. The manual should include: an overview of the materials, tests with answers, and any supplementary information thought to be useful to the instructors. It may also include a copy of the student manual and materials.

Intellectual skill A skill that requires some unique cognitive activity; involves manipulating cognitive symbols, as opposed to simply retrieving previously learned information.

Item analysis table A means of presenting evaluation data that show the percentage of learners who correctly answered each item on a test.

L **Learner performance data** Information about the degree to which learners achieved the objectives following a unit of instruction.

Learner specialist A person knowledgeable about a particular population of learners.

M **Mastery learning** Systematic approach to instruction based on students performing to a prespecified criterion level on a given unit of instruction before moving to the next unit of instruction.

Mastery level A prespecified level of task performance, with no gradations below it, that defines satisfactory achievement of an objective.

Media The physical means of conveying instructional content. Examples include: drawings, slides, audiotape, computer, person, model, etc.

Model A simplified representation of a system, often in picture or flowchart form, showing selected features of the system.

Module An instructional package with a single integrated theme that provides the information needed to develop mastery of specified knowledge and skills, and serves as one component of a total course or curriculum. May be referred to as a Learning Activity Package (LAP) or minicourse.

N **Need** A discrepancy between what should be and the current status of a situation.

Needs assessment The formal process of identifying discrepancies between current outcomes and desired outcomes.

Noninstructional solution Means of reducing performance discrepancies other than the imparting of knowledge; includes motivational, environmental, and equipment factors.

Norm-referenced test A test whose scores are interpreted by comparing students with each other.

O **Objective** A statement of what the learners will be expected to do when they have completed a specified course of instruction, stated in terms of observable performances. Also known as: performance objective; behavioral objective; instructional objective.

One-to-one evaluation The first stage in formative evaluation, referring to direct interaction between the designer and individual tryout student. Also known as clinical evaluation.

P **Posttest** A criterion-referenced test designed to measure performance on objectives taught during a unit of instruction; given after the instruction. Typically does not include items on entry behaviors.

Preinstructional activities Techniques used to provide the following three events prior to delivering instructional content:
- Get the learners' attention
- Advise them of the prerequisite skills for the unit
- Tell them what they will be able to do after the instruction

Pretest A criterion-referenced test designed to measure performance on objectives to be taught during a unit of instruction and/or performance on entry behaviors; given before instruction begins.

Procedural analysis A technique used with goals in the psychomotor skills domain to identify the sequence of actions needed to achieve the goal. For each step in the analysis, specific actions are identified by asking, "What would the learners be doing when they perform this step?" and identifying the required subordinate skills by asking, "What do the learners need to know or be able to do in order to perform this step efficiently?"

Psychomotor skill Execution of a sequence of major or subtle physical actions to achieve a specified result. All skills employ some type of physical action; the physical action in a psychomotor skill is the focus of the *new* learning, and is not merely the vehicle for expressing an intellectual skill.

R **Reliability** The consistency or dependability of a measure.

Research An investigation conducted to identify knowledge that is generalizable to many students at various times.

Revision The process of producing an amended, improved, or up-to-date version of a set of instructional materials.

S **Skill** An ability to perform an action or group of actions; involves overt performance.

Small-group evaluation The second stage of formative evaluation, referring to the use of a small number of tryout students who study an instructional program without intervention from the designer and are tested to assess the effectiveness of the instruction.

Student manual The collection of written materials given to the students to help them achieve the objectives. The manual should include the directions for using the instructional materials. It may also include some of the instructional materials, examples of test items, objectives, and practice tests.

Subject matter specialist A person knowledgeable about a particular content area. Also known as content specialist; subject-matter expert (SME).

Subordinate objective An objective that must be attained in order to accomplish a terminal objective. Also known as enabling objective; intermediate objective.

Subordinate skill A skill that must be achieved in order to learn a higher level skill. Also known as subskill, prerequisite, enabling skill.

Summative evaluation Evaluation designed and used after an instructional program has been implemented and formative evaluation completed. The purpose is to present conclusions about the worth of the program or product and make recommendations about its adoption or retention.

Superordinate skill Higher level competency that is comprised of and achieved by learning subordinate skills.

System A set of interrelated parts working together toward a defined goal.

Systems approach Procedure used by instructional designers to create instruction. Each step requires input from prior steps and provides input to the next step. Evaluation provides feedback that is used to revise instruction until it meets the original need or specification.

T **Target population** The total collection of possible users of a given instructional program.

Terminal objective An objective the learners will be expected to accomplish when they have completed a course of instruction, made up of subordinate objectives. Often, a more specific statement of the instructional goal.

Training A prespecified and planned experience that enables a person to do something which he or she couldn't do before.

Tryout students A representative sample of the target population; may be used to test an instructional program prior to final implementation.

U **Universal objective** An objective that meets the criteria for evaluating objectives, but does not convey any real information about the learned capability of the learners; an objective that is stated so broadly that it can be applied to any learning situation without modification.

V **Validity** The degree to which a measuring instrument actually measures what it is intended to measure.

Verbal information Requirement to provide a specific response to relatively specific stimuli; involves recall of information.

APPENDIX

Many of you are using this textbook as a resource for developing your own instruction. We thought it would be helpful for you to see the example products from each step in the design model collected together in one place. Therefore we have gathered the material related to our most complete example, writing stories using a variety of sentence types, and repeated it here in the Appendix. It should benefit those of you who are required to document your design process and develop materials as a course project. The following list will help you locate materials in the Appendix.

A

DESCRIPTION OF PROBLEM (NEED), PURPOSE OF INSTRUCTION, AND TARGET GROUP

PROBLEM (NEED)

During a middle school faculty meeting called to discuss problems of students' written composition, teachers decided to conduct a needs assessment study. Each teacher assigned a short essay for his or her students, to be written on a common topic. A newly formed evaluation team of teachers reviewed the themes to identify possible common problems. They reported that, generally, students use one type of sentence—namely, declarative, simple sentences—to communicate their thoughts rather than varying their sentence structure by purpose or complexity. Additionally, punctuation other than periods and commas was absent from students' work, and commas were rare.

PURPOSE

Teachers decided to design special instruction that focused students on (1) writing a variety of sentence types based upon sentence purpose, (2) writing using a variety of sentence structures that vary in complexity, and (3) using a variety of punctuation to match sentence type and complexity. Through instruction focused directly on the problems, they hoped to change the current pattern of simplistic similarity found in students' compositions. They decided to create two units of instruction with the following goals:

1. In written composition, students will use a variety of sentence types and accompanying punctuation based on the purpose and mood of the sentence.
2. In written composition, students will use a variety of sentence types and accompanying punctuation based on the complexity or structure of the sentence.

TARGET GROUP

The composition units with their special emphasis on sentence variety were judged most appropriate for sixth-grade classes that contain students presently achieving at average and above average levels of language expression. These groups will be very heterogeneous in their current writing skill; therefore, instruction on writing sentence types as well as on using sentence types in compositions should be included in the materials.

GOAL ANALYSIS OF THE INSTRUCTIONAL GOAL ON STORY WRITING
(FIGURE 3.5)

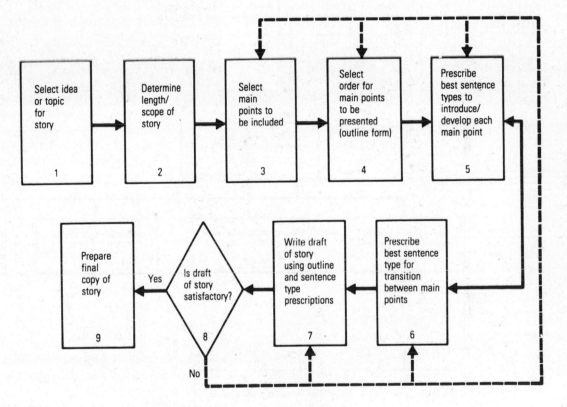

GOAL:

In writing short stories, use a variety of sentence types based upon sentence purpose and the idea or mood being communicated.

HIERARCHICAL ANALYSIS OF DECLARATIVE SENTENCE PORTION OF STORY-WRITING GOAL WITH ENTRY BEHAVIOR LINES (FIGURES 4.5 AND 5.3)

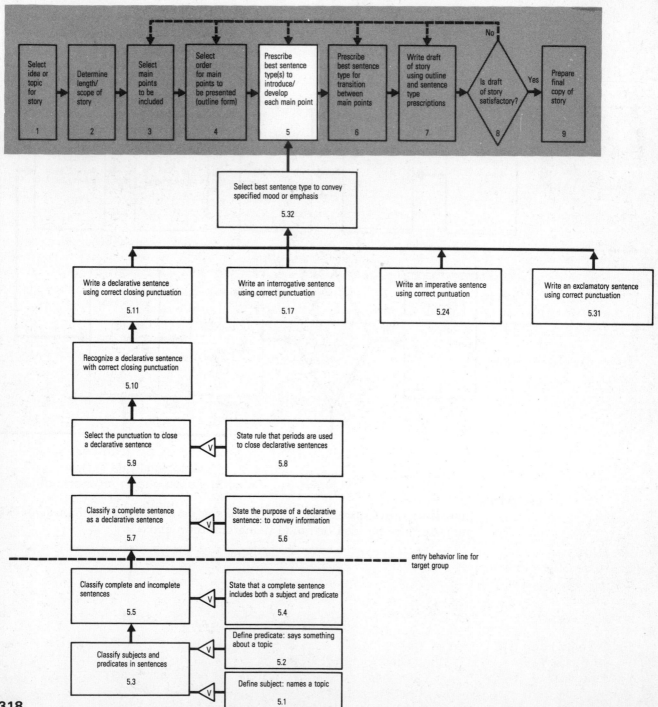

DESIGN EVALUATION CHART CONTAINING SUBSKILLS, PERFORMANCE OBJECTIVES (TABLES 6.1 AND 6.2), AND PARALLEL TEST ITEMS (TABLES 7.2 AND 7.3)

Subordinate Skills	Performance Objectives	Parallel Test Items
5.1 Define subject	5.1 Given the term *subject,* define the term. The definition must include that the subject names a topic.	1. Define the *subject* part of a sentence. 2. What does the *subject* part of a sentence do? 3. The *subject* part of a sentence names the _____.
5.2 Define predicate	5.2 Given the term *predicate,* define the term. The definition must include that the predicate says something about the subject or topic.	1. Define the *predicate* part of a sentence. 2. What does the *predicate* part of a sentence do? 3. The *predicate* part of a sentence tells something about the _____.
5.3 Classify subjects and predicates in complete sentences	5.3 Given several complete, simple declarative sentences, locate all the subjects and predicates.	Directions: Locate the *subjects* and the *predicates* in the following sentences. Draw *one* line under the *subject* and *two* lines under the predicate in each sentence. 1. The carnival was a roaring success. 2. The soccer team was victorious this season. 3. Susan got an after-school job weeding flower beds. 4. George's father was pleased with his report card.
5.4 State that a complete statement includes both a subject and a predicate	5.4 Given the term *complete sentence,* define the concept. The definition must name both the subject and the predicate.	1. Define a *complete sentence.* 2. What elements does a *complete sentence* contain? 3. A complete sentence contains both a(n)_____ and a(n) _____.
5.5 Classify complete and incomplete sentences	5.5.1 Given several complete and incomplete declarative sentences, locate all those that are complete	Directions: Locate complete sentences. Place an X in the space before each complete sentence.

Subordinate Skills	*Performance Objectives*	*Parallel Test Items*
		_____ 1. John closely followed the directions.
		_____ 2. The team that was most excited.
		_____ 3. The dogsled jolted and bumped over the frozen land.
		_____ 4. Found the lost friends happy to see her.
		_____ 5. The plants in the garden.
	5.5.2 Given several complete and incomplete declarative sentences, locate all those missing subjects and all those missing predicates.	Directions: Locate missing subjects and predicates. Place a P before all of the items that are *missing a predicate*. Place an S before all items that are *missing a subject*.
		_____ 1. John closely followed the directions.
		_____ 2. The team that was most excited.
		_____ 3. The dogsled jolted and bumped over the frozen land.
		_____ 4. Found the lost friends happy to see her.
		_____ 5. The plants in the garden.
		_____ 6. Played on the beach all day.
5.6 State the purpose of a declarative sentence	5.6 Given the terms *declarative sentence* and *purpose*, state the purpose of a declarative sentence. The purpose should include to convey/tell information.	1. What *purpose* does a *declarative sentence* serve? 2. The *purpose* of a *declarative sentence* is to _____.
5.7 Classify a complete sentence as a declarative sentence	5.7 Given several complete simple sentences that include declarative, interrogative, and exclamatory sentences that are correctly or incorrectly closed using a period, locate all those that are declarative.	Directions: Locate declarative sentences. Place the letter D in the space before the sentences that are *declarative*.
		_____ 1. Place the stamp in the upper right corner of the envelope.
		_____ 2. Are you hungry.
		_____ 3. Sarah selected a mystery book.
		_____ 4. The woods looked quiet and peaceful.
		_____ 5. Wow, look at that fire.
		_____ 6. Some birds do not migrate.
		_____ 7. Which of the birds migrate.

Subordinate Skills	Performance Objectives	Parallel Test Items
5.8 State that periods are used to close declarative sentences.	5.8 Given the terms *declarative sentence* and *closing punctuation*, name the period as the closing punctuation. The term *period* must be spelled correctly.	1. The closing punctuation used with a declarative sentence is called a _____. 2. Declarative sentences are closed using what punctuation mark?
5.9 Select the punctuation used to close a declarative sentence.	5.9 Given illustrations of a period, comma, exclamation point, and a question mark; the terms *declarative sentence* and *closing punctuation*, select the period.	1. Circle the closing punctuation used to end a declarative sentence. , ! . ?
5.10 Recognize a declarative sentence with correct closing punctuation	5.10 Given several simple declarative sentences with correct and incorrect punctuation, select all the declarative sentences with correct closing punctuation.	Directions: Locate correct punctuation for a declarative sentence. Place the letter D in the space before all the *declarative sentences* that *end* with the *correct punctuation* mark. _____ 1. John likes to read space stories? _____ 2. I ride two miles to school on the bus. _____ 3. I got an A on the spelling test! _____ 4. Juanita is traveling with her parents.
5.11 Write declarative sentences with correct closing punctuation	5.11 Write declarative sentences on: (1) selected topics and (2) topics of student choice. Sentences must be complete and closed with a period.	1. Directions: Write five declarative sentences that describe today's assembly. 2. Directions: Write five declarative sentences on topics of your own choice.

INSTRUCTIONAL STRATEGY FOR OBJECTIVE SEQUENCE AND CLUSTERS (TABLE 8.3), PREINSTRUCTIONAL ACTIVITIES (TABLE 8.4), AND TESTING ACTIVITIES (TABLE 8.5)

OBJECTIVE CLUSTERS (ONE HOUR FOR EACH)

1	2	3	4	5	6
5.6	5.12	5.18	5.25	5.11	5.32
5.7	5.13	5.19	5.26	5.17	
5.8	5.14	5.20	5.27	5.24	
5.9	5.15	5.21	5.28	5.31	
5.10	5.16	5.22	5.29		
5.11	5.17	5.23	5.30		
		5.24	5.31		

PREINSTRUCTIONAL ACTIVITIES FOR UNIT ON WRITING COMPOSITIONS

Preinstructional Activities:

MOTIVATION: A brief story will be used as an introduction. It will be on a topic of *high interest* to sixth graders, and it will contain all four sentence types to illustrate the point of variety and increased interest through varying sentence type.

OBJECTIVES: Each of the four types of sentences in the sample story will be highlighted and described in the introduction. The purpose of the unit, learning to write stories that contain a variety of sentence types, will be included.

ENTRY BEHAVIORS: Since there are several entry behaviors noted in the instructional analysis, a test including entry behaviors will be developed and administered to determine whether students have the required prerequisite skills.

TESTING ACTIVITIES FOR UNIT ON WRITING COMPOSITIONS

Testing:

PRETESTS: Administer a brief test of entry behaviors for subskills 5.1, 5.2, 5.3, 5.4, and 5.5. The test will be a short, paper-and-pencil test. If learners do not have prerequisites, then a lesson covering these subskills will be inserted as the first lesson in the unit. Two pretests will be administered after the first lesson, which will be used to motivate learners, inform them of the objectives, and provide example stories. For the pretests, students will be asked to write a brief story using all four sentence types as well as to complete objective questions on subordinate skills.

EMBEDDED ITEMS: Embedded items will be used in instructional materials to test each set of subskills included in the unit.

POSTTESTS: Two different types of posttests will be administered. An objective test will be administered following instruction on Objective 5 to facilitate diagnosis of problems students may be having with these subordinate skills. A second posttest, story writing, will be administered following all instruction in the unit.

INSTRUCTIONAL STRATEGY FOR THE INFORMATION PRESENTATION AND STUDENT PARTICIPATION COMPONENTS (TABLE 8.6) AND THE LESSON TIME ALLOCATION BASED UPON THE STRATEGY (TABLE 8.7)

OBJECTIVE 5.6 STATE PURPOSE OF DECLARATIVE SENTENCE	OBJECTIVE 5.7 CLASSIFY A COMPLETE SENTENCE AS DECLARATIVE
Information Presentation	*Information Presentation*
INFORMATION: Declarative sentences are used to convey information, to tell the reader something.	INFORMATION: Declarative sentences are used to convey information, to tell the reader something.
EXAMPLES: Joan likes to roller skate. It rained the day of the picnic. Fire drills are important. The roller coaster makes my stomach flutter.	EXAMPLES: 1. Tom enjoys space stories. 2. The kittens are all sold. 3. Mr. Jones is very tall. NONEXAMPLES: (Point out why each is not an example.) 1. What does Tom like to read? 2. Are the kittens still for sale? 3. How does Mr. Jones look?
Student Participation	*Student Participation*
PRACTICE ITEMS: What does a declarative sentence do? What does Joan like to do? How does a roller coaster make me feel? FEEDBACK: State that a declarative sentence is used to convey information. Point out what each sentence tells us.	PRACTICE ITEMS: Choose the declarative sentences: 1. How did the flowers smell? 2. Where was Julie going? 3. The traffic is noisy. 4. The sailboat is fun to ride. 5. This dog is very, very thin. FEEDBACK: State why declaratives 3, 4, and 5 are sentences, and 1 and 2 are not.

OBJECTIVE 5.8   STATE PERIODS USED TO CLOSE DECLARATIVE SENTENCE

Information Presentation

INFORMATION: Periods are used to close declarative sentences.

EXAMPLES:
The story is exciting.
The bear slinked through the campground.

Student Participation

PRACTICE ITEMS: What punctuation mark is used to close declarative sentences?

FEEDBACK: Restate that the period is used to close declarative sentences.

OBJECTIVE 5.9   SELECT PUNCTUATION TO CLOSE DECLARATIVE SENTENCE

Information Presentation

INFORMATION: Periods are used to close declarative sentences.

EXAMPLES:
The windows had cobwebs in them.
The zebra sounded like a horse.

NONEXAMPLES:
The poppies were red and orange?
The sunset was red and orange!

Student Participation

PRACTICE ITEMS: Select the punctuation mark—period (.), question mark (?), or exclamation mark (!)—to close these declarative sentences:
1. The frost covered the ground
2. Snow was piled along the road
3. The pond was covered with ice

FEEDBACK: State that periods should be used to close all the declarative sentences.

OBJECTIVE 5.10   RECOGNIZE DECLARATIVE SENTENCE WITH CORRECT PUNCTUATION

Information Presentation

INFORMATION: Only periods are used to close declarative sentences.

EXAMPLES:
1. The store had many different bicycles.
2. The store had several types of trains.

NONEXAMPLES:
What types of trains did the store have?
Put your trains away!
I feel so happy!

Student Participation

PRACTICE ITEMS: Which of the following are declarative sentences with correct punctuation?
1. Place your hands on the desk!
2. Begin on page one!
3. Where should we stop?
4. Camping can be fun.
5. Surfing is good exercise.

OBJECTIVE 5.11   WRITE A DECLARATIVE SENTENCE WITH CORRECT PUNCTUATION

Information Presentation

INFORMATION: Declarative sentences convey information and are closed using a period.

EXAMPLES:
1. The classroom was sunny and bright.
2. Everyone came to the party.

NONEXAMPLES:
1. Did John come to the party?
2. John, look out!

Student Participation

PRACTICE ITEMS:
1. Write five declarative sentences.
2. Change the following sentences to declarative.
   a. How did John look?
   b. Where did Billie go?
   c. The sky was very dark!

Student Participation	*Student Participation*
FEEDBACK: Indicate why 4 and 5 are declarative, and 1, 2, and 3 are not.	FEEDBACK: Provide students with list of criteria they can use to evaluate their sentences, e.g., has subject, has predicate, conveys information, and is closed with a period. Give examples of how 2a, b, and c could be rewritten as declarative sentences.

LESSON TIME ALLOCATION BASED UPON INSTRUCTIONAL STRATEGY

Activity	Time Planned	Activity	Time Planned
Session 1		**Session 5**	
1. Introductory, motivational materials 2. Entry behaviors pretest	1 hour	1. Pretest on objectives 5.18–5.24 2. Instruction on objectives 5.18–5.24	15 min. 40 min.
Session 2		**Session 6**	
1. Theme writing pretest	1 hour	1. Pretest on objectives 5.25–5.31 2. Instruction on objectives 5.25–5.31	15 min. 40 min.
Session 3		**Session 7**	
1. Pretest on objectives 5.6–5.11 2. Instruction on objectives 5.6–5.11	15 min. 40 min.	1. Review of objectives 5.11, 5.17, 5.24, and 5.31	1 hour
Session 4		**Session 8**	
1. Pretest on objectives 5.12–5.17 2. Instruction on objectives 5.12–5.17	15 min. 40 min.	1. Pretest on objective 5.32 2. Instruction on objective 5.32	15 min. 40 min.
		Session 9	
		1. Posttest on objectives 5.6–5.32	1 hour

APPENDIX G

SESSION 1: MOTIVATIONAL MATERIALS, UNIT OBJECTIVES, AND ASSESSMENT OF ENTRY BEHAVIORS

Component	***Subskill***	***Text***
Introduction/ Motivation (Strategy Table 8.4)		We can make stories we write more interesting by using different types of sentences when we write them. Using different types of sentences in our stories does not change the message, it only changes the way we tell it. Different kinds of sentences help the readers know exactly what we want to say and how we feel about what we have said. It involves them in what they are reading because it helps the story come alive. To show you how using several different kinds of sentences makes a story more interesting, we have written the same story two ways. Story A has all the same kind of sentences in it, while Story B has four different kinds of sentences in it. Read both stories and compare them.

Story A	Story B
(1) Yesterday, my Uncle Frank bought a present for me. (2) It was large, wrapped in fancy blue paper, and it had model cars on the ribbon. (3) The card said not to open it until my birthday. (4) I wondered what was inside the box. (5) I held the package, shook it, and turned it upside down. (6) My mother told me to stop playing with the package. (7) Later when she saw me holding the present, she took it and put it away. (8) I would like to find it.	(1) Yesterday, my Uncle Frank bought a present for me! (2) It was large, wrapped in fancy blue paper, and had model cars on the ribbon. (3) "Do not open until your birthday!" was written on the card. (4) What could be inside the box? (5) I held the package, shook it, and turned it upside down. (6) "Stop playing with your package," said Mother. (7) Later, when she saw me holding the present, she took it and put it away. (8) Where could she have hidden it?

Component	***Subskill***	***Text***
		Story B simply tells the same story in a more interesting way. When we write our own stories, we should remember that using several different kinds of sentences in them will make any story more interesting.
Objectives (Strategy Table 8.4)		During this unit you are going to learn to write stories that have different kinds of sentences in them. You will focus on four different kinds of sentences including:

Component	Subskill	Text
		1. Declarative sentences that tell the reader something 2. Interrogative sentences that ask questions 3. Imperative sentences that command, direct or request something 4. Exclamatory sentences that show emotion or excitement. Of course, writing stories that have all four kinds of sentences will require some instruction and lots of practice. The lessons that follow will teach you about each of the sentences and allow you to practice writing each one. After learning to write all four sentence types, you will use them together to create interesting short stories.
Prerequisites (Strategy Table 8.4)		Before learning to write different types of sentences, it is important for you to remember facts about complete and incomplete sentences. To help you remember these facts, answer the questions on the short quiz that follows. When you have finished the quiz, close your booklet and read quietly at your desk until your teacher tells you what to do next. *REMEMBER TO PUT YOUR NAME ON YOUR QUIZ PAPER*
Pretest on Entry Behaviors (Strategy Tables 8.4 and 8.5)	5.1 5.2	Define the following terms related to sentences. 1. A subject _____ _____ 2. A predicate _____ _____
	5.3 5.4	Locate subjects and predicates. In the following statements, draw *one line under the subjects* and *two lines under the predicates*. 3. The carnival was a roaring success. 4. The soccer team was victorious this season. 5. Susan got an after-school job weeding flower beds. 6. Define a complete sentence. _____ _____
	5.5	Locate complete and incomplete sentences. Place a C before all the following sentences that are *complete*. If the sentence is not complete, write an S to indicate that the *subject* is missing. Write a P to indicate that the *predicate* is missing. _____ 7. John closely followed the directions. _____ 8. The team that was most excited. _____ 9. The dogsled jolted and bumped over the frozen land. _____ 10. Found the lost friends happy to see her.

Session 2: Pretest story and checklist to evaluate stories (TABLE 9.2)

Component	Subskill	Text
Pretest Theme (Strategy Table 8.5)	Instructional Goal	Write a short, one-page story using a variety of sentence types to hold the interest of the reader and to strengthen the idea or mood of your story. In your story you should: 1. Use at least *two* of each of the following types of sentences: declarative, interrogative, imperative, and exclamatory. 2. Use only *complete* sentences. 3. Use the *correct punctuation* based upon sentence *type* and *mood*. 4. Select the best type of sentence to convey the idea you wish. Select one of the following titles for your theme.* 1. I Really Didn't Expect That! 2. He/She/You Shouldn't Have Done It! 3. I Will Think Twice Before I Do That Again! *The title does not count as one of your exclamatory sentences.

TOTAL
ERRORS
____ I. Declarative Sentences
    ____ 1. Number of declarative sentences
    ____ 2. Sentences complete
        ____ a. number of subjects incomplete
        ____ b. number of predicates incomplete
    ____ 3. Number of periods used to close sentences
    ____ 4. Sentence type appropriate for idea/mood conveyed
        ____ a. number appropriate

TOTAL
ERRORS
____ III. Imperative Sentences
    ____ 1. Number of imperative sentences
    ____ 2. Sentences complete
        ____ a. number of subjects incomplete
        ____ b. number of predicates incomplete
    ____ 3. Number of exclamation points used for strong requests, instructions
    ____ 4. Number of periods used for mild directions, requests

TOTAL
ERRORS

_____ b. number inappro-
priate
_____ 5. Transition smooth

TOTAL
ERRORS

_____ II. Interrogative Sentences
_____ 1. Number of interrogative
sentences
_____ 2. Sentences complete
_____ a. number of subjects
incomplete
_____ b. number of predi-
cates incomplete
_____ 3. Question marks used to
close sentences
_____ 4. Number of questions appropriate to lead reader
_____ 5. Number of questions appropriate to seek
information
_____ 6. Sentence type appropriate
for idea/mood conveyed
_____ a. number appro-
priate
_____ b. number inappro-
priate
_____ 7. Transition smooth

TOTAL
ERRORS

_____ 5. Sentence type appropriate
for idea/mood conveyed
_____ a. number appro-
priate
_____ b. number inappro-
priate
_____ 6. Transition smooth

TOTAL
ERRORS

_____ IV. Exclamatory Sentences
_____ 1. Number of exclamatory
sentences
_____ 2. Sentences complete
_____ a. number of sub-
jects incomplete
_____ b. number of predi-
cates incomplete
_____ 3. Number of exclamation
points used to close
sentences
_____ 4. Sentence type appropriate
for idea/mood conveyed
_____ a. number appro-
priate
_____ b. number inappro-
priate
_____ 5. Transition smooth

Session 3: PRETEST AND INSTRUCTION IN SUBORDINATE SKILLS 5.6 THROUGH 5.11

Component	Subskill	Text
Objective Pretest (Strategy Table 8.5)		The following short quiz has questions about declarative sentences on it. Put your name and the date on the top before you begin. Answer each question. If you are not sure of the answer, guess what the answer might be. Do not be upset if you do not know some of the answers, since you may not have had instruction on declarative sentences yet. When you finish the quiz, raise your hand and it will be collected. You may begin the lesson when you finish the quiz.
Instructions	5.6–5.11	
	5.6	1. The purpose of a declarative sentence is to _____.
	5.7	Determine whether the following sentences are declarative. If a sentence is declarative, mark a *D* in the space before the sentence.
		2. ____ Wow look at that fire 3. ____ Sarah selected a mystery book 4. ____ Did Sarah select a mystery book 5. ____ The woods look quiet and peaceful 6. ____ Are you hungry
	5.8	7. The punctuation mark used to close a declarative sentence is called a(an) _____.
	5.9	Place the punctuation mark that should follow these sentences in the blank to the left of the sentence.
		8. ____ Gina did not get a bike for her birthday 9. ____ Sam worked in the yard after school
	5.10	Identify declarative sentences with correct ending punctuation. Place a D beside each correct sentence.
		10. ____ Did George get many presents. 11. ____ The air was warm and balmy? 12. ____ Jenny was late for class. 13. ____ Ken was happy when they arrived. 14. ____ What is the first day of winter.

Component	Subskill	Text
	5.11	Write two declarative sentences with correct punctuation that describe today's class.
		15.
		16.
	5.11	Write two declarative sentences, with correct punctuation, on topics of your choice.
		17.
		18.

		Declarative Sentences
Information Presentation (Table 8.6)	5.6	A declarative sentence is used to convey information, to tell the reader something, or describe something. When you want to state a fact or describe something in a direct manner, you write a declarative sentence. Here are some declarative sentences used to state facts.
Examples		1. Joan likes to roller skate. 2. Fire drills are important.
		The first sentence tells us what Joan likes to do. The second sentence tells us that fire drills are an important activity.
Information		Declarative sentences can also be used to describe something. The following sentences are descriptions.
Examples		1. It rained the day of the picnic. 2. The roller coaster makes my stomach flutter.
		The first sentence describes the day as rainy and the second one describes how a roller coaster makes the writer's stomach feel.
	5.7	Look at the next two sentences. One is a declarative sentence and one is not.
Nonexamples		1. Tom enjoys reading space stories. 2. What does Tom want to read?
		The first sentence is declarative since it tells us what kind of stories Tom likes to read. The second sentence is not declarative. After reading this sentence, we do not know what Tom likes to read. Since the second sentence cannot give the reader information, it is *not* a declarative sentence.

Component	Subskill	Text
Practice	5.6 5.7	Read the following pairs of sentences. Which of the sentences are declarative and why? Are the kittens still for sale? The kittens are all sold. Mr. Jones is very tall. How did Mr. Jones look?
Feedback		In the first pair of sentences the declarative sentence tells us that the kittens are all sold. The other sentence does not tell us whether they are sold or not. Likewise, the declarative sentence tells us that Mr. Jones is very tall, but the other sentence does not provide any clues about how Mr. Jones looks.
Embedded Questions	5.6 5.7	1. What does a declarative sentence do? _____ _____ 2. Which of the following sentences are declarative? Place a *D* beside the declarative ones. ____ a. How did the flowers smell ____ b. Where was Julie going ____ c. The traffic is noisy ____ d. How do you do it ____ e. The sailboat is fun to ride
Information Presentation (Table 8.6)	5.8	Punctuation marks are used to close complete sentences. The period (.) is the punctuation mark that is always used to close a declarative sentence. When you see a period at the end of a sentence, it is a clue that the sentence *may* be a declarative one. Other types of sentences may use a period, but a sentence that (1) conveys information and (2) is closed with a period is always a declarative sentence. Here are some declarative sentences that are correctly punctuated. 1. The story is exciting. 2. The bear slinked through the campground. We know the first sentence is declarative because it describes the story and is closed using a period. The second sentence is declarative because it tells what the bear did, and it is closed with a period.
Information Presentation	5.9	If a sentence appears to be declarative because it tells something or describes something, yet the punctuation mark at the end of the sentence is not a period, then the sentence is not a declarative one. Some sentences tell the reader something, and this is a clue that they might be declarative. However, a period is not used to close the sentence. This means that they are *not* declarative. Look at these examples.
Nonexamples		1. He is huge! 2. My shoes are gone! Neither of these sentences is declarative because periods are not used to close them.

Component	Subskill	Text
Practice	5.8 5.9	Remember, to be a declarative sentence, it must tell the reader something, and it must close with a period. Consider these sentences. Which are declarative? _____ 1. The frost covered the ground! _____ 2. The frost covered the ground. _____ 3. What covered the ground?
Feedback		The first sentence is *not* declarative. Although it tells about frost on the ground, it does not end with a *period*. The second sentence is declarative. It tells about frost on the ground and it ends with a period. The third sentence is *not* declarative because it does not convey information and it does not end with a period.
Embedded Questions	5.8	3. What punctuation mark is used to close a declarative sentence? _____
	5.9	4. Place the *correct punctuation mark* at the end of these sentences. a. The sunset is red and orange _____ b. The snow was piled along the road _____ c. The pond is covered with ice _____
	5.10	5. Which of the following sentences are declarative? Place a *D* beside the declarative ones. _____ a. The poppies were red and orange. _____ b. Did the zebra sound like a horse? _____ c. The zebra sounded like a horse! _____ d. The windows had cobwebs in them. _____ e. I lost my key!
Information Presentation	5.11	You can write your own declarative sentences. To write correct declarative sentences, you should write them *to tell or describe something*, and you should always *close them with periods*.
		For each of the topics listed below, a declarative sentence has been written. Write a sentence of your own on each topic that is different from the one shown.
Examples and Embedded Test	5.11	**Topic** — **Sentence** Oranges — 1. Oranges grow on trees. 2. Mother — 1. My mother is a teacher. 2. School — 1. I like to go to school. 2. Friends — 1. My friends come to my house to play. 2. The Ocean — 1. Fish live in the ocean. 2.

Component	Subskill	Text
Embedded Test	5.11	Write four declarative sentences on topics of your own choice. 1. 2. 3. 4.
Answers to embedded questions 5.6, 5.7, 5.8, 5.9, 5.10, and 5.11 (These are not for students during field trials, but may be inserted later in instruction for use as feedback.)		1. A declarative sentence tells us something or conveys information. 2. ____ a. How did the flowers smell ____ b. Where was Julie going _D_ c. The traffic is noisy ____ d. How do you do it _D_ e. The sailboat is fun to ride 3. Period 4. a. The sunset is red and orange. b. The snow was piled along the road. c. The pond is covered with ice. 5. _D_ a. The poppies were red and orange. ____ b. Did the zebra sound like a horse? ____ c. The zebra sounded like a horse! _D_ d. The windows had cobwebs in them. ____ e. I lost my key!

Topic	Sentence
Oranges	1. Oranges grow on trees.
	2. Oranges grow in Florida and California.
Mother	3. My mother is a teacher.
	4. Mother goes to practice with me.
School	5. I like to go to school.
	6. School can be fun and boring.
Friends	7. My friends come to my house to play.
	8. I play games with my friends.
The Ocean	9. Fish live in the ocean.
	10. The ocean is very deep.

GROUP'S AND INDIVIDUALS' ACHIEVEMENT OF OBJECTIVES (TABLES 11.4, 11.5, 11.6, 11.7, 11.8, AND FIGURE 11.3) AND ATTITUDES ABOUT INSTRUCTION (TABLE 11.9)

STUDENT RESPONSES BY ITEM WITHIN OBJECTIVE ON THE ENTRY BEHAVIORS SECTION OF THE PRETEST

Objectives:	5.1	5.2	5.3			5.4	5.5							
Items →	1	2	3	4	5	6	7	8	9	10	Score	%	Obj.	%
Students ↓ 1							X		X		2	20	0	0
2			X	X	X		X		X		5	50	1	20
3			X	X	X		X		X		5	50	1	20
4	X		X	X	X		X		X		6	60	2	40
5	X	X	X	X	X		X	X	X	X	9	90	4	80
6	X	X	X	X	X	X	X	X	X	X	10	100	5	100
7	X	X	X	X	X	X	X	X	X	X	10	100	5	100
8	X	X	X	X	X	X	X	X	X	X	10	100	5	100
9	X	X	X	X	X	X	X	X	X	X	10	100	5	100
10	X	X	X	X	X	X	X	X	X	X	10	100	5	100
11	X	X	X	X	X	X	X	X	X	X	10	100	5	100
12	X	X	X	X	X	X	X	X	X	X	10	100	5	100
13	X	X	X	X	X	X	X	X	X	X	10	100	5	100
14	X	X	X	X	X	X	X	X	X	X	10	100	5	100
15	X	X	X	X	X	X	X	X	X	X	10	100	5	100
Total Right	12	11	14	14	14	10	15	11	15	11				
% Right	80	73	93	93	93	66	100	73	100	73				
% Object.	80	73	93			66	73							

Note: X = correct response; blank = incorrect response.

PRETEST FOR DECLARATIVE SENTENCES: STUDENT PERFORMANCE BY ITEM WITHIN OBJECTIVE

Objective	5.6	5.7					5.8	5.9		5.10					5.11				#		#	
Item	1	2	3	4	5	6	7	8	9	10	11	12	13	14	15	16	17	18	Score	%	Obj.	%
1			X		X		X	X	X	X	X	X							8	44	2	33
2			X		X		X	X	X	X	X	X							8	44	2	33
3			X		X		X	X	X	X	X	X							8	44	2	33
4			X		X		X	X	X	X	X	X							8	44	2	33
5			X		X		X	X	X	X	X	X			X	X	X		11	61	2	33
6			X		X		X	X	X	X	X	X			X	X	X		11	61	2	33
7			X		X		X	X	X	X	X	X			X	X	X		11	61	2	33
8			X		X		X	X	X	X	X	X			X	X	X		11	61	2	33
9			X		X		X	X	X	X	X	X			X			X	10	55	2	33
10	X		X	X	X	X	X	X	X	X	X	X			X	X	X	X	15	83	4	66
11	X	X	X	X	X	X	X	X	X	X	X	X	X	X	X	X	X	X	18	100	6	100
12	X	X	X	X	X	X	X	X	X	X	X	X	X	X	X	X	X	X	18	100	6	100
13	X	X	X	X	X	X	X	X	X	X	X	X	X	X	X	X	X	X	18	100	6	100
14	X	X	X	X	X	X	X	X	X	X	X	X	X	X	X	X	X	X	18	100	6	100
15	X	X	X	X	X	X	X	X	X	X	X	X	X	X	X	X	X	X	18	100	6	100
# Right	6	5	15	6	15	6	15	15	15	5	15	15	15	5	7	10	10	11				
% Right	40	33	100	40	100	40	100	100	100	33	100	100	100	33	46	66	66	73				
% Mastering	40			26			100	100				33					40					

STUDENT PERFORMANCE BY ITEM WITHIN OBJECTIVE ON EMBEDDED QUESTIONS FOR DECLARATIVE SENTENCES

Item	5.6		5.7				5.8	5.9			5.10					5.11									Raw Score (24)	Percent Correct	# obj (6)	% obj
	1	A	B	C	D	E	3	A	B	C	A	B	C	D	E	1	2	3	4	5	6	7	8	9				
1	X	X	X	X	X	X	X	X	X	X		X	X	X	X		X			X		X	X	X	19	88	4	66
2	X	X	X	X	X	X	X	X	X	X	X	X	X	X	X		X		X	X	X	X	X	X	22	92	5	83
3	X	X	X	X	X	X	X	X	X	X	X	X	X	X	X	X	X	X	X	X	X	X	X	X	24	100	6	100
4	X	X	X	X	X	X	X	X	X	X	X	X	X	X	X	X	X	X	X	X	X	X	X	X	24	100	6	100
5	X	X	X	X	X	X	X	X	X	X	X	X	X	X	X	X	X	X	X	X	X	X	X	X	24	100	6	100
6	X	X	X	X	X	X	X	X	X	X	X	X	X	X	X	X	X	X	X	X	X	X	X	X	24	100	6	100
7	X	X	X	X	X	X	X	X	X	X	X	X	X	X	X	X	X	X	X	X	X	X	X	X	24	100	6	100
8	X	X	X	X	X	X	X	X	X	X	X	X	X	X	X	X	X	X	X	X	X	X	X	X	24	100	6	100
9	X	X	X	X	X	X	X	X	X	X	X	X	X	X	X	X	X	X	X	X	X	X	X	X	24	100	6	100
10	X	X	X	X	X	X	X	X	X	X	X	X	X	X	X	X	X	X	X	X	X	X	X	X	24	100	6	100
11	X	X	X	X	X	X	X	X	X	X	X	X	X	X	X	X	X	X	X	X	X	X	X	X	24	100	6	100
12	X	X	X	X	X	X	X	X	X	X	X	X	X	X	X	X	X	X	X	X	X	X	X	X	24	100	6	100
13	X	X	X	X	X	X	X	X	X	X	X	X	X	X	X	X	X	X	X	X	X	X	X	X	24	100	6	100
14	X	X	X	X	X	X	X	X	X	X	X	X	X	X	X	X	X	X	X	X	X	X	X	X	24	100	6	100
15	X	X	X	X	X	X	X	X	X	X	X	X	X	X	X	X	X	X	X	X	X	X	X	X	24	100	6	100
Number of students	15	15	15	15	15	15	15	15	15	15	14	15	15	15	15	13	15	13	14	15	14	15	15	15	$\overline{x} = 17.8$			
Percent of students correct	100	100	100	100	100	100	100	100	100	100	93	100	100	100	100	86	100	86	93	100	93	100	100	100				

X = Correct
A blank space reflects an incorrect response

STUDENT PERFORMANCE ON OBJECTIVES ON THE PRETEST, EMBEDDED TEST ITEMS, AND POSTTEST

Objective	5.6			5.7			5.8			5.9			5.10			5.11		
Content	Purpose			Identify			Name Punctuation			Punctuate			Recognize			Write		
Test	Pre	Emb	Post	Pre	Emb	Post	Pre	Emb	Post	Pre	Emb	Post	Pre	Emb	Post	Pre	Emb	Post
1		X	X		X	X	X	X	X	X	X	X		X				
2		X	X		X	X	X	X	X	X	X	X		X			X	
3		X	X		X	X	X	X	X	X	X	X		X	X		X	
4		X	X		X	X	X	X	X	X	X	X		X			X	
5		X	X		X	X	X	X	X	X	X	X		X	X		X	
6		X	X		X	X	X	X	X	X	X	X		X	X	X	X	X
7		X	X		X	X	X	X	X	X	X	X		X	X	X	X	X
8		X	X		X	X	X	X	X	X	X	X		X	X	X	X	X
9		X	X		X	X	X	X	X	X	X	X		X	X		X	X
10	X	X	X		X	X	X	X	X	X	X	X		X	X	X	X	X
11	X	X	X	X	X	X	X	X	X	X	X	X	X	X	X	X	X	X
12	X	X	X		X	X	X	X	X	X	X	X	X	X	X		X	X
13	X	X	X	X	X	X	X	X	X	X	X	X	X	X	X	X	X	X
14	X	X	X	X	X	X	X	X	X	X	X	X	X	X	X	X	X	X
15	X	X	X	X	X	X	X	X	X	X	X	X	X	X	X	X	X	X
Number of students passing	6	15	15	4	15	15	15	15	15	15	15	15	5	15	12	8	14	10
Percent of students passing	40	100	100	27	100	100	100	100	100	100	100	100	33	100	80	53	93	66
Differences	+60		0	+73		0	0		0	0		0	+67		−20	+40		−27

X = Objective passed

ENTRY BEHAVIOR ITEMS, PRETEST, EMBEDDED TEST, AND POSTTEST BY PERCENTAGE OF POSSIBLE ITEMS AND BY PERCENTAGE OF POSSIBLE OBJECTIVES

	Percentage of Total Items					*Percentage of Total Objectives*			
Student	Entry behavior	Pretest	Embedded Test	Posttest	Student	Entry behavior	Pretest	Embedded Test	Posttest
1	20	44	79	80	1	0	33	66	66
2	50	44	92	80	2	20	33	83	66
3	50	44	100	85	3	20	33	100	83
4	60	44	100	80	4	40	33	100	66
5	90	61	100	85	5	80	33	100	83
6	100	61	100	100	6	100	33	100	100
7	100	61	100	100	7	100	33	100	100
8	100	61	100	100	8	100	33	100	100
9	100	55	100	100	9	100	83	100	100
10	100	83	100	100	10	100	66	100	100
11	100	100	100	100	11	100	100	100	100
12	100	100	100	100	12	100	100	100	100
13	100	100	100	100	13	100	100	100	100
14	100	100	100	100	14	100	100	100	100
15	100	100	100	100	15	100	100	100	100
# items	10	18	24	24	# obj	5	6	6	6

STUDENTS' PERFORMANCE PLOTTED BY OBJECTIVE ON PRETEST, EMBEDDED TEST ITEMS, AND POSTTEST

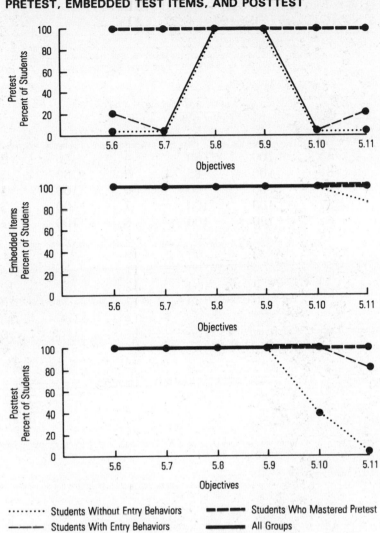

.... Students Without Entry Behaviors   ▬ ▬ ▬ Students Who Mastered Pretest

— — — Students With Entry Behaviors   ▬▬▬▬ All Groups

SUMMARY OF STUDENTS' RESPONSES ON ATTITUDE QUESTIONNAIRE BY GROUP

Name _____ *Summary* _____ Date _ *1-16* _ Class _ *Small Group*

Attitude Questionnaire

Please answer the following questions to help us understand what you think about the lessons on writing different kinds of sentences. Your opinions will help us make better lessons for you.

A. Motivation

1. Did you enjoy the story about the birthday present?
   _*15*_ Yes //// LHT / HHT
   _____ No

2. Did you think the version of the story that had all types of sentences included (B) was more interesting than the first (A)?
   _*15*_ Yes //// LHT / LHT
   _____ No

3. Did reading the story make you want to try to write more interesting stories yourself?
   _*15*_ Yes //// LHT / HHT
   _____ No

4. What kinds of stories do you most like to read?
   *horses, pets, space, sports, nature, cars, mysteries*

B. Objectives

1. Did you understand that you were going to learn to write stories that were more interesting?
   _*15*_ Yes //// LHT / HHT
   _____ No

2. Did you understand that you were going to learn to use four different kinds of sentences in your stories?
   _*15*_ Yes //// LHT / HHT
   _____ No

3. Did you want to write different kinds of sentences?
   _*15*_ Yes //// HHT / HHT
   _____ No

C. Entry Behaviors

1. Were the questions about subjects, predicates, and complete sentences clear to you?
   _*15*_ Yes //// LHT LHT
   _____ No

2. Did you already know about subjects, predicates, and complete sentences before you started?
   _*14*_ Yes /// LHT / HHT
   _*1*_ No /

3. Do you wish information about subjects, predicates, and complete sentences had been included in the lesson?
   _____ Yes
   _*15*_ No //// LHT LHT

D. Tests

1. Did you think questions on the pretest were clear?
   _*8*_ Yes /// HHT *Didn't know the answers*
   _*7*_ No //// /// *Vocabulary clear*

2. Did you think you knew most of the answers the pretest?
   _*9*_ Yes / /// LHT
   _*6*_ No /// ///

3. Were the questions on the posttest clear or confusing?
   _*15*_ Clear //// LHT / LHT
   _____ Confusing

4. Did you think questions within the lesson were clear or confusing?
   _*15*_ Clear //// LHT / HHT
   _____ Confusing

E. Instruction

1. Was the instruction interesting?
   _*15*_ Yes //// HHT / LHT
   _____ No

2. Was the instruction clear?
   __15__ Yes //// LHt / HH
   _____ No
   If not, what wasn't clear? _____ *Where were the stories?* _____

   _____

3. Were the example questions helpful?
   __10__ Yes //// HH /
   __5__ No   HH

4. Were there too many examples? Too Few?
   __5__ Yes   __3__ Yes
   __10__ No   __7__ No

5. Did the practice questions in the instruction help you?
   __10__ Yes //// HH /
   __5__ No   HH
   If not, why not? _____

   _____

6. Did the feedback exercises in the instruction help you?
   __10__ Yes //// HH /
   __5__ No   HH
   If not, why not? _____

   _____

F. Overall

1. Generally, did you like the lesson?
   __15__ Yes //// HH / HH
   _____ No

2. Did you learn to do things you couldn't do before?
   __10__ Yes //// HH /
   __5__ No   HH

3. What do you think would improve the lesson most?

   More example stories to see; pick out declarative
   sentences in stories; the lesson wasn't about
   writing stories

   _____
   _____
   _____
   _____

Materials Revision Analysis Form (Table 11.10)

Component	Problem	Change	Evidence and Source
Motivational introductory material	None	Perhaps add another example story to the material	Students reported enjoying illustrative story and understanding the purpose for the unit (attitude questionnaire). All groups reported wanting to read more example stories on the questionnaire and in the debriefing session.
Entry behaviors items	None	None	1. Items did identify students who would have difficulty with first lesson (comparison of entry behavior scores and posttest scores). 2. Test fits time frame. 3. Students understood vocabulary used and question structure.
Pretest on Instructional Objectives	None	None	1. Pretest did separate students who knew the materials from those who did not. 2. Vocabulary level OK. 3. Time frame OK. 4. Question format OK.
Materials content	1. Instruction on punctuation (5.8 and 5.9) not needed by any students	Potential removal of punctuation objectives from lesson	Observe problems with periods used to close imperative and exclamatory sentences

Component	Problem	Change	Evidence and Source
			in subsequent lessons—may provide foundation here.
	2. Entire lesson not needed by students who mastered pretest	Possibly have high ability students begin with lesson two	Five students did not need lesson (pretest, embedded test, posttest, attitude questionnaire).
	3. Entry behaviors skills and sentence writing skills not mastered by some members of the group	Develop a set of remedial materials for these students to cover entry behaviors as well as provide more practice in writing sentences	1. Four students had difficulty recognizing complete sentences, subjects, and predicates (pretest). 2. Four students had difficulty writing sentences (posttest, objective 5.11).
	4. Students lost focus on story writing in lesson on sentences	Add stories from which students can classify declarative sentences. Have students write declarative sentences for given stories	Debriefing session and questionnaire.
Embedded Tests	Predictive Validity (embedded items did not indicate eventual problems on posttest for same items)	Insert embedded test items on recognizing complete sentences and writing sentences in materials a distance from instruction and examples	Embedded test items functioned well in the materials, *but* they did not predict students who would have difficulty on the posttest. This may be related to students' ability to mimic sentences in the embedded tests (embedded and posttest scores).
Posttest	None	None	1. Test did identify students having difficulty with objectives 5.10 and 5.11. 2. Time OK. 3. Question format OK. 4. Vocabulary OK (posttest data).
Attitude Questionnaire	None	None	1. Did detect dissatisfaction of

Component	Problem	Change	Evidence and Source
			high-ability students with lesson.
			2. Information corroborated correct level of difficulty for students with prerequisite skills.
			3. Information from students without the prerequisites (guessing) was corroborated with test data.

INDEX